St. Louis Community College

Forest Park
Florissant Valley
Meramec

Instructional Resources
St. Louis, Missouri

GAYLORD

The Bubbling Cauldron

The Bubbling Cauldron

Race, Ethnicity, and the Urban Crisis

Michael Peter Smith and
Joe R. Feagin, editors

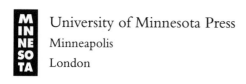

University of Minnesota Press
Minneapolis
London

Chapter 2, "Dictatorship, Democracy, and Difference: The Historical Construction of Racial Identity," first appeared in Howard Winant, *Racial Conditions: Politics, Theory, Comparisons* (Minneapolis: University of Minnesota Press, 1994), copyright Howard Winant, reprinted by permission.

Published by the University of Minnesota Press
111 Third Avenue South, Suite 290, Minneapolis, MN 55401-2520
Printed in the United States of America on acid-free paper

Library of Congress Cataloging-in-Publication Data

The bubbling cauldron : race, ethnicity, and the urban crisis /
   Michael Peter Smith and Joe R. Feagin, editors.
      p.   cm.
   Includes bibliographical references and index.
   ISBN 0-8166-2331-7 (acid-free paper)
   ISBN 0-8166-2332-5 (pbk. : acid-free paper)
   1. United States — Race relations.   2. United States — Ethnic
relations.   3. Race discrimination — United States.   4. Ethnicity —
United States.   5. Minorities — United States.   6. United States —
Social conditions — 1980–   I. Smith, Michael, P.   II. Feagin, Joe
R.
E184.A1.B89   1995
305.8'00973 — dc20   95-13450

Contents

Part I

Introduction

1 / Putting "Race" in Its Place

Michael Peter Smith and Joe R. Feagin

Why is "race" a central source of meaning, identity, and power in U.S. society? How does the way we talk about racial difference articulate with the interplay of power and knowledge in the structuring of class, gender, and ethnic relations in contemporary society? Who has the power to construct the dominant racial categories that structure social opportunities and constraints? How much of the past is present in today's racialized opportunity structure? How is the multiplicity of racial and ethnic groups, brought to our shores by the explosion of transnational migration in today's global epoch, being inserted into dominant discourses about racial-ethnic identities and the hierarchies of power shaped by these discourses? What new complexities have been added to the ever-present role of the state in the processes of racial formation by the internationalization of the economy and the globalization of culture?

Race and ethnicity are sometimes erroneously conceived as primordial essences likely to be erased by the inexorable march of "modern times" and various material driving forces (for example, capitalism, market relations, the media, and the bureaucratic state). Racial and ethnic identities have often been deployed as a trope for local and premodern vestiges of the past. Both Marxian and free market modernists have anticipated their disappearance as the spread of the world market reduces all nonmarket identities to the cash nexus and condenses all differences of color into the one color, green. Likewise, those who have seen the formation of the nation-state system as the quintessential sign of "modernity" have envisaged the construction of "citizenship" by state structures as eventually erasing the divisive particularisms of ethnic nationalism. In the face of the racial and ethnic antagonisms stirred up everywhere by the globalization of the capitalist economy and the end of the cold war, the "melting pot" notion of the declining significance of racial and ethnic consciousness no longer has much purchase. In the reinvigorated view of race and ethnicity used in *The Bubbling Cauldron,* the politics of racial and ethnic formation is conceived as a dynamic arena of domination and resistance, division and self-definition in a "cool" world where people have lost compassion for the distant other. These are spheres within which individuals and groups deal with the forces and practices of domination, contest large-scale structural and cultural processes, modify their social contexts, and even reconstruct their very selves.

We conceptualize racialization as a contested process of ordered social relations. Racialization is a historical structure of domination-subordination within community and societal formations whose contours mark the fault lines of cultural and political resistance to dominant representations of racial-ethnic difference. At the group level, racial and ethnic consciousness, like all forms of collective identity, does not spring sui generis from conditions such as nationality, geographical origin, or intergroup attributes. Just as class consciousness does not arise automatically out of the mode of production (which is itself a socially and politically mediated construct), racial and ethnic consciousness is also a relational construct made possible through sociopolitical practice. Racial and ethnic differences, and hence patterns of racial and ethnic domination, conflict, and accommodation, are socially produced through recurring group-level and institutional-group interactions that are changed over time by human practice. These interactive practices establish the racial or ethnic identity of a group by specifying its relations with other groups. As a form of "imagined community," racial and ethnic consciousness is continually shaped and reshaped by socially and politically contested representations of difference.[1]

The identification of different modes of accommodation and resistance to similar structural constraints and forms of social control places the motif of domination-accommodation-resistance at the center of recent trends in the analysis of racial and ethnic formation. The centrality of this motif marks the kind of recombinant political economy and postmodern ethnography used by several of the authors in this book as different from traditional ethnography and purely structural analysis. The advantage of this motif is in providing a central theme and a research strategy that address rather than elide the structure-agency dialectic in social theory. By refocusing scholarly inquiry amid worldwide social change upon the domination-accommodation-resistance motif, the approach informing this essay and this book provides an intelligible starting point, at the intersection of social structure and human agency, for understanding the complex dynamics by which new racial and ethnic identities and new forms of racialization emerge in and through, for and against such global phenomena as urban sociospatial restructuring, transnational migration, and ethnic and racial conflict itself.

Since racial and ethnic consciousness springs from people's historical and material circumstances and from their perceptions and cultural understandings of these circumstances, the detailed case study and the ethnographic approach are indispensable methodological routes to knowledge of the ways in which ethnic and racial consciousness are actually formed and how they change over time and space. They are necessary interpretive complements to more conventional means by which social scientists study ethnic and racial relations such as survey research, demography, and macrosocial analysis. The richness found in the single case study chapters of *The Bubbling Cauldron* by Roger Waldinger and by Harold Brackman and Steven Erie and in the ethnographic chapter by Leslie Inniss; the nuanced combined ethnographic and case study approach deployed in the chapters by Michael Peter Smith, Bernadette Tarallo, Michael Hodge, Joe R. Feagin, and Edward Murguia; and the use of ethnographic data to ground the more theoretical essays by Michael Kearney and Néstor Rodríguez are signs of a qualitative turn in the field of racial and ethnic research that does not lose sight of larger structures within which human agency is expressed.

Having said this, we do not believe that it is necessary to pose a binary antagonism between "qualitative" and "quantitative" research that excludes either as a window to advance perception and understanding of the causes and consequences of racial and ethnic formation in today's more complicated global context. The contributions to *The Bubbling Cauldron* by Norman Fainstein, James Button, Cedric Herring, and Sharon Collins give testimony to the continuing usefulness of intellectually nuanced quantitative research designed and executed to detail the material consequences of socially constructed racial and ethnic hierarchies. Such research also pointedly illustrates the tangible distributional consequences of state policies in the realms that count most in the determination of the material life chances of different racial and ethnic groups, namely housing, employment, education, neighborhood services, and their attendant avenues of access to social space and basic respect.

Racial Representation and the State

Racial and ethnic identities are locally constructed at particular historical times and places through a politics of representation in which the role of the state looms large. State power has often been the object of the politics of racial representation; and state policies, the means used to enforce relations of racial and ethnic domination-subordination. In the American case, the archetypal foundation for centuries of subsequent racial-ethnic incorporation, negotiation, and conflict began with the early colonial struggles between European settlers and Native Americans and between the settlers and their imported African slaves. State policies of genocide and exclusion from white spaces were developed for the native population, while a policy of highly ideologized, labor-oriented oppression within white communities was developed for the Africans. The latter involved a multilayered construction of dominance and oppression that cut across all major institutions. It was reflected in a postcolonial "democratic" republic, whose foundational features — the Declaration of Independence, the Constitution, the Supreme Court, and early slaveholding presidents — all defined African Americans as noncitizens, and any known African ancestry generated a noncitizen status. This social construction of black subordination and exclusion from civil society was comprehensive and long lasting, and was replicated in the economy, education, housing, and public accommodations.

Not only did the state policies regarding slavery and Native American exclusion enshrine a racialized social order, but, in addition, a long series of subsequent uses of state power reinforced that order. For example, the Naturalization Law of 1790 declared only "white" immigrants fit for naturalization. The Alien and Sedition Acts of 1798 gave the president the power to expel politically "dangerous" immigrants. Subsequently, non-European immigrants, including Africans and Asians, were prevented from becoming citizens, Asians until the 1950s.

Once in place, the archetypal system of state-institutionalized racialization became the framework for the incorporation of subsequent non-European groups. Thus, although Asian and Pacific peoples were imported as contract workers in the nineteenth century and the early twentieth century, they were officially constructed as "nonwhite" and thus as noncitizens. Strikingly, in 1854 the California Supreme Court ruled that the new Chinese immigrants were to be classified officially as "Indians" and thus as ineligible for the rights of citizenship. Fostered by federal decrees and military protection, the westward expansion of the nation-state in the nineteenth century brought Native American and Mexican peoples and lands new orbits of exploitation. After the forcible conquest of northern Mexico, agricultural development in the West and Southwest, from then to the present, was fueled by state-sanctioned labor from Mexico.[2]

Since the late nineteenth century, particularly during war periods, there has been a great expansion of the national government bureaucracies. The state has grown in relationship to military involvements and adventures overseas and in relationship to large-scale transnational migration. The racial-ethnic power hierarchy has been critical in shaping state action in regard to each new period of immigration. State policies, both shaping and shaped by white majority public opinion, have launched military invasions overseas and drafted restrictive immigration laws. Expansionism overseas, as for example in the Philippines or Puerto Rico in the late nineteenth century or in Korea and Southeast Asia during the cold war epoch, has shaped the pattern of immigration to the United States by peoples from the regions of state intervention. Such state actions, linked to and undergirding variations in class relationships and interstate relations, have significantly affected the ways in which new immigrants enter, adapt to, resist, or avoid the prevailing racial-ethnic hierarchy.

In the late nineteenth and the early twentieth centuries, national government policies actually legitimated state actions to exclude "immoral" aliens, those with diseases, political radicals, and immigrants from China and Japan. These laws reflected prevailing stereotypes of immigrants not from northern Europe. A 1917 act even created an Asiatic barred zone, from which no immigrants could enter. The most important anti-immigrant legislation, the 1924 National Origins Act, set up quotas favoring northern European countries, limiting immigration from southern and eastern European countries, and solidifying the exclusion of all Asians. A coalition of anti-immigrant, labor, and business groups, with the background support of executives from large capital-intensive corporations, lay behind the passage of this explicitly racist legislation, which was to remain the law of the land until 1965.

The interplay of state power and global capitalistic development and expansion have shaped the context and character of immigration to the United States and subsequent patterns of racial-ethnic relations. Historically, for example, the U.S. government has defined for employers many categories of Mexican immigrant labor, not only the regular legal immigrants but also temporary braceros (seasonal farm workers), commuters who live in Mexico but work in the United States, and "border crossers" with short-term work permits.[3] It continues today to channel temporary "nonimmigrant" skilled workers into the United States in such high-tech fields as computer science and engineering while introducing increasing barriers against the legal entrance of immigrant workers who lack skills.

As the Mexican case illustrates, the labor needs of employers have been central to the determination and character of many migration flows. The actions of capitalist employers in one period, such as the extensive recruitment of large numbers of immigrant laborers from one section of the globe, can in the next historical period mean conflict between older immigrant laborers and newer immigrant laborers imported by later employers. In this fashion, intraclass conflicts within the U.S. working class, such as between white European and black, Mexican, or Asian workers, have played their part in the often violent U.S. history of racial and ethnic relations. Anti-immigrant agitation and subsequent state action have usually been correlated with the economic cycles of the global capitalist economy and its shifts in job creation and labor demand. As Albert Szymanski has noted, "In times of real labor shortage the state imposes few obstacles on immigration."[4]

Until the civil rights revolution of the 1960s, the status system underlying such state policies was rationalized by an extensive ideology of binary racial difference, elements of which, as many of the articles in this book reveal, have been reappropriated in today's fluctuating context of identity formation to justify newer forms of privilege and exclusion. All subsequent peoples of color have faced this binary mode of thought as a starting point in the negotiation and construction of their racial and ethnic identities. Whether migrating in response to changing global labor demand or to flee political persecution in their homelands, newcomers to U.S. shores faced laws, ideologies, and political arrangements that have viewed them on the "black" side of the binary racial divide. Over time these groups were often able to negotiate a higher status for themselves entailing less discrimination than that faced by African Americans. Yet "higher" has not meant equal, for equal political and economic citizenship, the hope of the civil rights movement of the 1960s, has not yet been effectively won by any groups of color. This point is well documented in this book.

Historically, the persistent exclusion of racially defined minorities from a significant place in civil society and, until the 1960s, from formal citizen rights reflected the dominant white culture's enduring interest in maintaining structures of domination and securing what George Lipsitz has termed its "possessive investment in whiteness." The formal citizenship rights created by the equal rights discourse and laws of the 1960s formed a key basis, as Howard Winant's chapter shows, for the self-organization of political unity out of internal difference by excluded peoples of color to challenge this possessive white interest. Yet as Adolph Reed's chapter documents, the unity necessary to break down exclusionary walls does not easily translate into the construction of a coherent political agenda on behalf of social equality once formal, legal barriers to minority social and political participation are removed. The informal racial barriers that coexist with or replace the formal barriers are increasingly complex and require different strategies to overcome.

Today, for example, the complexity of contemporary racial and ethnic divisions can be seen in the often vigorous opposition to Latino immigrants, legal and undocumented. In the last two decades public debates have reappropriated racist anti-immigration arguments of the past but have cast them in more neutral-sounding language. Fearing labor market competition, many native-born Americans, including some members of native-born minority groups (for example, blacks and Mexican Americans) are concerned that the United States cannot economically incorporate so many immigrants in currently uncertain economic times. Implicit in many discussions of "new immigrants" among the white voting majority is a further sociocultural concern, couched as an "absorption problem," that most of today's newcomers exceed the nation's "carrying capacity," because they are from Latin America and Asia — that is, that they are not white or English speaking. As a result, legislators and state bureaucrats have imposed significant restrictions on legal immigration from Mexico in the form of additions to the 1965 Immigration Act and in the 1986 Immigration Reform and Control Act. The governors of Florida, California, Texas, and other states experiencing high rates of transnational migration are currently even suing the federal government to get them to compensate the states for the claimed high "fiscal costs" of immigration and are demanding that the national government enforce ever tighter restrictions on the entry of new immigrants and political refugees. These pressures have culminated most recently in the passage of Proposition 187, a referendum targeted against "illegal" immigrants in California that would deny public education and health services to the U.S.-born children of undocumented immigrants. The complexity of the new social divisions revealed in the current immigration debate illustrates the limits of political strategies based on rhetorical calls for rainbow coalitions, greater compassion, or enforcement of existing civil rights laws.

Racial Ideology and Intergroup Violence

A clear legacy of the state-sanctioned racial and ethnic opportunity structure in contemporary American society is the resilience of historically produced racial and ethnic stereotypes. In a recent influential book Patricia Hill Collins has underscored the negative stereotypes of black women still dominant in white society — the stereotypes of the docile mammy, the domineering matriarch, the promiscuous whore, and the irresponsible welfare mother.[5] Recent survey research findings reveal persisting white stereotypes of black men and women. When whites in a 1990 survey were asked to evaluate on a scale of one to seven how violence-prone blacks were, 51 percent chose the violent end of the spectrum. When asked to rank blacks on preference for welfare (as opposed to working), 55 percent of whites ranked blacks toward the welfare end of the spectrum. Asked to rank blacks on "intelligence," 29 percent of whites placed blacks toward the unintelligent end of the continuum. Given the persistence of these negative stereotypes, it is hardly surprising that in recent weeks a "black male" was the scapegoat chosen to cover up a heinous murder of two white children by their mother in South Carolina. Such stereotypes help explain why "the end of welfare as we know it" now has bipartisan political support and why genetic explanations of racial inequality, like Richard Herrnstein and Charles Murray's *The Bell Curve,* are once again in vogue.[6]

Other minority groups suffer similar stereotypes. Many whites have come to hold stereotypes about the alleged laziness, backwardness, and culture of poverty of what they once called the Mexican "race." Early on, white settlers in the Southwest rationalized the subordination of dark-skinned Mexican Americans with terms of inferiority such as "Greaser." With the heavy Mexican immigration after 1900 came even more hostile stereotyping, which was linked to violent attacks. Labor camps were raided by white supremacist groups and Mexican workers were beaten. In recent decades anti-Mexican stereotypes have persisted. Images of drugs, laziness, and gang criminality are still commonplace. A California study found that a quarter of whites would find it distasteful to eat with a Mexican and that 37 percent felt that "Mexicans are shiftless and dirty."[7] U.S. movies continue to cast Mexicans as criminals or señoritas. Protests from Mexican American political organizations have sometimes successfully targeted stereotypical depictions of Mexican Americans in advertising and the media. For example, in 1991 community protests forced a restaurant chain in Houston to discontinue a TV ad containing a stereotypical Mexican figure.[8]

Asian Americans have also been targets of recurring stereotypes. They have been widely depicted by workers and politicians alike as devious, inscrutable, and drug oriented. Asian Americans currently report that many whites often view them as "foreigners," even telling them to "go back home."

A recurring stereotype is that all "Asians" are essentially the same physically and culturally. Japanese Americans are often mistaken by whites for Chinese Americans, who may be mistaken for Vietnamese or Korean Americans. This scenario was recently played out effectively in oppositional terms in the film version of Amy Tan's recent novel *The Joy Luck Club*.

An unfortunate legacy of these persisting constructions of racial and ethnic difference is the rising incidence of antiminority violence. Racial harassment, vandalism, and violence have been directed against Asian Americans since the earliest days of Asian immigration and persist to this day. Indeed, reported incidents of anti-Asian assaults and vandalism have increased since 1980. Moreover, the number of cases reported is only a small portion of the actual number because many Asian Americans distrust the police and because few cities have collected systematic data on such ethnic violence.[9]

During the 1980s and 1990s hundreds of acts of vandalism and intimidation were directed not only against Asian Americans but also against black and other minority Americans. One of the most notorious cases occurred in 1986 in the Howard Beach area of New York City, when three black men were beaten by white youths. One died when chased into the path of a car.[10] The FBI's first hate crime report, mandated by the Hate Crime Statistics Act, counted 4,558 attacks for the year 1991, with fewer than a fifth of enforcement agencies reporting. The largest proportion of these were antiblack crimes, ranging from intimidation and property damage to assaults.[11] Although most hate crimes are carried out by whites against racial and ethnic minorities, the recent shooting of white and Asian American commuters traveling on the Long Island Railroad by a disaffected black immigrant from Jamaica is a sign of the explosive state of racial and ethnic relations in the United States today, as the bubbling cauldron of "race" continues to inform the character and quality of the everyday social relations of race and ethnicity.

The Politics of Racial Representation: Socially Constructing Identity and Difference

It is now widely recognized that the racial and ethnic "interests" contested in the politics of racial representation are never simply materially preordained but are always mediated and constructed by politics and culture. In the contemporary U.S. political economy, six sites of institutional power constitute the political space where contests over the meaning of racial and ethnic difference are normally fought out. These make up a nexus of domination and a social space of actual and potential resistance. This multifaceted political space where the contested politics of racial representation is fought out includes

1. the national, state, and local political party arenas where policy debates in both major parties have for a long time been fraught with racially coded representations of crime and urban violence and more recently of "illegal" immigration, the "underclass," and a "family crisis" requiring welfare reform;

2. the media of mass communications that constantly deploy representations of racial and ethnic otherness and difference, and constitute the technological space for connecting local to national and global signifying practice;

3. the local politics of crime, policing, and the courts, where actions and practices, undertaken under the legitimate color of the law, entail the discretionary power not only to regulate but also to publicly characterize the behaviors of the individuals with whom local police forces deal as group attributes, thereby stigmatizing these groups and contributing to the social construction of racial and ethnic others (for example, the police discourse on the black "underclass"; black, Latino, and Asian "gangs"; and "illegal" Latino immigrants);

4. national sociocultural elites, including social scientists who have contributed to the discourse on racial relations in the United States by inserting their constructions of the "underclass," the "black versus brown" dimension of the new immigration, and the "chain reaction" of the white

backlash into public debate, as well as educators at all levels who deploy consequential understandings of racial, class, ethnic, and gender differences not only by their explicit communications about social (in)equality but also by their daily interactions with young men and women, including whites and people of color, and those of differing class and national backgrounds;

5. economic elites, particularly employers in the mainstream and ethnic economies whose hiring practices segment and stratify labor markets by race, ethnicity, and gender, thereby dividing the interests of the working population and creating new divisions and sources of antagonism, as well as controllers of credit who use racialized criteria to inform lending practices for home ownership and business enterprise; and,

6. state bureaucrats whose census counting, entitlement, and regulatory categories render our multicultural society more manageable by reducing an immense cultural mosaic into five color-coded (and policy-relevant) categories of white, black, brown, red, and yellow.

In present-day political struggles over the meaning of "multiculturalism," the state's role in racial formation especially involves the making of public policies designed to reduce the enormous heterogeneity of nationalities now part of the U.S. social system in the global epoch. The state institutionalizes a color-coded handful of manageable racial and ethnic categories around which its material benefit, regulation, and control systems can be more readily constructed, while masking the exclusions that this entails in a rhetoric of "diversity."

All of the contributors to *The Bubbling Cauldron* speak to the central role of these institutional centers of power in mediating the politics of racial and ethnic representation. The party politics of racial and ethnic incorporation is a process that is multilayered and operates at different geographical scales. At the urban scale, the chapter by Harold Brackman and Steven Erie focuses on the political incorporation of Asian and Pacific Island groups into mainstream urban politics in Los Angeles. Brackman and Erie comprehensively discuss the barriers to and opportunities for the political incorporation of this diverse panethnic category into the benefit systems controlled by city of Los Angeles. Edward Murguia's complementary chapter offers a theoretically rich discussion of the achievements and limits of the accumulation of local "political capital" by an economically poor Yaqui (Catholic and Native American) Mexican origin community living in a township in Arizona bordering on, but excluded from the services of, the cities of Phoenix and Tempe. The chapters by political scientists Adolph Reed Jr. and James Button assess a second face of political incorporation. In different ways Reed and Button offer skeptical assessments of the long-term policy and political gains won by the civil rights revolution of the 1960s and subsequent political incorporation of black citizens at both the national and the urban level into what Reed dubs the new urban regime of "race relations management."

At the wider scales of the nation-state and the international political economy, Sophie Body-Gendrot's comparative analysis of modes of integration of new immigrants in France and the United States illustrates the changing role of the state in ideology and practice as a maker of citizenship and regulator of cultural diversity. She examines the national political party discourses, media representations, and urban policies that mediate the immigration question in the face of rising global migration to both nations.

The rising significance of the mass media in communicating representations of racial-ethnic identity and difference is a recurring motif in social science and cultural studies. Several contributions to *The Bubbling Cauldron* shed light on the media politics of racial representation. The channels of privileged access to reporters that shape local print media representations of ethnicity, youth violence, and crime are focused on by Michael Peter Smith and Bernadette Tarallo in their examination of the social construction of the Vietnamese "other." Smith and Tarallo's ethnographically grounded narrative provides a dramatic account of the contested politics of representation following the eruption of violence between local police forces and Vietnamese youths in a Southeast Asian enclave in Sacramento, California. Their chapter combines political economy and ethnographic analysis to underline the symbiotically linked character of representations by local police and media elites of racial and ethnic difference and the highly politicized character of these representations. Smith and Tarallo's structurally situated ethnography illustrates the interaction between local law enforcement authorities and the local media, and between both and political elites, in deploying racialized images of Southeast Asian youths as dangerous "others" in reports on crime and violence. Their case study illustrates as well the symbolic politics underlying the emergence of grassroots oppositional voices capable of challenging such officially constructed identities.

At the national level Adolph Reed documents a similar symbiotic convergence of sensationalist journalists and self-styled "tough-minded" social scientists in enshrining "underclass" rhetoric as the current discursive frame for discussing poverty and racial inequality. This dominant focus shifts attention from structural sources of inequality to the behavioral "dysfunctions" of the putative members of the stigmatized "underclass." Like its predecessors (for example, the "culture of poverty" thesis of Oscar Lewis and Edward Banfield), the cultural construction of ethnicity positioned centrally in the "underclass" thesis ends up attributing economic inequalities and differential rates of mobility to differences in cultural norms and behavioral practices between those inside and outside the constructed group. It is a short step from blatant victim blaming by journalists and public intellectuals to unmediated racial-ethnic antagonism by those constructed as excluded from the stigmatized "underclass" other.

The chapters by Norman Fainstein, James Button, and Howard Winant also address the role of social scientists and other public intellectuals in shaping the discourses on "race" and the racialized "underclass" in political debate and public policy analysis. Reed's and Fainstein's arguments show how social science constructions and discourses do not occur in a vacuum. They are framed within the context of a wider national political discourse on race, poverty, and the urban underclass that has reached hegemonic proportions. Political party elites, welfare bureaucrats, employers, poverty intellectuals, and the national and global mass media have all played prominent roles in the social production of this antipoor, antiminority ideology.

The current academic and public debate surrounding William Julius Wilson's controversial formulation of the "underclass" social construct,[12] as well as the relative importance of race, class, and status in shaping racial relations today, is especially well joined in the critical articles by Reed and Fainstein on the one hand and the Wilsonian article by Martín Sánchez Jankowski on the other. The latter offers an emphasis on status stratification among African Americans today as an explanation for racial discrimination and inequality. This status stratification among middle-class, "coping stratum," and poor urban blacks is also acknowledged by Winant, but is theorized quite differently in terms of "modes of identity" and "sets of interest" politically dividing African Americans. Winant's interpretive essay maps the basic contours of racial conflict in America today. He points out that many contemporary struggles about the meaning of race and ethnicity now occur in the domain of "identity politics," pitting those who challenge the prevailing boundaries of racial identity against those who wish to reinforce those boundaries from different ideological and institutional locations.

In a related empirical chapter Cedric Herring and Sharon Collins provide a quantitative analysis of survey data that offers a powerful rebuttal to neoconservative interpretations of affirmative action policies as "reverse discrimination" hurting white males. The fact that their study was framed

to test a widely accepted hypothesis that is part of a denial of the significance of racism by many intellectuals and political journalists (for example,
Nathan Glazer, William Julius Wilson, Thomas and Mary Edsall, Stephen
Carter, and Jim Sleeper), as well as a sizable percentage of white public opinion, is testimony to the powerful impact that public intellectuals have had
on the politics of racial representation.

Leslie Inniss's ethnographic account of the psychological damage done
to the first generation of black children experiencing the trauma of desegregation poignantly illustrates the racializing role of another social-cultural
elite group — educators. In Inniss's view the many forms of white resistance
to integration and denial of racism experienced by blacks have led many
African Americans today, including the early desegregation pioneers, to
abandon the dream of an integrated society in favor of multiculturalism as a
social policy and an Afrocentric curriculum in separate black schools.

Not surprisingly, in a capitalist society economic elites continue to
play a pivotal role in the differential distribution of life chances by ethnicity
and race. The article by Michael Hodge and Joe R. Feagin on the structural economic barriers to black entrepreneurship provides telling ethnographic evidence of the difficulties black businesspeople face in obtaining
contracts, supplies, bonding, and sufficient credit to run a successful business,
even with collateral comparable to that of whites. This and other evidence
suggest that discrimination in lending on the basis of racial groups for commercial purposes and for residential housing is a pervasive feature of late-
twentieth-century capitalism in the United States. In a recent pathbreaking
book, Douglas Massey and Nancy Denton have demonstrated that racial
discrimination by realtors and bankers in the institutional arena of housing
is still so widespread and entrenched as to structure a racialized system they
call "American Apartheid."[13]

Roger Waldinger's comparative historical study of the economic niches
made by four successive waves of new immigrants to New York City — Irish,
Jews, blacks, and Koreans — shows how ethnic segmentation in specialized
employment realms as a means of group upward mobility has been a double-
edged sword. On the one hand, ethnic specialization over time produced
some economic mobility for Irish public-service workers, Jewish clothing
makers and public-school teachers, black government employees, and Korean small business owners. On the other hand, each group's successful mo-
nopolization of occupational niches has sometimes pitted them against other
racial-ethnic groups in competitive contests for scarce resources (for example,

competition for civil service jobs) and structurally antagonistic and conflictual relationships (such as Jewish teachers versus black students; black customers versus Korean merchants).

Recent studies by Paul Ong, Edna Bonacich, and Min Zhou and John Logan suggest that in today's postindustrial context, without a large-scale factory system to absorb new immigrant workers, the pursuit of collective empowerment strategies by economically advantaged classes within ethnic groups (such as Chinese restaurant owners and Korean contractors and sweatshop owners) can lead to structurally exploitative relations of employment with their ethnic co-workers. Bonacich and Ong contend that serious class-based antagonisms are masked by cultural appeals for ethnic solidarity on the part of enclave employers in order to dampen class awareness.[14] A recent comparative ethnographic study of new Asian and Latino immigrants by Smith and Tarallo suggests that, in California at least, it may be lack of citizen rights and the unavailability of English-language acquisition programs in the globalized context of today's hypermigration rather than the absence of class awareness that prevents low-paid new Asian immigrant workers in the ethnic enclave economy from voicing their discontent in intraethnic labor struggles.[15]

The Globalization of Racial and Ethnic Relations

Despite our focus on the role of intersocietal interactions in the emergence of racial and ethnic structure, identities, and conflicts, we recognize that under contemporary historical conditions of globalization, social and cultural phenomena can no longer be understood solely at the level of the nation-state. Much of the foregoing analysis and many of the contributions to this book shed light on the tension between people of color and state bureaucrats seeking to define them in racialized ways. Yet in today's global epoch, the very power of nation-states to command loyalty and regulate the flow of people in and out of their borders is increasingly challenged by the globalization of the economy from above and the rising tide of transnational migration "from below."

The implications of globalization for the processes of racial and ethnic formation have been well stated by Roger Rouse. "We live in a confusing world," notes Rouse, "a world of crisscrossed economies, intersecting systems of meaning, and fragmented identities. Suddenly, the comforting modern imagery of nation-states and national languages, of coherent communities and consistent subjectivities, of dominant centers and distant margins no longer seems adequate.... [W]e have all moved irrevocably into a new kind of social space"[16]

In short, cultures, as socially constructed systems of representation and meaning, must now be conceptualized comparatively in all of their global scope and complexity. Contests over the representation of personal and collective identity and the categories through which identity is filtered — class, race, gender, ethnicity, and nation-state — must recognize that the world is increasingly a single social space.

Two of the most intriguing contributions to *The Bubbling Cauldron* addressing this theme are Michael Kearney's analysis of the formation of Mixtec ethnic identity in California agriculture and Néstor Rodríguez's study of undocumented transnational migration from Central America to U.S. metropolitan areas. Rodríguez and Kearney deal in different ways with the limits of state action in socially constructing ethnic and racial identities in today's global era. Not only have production systems and labor markets become crisscrossed and globalized, but so too have social networks from below and personal identities from within. Rodríguez and Kearney acknowledge the continuing policing (and thus racializing) role of the nation-state in regulating the flow of immigration within national boundaries and in enforcing a sense of national collective identity on new immigrants and refugees. Yet each also expresses an oppositional imagination by characterizing the transnational migration patterns they have studied as "stateless." In their view, the multiple sites through which transnational migrants move as they reconstitute their lives has thus far allowed them to escape, to varying degrees, official categories of identity constructed by U.S., Mexican, and Central American nation-states to regulate racial-ethnic relations within their borders.

Other concrete examples of the globalization of racial and ethnic relations in the United States abound. In the aftermath of the Los Angeles rebellion it has become clear that unfavorable media representations of minority Americans are both a domestic and a global phenomenon. As a result of U.S. military interventions over the past forty years, U.S. films, videos, and television shows distributed overseas have provided racist stereotypes of black Americans in advance to (South) Koreans and immigrants from other former U.S. "colonies." Their antiblack views often predate actual experiences with African Americans and predetermine their negative reactions to black clients, customers, and neighbors.[17]

Having said this, it is also increasingly clear that the politics of racial and ethnic representation in the global era is not a one-sided story of global elite domination of the mass media. On the oppositional side of the media dialectic, for example, Rodríguez describes how an alternative transnational Latino media has been created, as both a medium and an outcome of accelerated transnational migration between the United States and Latin America. He illustrates that media politics is a two-way street and a site of struggle in the politics of racial representation.

At the level of the global-local interplay, Kearney's chapter shows that even the "remote" hinterlands of Meso-America, once a quintessential site of "traditional culture," are now connected to circuits of user-friendly mass and two-way communication devices, ranging from satellite dishes to VCRs, camcorders, teleconferencing systems, electronic banking, and e-mail. The recent Zapatista uprising in Chiapas, Mexico, is instructive in this regard. The media politics of this struggle reveals how well aware the rebel forces were of the importance of global media politics and how quickly representatives of global media tried to name the rebellion in their own racial-ethnic terms and thus undercut its indigenous Native American character. Global media reports frequently described one of the rebellion's leaders, Subcommandante Marcos, as "light-skinned," "green-eyed," and "revered" and dubbed him "the region's first postmodern guerrilla hero."[18] In short, the global media (thus far unsuccessfully) are replaying the outside-agitator theme often used by white police officials and political leaders to try to discredit activists in the U.S. civil rights movement and participants in urban black rebellions.[19]

The constitution of global space, of course, is not entirely new. The globalization of economic relations began in the late 1400s with the expansion of the capitalist world economy, which began in Europe but spread rapidly over the next few centuries until it now encompasses virtually every national, racial, and ethnic group around the globe. Balandier notes that "until very recently the greater part of the world's population, not belonging to the white race (if we exclude China and Japan), knew only a status of dependency on one or another of the European colonial powers."[20] Many society-colonies eventually became independent of their colonizers but continued to have their economies and media cultures shaped by the dominant institutions of the former colonial powers, which in turn continued to influence local racial and ethnic tensions and conflicts. In addition, the former colonies often supplied large numbers of immigrants to the colonial societies. Colonialism has played a central role in creating or exacerbating racial and ethnic oppression within many existing nation-states across the globe.

What is new, however, is the sense of "confusion" alluded to by Rouse over the future course of social relations (including racial and ethnic relations) in an epoch when new social spaces for the formation of meaning, identity, and social action seem to be in a constant state of formation and emergence. The globalization of economic and sociocultural processes, combined with the political restructuring following the end of the cold war, has created a world of ever more complicated endings and beginnings. In this ever-changing context, political space, like economic and cultural space, is constantly shifting ground. Class formation and class-based national and urban politics, for example, have been immensely complicated by the effects of interrelated global developments impinging on national and local racial-ethnic relations. These include the trans-territorialization of production, the restructuring of labor processes and the attendant fragmentation of national working classes, the global speed and instantaneity of mass communications, global geopolitical restructuring, and the renewed acceleration of transnational migration.

Historically, the policies and practices of both capitalist and state actors have linked these processes of economic and sociocultural restructuring. For example, the austerity policies of international banks, cold war counterinsurgency policies, and growing regional and income inequality promoted by the export-oriented development strategies of the World Bank made it difficult for many households in the postcolonial countries affected by these policies to maintain nationally based survival strategies. This led to the formation of binational households capable of tapping into income-producing capacities of labor demand in societies such as the United States. Despite recent efforts by the U.S. state to "police the borders," this continues to be an active survival strategy pursued by households from Central America and Mexico. Such transnational survival strategies, as the contributions by Rodríguez and Kearney make clear, are sustained by transnational social networks extending across national borders, thereby circulating both material and symbolic capital across global space.

Dramatic sociospatial changes such as these have affected prevailing structures of work, residence, and social intercourse at the level of the locality, impinging on peoples' everyday experience of social life. They have reconstituted the opportunities for and constraints on communication. The global-local interplay has thus become a driving force in both the structuring of cultural practices at the level of the locality and the move to integrate analysis of the local practices of everyday life into research on the political economy of racial and ethnic formation. The complex global changes have created new material and cultural conditions conducive to the production of a multiplicity of voices, including oppositional voices to dominant modes of power and symbolism. Under these conditions, the differences of racial group, class, gender, ethnicity, locality, and region—and their complex interplay in discourses where personal and group identities are formed—have again become social bases for the emergence of new or refurbished antisystemic political movements, as the chapters by Kearney, Smith and Tarallo, and Rodríguez make clear.

What are the implications of these transformations for our understanding of the sociology and politics of racial and ethnic identity? Today, the demographic transformation of localities by the accelerated flows of transnational migration is modifying the social relations of race, ethnicity, and community that had once grounded traditional community research in particular social spaces of cultural production and place. Consistent with Rouse's analysis, Rodríguez describes a multiplicity of new social spaces that have been constituted and linked together by the daily practices of transnational migrants to North American cities from Mexico and Central America. His narrative links the globalization of everyday life in postcolonial communities and regions, via global migration and remittances, to new racial and ethnic group formations, to cooperation and conflict in U.S. cities, and to the emergence of autonomous communities made up of poor households that bridge localities and social structures across nation-state borders, demonstrating the artificiality and political construction of such border lines. The anthropological, sociological, and political science literature exploring other instances of emergent transnational spaces of daily life and political practice in today's global context is now extensive.[21] Kearney's article reviews the main contributions of this literature as a prelude to his development of the term *Oaxacalifornia* to designate the new binational social space that has been created by the everyday practices and political strategies of Mixtec migrant workers.

The Politics of Culture and the Cultural Politics of Difference

In the political sociology of ethnic and racial formation targeted in this book, the presumed global cultural homogenization of what is often called the "consumer society" is strongly challenged. Like past criticisms of the totalizing tendencies of various versions of modernization and development theory, we recognize cultural differentiation and the multiplication of forms of social agency as accompaniments and modes of resistance to the homogenizing logic of global consumer societies. In response to the globalization of U.S. localities, an emergent body of research has focused on the interplay between observed globalizing trends and local contextual experiences in the negotiation of racial and ethnic relations at the local level. As noted at the outset, this research has sought to unearth the recombinant possibilities of contemporary social life by studying the ways that in daily life people in various life situations appropriate, accommodate to, or resist the structural imperatives and capital logics of their own time and place in forging emergent race, class, ethnic, and gender identities.

The case of Korean American shopkeepers and their relationship with African Americans in large cities like Los Angeles is an intriguing case in point. Because of the export-oriented development strategy of the South Korean state and the inability of that economy to absorb upwardly mobile professionals, many Korean professionals whose mobility was blocked in their homeland immigrated to the United States. The occupational niches in the U.S. economy that were open to them were limited, since their professional credentials were often not readily transferable and they often faced anti-Asian discrimination. The economic niches these small capitalists were able to find, using household resources or capital borrowed from ethnic associations, placed them in large U.S. cities like New York and Los Angeles in potentially antagonistic relationships with other minorities, for example, as convenience store and liquor store owners in black neighborhoods, as contractors and sweatshop owners with Latino workers, and even as employers of fellow Koreans from less privileged class backgrounds. The fact that many Korean immigrants had absorbed into their conceptual repertoires negative images of the Americans, such as black Americans, from the globalized U.S. media even before they left their home country set the stage for antagonistic relations with the people whom they would serve.[22]

Following the 1992 Los Angeles rebellion, targeted by blacks and Latinos, in part, against Korean American small businesses, the once politically quiescent Korean merchants in Los Angeles protested against an ordinance passed by the city council at the urging of black neighborhood organizations to limit the rebuilding of liquor stores in South Central Los Angeles. They stood in front of city hall for two weeks and beat drums to demand a meeting with the mayor about removing the limits. They got their meeting but the ordinance stood.[23] In this example the class structure and interethnic dimensions of the L.A. rebellion were masked by the exclusive media construction of the rebellion as a "race riot" involving blacks against whites. Likewise, the class dimension of this ethnic political mobilization of the Korean merchants is masked by their ethnic homogeneity and the style of protest they brought from Korea. As for the Korean American poor, they are silent and invisible in dominant "race relations" narratives.

We have chosen the Korean American example to underscore our basic argument that race-ethnic-class relations are globally shaped, inextricably interwoven, and historically particular. Michael Omi and Howard Winant have suggested the concept of "social rearticulation," the recurring historical process of rupturing and reconstructing the understandings of racial-ethnic relations. The protest movements of various racial and ethnic groups periodically challenge the governmental and institutional elite definitions of racial-ethnic realities, as well as individual definitions of the same realities. The 1960s civil rights movement rearticulated traditional cultural and political ideas about race in the United States, and in the process changed the U.S. government and broadened the involvement of minority Americans in the politics of that government. New social movements regularly emerge, sometimes bringing new identities and political norms.[24] The Korean American protests are yet another example of this rearticulation process.

The play of difference and contests over the meaning of ethnic and racial identity operate within various groups often socially constructed in popular discourse as "marginal." Yet as the previous example illustrates, racial and ethnic groups are not pure, monolithic, essentialist entities. Rather, different-gendered relations; generational, occupational, and local residential experiences; and divisions of labor operate within households at all social levels and among all social groups. This means that even within the same household unit the implosion of macrostructural social divisions, contradictions, and systems of signification are subject to interpretation by differently situated social actors. This tends to produce varied responses to perceived situations of domination and marginality.[25]

Internal differences within historical and contemporary racial and ethnic groupings constitute an important form of resistance to the homogenization by dominant centers of power of "nonwhite others" in order to essentialize (that is, to define as fundamental) this single component of group identity. Such homogenization of racial and ethnic groups in law, custom, and everyday practice constitutes what Winant terms "white institutionalization of racial difference." For example, the elevation of "racial" difference to a fundamental component of both personal and group identity can lead to the neglect, in both research and practice, of the historically specific circumstances, conditions, and needs of both women of color and white women of different social classes. Essentializing racial difference causes insufficient attention to be given to the importance of class, gender, and generational relations within racialized groups.

The dominative structures imposing racial essentialism are contested. Voices from within racial and ethnic groups often articulate counternarratives to institutionalized racialization. Yet, precisely because of the internal differentiation among social groups, it is by no means an easy task to fulfill the exhortation to let subordinated groups "name themselves" through their voices and everyday practices. The collective self named in this way often represents a partial, selective recovery of past understandings deployed in social contests over group identity. As the chapter by Adolph Reed and the Korean American example just discussed illustrate, efforts to give voice to "authentic" racial or ethnic sensibilities are complicated by the conflation of ethnicity, race, class, and culture often encountered in internal conflicts over group identity.

Reed's powerfully argued essay lucidly underlines this complication. He shows that the essentialization of "the black community" in white and black political discourse is a basic source of black demobilization that undercuts possibilities for forming wider coalitions based on public issues of policy and governance that transcend communitarian mythology. All racial and ethnic groups are internally differentiated in salient ways. Thus, for example, Smith and Tarallo's analysis stresses the crucial internal conflicts between first-wave and second-wave Vietnamese refugees based on the different class, regional, and ideological bases of the two migrations. Winant, Brackman, and Erie note that an awareness of internal differentiation is crucial to our understanding of the prospects for the construction of panethnic identities like "Asian-American" or "Latino." For instance, residual home country historical antagonisms between Japanese and Koreans, Vietnamese and Chinese, Mexicans and Central Americans, Cubans and Puerto Ricans can be barriers to the construction of communitarian panethnic identities constructed from below as well as from above.

Moreover, it is not only internal differences but also the ways in which some potential coalition members are stigmatized in the wider world that stand in the way of the formation of politically viable panethnic social movements. For example, one barrier to the formation of a panethnic Asian

American consciousness is the current construction of poor refugees from rural parts of Southeast Asia as socially dysfunctional members of American society. While heretofore the racialized "underclass" discourse discussed earlier has largely stigmatized unemployed or underemployed black and (less often) Latino men and women, in the global era it is being extended more broadly by U.S. social welfare bureaucrats and policy intellectuals to encompass a growing number of second-wave Southeast Asian refugee families from Laos, Cambodia, and Vietnam, groups that have become dependent on public assistance for household survival in recent years. This development, along with the rise of Southeast Asian youth gangs in some cities, leaves these groups vulnerable to the "underclass" rhetoric. These developments, in turn, make other Asian American nationalities and classes less likely to incorporate these groups into a multiclass, panethnic coalition.

Despite Reed's subtly inflected critique of black essentialism, the text and the subtext of his contribution express skepticism concerning the trend to import conceptual tools from cultural studies into social science analyses of "cultural politics." It is useful to heed Reed's warning against a turn toward romanticism in the study of cultural politics. Nevertheless, several contributions to this volume, notably those by Fainstein, Kearney, Rodríguez, and Smith and Tarallo, add another layer of complexity to the debate on cultural politics by considering the current impact of representations of racial-ethnic differences in the mass-mediated spaces of popular culture. Even the more economically focused ethnography by Hodge and Feagin enters the domain of cultural politics by powerfully contesting the image by neoconservatives that black businesspersons lack an entrepreneurial culture, rather than just fair access to supplies, credit, and capital.

At least since the 1980s resurrection of the once-discredited "culture of poverty" thesis, and its use by neoconservative media commentators as a mechanism to blame subordinated groups (mainly blacks, Mexican Americans, and Puerto Ricans) for lacking the "entrepreneurial culture" of Jewish, Korean, and Cuban Americans, it has become clear that the domains of cultural politics and institutional politics are inextricably joined. In the mass-mediated society in which we live, the politics of representation contained in gangster-rap videos and MTV necessarily spills over into the political space of public policy discourse on poverty, race, crime, law, order, and governance. In the last instance, therefore, there is an unavoidable interplay between immediate and mass-mediated communications, power and symbolism, and state structures and the commercial marketplace in the reconstitution of racial-ethnic identity and difference. In the same sense that all politics is local, all politics is also "cultural," and necessarily so, if the democratic voices needed to put "race" in its place are to be heard.

Notes

1. See Michael Peter Smith, "Postmodernism, Urban Ethnography, and the New Social Space of Ethnic Identity," *Theory and Society* 21 (1992): 493–531.

2. This and the next several paragraphs draw in part on Joe R. Feagin and Clairece B. Feagin, *Racial and Ethnic Relations,* 4th ed. (Englewood Cliffs, N.J.: Prentice-Hall, 1993), 43–44, 213–404.

3. See U.S. Department of Justice, Immigration and Naturalization Service, *Annual Report* (Washington, D.C.: GPO, 1975), 62–64; and Julian Samora, *Los Mojados: The Wetback Story* (Notre Dame, Ind.: University of Notre Dame Press, 1971).

4. Albert Szymanski, *The Capitalist State and the Politics of Class* (Cambridge, Mass.: Winthrop, 1978), 187–88.

5. Patricia Hill Collins, *Black Feminist Thought: Knowledge, Consciousness, and the Politics of Empowerment* (Boston: Unwin Hyman, 1990), 40–48.

6. National Opinion Research Center, 1990 General Social Survey, tabulations by Joe R. Feagin; Don Terry, "Woman's False Charge Revives Hurt for Blacks," *New York Times,* November 6, 1994; Richard J. Herrnstein and Charles Murray, *The Bell Curve* (New York: Free Press, 1994).

7. Ozzie G. Simmons, "The Mutual Images and Expectations of Anglo-Americans and Mexican-Americans," in *Introduction to Chicano Studies,* ed. Livie I. Duran and H. Russell Bernard (New York: Macmillan, 1973), 387–97.

8. Feagin and Feagin, *Racial and Ethnic Relations,* 266.

9. U.S. Commission on Civil Rights, *Recent Activities against Citizens and Residents of Asian Descent* (Washington, D.C.: GPO, 1986), 7, 43–44; U.S. Commission on Civil Rights, *Civil Rights Issues Facing Asian Americans in the 1990s* (Washington, D.C.: GPO 1992), 25–28.

10. "Tension Rises in New York in March over Black's Death," *Austin American-Statesman,* December 28, 1987, A3.

11. Reported in "FBI Issues First Data on Hate Crimes," *Race Relations Reporter,* March 15, 1993, 8.

12. William Julius Wilson, *The Truly Disadvantaged* (Chicago: University of Chicago Press, 1987); for a critique of the underclass concept, see Joe R. Feagin and Leslie Inniss, "The Black Underclass Ideology in Race Relations Analysis," *Social Justice* 16 (Winter 1989), 12–34; see also Adolph Reed Jr., "The Underclass as Myth and Symbol," *Radical America,* January 1992, 21–40.

13. Douglas S. Massey and Nancy A. Denton, *American Apartheid: Segregation and the Making of the Underclass* (Cambridge, Mass.: Harvard University Press, 1993), 221–23. For a theoretical explanation of this institutional dynamic, see Michael Peter Smith, *City, State and Market* (Cambridge, Mass., and Oxford: Basil Blackwell, 1991), 9–14.

14. Edna Bonacich, "The Social Costs of Immigrant Entrepreneurship," *Amerasia Journal* 14, no. 1 (1988): 119–28; Paul Ong et al., *Beyond Asian American Poverty* (Los Angeles: Asian Pacific Public Policy Institute, 1993); see also Min Zhou and John R. Logan, "Returns on Human Capital in Ethnic Enclaves: New York City's Chinatown," *American Sociological Review* 54 (1991): 809–20.

15. Michael Peter Smith and Bernadette Tarallo, *California's Changing Faces: New Immigrant Survival Strategies and State Policy* (Berkeley: California Policy Seminar, 1993), 130–41.

16. Roger Rouse, "Mexican Migration and the Social Space of Postmodernism," *Diaspora,* Spring 1991, 1–23.

17. Hsiao-Chuan Hsia, "Imported Racism and Indigenous Biases: The Impacts of the U.S. Mass Media on Taiwanese Images of African Americans" (paper presented at the American Sociological Association meetings, Los Angeles, Calif., August 1994); Sumi K. Cho, "Korean Americans vs. African Americans: Conflict and Construction," in *Reading Rodney King, Reading Urban Uprising,* ed. Robert Gooding-Williams (New York and London: Routledge, 1993), 199.

18. Tim Golden, "The Voice of the Rebels Has Mexico in His Spell," *New York Times,* February 8, 1994, A3; see also *San Francisco Examiner,* February 21, 1994, A12.

19. On the use of the outside agitator ideology, see Joe R. Feagin and Harlan Hahn, *Ghetto Revolts* (New York: Macmillan, 1973).

20. G. Balandier, "The Colonial Situation: A Theoretical Approach," in *Social Change,* ed. Immanuel Wallerstein (New York: Wiley, 1966), 35.

21. See Arjun Appadurai, "Disjuncture and Difference in the Global Cultural Economy," in *Global Culture,* ed. Michael Featherstone (London: Sage, 1990), 295–310; Carol Nagengast and Michael Kearney, "Mixtec Ethnicity," *Latin American Research Review* 25, no. 2 (1990): 61–91; Rouse, "Mexican Migration and the Social Space of Postmodernism"; and Michael Peter Smith, "Can You Imagine? Transnational Migration and the Globalization of Grassroots Politics," *Social Text* 39 (Summer 1994): 15–33.

22. See Ong et al., *Beyond Asian American Poverty,* and Cho, "Korean Americans vs. African Americans."

23. Raphael J. Sonenshein, *Politics in Black and White: Race and Power in Los Angeles* (Princeton, N.J.: Princeton University Press, 1993), 255.

24. Howard Winant, "Racial Formation Theory and Contemporary U.S. Politics," in *Exploitation and Exclusion,* ed. Abebe Zegeye, Leonard Harris, and Julia Maxted (London: Hans Zell, 1991), 130–40.

25. Smith, "Postmodernism, Urban Ethnography."

Part II

The Social Construction of Racial and Ethnic Difference

2 / Dictatorship, Democracy, and Difference

The Historical Construction of Racial Identity

Howard Winant

Introduction: The Sources of Racial Identity

A quarter-century after the peak of the civil rights movement, the theme of race continues to occupy a central place in U.S. cultural, political, and economic life. But what does race *mean* in the United States today? How can a concept with no scientific significance, a concept that is understood in such varied and often irrational ways, retain such force? Why is race such an important source of meaning, identity, (dis)advantage, power, and powerlessness?

In U.S. society, and in many others as well, race is a fundamental organizing principle, a way of knowing and interpreting the social world. As we watch the videotape of Rodney King being beaten by Los Angeles police officers; compare real estate prices in different metropolitan area neighborhoods; select a radio channel to enjoy while we drive to work; size up a potential client, customer, neighbor, or teacher; or carry out a thousand other normal tasks, we are compelled to think racially, to use the racial categories and meaning systems into which we have been socialized. Despite exhortations both sincere and hypocritical, it is not possible to be "color-blind," for race is a basic element of our identity. Indeed, when one meets a person who is difficult to classify racially, the result is often a "minicrisis" of identity:

not knowing to what race someone belongs is like not knowing to what sex they belong. For better or for worse, without a clear racial identity, an American is in danger of having no identity.

The problem, though, is that a clear racial identity does not, and cannot, exist. At the moment, the U.S. "racial rules" offer us a choice of five racial categories: white, black, brown, yellow, and red. Stripped of euphemism, these color categories, absurd as they are, define the racial universe. Unfortunately, many people don't fit in anywhere. Where should we classify Arab Americans, for example, or South Asians, or Brazilians? What about people with more than one racial characteristic, for example black Puerto Ricans? Are they "African American" or "Hispanic"? Such questions can be multiplied indefinitely.

In this chapter I explore the logic of racial identity as it has evolved in the United States, from the aftermath of the Civil War to the present. I emphasize four basic themes: first, in the United States there has always and necessarily been a deep relationship between nonwhite and white identities. Second, until about the end of World War II the United States was a *herrenvolk* democracy,[1] a de facto racial dictatorship constituted by the denial of basic democratic rights to racially defined minorities (and to women, although that is not my focus here). Third, movement-based democratic challenge to this increasingly atavistic racial order necessarily transformed all U.S. racial identities, in the process of reducing, although not eliminating, white supremacy. Fourth and finally, in the aftermath of that ruptural moment, or if you prefer, in the post–civil rights era, racial identity is experienced at unprecedented levels of tension, for it can be neither fully affirmed nor denied.

While the chapter is intended as an overview of the historical processes through which racial identity developed in the United States, it makes no attempt to be comprehensive. I pursue what I consider to be central political and cultural themes in the construction of the racial present out of the past, and ignore others. Indeed it could not be otherwise with a topic of this size. Finally, in a brief conclusion entitled "Democratizing Racial Identity," I offer some notes on the contemporary politics of racial identity. The relational and increasingly complex nature of racial identity — and the centrality of a conception of identity to the ongoing struggle for racial democracy and social justice — continues to preoccupy us today. These forces now at play in the construction of contemporary racial identity are descended from a past that we ignore or misinterpret at our peril.

Historical Racialization

By now it is a commonplace to note the centrality of racial slavery in the development of notions of freedom and democracy in the United States[2]. The racialization of these political categories (and their genderization, as well) was already well codified by the time the United States was founded. Similarly, arguments about the relationship of race and class may be traced back to the contradictory relationship between enslaved and "free" labor. The classical Marxian position, that "labor cannot emancipate itself in the white skin where in the black it is branded,"[3] unquestionably recognized an important truth, one that resulted in considerable support among white workers for the cause of the North in the U.S. Civil War. Yet, despite their occasionally enthusiastic support for emancipation, these workers were determined to maintain the separate and elevated status the designation "white" bestowed upon them. Why?[4]

It is not enough to argue that whites were protecting their jobs and higher wage levels, although this is of course significant. This "split labor market" analysis (which I have criticized elsewhere) cannot be seen as operating in a vacuum or as automatically determining political orientation, cultural reference points, or notions of identity.[5] As several decades of crucial work in social history and social theory have taught us, "interests" are never obvious, never objective, never simply given. They are always mediated by politics, culture, subjectivity; they are always constructed.

So it is not surprising that race was already present in the way *white* workers recognized themselves in the nineteenth century. Why else would they have been more threatened by emancipated black labor (or conquered Mexican labor or immigrant Asian labor) than by the flood of European immigrants in the later nineteenth century? Why else would they have adopted — with a few noble but short-lived exceptions — racially exclusive forms of organization? Their class identity was itself racialized, and the class formation process that issued in this situation drew not only upon fears of economic competition — wage-cutting and even replacement by nonwhite labor — but also upon larger fears of a political, cultural, and even sexual nature. Such ideas were deeply embedded in nineteenth-century biologistic notions of race.

White workers defined themselves through various cultural forms — notably minstrelsy — accepting the disciplinary regime of industry, "hardening" themselves against any weakness (perceived as effeminate) and against the idleness and ease they associated with blacks, the sunny southland, and so on. The outcome of these transformations was a racialization of working-class identity as white. This racializing process worked to organize both resentment and desire, in the service of an essentially tragic but noble whiteness that was constantly threatened by "weakness" and "longings" no amount of discipline could ever fully dispel. Such was the legacy for whites of enslavement and emancipation. The consequence was *herrenvolk* democracy and a system of racial difference as monolithic — because of its deep psychological embeddedness in the working class — as any in the world.

Parallel processes occurred in other spheres of nineteenth-century U.S. race relations. In the Southwest, for example, where the problem was conquest, not enslavement,[6] the construction of Anglo and Mexicano racial identities was a prolonged and occasionally violent process. As David Montejano writes: "In the 'liberated' and annexed territories, Anglos and Mexicans stood as conquerors and conquered, victors and vanquished, a distinction as fundamental as any sociological sign of privilege and rank. How could it have been otherwise after a war?"[7]

From the end of the war with Mexico onward the region underwent a lengthy transition from ranching to commercial agriculture (and ultimately to industrialization), all undertaken under the heavy legacies of conquest, the defeat of the South in the Civil War, and the Mexican revolution. Locally this brought about a varied combination of antidemocratic forms of rule, incorporating not only coercive labor systems and widespread discrimination, but also creating what Montejano defines as a "race situation": "a situation where ethnic or national prejudice provided a basis for separation and control."[8] The system of racial rule in the Southwest was certainly coercive and arbitrary, but retained a distinctiveness and paternalism that derived from the semicolonial status of the area — in which a white settler minority ruled over a racialized "native" majority — and from the presence of the border.

After the conquest, the native Spanish-speaking Tejanos outnumbered the white settlers, and they resisted land usurpations and other indignities in the "Cortina Wars" (1859–60, 1873–75) and the El Paso "Salt War" (1877), as well as innumerable skirmishes. Eventually terms of accommodation developed (although not for decades in some areas) that involved de facto segregation, a recognition of citizenship rights combined with significant disenfranchisement of ordinary Mexicanos, and a limited conciliation among the Anglo and Mexicano elites. While perhaps less harsh than the repressive regime of the Deep South, this system was nevertheless of the *herrenvolk* variety.[9]

On the West Coast, *exclusion* also provided the basis for coercive racial control, crystallizing a complex pattern of white fears and exploitation of Asians.[10] Asian subordination was unlike that of blacks or Mexicans, since it distinguished among racialized groups on a national basis. Great variation also existed among particular locales and over historical time. Filipinos, for example, were subject to anti-Asian racism but were less easily excluded, since the Philippines were a U.S. territory after 1898. The chief motivation for exclusionist policies came from demands made by white workers, but here too the construction of working-class identity and political collectivity was intensively racialized. The labor historian Selig Perlman suggested some of the ferocity and complexity of this process when he wrote:

> The political issue after 1877 was racial, not financial, and the weapon was not merely the ballot but also "direct action" — violence. The anti-Chinese agitation in California, culminating as it did in the Exclusion Law passed by Congress in 1882, was doubtless the most important single factor in the history of American labor, for without it the entire country might have been overrun by Mongolian [sic] labor and the labor movement might have become a conflict of races instead of one of classes.[11]

As this passage makes clear, the labor movement *did* in fact become a conflict of races. And there was never a chance that Asians might immigrate in the numbers that Europeans did; Perlman reflects some of the fears his white working-class subjects felt.

In fact, exclusionary policies merely formalized the anti-Asian mobilization — chiefly based in the labor movement — that had been building on the West Coast for decades. The various laws and policies aimed at restricting immigration — the 1882 Act (renewed in 1892 and made permanent in 1907), the "Gentlemen's Agreement" of 1907 sharply restricting Japanese immigration, and the 1924 immigration law — were only the most prominent anti-Asian measures. Restrictions on citizenship, outmarriage, land ownership, and legal rights in general had little to do with immigration and everything to do with widespread fears of the "yellow peril." Anti-Asian agitation also had a *herrenvolkish* character that went far beyond labor market competition. It relentlessly emphasized the *alien* qualities of Asians, their necessary and presumably permanent incompatibility with the North American (that is, white) way of life. The California Supreme Court articulated these concepts in quintessential form as early as 1854 in *People v. Hall.*

At times anti-Asian agitators stressed degeneracy and disease or harped on sexual fears. For example, such themes as opium use, prostitution, and "white slavery" were constantly invoked in anti-Chinese propaganda. Here is a certain parallelism with the construction of whiteness as antiblackness in the same historical epoch. While the particular arguments of anti-Asian rhetoric varied, the underlying theme of otherness was always present. The Asian immigrant was seen as irremediably alien, the "stranger from a distant shore," whose acceptance in the United States was almost unimaginable.

Constructing the Present

Enslavement, conquest, and exclusion, then, were the chief means through which U.S. society was racialized beginning with its colonial origins. Racialization varied over time, across regions, and in respect to particular groups. But it was always present, always crucial to the construction of what Saxton calls "the white republic." Racialization can be understood in many ways: as a repertoire of coercive social practices driven by desires and fears, as a framework for class formation, or as an ideology for nation building and territorial expansion, to name but a few.

Here I wish to emphasize the political consequences of racialization: beyond class formation, beyond territorial expansion, beyond the biologism that informed the building of a *herrenvolk* society, racialization organized a basic U.S. social structure: it established the overall contours, as well as the particular political and cultural legacies, of subordination and resistance. It restricted or even eliminated the political terrain upon which racially defined groups could mobilize within civil society, thus constituting these groups as outsiders. It denied the existence of commonalities among whites and non-whites—such as shared economic activities, shared rights as citizens, even on occasion shared humanity—thus constructing race, at least typically, in terms of all-embracing social difference. Racialization, then, also tended to homogenize distinctions among those whose difference with whites was considered the only crucial component of their identities. Over time, then, this white-versus-other concept of difference created not particular and unchanging racial identities—for these are always in flux—but the potentiality, the social structures, indeed the necessity, of universally racialized identities in the United States. Elsewhere Omi and I have described this process, drawing on Gramsci, as *racial war of maneuver*: a conflict between disenfranchised and systematically subordinated groups, whose principal efforts are devoted to self-preservation and resistance, and that of a dictatorial and comprehensively dominant power.[12]

Paradoxically, white institutionalization of racial difference; white refusal to grant such basic democratic rights as citizenship, access to the legal system, and the vote; and white resistance to the participation by racially defined minorities in civil society, permitted — and indeed demanded — the organization and consolidation of excluded communities of color. Because it had so comprehensively externalized its racial others, *herrenvolk* democracy helped constitute their resistance and opposition. It set the stage for its own destruction, because, over centuries, whites forced nonwhites to forge their own collective identities, to suppress their differences, and to unite outside the high walls of a supposedly democratic society whose rights and privileges were systematically restricted on the basis of race.

Disruption of Identity

It would be too optimistic to assert that at some point the walls came tumbling down. Indeed in many respects the racial walls remain impenetrably thick today. Yet clearly with emancipation, with the consolidation — at often terrible costs — of racially identified communities whose permanent presence on these shores was no longer in serious doubt, with the development of racial *war of maneuver*, the preconditions of the political movements of our own time had been created. The pioneering movement, of course, was the black movement.[13]

Beginning in the 1950s, the modern civil rights movement transformed the American political universe, creating new organizations, new collective identities, and new political norms; challenging past racial practices and stereotypes; and ushering in a wave of democratizing social reform. This transformation, which at first affected blacks, but soon touched Latinos, Asian Americans, and Native Americans as well, permitted the entry of millions of racial minority group members into the political process. It set off the "second wave" of feminism, a new anti-imperialism and antiwar movement, movements for gay and disability rights and even for environmental protection. The black movement deeply affected whites as well, challenging often unconscious beliefs in white supremacy and demanding new and more respectful forms of behavior in relation to nonwhites.

These changes can be understood as the eruption of a racial *war of position,* supplanting the war of maneuver that had largely shaped previous racial conflict in the United States. Gramsci understands war of position as political and cultural conflict, undertaken under conditions in which subordinated groups have attained some foothold, some rights, within civil society; thus they have the leverage, the ability to press some claims on the state.[14]

In transforming the meaning of race and the contours of racial politics, the movement shifted the rules of participation and the organizing themes of American politics itself. It made identity, difference, the "personal," and language itself political issues in very new ways. By the mid-1960s, popular support for the main principles of the "civil rights revolution" had been secured and legislation passed.

Yet this triumph was partial and contradictory. The movement agenda had been accepted, but only in its most moderate form. A significant distance remained between the formal acknowledgment by Congress or the Supreme Court of black *rights* to equal justice, education, housing, or employment and the actual *achievement* of those rights. The unity of the movement eroded rapidly as its mainstream liberal supporters — and most of its white adherents — congratulated themselves on their victory, while many movement activists — and much of its black membership — wondered how much change civil rights could bring, absent significant redistribution of income and major efforts to eradicate poverty. These veterans wanted not only rights, but also the power and resources to achieve dramatic social change; they demanded not simply abstract and often unrealizable opportunities, but concrete results.

Perhaps most important, movement moderates sought to downplay the significance of racial identity, while movement radicals tried to reemphasize it. The debate over identity focused in crucial ways on black views of whites: would they be able to move beyond their own racism, their own dependence, often unconscious, on the privileges conferred by white skin in the United States? Was American democracy, in the familiar dichotomy articulated by Martin and Malcolm respectively, a "dream" or a "nightmare"?

These divisions between moderates and radicals over matters not only of policy but also of identity were the inheritance of centuries-long conflicts in the U.S. social structure. They reflected the submerged but still powerful legacy of *herrenvolk* democracy, of the institutionalization of racial categories at the base of North American society. Simultaneously, they epitomized the unraveling of these structures, the impossibility of sustaining a racial dictatorship, and the potential for an even more serious explosion of racially . based movement opposition if serious reforms were not undertaken. Such ferocious divisions, rooted in the framework of U.S. society and history, could hardly be resolved by the movement; they could only be mirrored within it. They would continue to sunder not only the black movement, but all racially based movements in the post-civil-rights period. They would continue to divide racial identities — *all* identities, including those of whites — from the 1970s onward.

In the aftermath of the civil rights reforms, the forces of racial reaction also had to regroup. They could no longer sustain an implacable resistance to black demands for basic social rights, for such a posture risked their marginalization at the far right of the political spectrum. On the other hand, although white supremacy had certainly been shaken, it had not been destroyed. The cultural framework that supported it — the racial subjectivities, representations, and cognitive capacities of the U.S. populace — had not been comprehensively transformed. So the racial right, like its movement antagonists, was divided.

The nascent *new right* recognized that white supremacy was not dead, but only wounded. It therefore attempted to tap into repressed but still strong currents of racism in order to counter the black movement's egalitarian thrust. Born in the campaigns of George Wallace and Richard Nixon's 1968 "southern strategy," the new right developed a new subtextual approach to politics, which involved "coding" white resentments of blacks, and later of other minorities, women, and gays.

Another approach was developed by the *neoconservatives,* former liberals who had been affiliated with the moderate wing of the civil rights movement but were disaffected by its post-1965 nationalist and class-based radicalisms. Marked by their white ethnicity, their experience as the children of immigrants, and in particular their youthful leftism and their struggles against anti-Semitism (many key neoconservatives were Jews), neoconservative thinkers and politicians had made visceral commitments to what they saw as the core political culture of the United States: pluralism, consensus, gradualism, and centrism. They subscribed to an ethnicity-based model of race, derived quite consciously from the "immigrant analogy."[15] Their opposition to the outright institutionalized prejudice of Jim Crow, which had temporarily allied them with the pre-1965 civil rights movement, thus had sources very different from that of their erstwhile movement allies. The idea of white supremacy as an abiding presence in American life was anathema to the neoconservatives, for it called into question their idealized view of U.S. political culture.

Neoconservatives abhorred the arguments of black militants as typified in Malcolm's statement: "I don't see any American democracy. All I see is American hypocrisy." In a striking way, they reproduced the fearful and compensatory allegiance to whiteness exhibited in the late nineteenth century. Just as many whites in the nineteenth century had opposed slavery but resisted a comprehensive reorganization of their privileged status vis-à-vis emancipated blacks, so too the neoconservatives opposed overt discrimination, but resisted an in-depth confrontation with the enduring benefits that race conferred on whites. Thus they sought to confine the egalitarian upsurge, to reinterpret movement ideas more narrowly and individualistically, and to channel them in more conservative directions. Their views aligned them with the white ethnics whose integration into mainstream American society resulted in conservative politics and a sense of "optional" ethnicity, amounting in practice to a denial of the significance of race in American life.

So the racial reaction, too, was beset by divisions, in this case between the new right and the neoconservatives. Should the legacy of racial dictatorship and white supremacy, of *herrenvolk* democracy, be exploited or suppressed? Should the state uphold the civil rights legacy or undermine it? Should whites be mobilized qua whites — in defense of their racial privilege — or should the erosion of that privilege be anticipated or even encouraged? These questions sharply problematized white identities in the post-civil-rights period and created serious difficulties for nonwhites, as well.[16]

Tension Rules, OK?

The racial sea change wrought by the movement was incomplete; it was immediately challenged by "backlash" and a resurgent racial right, and the movement was itself split between moderates and radicals. Therefore the meaning of race in the United States and the ongoing significance of race for North American identities remained as problematic as ever, as the civil rights legacy was drawn and quartered, beginning in the late 1960s. The tugging and hauling, the escalating contestation over the meaning of race, resulted in ever more disrupted and contradictory notions of racial identity. The significance of race ("declining" or increasing?), the interpretation of racial equality ("color-blind" or color conscious?), the institutionalization of racial justice ("reverse discrimination" or affirmative action?), and the very categories — black, white, Latino/Hispanic, Asian American, and Native

American — employed to classify racial groups were all called into question as they emerged from the civil rights "victory" of the mid-1960s.

In the post-civil-rights period, what did it mean to be "black"? The term "Negro" had once been asserted with pride as a token of independence and resistance to racism, but in the era of black power it was tainted by its long association with the old-line civil rights organizations such as the NAACP and the Urban League, groups that came to be seen as co-opted, even as "Toms." The reassertion of the term "black," then, symbolized race consciousness and pride.[17] Black psychologists noted a "negro-to-black conversion experience."[18] Indeed, in the wake of the black power revolt, debates over what constituted a "true" black identity expanded vigorously into every area of social and cultural life: language, skin color, taste, family life, and patterns of consumption all became testing grounds of blackness. Prescribing criteria for identity formation became one of the chief preoccupations of so-called cultural nationalism.[19] Radical nationalisms could not consolidate themselves politically, however, although they continued to exercise important cultural influences. Nationalism also appeared to thrive in the conservative framework of the Nation of Islam.

The decline of the organized black movement in the 1970s and the wholesale assaults against the welfare state initiated by Ronald Reagan during the 1980s created a black community sharply divided along class lines. A small but relatively secure black middle class, a "coping stratum" of black workers increasingly threatened by deindustrialization and the erosion of public services, and a marginalized sector dubbed "the urban underclass" by William J. Wilson and others offered three quite different models of identity, and indeed embodied three disparate sets of interests.

Middle-class blacks were unable and unwilling fully to integrate, and they still faced significant levels of discrimination, yet the range of opportunities available to them would have been unimaginable only a few years before. The dilemmas of racial identification thus hit them with special force.[20] Sharply distinguished from the professionalized and upwardly mobile middle class was the "coping stratum" of working-class blacks, who struggled to survive the continuing threat of declining neighborhoods, worsening schools, and eroding employment markets.[21] Meanwhile the desolation of the poor increased steadily, interrupted only by periodic revivals of victim blaming.[22]

Although divided by status, these sectors were united by a residual racial solidarity, rooted both in the complex web of social ties — provided by family, work, religion, and so on—and in the recognition that white supremacy and racial inequality were far from dead. But without question black experience in the post–civil rights period was characterized by greater division than the community had ever known before.

Without extolling the racist ethos of the period, it is undeniable that the black community in the Jim Crow era experienced a certain *organic* interrelatedness—especially in the urban context[23]—that the winning of civil rights reforms tended to erode. The significance of disrupted black identity is therefore complex, even contradictory. On the one hand, the emergence of diverse and even conflicting voices in the black community is welcome, for it reflects real changes in the direction of mobility and democratization. On the other hand, the persistence of racism, of white supremacy, and of glaring racial inequality demands a level of concerted action that division and discord tend to preclude.

In the post-civil-rights period, what did it mean to be "yellow" or "brown"? The civil rights reforms had tremendous demographic and political effects on racialized groups of Asian and Latin American origins. The reforms included passage of a new immigration act in 1965, which abolished many overtly racist features of the previous 1924 law. As a result these communities began to grow rapidly. Politically, the black movement—and the victories it won—exerted a substantial influence upon Asians and Latinos, sparking substantial panethnic currents. Previously isolated in enclaves based on language and national origin, Koreans, Filipinos, Japanese, and Chinese underwent a substantial racialization process from the late 1960s onward, emerging as "Asian Americans."[24] Thenceforward, the racism they had previously experienced as separate groups would be seen in a more common light, although the conflicts among these groups did not entirely abate. Similar shifts overtook Mexicans, Puerto Ricans, Central Americans, and even Cubans as the "Latino" and "Hispanic" categories were popularized. The destruction of formal segregation in Texas had a profound impact on Mexican Americans there, while the brief rise of militant black nationalism greatly influenced the development of Chicanismo in California,[25] as well as affecting Puerto Rican groups in the Northeast.

But for both Asian Americans and Latinos this new racial identity was fraught with contradictions. Apart from long-standing antagonisms among particular groups—for example, Cubans and Puerto Ricans, or Koreans and Japanese—significant class- and gender-based conflicts existed as well. Tendencies among long-established residents to disparage and sometimes exploit immigrants who are "fresh off the boat" or for group ties to attenuate as social mobility increased suggest the centrality of class in immigrant life.[26] The liberating possibilities encountered by immigrating women and their greater proclivity to settle in the United States rather than to return to their countries of origin suggest the centrality of gender in immigrant life.[27]

Knit together by "racial lumping" and by a series of common political concerns—in the Asian American case, continuing anti-Asian violence[28] and recession-driven increases in prejudice; in the Latino case, hostility to immigrants, the "English only" movement, and so on[29]—these groups were also uncomfortable with the new terms in which their identities were racialized. Japanese Americans, and all Asian Americans by extension, were faced with hostility they had not experienced since World War II as Japanese economic competition revived working-class anti-Asian prejudice and new talk of exclusion, for example in the universities.[30] At the same time Asian Americans were held up as "model minorities," and their accomplishments were used (and often distorted) to justify neoconservative racial politics and policies. The realization that racism can stigmatize one not only as inferior but also as superior was startling.

Some parallel tensions erupted among Latinos and blacks, who were often pitted against each other in local electoral contests (particularly in California and Texas, but also in other areas) and in struggles for influence over such city and county agencies as school systems and police departments. Many of Latin American descent resisted the very categories "Latino" and "Hispanic," in recognition of the sharp disparities between the racial order in their countries of origin (or of their parents' origin) and the system of racial classification in the United States.[31] When they returned the 1990 census questionnaire, for example, many Puerto Ricans checked the box marked "Other" rather than selecting a "Hispanic" category.[32]

Thus Asian Americans and Latinos frequently found themselves caught between the past and the future. Old forms of racism resurfaced to confront them, and it was sometimes intimated that they lacked the rights of whites, as in the Asian admissions controversy. Yet at the same time their newly panethnicized identities brought them face to face with challenges that were quite distinct from anything faced in the past. Some examples of these challenges were the dubious gift of neoconservative support, the antagonism of blacks, and the tendencies toward dilution of specific ethnic-national identity in a racialized category created by a combination of "lumping" and political exigency.

In the post–civil-rights period, what did it mean to be "white"? This is a difficult question. Recent research shows the components of classical white *ethnicity* to be in inexorable decline. Large-scale European immigration is a thing of the past (although contemporary upheavals in Eastern Europe may reverse this); while urban ethnic enclaves continue to exist in many major cities, suburbanization and gentrification are taking their toll. Communal forms of white ethnic identity are eroded not only by outmarriage but also by the very situation that generates it: heterogeneous contact in schools, workplaces, neighborhoods, religious settings, and so forth.

The result of these trends is the development of a new, catchall category, the "European American."[33] This designation may seem merely a synonym for "white," but according to the best recent studies, it incorporates not only a residual commitment to racial "status honor,"[34] but also a certain set of cultural tools allowing the bearers to identify with American individualism and with the ideology of opportunity so basic to U.S. culture.

Ironically, retention of some ethnic identification becomes more important as the communal supports for ethnicity erode. According to Waters, the quest for an ethnic identity helps counteract the experience of homogenization that accompanies white middle-class existence, which is often culturally deracinated. "Symbolic ethnicity" revitalizes and individualizes one's sense of self.[35] But because ethnicity remains largely symbolic for whites, it is fundamentally different from race. This is a point whites frequently don't understand. "They enjoy many choices themselves, but they continue to ascribe identities to others — especially those they can identify by skin color."[36] White identity is undergoing a crisis that is at bottom deeply political. The destruction of the communal bases of white ethnicity is far advanced, yet whiteness remains a significant source of "status honor." This white privilege — a relic of *herrenvolk* democracy — has been called into question in the post–civil-rights period, without being entirely destroyed. The result has been significant anxiety and a drift to the right, a tendency quite manipulable by modern, more subtle, race-baiters.

What are the limits of the rightward drift in white identity politics? Clinton's election in 1992 seemed to indicate that the Democratic coalition of working-class whites and racially identified minority voters, which had split apart first in 1968 and then again in 1980, could be revived. Two years later, though, that coalition was in shambles once again. The 1994 elections featured renewed race-baiting from both Republicans and Democrats, particularly on the issues of crime and welfare. The bills for the Democrats' move to the right in 1992 now came due: Clinton's effort to accommodate the white suburbs and the "Reagan democrats" resulted in the reappearance of venerable traditions of racial scapegoating, combined with apathy among traditional Democratic voters.

Yet it is unclear how much race-baiting can accomplish thirty years after the passage of civil rights legislation. While the suburban drift rightward certainly reflects racial fears, it also expresses the anxieties of a working class whose economic security is now in greater jeopardy than at any time since the 1930s. And while the civil rights agenda has hardly been fulfilled — witness the nearly complete absence of residential desegregation — on other levels racial integration has unquestionaby advanced, and tolerance is not dead, even in the suburbs. Millions of white women and gays understand something about the ongoing realities of discrimination, for example. White identities remain uneven and contested: white ethnics are not uniformly "Reagan democrats"; conservative whites may be antiracist; class and gender play important parts in determining racial attitudes; and other factors such as age, work experience, and neighborhood are also involved. The volatility of contemporary white identities, not their consolidation, is what must be emphasized.

Toward Racial Democracy

Not since the aftermath of the Civil War, and possibly not since Europeans first landed on these shores, has racial identity has been more problematized and contested. The contest is a truly epochal one, whose origins are simultaneously age-old and contemporary.

Over the past few decades, after preparatory labors lasting a century and more, a fundamental challenge was finally posed to the long tradition of racial dictatorship, of *herrenvolk* democracy, in the United States. This challenge, and the reaction to it, deeply disrupted the sense of racial identity, of what it means to be black, white, Latino, Asian American, or Native American. Initiated by the civil rights movement but not limited to blacks — indeed not limited to racially defined minorities — this challenge sought to open up the floodgates of democracy and social justice, to sweep away the legacy of white male privilege. It was only partially successful. It achieved many political reforms, and it significantly reshaped social and cultural life, but it did not accomplish the destruction of white supremacy. Nor could it have, for such a thoroughgoing social change is the work of many years. The struggle continues.

Nor could the movement have succeeded for another reason: it was it-self deeply divided over the meaning of race. The movement's limitations created openings for racial reaction, which fashioned its defense of white supremacy as a conservative egalitarianism, sometimes upholding a vision of a color-blind society, sometimes blatantly manipulating racial fears. Thus, for roughly two decades (say, 1970 to 1990), the disruption of racial identi-ties did not result in the upsurge of democracy desired by the movement. Rather, it *increased* racial tensions, both in U.S. society at large and among (and within) racially defined groups. Such tensions combined advances and setbacks, progress and defeats, for the cause of racial democracy and democ-racy in general.

The task today is to reignite the movement for greater democracy. To achieve that is not the work of an essay, but I would like to offer one sug-gestion, to contribute one idea, to that effort, as a concluding thought based on the analysis offered here. It is this: *racial democracy involves the democratiza-tion of racial identity.* What this means above all is that open discussion is needed about the commonalities and differences that exist not only among distinct racially defined groups, but also within each group. As I have ar-gued, today divisions within each group are greater than ever before, yet this does not in any way place U.S. society "beyond" race. Events like the L.A. riots and the Thomas-Hill hearings demonstrate the significance of class- and gender-based differences for contemporary racial identities and the fallacies of invoking criteria of "racial authenticity" in making political or ethical judgments about individuals or events.[37] But they also demon-strate the persistence and adaptability of racism.

Nearly a century ago Du Bois analyzed "double consciousness" as a basic tension in black identity produced by the painful but ineluctable pres-ence within black subjectivity of white attitudes and prejudices. Today we may reasonably extend this insight to propose the existence of a "multiple consciousness" through which most North Americans necessarily experi-ence their racial identities. Although uneven — and for many whites still quite remote — our sense of ourselves and each other as racially identified persons and groups always potentially involves not only external differentiation (I am different from another), but also internal differentiation (I contain dif-ferences within myself). This is a crucial lesson of the post-civil-rights pe-riod in U.S. history. The ongoing transformation and increasingly complex construction of racial identities in the contemporary United States is an ac-complished fact. The big question is how this perception is to be inter-preted politically. Will it take the form of increasing distrust and defensive

mobilization of difference and division? Will it revert to a "blame the victim" mentality, which frankly or subtly exculpates the beneficiaries of white
privilege from responsibility for the fate of the underprivileged? Will it be
manifested in efforts to "police the boundaries" of racial identity and to
deny voice and rights to those who do not meet increasingly archaic criteria of racial authenticity? Or will a future politics of race take the form of
democratic solidarity, granting equal access to all the institutions of society,
recognizing differences, and carrying out the commitment made so long
ago to rid this nation of the last vestiges of racial dictatorship?

Notes

A longer version of this chapter appeared in Howard Winant, *Racial Conditions: Politics,
Theory, Comparisons* (Minneapolis: University of Minnesota Press, 1994).

1. This is a phrase coined, as far as I know, by Pierre van den Berghe in regard to
apartheid. See Pierre L. van den Berghe, *Race and Racism* (New York: Wiley, 1967). David
Roediger prefers the term *"herrenvolk* republicanism," since this brings in the notion of small
(white) producers and artisans fighting for their rights—in this case against encroaching blacks.
See David R. Roediger, *The Wages of Whiteness: Race and the Making of the American Working
Class* (New York: Verso, 1991).

2. David Brion Davis, *The Problem of Slavery in the Age of Revolution, 1770–1823* (Ithaca,
N.Y.: Cornell University Press, 1975); George M. Frederickson, *The Black Image in the White
Mind: The Debate on Afro-American Character and Destiny, 1817–1914* (Middletown, Conn.:
Wesleyan University Press, 1987); Toni Morrison, *Playing in the Dark: Whiteness and the Liter-
ary Imagination* (Cambridge, Mass.: Harvard University Press, 1992).

3. Karl Marx, *Capital,* vol. 1 (New York: International Publishers, 1967), 301.

4. I rely throughout the following section on Roediger, *The Wages of Whiteness,* and
Alexander Saxton, *The Rise and Fall of the White Republic: Class Politics and Mass Culture in
Nineteenth Century America* (New York: Verso, 1990).

5. Michael Omi and Howard Winant, *Racial Formation in the United States: From the
1960s to the 1980s,* 2nd ed. (New York: Routledge, 1994), 29–35.

6. Racial slavery of course existed in Texas, but did not have the extensive roots it
had established elsewhere in the South.

7. David Montejano, *Anglos and Mexicans in the Making of Modern Texas, 1836–1986*
(Austin: University of Texas Press, 1987), 5.

8. Ibid., 82.

9. Ibid., 30–41.

10. Alexander Saxton, *The Indispensable Enemy: Labor and the Anti-Chinese Movement in
California* (Berkeley: University of California Press, 1971), remains the best single study of
anti-Asian politics in the United States; Asian exclusion is treated in depth in Ronald Takaki,
Strangers from a Distant Shore: A History of Asian Americans (New York: Penguin, 1990); see
also Stanford M. Lyman, *The Asian in the West* (Reno and Las Vegas: University of Nevada,
1970).

11. Selig Perlman, *The History of Trade Unionism in the United States* (New York: Augustus
Kelley, 1950), 52.

12. Omi and Winant, *Racial Formation,* 80–81. A certain adaptation of Gramsci's conception of "war of maneuver" and of the related "war of position" is required before these

terms can be applied to U.S. conditions. Gramsci's frame of reference is mainly that of the bourgeois revolution in Europe and occasionally that of the Russian revolution. See, for example, Antonio Gramsci, *Selections from the Prison Notebooks,* ed. Quentin Hoare and Geoffrey Nowell Smith (New York: International, 1971), 238–39.

13. Space does not permit discussion of the long gestation of the modern civil rights movement or of the deep religious, intellectual, and political roots that nurtured and shaped it. The historical literature on the early civil rights movement is voluminous. A few good accounts are Vincent Harding, *There Is a River: The Black Struggle for Freedom in America* (New York: Vintage, 1981); August Meier and Elliot Rudwick, *CORE: A Study in the Civil Rights Movement, 1942–1968* (New York: Oxford University Press, 1973); John Hope Franklin, *From Slavery to Freedom: A History of Negro Americans* (New York: Vintage, 1969).

14. Omi and Winant, *Racial Formation,* 81.

15. Ibid., 16–17; see also Robert Blauner, *Racial Oppression in America* (New York: Harper and Row, 1972), 51–81.

16. I am thinking here of the upsurge, beginning in the early 1970s, of neoconservatism among racially defined minorities. This fascinating subject is beyond the present chapter's scope. For a good treatment, see Thomas D. Boston, *Race, Class, and Conservatism* (Boston: Unwin Hyman, 1988).

17. "When we were in Africa we were called Africans or blacks; when we were in Africa we were free. When we were captured and stolen and brought to the United States, we became Negroes" (Stokely Carmichael, *Stokely Speaks: Black Power Back to Pan-Africanism* [New York: Vintage, 1971], 149–50).

18. For a comprehensive review and reinterpretation of studies on black identity formation in the United States, see William E. Cross Jr., *Shades of Black: Diversity in African-American Identity* (Philadelphia: Temple University Press, 1991).

19. See, for example, Imamu Amiri Baraka, *Raise, Race, Rays, Raze: Essays since 1965* (New York: Vintage, 1972).

20. Black psychiatrist Alvin Poussaint has pointed out, "There's a lot of pressure on the black middle class to stay black.... It's kind of a contradiction. Your kids are living in an integrated community, and you want them to feel part of the community, participating equally in it. Then you feel very ambivalent about it psychologically, when they do" (quoted in Joel Garreau, "Competing Bonds of Race and Class," *Washington Post,* November 30, 1987); see also Joe R. Feagin, "The Continuing Significance of Race: Antiblack Discrimination in Public Places," in *American Sociological Review* 56 (1991); Bart Landry, *The New Black Middle Class* (Berkeley: University of California Press, 1987); David Dent, "The New Black Suburbs," *New York Times Magazine,* June 14, 1992.

21. Martin Kilson notes the increasing division of the black working class into "coping" and "non-coping" strata; see Martin Kilson, "Problems of Black Politics: Some Progress, Many Difficulties," *Dissent,* Fall 1989; Martin Kilson and Clement Cottingham, "Thinking about Race Relations: How Far Are We Still from Integration?" *Dissent,* Fall 1991.

22. Charles Murray, *Losing Ground: American Social Policy, 1950–1980* (New York: Basic Books, 1984); Jim Sleeper, *The Closest of Strangers: Liberalism and the Politics of Race in New York* (New York: Norton, 1990); Mickey Kaus, *The End of Equality* (New York: Basic Books, 1992).

23. St. Clair Drake and Horace Cayton, *Black Metropolis: A Study of Negro Life in a Northern City,* 2nd ed., 2 vols. (New York: Harper and Row, 1962).

24. Yen Le Espiritu, *Asian American Panethnicity: Bridging Institutions and Identities* (Philadelphia: Temple University Press, 1992).

25. On the "demise of Jim Crow" in Texas, see Montejano, *Anglos and Mexicans,* 262–87. Carlos Muñoz argues that it was the cultural nationalist currents of black power that most

attracted young Chicanos (Carlos Munoz Jr., *Youth, Identity, Power: The Chicano Movement* [New York: Verso, 1989], 86).

26. Alejandro Portes and Robert L. Bach, *Latin Journey: Cuban and Mexican Immigrants in the United States* (Berkeley: University of California Press, 1985); Takaki, *Strangers.*

27. Sherri Grasmuck and Patricia R. Pessar, *Between Two Islands: Dominican International Migration* (Berkeley: University of California Press, 1991).

28. A key role in rallying Asian Americans around the issue of anti-Asian violence was played by the Vincent Chin case, in which a young Chinese American man was murdered in Detroit by several auto workers after getting into an altercation at a bar. The attackers apparently mistook Chin for Japanese (Espiritu, *Asian American Panethnicity*, 141–55). Also crucial in this regard is black antagonism to "middleman minorities," often Korean Americans, who operate small stores in ghetto neighborhoods. The spring 1992 L.A. riot was the most extreme example of this, but cases of black-Korean tensions have flared from coast to coast.

29. Jack Miles, "Blacks vs. Browns," *Atlantic Monthly,* October 1992; Wanda Coleman, "Blacks, Immigrants, and America," *Nation,* February 15, 1993.

30. Dana Y. Takagi, *The Retreat from Race: Asian Admissions and Racial Politics* (New Brunswick, N. J.: Rutgers University Press, 1993).

31. Suzanne Oboler, *Labeling Hispanics: The Dynamics of Race, Class, Language, and National Origins* (Minneapolis: University of Minnesota Press, 1995).

32. Clara E. Rodriguez, "Racial Classification among Puerto Rican Men and Women in New York," *Hispanic Journal of Behavioral Sciences* 12, no. 4 (November 1990).

33. This account draws heavily on Richard D. Alba, *Ethnic Identity: The Transformation of White America* (New Haven, Conn.: Yale University Press, 1990); Mary C. Waters, *Ethnic Options: Choosing Identities in America* (Berkeley: University of California Press, 1990).

34. This Weberian term puts a positive spin on the matter; a recent negative reading that invokes the "white privilege" argument is Andrew Hacker, *Two Nations, Black and White, Separate, Hostile, Unequal* (New York: Scribner, 1992).

35. Waters, *Ethnic Options,* 147–55. "Symbolic ethnicity" is a phrase coined by Herbert J. Gans; see Herbert J. Gans; "Symbolic Ethnicity: The Future of Ethnic Groups and Cultures in America," *Ethnic and Racial Studies* 2 (January 1979).

36. Waters, *Ethnic Options,* 167.

37. Cornel West, "Black Leadership and the Pitfalls of Racial Reasoning," in *Race-ing Justice, En-gendering Power: Essays on Anita Hill, Clarence Thomas, and the Construction of Social Reality,* ed. Toni Morrison (New York: Pantheon, 1992); Michael Omi and Howard Winant, "The Los Angeles 'Race Riot' and Contemporary U.S. Politics," in *Reading Rodney King, Reading Urban Uprising,* ed. Robert Gooding-Williams (New York: Routledge, 1993).

3 / Who Are the "Good Guys"?

The Social Construction of the Vietnamese "Other"

Michael Peter Smith and Bernadette Tarallo

At 1:30 in the afternoon on April 4, 1991, four Asian American youths entered a Good Guys electronic store located in the Florin Center Shopping Mall in south Sacramento, California. The young men, who were armed, held forty-one people hostage, negotiating with the Sacramento County Sheriff's Department for, among other demands, passage out of the country to enable them to fight Communists in Southeast Asia. Before the siege ended eight and a half hours later, the youths killed three hostages and wounded eleven others as the sheriff's SWAT team stormed the building from outside and within. In a spray of cross fire, SWAT officers killed three of the youths and seriously injured the fourth. The incident ended as a member of the SWAT team shouted, "We have four bad guys," a code message meaning it was over and clear, as medics rushed onto the scene.[1]

The story of the Good Guys hostage taking, its ensuing violent ending, and the subsequent representations of its meaning and significance are important to analyze, not only to understand how such a tragedy could have occurred, but also for what it might reveal about the complex conditions shaping the social construction of ethnic identity among America's new immigrants and refugees. These include not only structural economic and sociocultural conditions, considered so crucial by students of immigration, but how these conditions become refracted in the life-worlds of the individual transnational migrant in the reshaping of personal and ethnic identity. These processes of identity construction, in turn, are mediated by the changing context of the reception of new immigrants and refugees by powerful institutional actors, including the representations of group identity and difference deployed by the state, the media of mass communications, and political elites.[2]

As a nation constituted since its inception by successive waves of "new" immigrants from distant shores, global migration to the United States has always been fraught with cultural misunderstandings, racial and ethnic conflict, and the need to negotiate workable modes of social integration in the face of contested representations of racial and ethnic difference. The state, likewise, has always played a central role in the formation of U.S. racial and ethnic relations.[3] In the contemporary global era, however, the misunderstandings, conflicts, and patterns of adjustment are more complex than those described in the existing literature on racial and ethnic relations, and the state is less well situated to manage the process of social integration.

The conventional literature on the racialization of Asian Americans underlines the extent to which second-generation Asian Americans have faced an especially coercive adjustment to the dominant Anglo culture, replete with both negative and positive stereotypes of Asian Americans, making it difficult for them to fit either stereotype.[4] The Southeast Asian refugee children who make up a large portion of today's second-generation Asian Americans face an even more complex adjustment. The society in which their parents were born and with which they often continue to identify no longer exists and, for now, holds little hope for return. At the same time these second-generation youths must adjust to a dominant U. S. culture that is presently in the throes of a profoundly unsettling economic, political, and cultural transformation, sometimes ironically referred to as "the New World Disorder." Their very presence is a marker of the nation's loss of global hegemony in the post–cold war period. They must construct a new ethnic identity in the context of economic restructuring, intensifying racial and ethnic division, and growing anti-immigrant sentiment. Compounding these contextual pressures is their generational status—that is, the normal adolescent adjustment questions along with their need to make sense of and construct a meaningful cultural identity out of the contradictory images of race, ethnicity, class, gender, and power emanating from the mass media.

A central theme of this chapter is that the accelerated pace, scale, and diversity of transnational migration in the past two decades has led to the globalization of U.S. race relations. Contemporary global migration has been driven by several overlapping structural transformations in the international political economy. The main driving forces are the declining capacity of peripheral economies to absorb the labor that is created within their borders; the austerity policies imposed on developing states and societies by international banks; the production of refugees from Central America and Southeast Asia as a legacy of cold war military struggles; and the globalization of the media of mass communication, including television, film, videos, and music, which scatter the symbolic ingredients of "imagined lives" and modes of self-empowerment at the "core" to even the remotest of peripheral hinterlands, thereby making the theoretical distinction between core and periphery increasingly problematic. Taken together, these globalizing trends have reconstituted the sociocultural landscape and eroded the boundary-setting capacities of the nation-state.

Changing global geopolitical relations have played a central structural role in the expansion of the scale and diversity of contemporary transnational migration to U.S. shores. In light of the prominent role that U.S. military intervention played during the cold war, it is not surprising that a substantial portion of today's transnational migrants to the United States are political refugees. Since then, the disintegration of the state structures of former Communist states has produced new refugees, expanded the diversity of transnational migration, and further contributed to the globalization of race relations in the United States.

Not only economic restructuring and changing geopolitical alignments but also modes of cultural production are more spatially and territorially unbounded in the post–cold war epoch. This cultural fluidity is quite apparent in the case of transnational refugees now living in the United States who are currently seeking to orchestrate meaningful lives under conditions in which their life-worlds are neither "here" nor "there" but at once both "here" and "there." Many have observed that for transnational migrants who have entered the migrant stream voluntarily and remain connected to transnational networks of affiliation, symbolic and material interdependence, and mutual support (for example, circular migrants between the United States and Mexico), the social space for cultural reproduction has become bifocal and transnational.[5]

This condition of cultural bifocality, of course, can be the source of much psychic pain where the initial source of migration has been forced, as in the case of many Vietnamese refugees to the United States. Their ability to return or to move between "here" or "there" has been precluded by military defeat, but they must nevertheless forge a meaningful ethnic identity and find a niche in the contemporary American milieu, which is both race conscious and highly racially divided. As we will show, the analysis of the social process of construction of ethnic identities must take into account the role of powerful state and societal actors, in this case the police and the mass media, who are crucial players mediating the process of racial and ethnic formation precisely because of the uncertainty produced by the globalization of race and state relations.

A second purpose of our chapter is to recount a compelling story that illustrates the impossibility of social research remaining detached from the social world of which one is attempting to make sense. The Good Guys shooting took place in the Lemon Hill neighborhood of Sacramento, which we had been studying for other purposes for the past two years.[6] Our political-economic and ethnographic research on the formation of this new Southeast Asian ethnic enclave provided us with a wider context within which to interrogate and interpret the local events of the episode as elements in the global processes of transnational migration, refugee resettlement, and ethnic and racial formation. Accordingly, we were uniquely positioned to assess the representations of the events in question by the police, the media, and political elites.

Our choice eventually drew us into the aftereffects of the episode as participants rather than observers, bringing home to us the collapsing of the distinction between "inside" and "outside" that has become such a prominent feature of poststructuralist social criticism.[7] Before the Good Guys incident occurred, we had been writing a research paper on cultural misunderstandings involved in the migration experiences of Southeast Asian refugees.[8] The paper was slated for presentation at an Asian American Studies Association Conference in late May 1991. When the Good Guys incident occurred in early April, we decided to include it in our paper because it concretely illustrated cultural representations and misunderstandings much broader than the hostage siege. Following the conference, we sent the paper to the University News Service in response to a routine request for copies of our recent work. Their news release prompted a call from a feature reporter from the *Sacramento Bee*. We granted her an interview and gave her a copy of the paper. A few days later, on August 6, 1991, an article appeared in the *Bee* on the front page of the metro section under the headline, "UCD Team Criticizes Handling of Good Guys Siege." The article represented our paper largely as a criticism of police handling of the incident. This, in turn, prompted a series of additional requests for interviews and copies of our paper by other major players in the ensuing trial of the surviving hostage-taker—including the public defender's office, one of the potential judges, and the district attorney's office. To our surprise, it also provoked a series of highly critical letters to the editor in the *Bee* from citizens defending the police action, denouncing our "ivory tower" positionality, criticizing our "report" as characterized by the *Bee,* and even denouncing the fact that we had traveled to Hawaii to deliver the paper.

Shortly thereafter, we received a call from Captain Donald Savage, the head of the Sacramento County Sheriff's Department SWAT team. The captain, who had received our paper from an unspecified source, was heated in his criticism of our paper's description of the Good Guys shooting. He said that the first few pages, characterizing his SWAT team, were different in tone from the more measured analysis in the rest of the paper. We suggested that our research team would be happy to meet with him and his team to listen to their concerns.

The police in U.S. society occupy a privileged position as major institutional actors in the social construction of urban gangs, ethnic difference, and street violence. This position is enhanced by the extensive reliance of newspaper reporters on police authorities as sources of information and interpreters of "reality." We initiated this meeting because we felt that it was crucial to our evolving project to learn the predominantly white police force's (and by implication, the state's) understanding of the episode and their deployment of representations of it and of new Asian immigrants to others.

The body of our chapter is divided into five parts. The first reconstructs the events of the Good Guys incident and examines the narrow institutional matrix and separate language game in which the SWAT team's understanding both of the event and of urban violence more generally is embedded.[9] The second contextualizes the event as part of a larger resettlement story grounded in our ethnographic conversations with Vietnamese refugees. The third illustrates and critiques media attempts to lump the Good Guys shootout with stories of emergent Southeast Asian gangs in other places, to construct the social problem of "Asian gangs" in California and the nation. We then illustrate the inappropriateness of this construct and the attendant harmful ethnic stereotyping of "boat people" that it entails. Finally, we offer our own understanding of the realities in question.

Reconstructing the Episode and the Police Reading

The Good Guys electronics store is located on the south side of Sacramento, an area consisting of neighborhoods of long-term minorities, blacks and Latinos, and now a large concentration of newly arrived Southeast Asians. Numerous shopping centers line the large surfaced streets in the south area, containing supermarkets, department stores, and large discount houses, such as the Good Guys, the new temples of consumer capitalism.[10] A preponderance of bail bondsman outfits also dot various corners, indicating the different types of activity and clientele found in Lemon Hill. In addition, the landscape is being reconstituted by a burgeoning number of Southeast Asian restaurants and commercial businesses, created by and catering to the needs of new immigrants and refugees. The children of long-term residents and newly arrived Southeast Asians attend the local schools, which are now over 50 percent nonwhite. The area is a sea of diversity, with waves of newcomers raising children, working, doing business, shopping, and socializing in these contiguous neighborhoods, settling into an apparently uneasy coexistence with long-term residents.

The youths' backgrounds and the nature of their demands, the carrying out of the siege, and the handling of the hostage situation by law enforcement and the media shed important light on changing cultural representations and misunderstandings surrounding new immigrants and refugees. The choice of a global discount electronics store, a chain discount house specializing in audio and video equipment, as the place to carry out the siege is emblematic of the social transformation underlying the emergence of postindustrial consumer society. The electronics business is a foremost enterprise of postindustrial society, offering the distinctive commodities of advanced consumer capitalism that create and provide information, entertainment, and instant culture. For most children growing up in the United States in the 1990s, even a rudimentary understanding of the electronic media through TV and video games unveils its power. Throughout the eight-and-a-half hour ordeal, the youths occasionally watched themselves on the television sets that lined the walls. They once directly used the media to demand bullet-proof vests, insisting that a local television station air their messages. Moreover, from late afternoon onward, the event was televised on all the local stations, enabling the general public, as well as the family and friends of the hostages and the youths, to watch the chilling drama unfold. In a particularly dramatic moment, one of the hostages was shot in the leg and then crawled to safety outside the store to deliver a message on camera from the youths: "They want three bullet proof jackets, a helicopter and firearms. They already shot me. That's all I have to say." [11]

From the outset, the incident was filled with confusion, as law enforcement officials at first had difficulty in determining the youths' ethnicity. As one news article reported, "The gunmen spoke a foreign language to each other but spoke English to the hostages."[12] One of the youths' demands was air passage to Thailand to enable them to fight Communists. A Thai interpreter and a Buddhist priest were brought in to communicate with the youths, but were later dismissed when officials discovered the boys were Vietnamese and Chinese Vietnamese. Ironically, the only Vietnamese member of the sheriff's office, all of whose leaders were white, was out of state, attending a police-sponsored conference in Seattle on Asian gangs.

After identifying the youth, a sheriff's deputy contacted the father of three of the youths who were brothers for the purpose of making a positive identification. After this police contact the parents recognized their sons on television. The terrified mother then drove to the store. Yet, in a surprising twist of the story, the parents were never allowed to talk to their sons. Pleading with officials to speak to their sons, the mother was informed by deputies that the youths refused to speak to their parents. The mother returned to her home, and with her husband and the rest of the public, watched the last horrifying moments as two of their sons were killed. Later, the mother agonized through an interpreter, "If they had let me talk to my son, I could have talked him out of it, to lay down their weapons ... they wouldn't shoot me." The father agreed, saying his sons "always listen to their mother."[13]

The nature of the youths' demands, their complaints to the hostages, and their volatile behavior all indicated that this was not a simple robbery. Negotiating with a team of deputies, the youths raised a series of demands that seemed like an odd combination of past political events in Southeast Asia and media-derived fantasies of wealth and power: four bullet-proof vests, four million dollars in cash, passage to Thailand in order to fight Vietcong, a helicopter to seat forty people, and ginger plants to prepare tea.

The demand for air passage to Thailand initially was taken by law enforcement officials as a sign that the hostage takers were Thai. This misconstruction not only overlooked the fact that Thais have not settled in significant numbers in Sacramento, it also displayed lack of awareness of the fact that Bangkok is one of the major Southeast Asian cities (along with Manila and Singapore) that has regularly scheduled flights to Ho Chi Minh

City. The hostage takers, on the other hand, may have been familiar with this itinerary. This route is reportedly fully booked months in advance by Vietnamese living in the United States who wish to return to Vietnam.[14] Such forms of return have been described as an "open secret" in Asia, and have been openly condemned by conservative Vietnamese refugee leaders who regard this as a treasonous accommodation to the current Communist regime. Tying their demand for passage to Thailand to the rightist goal of military confrontation with that regime suggests a possible recognition by the four youths of the scarce supply of such bookings in relation to demand, and an accommodation to and/or partial appropriation of the political agenda of the rightist faction of the Vietnamese refugee leadership.

The complaints of the four youths to the hostages inside the store were more immediately grounded in their everyday experiences in Sacramento. They expressed deep dissatisfaction with their lives in the United States, claiming that they could not find steady jobs because they did not have high school diplomas. They characterized the United States as a "bad country." According to a former hostage, "I think they just felt that they'd never gotten anything in their life and they came here (to the store) to do something."[15] In reviewing his decision to storm the store, the sheriff stated that the negotiating team offered the youths help in finding jobs and lighter jail sentences to end the siege peacefully. Yet he admitted that the negotiations, conducted in English, were hampered by "cultural misunderstandings" on both sides and by the inability of the youths to focus on what they really wanted.[16]

As a result of our three-hour meeting with Captain Savage, his chief SWAT team negotiator, another SWAT team member, and the department's only Vietnamese employee, we realized that the gap between American and Vietnamese culture was not the only fault line in this situation. The SWAT team members' explanations of their practices and actions during the hostage negotiations revealed to us the ways in which their everyday work life is shaped and constrained by a relatively narrow set of discursive practices. For example, their understandings of the options open to them in negotiating with the youth were circumscribed by their appropriation of what they described as "standard police practices" in hostage situations, namely procedures developed by the FBI for dealing with "domestic terrorism." The actual danger they face thus prompts them to invoke a set of ritualistic procedures for dealing with all hostage takings as potential acts of "terrorism." This in turn, both escalates the volatility of an already volatile situation and narrows the range of options available for defusing it. In this instance, for example, we were told that the team would never allow the mother of the three hostage takers to directly speak to her sons to avoid "loss of control" of the negotiations. They argued that it is "standard operating procedure" in hostage situations to offer relatives of hostage takers the opportunity to make a tape that the police might use at their discretion, at a later stage of negotiating. Because they did so in this case they insisted to us that they had not denied the mother the right to speak to her sons. From their view, driven by a perceived need to maintain "control" at all costs, the mother of the hostage takers was being uncooperative by refusing to turn her voice over to them and "storming out of the building." From the parents' point of view, as described earlier, the sheriff's SWAT team refused to give the mother, who was a strong influence on her sons, a chance to talk them into surrendering peacefully.

The problem with the deployment of "standard police procedures" to deal with hostage taking rests not only on the fact that it produces misunderstandings such as this but also on the fact that the standardization narrows perspective and excludes possible avenues for de-escalating conflict. The universalization of these FBI procedures for dealing with "domestic terrorism" decontextualizes hostage taking episodes. This makes it exceedingly difficult for police to develop sufficient tactical flexibility to differentiate between different types of hostage taking, for example, those related to actual organized terrorism, to isolated idiosyncratic grievances, or to robbery attempts gone sour. This, in turn, reduces the possibility of nonviolent resolution for both sides. The limits of these procedures was made strikingly clear in the recent apocalyptic outcome of police actions in Waco, Texas, where federal law enforcement officials deployed the same "domestic terrorism" procedures to deal with the Branch Davidians, a messianic religious group.

In light of the decontextualization present in this case it is important both to place our unfolding story in its immediate urban context of Vietnamese resettlement in Sacramento and, in turn, to place this local context within the wider historical and geopolitical circumstances in which Southeast Asian refugee resettlement in the United States has unfolded during the past two decades. Accordingly, our next section draws upon ethnography and history to contextualize our story in time, place, and space.

Contextualizing the Story

Although at first seemingly wild-eyed and erratic in nature, the youths' demands and complaints point to deep-seated, interacting problems within and between the transnational migrant community and the host society. These problems may shed some light on the level of alienation experienced by the youths, which escalated out of control. Upon closer examination of the youths' backgrounds, various problems and at least two sets of images emerge.

The family of the three youths who were brothers escaped Vietnam in the late 1970s by fishing boat. Fleeing first to Malaysia and a Southeast Asian refugee camp, the family of eight came to the United States, settling first in San Jose, California, and then moving to Sacramento in 1980. The father was a former soldier in the South Vietnamese army. The family lives in a two-bedroom apartment, approximately one half mile from the Good Guys store, in a neighborhood where many other Southeast Asians reside. Although the apartment is cramped and typical of the housing in which many low-income immigrants live, symbols of the past and present adorn the home. A South Vietnamese flag hangs from the TV set, signifying the father's ideological stance and prior occupational background, a soldier and staunch anti-Communist. An altar is displayed in the living room for paying tribute to ancestors, surrounded by a crucifix and statues of saints signifying the family's active status in the Vietnamese Catholic Martyr Church, where the father serves as a deacon.

The fourth youth involved in the hostage incident was from a more affluent family. Of Chinese Vietnamese extraction, the boy lived with his parents in a new four-bedroom home in a residential subdivision of two-hundred-thousand-dollar houses in the south area. Both parents are small business owners. The mother owns and operates a manicurist shop in South Sacramento; the father owns a restaurant in San Francisco, living there five days a week and commuting from San Francisco to Sacramento on the weekends. The mother is a member of the Buddhist temple.[17]

The youths' backgrounds indicate the diversity found in the Vietnamese community, a diversity that is often masked by the popular media's promotion of the Vietnamese as the contemporary model minority through images of strong family unity, children as valedictorians, and wildly successful businessmen, as well as in the academic literature measuring economic adjustment. In fact, discussing the Vietnamese by extrapolating from the backgrounds and experience of the most well equipped first-wave settlers tends to ignore the splits both within and between first- and second-wave refugees, masking many adjustment problems, particularly among the second wave. Although often exaggerated and oversimplified, the adjustment of the first wave is in part attributable to their social backgrounds in Vietnam: many refugees were from urban areas, educated, with professional and military backgrounds. Although their occupational skills from Vietnam were not immediately transferable, many first-wave refugees were eventually able to adapt their abilities and skills to jobs where there was some carryover after developing a functional command of the English language. Their relatively high educational and occupational backgrounds, substantial capital and family assets, and familiarity with urban living and exposure to Western culture helped to contribute to their relatively successful adaptation.[18]

The situation of second-wave refugees, of which the family of the three brothers involved in the Good Guys incident is fairly typical, is quite different. Arriving from 1979 onward, and often referred to as "boat people," they are generally less educated, financially less well off, and often from rural areas with limited exposure to Western culture or to a technical and urbanized way of life. In many cases, illiteracy and unfamiliarity with the concept of classroom learning, particularly in acquiring English language skills, is a major obstacle. Furthermore, the conditions of their escape left them with few financial resources, with deep emotional scars, and in many more ways less prepared than the first wave to make a transition to life in the United States.

Our two years of ethnographic interviews with second-wave refugees in Sacramento reveal that these settlers tend to be isolated, not only from the mainstream society but also from first-wave settlers in their own community. Our second-wave respondents have expressed surprisingly little interest or involvement in established local Vietnamese associations and the services they offer. The differences in the backgrounds between second- and first-wave settlers, stemming not only from economic, social, and ethnic factors but also from the vast regional differences found in Vietnam, often make it difficult for second-wave refugees to relate to first-wave settlers. Moreover, given the political history of Vietnam, the second wave often displays a distrust of former government officials found in the first wave, and it is these settlers who tend to dominate and run Vietnamese associations and clubs. Perhaps most significant, according to one of our informants, an active Vietnamese community member involved in social service provision, first-wave settlers running the Sacramento Vietnamese associations tend to lose sight of, or are out of touch with, the concerns and problems facing the majority community of second-wave immigrants, not least of which are problems confronting youth in attempting to figure out what it means to be both Vietnamese and American. Lack of knowledge about and/or inability to identify with the perceived purpose and interests of Vietnamese associations has contributed to the second wave's lack of participation in formal social networks created by the first wave, further increasing their isolation.

The isolation experienced by second-wave settlers and their lack of social networking may be attributed in part to the nature of the Sacramento community. Although many second-wave immigrants tend to settle in the Lemon Hill neighborhood of South Sacramento, there is no overreaching Vietnamese organization or even industry (such as electronics in San Jose, California) binding them together. If participation in formal networks by second-wave immigrants has been minimal, their creation and use of informal networks is also weak. The majority of our respondents have reported that they do not know their neighbors, whether Asian or Anglo, except for passing hellos. When questioned if he knew his neighbors, one Vietnamese settler's response was typical: "No. I usually just greet or nod at them. They have black hair [meaning that they are Asian], but I do not know their nationality. I also know other Americans who live in the area, but not very well."

The pattern that is emerging for second-wave settlers in Sacramento is an extreme reliance on the immediate family in its various stages of construction (as many families are only now being unified through the Orderly Departure Program) and on government services for which they are entitled but that are sorely inadequate, as incoming refugee aid is now limited to four months, in comparison to the eighteen months of benefits available to most first-wave refugees in an earlier and more receptive political and economic climate. Older parents tend to supplement welfare with informal work in jobs where English-speaking ability is not essential, such as gardening, restaurant work, sewing, and cosmetology. Parents place their hopes for success on their children. After initially receiving welfare, the children in our sample tend to get jobs to put themselves through school and contribute to the family income. As we shall see, this heavy reliance on familial networks is placing a strain on relations within the Vietnamese family, as well as on youth in their self-formation and in making choices in the wider society.

One additional division affecting the Sacramento Vietnamese community needs to be mentioned. Since the late 1970s, Sacramento has been the site of a virulent anticommunist movement in northern California, promoting a return to and recapturing of Vietnam. The leaders of this movement, former colonels in the South Vietnamese army who resettled in Sacramento (others in San Jose and southern California), self-consciously set themselves apart and opposed more moderate community leaders who advocated adjustment in their new country while retaining values and cultural knowledge of Vietnam with the hope of blending these into a bicultural identity. In the early 1980s, the anticommunist leaders targeted a respected and beloved religious community leader in the moderate camp, maligning his character and splintering the community around allegiance to Vietnam.

In a further twist to the Good Guys incident, one of our informants revealed that the father of the three brothers involved is an active supporter of the anticommunist faction. Thus, the seemingly strange request of the youths for passage to Thailand to fight Vietcong becomes more understandable in light of their growing up in a close-knit household that kept alive the hope of returning not just to Vietnam, but to a precommunist Vietnam where the father, now on welfare, held a position of authority. Although the boys were toddlers when they came to the United States and would have little if any physical recollection of Vietnam, the question can be raised, given the family's political bent, as to what became identified as "home" for the youths — or at least was used as a rationalizing or reference point for identity, especially when life in a new society became so difficult. At the very least, deep confusion on the part of the youths is evident in facing the new society.

Although the youths were from different backgrounds and experiences in the United States, mirroring the diversity of circumstances in the Vietnamese community, all four boys were having problems with school, employment, and language. It is important to stress that the tragic outcome of these problems was extreme and aberrant in nature and has already resulted in incidents of backlash and discrimination in Sacramento's Vietnamese community. At the same time, the incident focuses attention on the tensions experienced between parents and children in many Vietnamese families as they face the adjustment process. An overwhelming concern consistently expressed by our respondents is parents' concern for and lack of control over their children's behavior in the new society. Typical of these responses is one mother's concern when asked if it is more difficult to raise children in the United States than in Vietnam:

> Yes, I think so because it's so free in America. I feel that I don't have that much control over my children since I can't afford to pay for their education. It's not like in Vietnam, I pay for their education, so they have to listen to me. Also, my children are self [sufficient], I have no control over when and where they go. The time they spent at home is minimal. They can't do that in Vietnam, they have to be home after school. Furthermore, since my chil-

dren were not so financially independent, they had to ask me for money to buy certain things. Therefore, I had more control and supervision over them.

Another respondent, a father, put it even more pointedly:

According to my understanding, in the American way of life, children have many misguided thoughts. They are free in an excessive sense. [Life] experience is very expensive to buy. Vietnamese say "a child disobey their parents, a child is delinquent in hundred ways." In reality, if a child is still alive, his mistake will affect him over time, and slow. But for example, in the recent case of a child drowning in the American River, the child died because he disobeyed his parents. When he died, that's it. No more. If he did not die, he will get into other troubles later on in life, who know what. Therefore children is the issue of gravest concern for Vietnamese family.

If parents are expressing difficulty in coping with the conflicts between the relative openness of the new society and their traditional parental roles, children face a set of conflicting expectations and often confusing choices. In addition to such practical issues of adjustment as learning a new language, becoming accustomed to the U.S. school system and meeting new peers, they face a host of social-psychological issues in straddling or negotiating conflicting Vietnamese values and expectations of filial respect and authority and the expectations of independence, self-satisfaction, and questioning of authority encouraged by their new society. As Nazli Kibria notes in her research on Vietnamese settlers in Philadelphia, the biggest challenge to adjustment for Vietnamese youth will be carving out an identity and place in their own families and becoming Vietnamese American in the larger society.[19]

In a community forum in Sacramento convened by civic and religious leaders to try to understand the Good Guys incident, a Vietnamese community leader posed the problem in language that we could all understand: "Parents keep telling their children to go slow, go slow, while their peers keep telling them to go faster, go faster." A Vietnamese teacher in the South Sacramento school system revealed the level of cultural misunderstanding that exists between recently arrived refugee families and the U.S. school system: when a note is sent home from the teacher discussing a student's progress it is often interpreted by the parents as a criticism of them. In the absence of government services or school and youth counseling programs to bridge these gaps, it is no wonder that many recently arrived families feel frustrated and overburdened.

The Good Guys incident undoubtedly fueled these fears with regard to a problem affecting the Vietnamese community and their children. In an undocumented and highly controversial but widely circulated media assertion, the boys involved in the hostage taking were reported to be members of a Southeast Asian youth gang.

The Media Construction of a "Southeast Asian Crime Wave"

In a particularly inflammatory article in the *San Francisco Examiner* published three weeks after the Good Guys incident, the Good Guys hostage taking and the ensuing violence were mistakenly treated as epiphenomenal of the wider social problem of Vietnamese gangs. On April 28, 1991, a front page "special report" by Steven Chin and Andy Furillo appeared under the banner headline: "Viet Gangs a Growing Threat in State, U.S." Most of the report dealt with various criminal activities such as extortion, street crime, and "home invasion" robberies, which have been identified with Vietnamese or Chinese Vietnamese gangs in press accounts throughout the early 1990s. After raising the spectre of a "Southeast Asian crime wave" by rootless Vietnamese youth gangs, the press report directly linked the Good Guys shooting to the reporters' construction of the growing threat to California and the nation posed by these gangs, despite the fact that the four youths were not gang members. The connection was made as follows:

> The April 4 shoot-out at a Good Guys electronics store in Sacramento, in which four Vietnamese *gang members* shot and killed three hostages before three of them were killed by sheriff's deputies, focused national attention on the country's *newest gang problem.*
>
> California, with a population of 379,000 Vietnamese refugees, is *bearing the brunt of the assault.*[20]

The special report made no effort to distinguish the Good Guys shooting from Vietnamese gang-related activities such as "home invasions." Indeed, it rhetorically conflated the two by calling the incident "the country's newest gang problem" and characterizing the shoot-out as part of a nationwide trend of violent assaults by Southeast Asian youth gangs. Later in the story, this representation of the Good Guys hostage taking as a gang activity was reinforced by conjoining it with a number of "home invasion" robberies that had occurred in other California cities the same month. In a slippery yet unmistakably inflammatory construction of a "crime wave" by Vietnamese gangs, the reporters state: "The trend shows no signs of abating. In the first 10 days of this month, there were five invasions in Northern California — three in Stockton, one in San Francisco, one in San Jose, *not to mention the Good Guys drama in Sacramento.*"[21]

Another unfortunate misrepresentation made in this story has to do with the targets of the growing threat it envisages. It is clear from a close reading of this story that all of the victims of "home invasion" robberies have been other Southeast Asian refugees. Yet the tone of the special report leaves the overall impression, punctuated by the Good Guys shooting, that the threat posed by the gangs is being borne by the American cultural mainstream, particularly by "California," which, because of its large population of Vietnamese refugees, is "bearing the brunt of the assault."

In representations such as these, a new stereotype, that of the second-wave Vietnamese refugee youth as nomadic gangsters, is being inserted into the popular media. From 1975 until the mid-1980s, the "model minority" image of first-wave Vietnamese refugees, drawn on the basis of the selective success of those first-wave refugees who came to the United States with money, connections, language skills, and cultural capital, caused many to overlook important differences among refugee households in social capital, cultural adaptation, and socioeconomic mobility. In the early 1990s, the "nomadic gangster" image of second-wave refugees, drawn on the basis of the real but partial story of the social dysfunctions experienced by a small segment of them, known as *bui doi* gangs, is being used as a representation that fosters fear, intolerance, and exclusion.

In discourses such as the special press report the rhetoric of "threat" serves to oversimplify the complex, highly differentiated, and rapidly changing social experiences of Vietnamese refugees. Every "reality" is also a social construction. In this instance, the existence of *bui doi* youth gangs is being used as a category of meaning that obscures and thus denies significant differences in class, ethnicity, household structure, and cultural and historical experience *within* the category "Vietnamese refugee" as "other" when used in binary opposition to an equally undifferentiated, socially constructed, mainstream American "us." Ironically, the image that conflates "boat people" with sociopathic vagabond gangs is based on the life experiences of a small segment of "others" whose life has indeed been a series of exclusions — the experience of *bui doi,* or "dirt in the wind," gang youth who, as children in Vietnam, were doubly excluded: as orphans in a family-centered social system and as ethnic minority Chinese in a race-conscious society, many of whom "came up" by spending time in the squalid and parasitic refugee camps of Southeast Asia and now survive on the mean streets of American cities and their suburban ethnic enclaves by preying on the weaknesses of fellow second-wave refugees.

Global Reproduction:
The Social Origins and Practices of *Bui Doi* Gangs

In light of the dangers entailed in this social construction of ethnic "otherness," it is important to address several distinct questions: (1) What in general do we know about the social origins and practices of *bui doi* Vietnamese gangs? (2) Who have been their victims? (3) How have these gangs operated locally in Sacramento? Once these questions are answered we will be able to address the question of the relationship, if any, between *bui doi* gang activities and the Good Guys hostage taking and to assess the validity of police and media social constructions of the Vietnamese "other."

The prevalent image of the typical *bui doi* Southeast Asian gang member is that of a rootless vagabond, separated from household social structure and "normal" family life by war, migration, and an orphaned existence in violent, chaotic, and unsafe refugee camps. How well grounded is this image? Our ethnographies support the prevalent image of daily life in refugee camps. They give voice to the wretched experiences faced by second-wave refugees in the camps which were part of their rite of passage to American life. One Vietnamese youth, who is now twenty-one and who spent one of his teenage years in a refugee camp in Hong Kong, described his experience in the following exchange:

I stayed in Hong Kong for one year. I forgot the name of the camp but it was a closed camp.

Q: How was your life like in Hong Kong?

A: It was miserable. It was like being in jail. Everyday, we went to line up to pick up our meals. Besides that, we waited around to be called to interview. As for myself, I studied English. Since it was a closed camp, people were not allowed to go out of the camp. If one had relatives outside the camp, then the relatives could ask for permission to visit their people inside the camp.

Q: Were the camp officers nice to you?

A: I heard that they were very nice before but not now. We weren't beaten up or anything but the camp was very chaotic. The Vietnamese people fought against one another.

Q: After you left Hong Kong, where was your next stop?

A: Our next camp was in Philippines. I stayed there for four months. We were put in the camp to study English. Life was basically the same like in Hong Kong.

Another of our ethnographic subjects, an ethnic Chinese youth from Vietnam born in 1963, was separated from his family after the fall of Saigon in 1975 and spent time in the camp in the Philippines. This American-managed camp is intended to acculturate Southeast Asian refugees before they reach U.S. shores. He pointedly describes that camp experience in the following way: "Philippines is just as poor as Vietnam. There were always fights in the camp. One would often hear the news of a Vietnamese or a Laotian died of something. It was so chaotic, so disordered in the camp. The camp lacked policemen, its security system was bad, therefore people kept slaughtering one another. A small problem would be blown up to lead to a fight."

A young Amerasian orphan youth interviewed in our study described some of the intended and unintended lessons learned in the six months he spent in the Philippines camp:

Q: How is life in the Philippines camp?

A: It's interesting. We supposed to stay there to study English and about American life for six months. We were given rice and fresh food to cook our own meals. It is very chaotic there. We were taught by the Philippines and the Americans. But some people discriminate against the Philippines staffs. I don't know what the story was but I guess the people who came before us must have done something disgraceful. We also have problems communicating with the staffs. One day in the camp is the drag on of misery. There are different types of people in the camp: the Amerasians, the ODP people, the boat people.

Q: What did you learn in Philippines?

A: I learnt English ha . . . ha . . . "Yes, yes, no, no, . . . six months to go" . . . or "goodbuy pesos hello dollars" . . . just kidding. They taught us about life in the U.S., of what to expect. At the same time, there are the bad people who would interfere with our lives in the camp. Some of them will stop you on your way home from class and ask you for money. It happened to me once. They hadn't taken any money from me, I already knocked them out. I feel sorry for the ones who can't defend themselves. Sometimes I saw they did it to people. They would hit the people if they didn't give them the money. I interfered several times. The security system was very lacking.

It is conditions such as these which have provided a contextual opportunity for the reproduction of the *bui doi* gang scene as a parasitic dimension of the second-wave Vietnamese transnational migration experience. How extensive is this gang scene in the United States today and how did it originate? By the highest available estimate, the inflammatory Chin and Furillo piece, the *bui doi* gangs consist of under a thousand nomadic youth nationally. The *bui doi* scene originated in ethnic Chinese enclaves in Vietnam like Cholon, an ethnic Chinese suburb of Saigon. *Bui doi* gang members have been multiply excluded—first by postwar Vietnamese society, when many of the not fully integrated ethnic Chinese minority were forced to leave the country during Vietnam's short but fierce border war with China in 1979; then by other Southeast Asian refugee families forced to live together under the atomized and chaotic conditions of refugee camps just described; next by both first-wave Vietnamese-Americans and by established Chinese American communities in the United States; and finally by mainstream American cultural institutions, where they experienced school difficulties and high dropout rates and acquired only limited English language proficiency. The gangs, started as orphaned street youth, reestablished ties with the only social network available to them, other isolated youths whom they had known on the streets of places like Cholon and in the camps. Those current gang members who were not orphaned in the camps, nevertheless, have lacked adult supervision in the United States because of the economic pressures on second-wave refugee families, where each of the resident adult members of traditional extended family households must work, often moonlighting at more than one job in order to survive.[22]

"Fitting in" nowhere, neither advantaged by the "model minority" social construction of Vietnamese ethnicity exemplified by first-wave Vietnamese professionals, entrepreneurs, and "community" leaders, nor constrained by the cultural misunderstandings impeding the social mobility of many less affluent second-wave immigrants, the *bui doi* have carved out a new social space of the "excluded other" driven by dreams of endless riches and intoxicated by media fantasies of unlimited power.

In California the *bui doi* Southeast Asian gangs operate quite differently from other ethnic gangs. Their practices are delocalized. They seek neither to obtain nor defend local "turf." Their internal social structure is based on the reproduction of social networks that transcend locality, community, and place. They are nomads rather than settlers. They move from place to place where Southeast Asians are concentrated, using the easy exit option of freeways and airports to escape identification and capture. Their "home," both in transit and when operating in the scattered ethnic neighborhoods they victimize, is the motel. While "living in the 'mo'" they prey upon localized ethnic households, exploiting their knowledge of the general cultural understandings and misunderstandings that handicap the least adapted segments of these communities. These vagabond gangs appropriate globalized images readily available on "Kung Fu" movies and videos to glamorize the brutal tactics they use to coerce their victims.

Moving beyond their original historical basis in conflictual interethnic relations between pure Vietnamese and ethnic Chinese in Vietnam, these gangs have been depicted in a recent government report issued by the California Bureau of Organized Crime and Criminal Intelligence as starting to recruit members from other Southeast Asian ethnic groups, such as the Khmer, Lao, and Hmong, and expanding their operations from home invasion robberies and extortion to more sophisticated high-tech crimes such as the theft of computer chips.[23] Police officials in the city of Sacramento, where the Good Guys shooting took place, have said that Southeast Asian gang activities in that city have been limited largely to burglaries and home invasions. They estimate that fifty or sixty youths have been involved in these activities in the Sacramento area.[24]

In early 1990, a series of extortion attempts and residential "home invasion robberies" began in the Lemon Hill neighborhood of Sacramento and in nearby suburbs with Vietnamese enclaves. The *bui doi* gangs in Sacramento are largely made up of ethnically Chinese Southeast Asian refugee youth who prey upon older refugee families reluctant to contact police because they mistrust formal institutions of law enforcement and fear reprisals. The victims are chosen for "home invasions" precisely because of their isolation from and misunderstanding of mainstream American institutions. Unfamiliar with or mistrustful of banks, many second-wave refugee families keep their life savings in cash or commodities like gold and jewelry hidden in their homes. *Bui doi* gang members target such households for invasion, often torturing their robbery victims to get them to reveal the hiding place of their store of capital. Once robbed in this way, the victims' cultural mis-understanding of the legal practices of bail bonding and probation leads them to assume that their assailants have bribed police officials to obtain release from jail. They thus transfer their knowledge of corrupt practices common in Vietnam both before and since the fall of Saigon into a differ-ent cultural context, where it is less appropriate because it reinforces their suspicion and mistrust of potentially useful institutions and impedes the ability of the legal system to try, convict, and incarcerate a basically parasitic segment of the refugee population.

Ironically, the tactics used by law enforcement officials in Sacramento to combat the recent "home invasion" robberies have reinforced rather than overcome this reluctance to use the legal system. Despite the fact that, by their own accounting, the home invasions were perpetrated by nomadic gangsters who lived nowhere in particular, except "the mo," Sacramento city police officials engaged in a series of indiscriminate searches of local Vietnamese residents during random "sweeps" of all the patrons of restau-rants, clubs, pool halls, and other establishments frequented by local Viet-namese refugees. In a three-week period during March 1990, scores of pa-trons were detained, photographed, and interrogated, although there was no evidence linking them to any crimes. Although challenged by civil lib-erties advocates for ignoring the "probable cause" for search requirement, these sweeps were justified by law enforcement officers, who waxed enthusi-astically about their effectiveness. In defending the need for the sweeps and their legality, officers used phrases like "turning up the heat," "shaking the trees," and "putting on the pressure" in reference to the raids. Despite this implicitly intimidating rhetoric, detectives in charge of the robbery investi-gations asserted that the purpose of the raid was legitimate—"We did not do this for intimidation, but for identification and intelligence gathering."[25]

In a further irony, some segments of the first-wave Vietnamese refugee community defended these raids. For example, Hung Le, an administrative aide to Sacramento Assemblyman Phillip Isenberg, blithely minimized the civil liberties violations and stigmatizing effects of the raids by telling the press: "Personally, I don't think it [the raids] violated their civil rights. Hey, compared to Vietnam it's nothing. I feel those actions are necessary. It doesn't sound like democracy, but, hell, it works."[26] Needless to say, such rhetorical strategies are unlikely to reduce the mistrust of law enforcement agencies that enables the *bui doi* to operate. Indeed, their modus operandi depends on precisely such mistrust. The tactics, and their defense by more privileged first-wave refugees, reinforce the mistrust and hence the vulnerability of the most isolated second-wave families facing the pressures of adjustment.

Representing Difference: What Future?

A key issue that requires resolution is the relationship, if any, between the Good Guys incident and the activities of the *bui doi* gangs. In the immediate aftermath of the Good Guys shootings, representatives of community organizations assisting Southeast Asian refugees in resettlement, as well as some experts on Asian gang activities, challenged media representations that had closely linked the two phenomena in stories asserting that Asian gang activities in the United States had reached crisis proportions. The handling of the siege by law enforcement officials was also challenged. For example, questioning frequent media references to the four youths as "gangsters," Vu-Duc Vuong, the executive director of the Southeast Asian Refugee Resettlement Center and a past candidate for the San Francisco Board of Supervisors, noted that if the four youths were gang members, it is doubtful they would have had to buy the weapons they used in the siege a week before the incident. Gang experts also cast doubt on the four youths' self-description as members of the "Oriental Boys" gang in Sacramento. One gang expert noted that most Asian gangs do not even have names, except those given to them by law enforcement agencies for easy identification. Sacramento County sheriff's office spokesman Ed Close, who remained "confident" in the view that the hostage takers were gang members, was prompted by such criticisms to deny that the Good Guys siege was "gang orchestrated."[27] Close nevertheless glibly dismissed the youths' claim of wanting to go to Southeast Asia to fight Communists as "garbage."

In the wake of the perceptual impasse exemplified by such comments, the representation of the Good Guys incident as a "gang-related" activity has inexorably become highly politicized. So too has the forceful police assault that flowed, in part, from this social construction of reality. On May 22, 1991, a coalition of twelve ethnic organizations in Sacramento, termed the Coalition for Equity for Minorities, called for a grand jury investigation of the sheriff's department's handling of the Good Guys shoot-out. While not directly blaming sheriff's deputies for the outcome of the incident, coalition spokespersons raised a series of questions that they said were sufficiently problematic to justify an independent inquiry. Several of these are pertinent to our foregoing discussion. They asked whether bicultural resources were adequately used during the negotiations with the hostage takers. They questioned the decision not to use the mother of three of the youths during the negotiations, asking whether or not it had been made "with the assistance and advice of bilingual and bicultural professionals in the community."[28] They also asked whether the positioning of law enforcement personnel had increased or decreased the chances that hostages would be caught in a crossfire.

The coalition did not form solely to address this single issue. It had been researching charges of excessive force by city police and county sheriff's deputies in Sacramento since the police "sweeps" occurred over a year earlier. The organization's goal has been the establishment of a nonpartisan civilian review commission with the power to independently monitor complaints against law enforcement agencies. The Good Guys incident simply catalyzed the coalition, whose leaders have treated the incident as exemplary of a pattern of police brutality rather than gang violence.

There are signs that this alternative construction is beginning to take root in Sacramento in the contested political space that has emerged since the Good Guys shootings. In an unexpected development, Peter Torres, the brother of one of the slain hostages, Fernando Gutierrez, and uncle to two nieces also held hostage, welcomed the coalition's call for an independent investigation, stating: "We don't blame the Vietnamese community at all.... We blame the Sheriff's Department."[29]

In light of these developments, the arguments and evidence presented in this chapter have several important implications. First, our research casts doubt on the sheriff's department's initial glib dismissal of the political content of the youths' demands as "garbage." We have shown that the father of three of the four youths was active in the anticommunist faction of the Vietnamese refugee community. At the very least, it can be assumed that the political ideas informing this faction were present in the household in which three of the youths were raised, as exemplified by the prominently displayed South Vietnamese flag that hung in their home. Accordingly, it seems more reasonable to assume that the political beliefs underlying this faction were an element of the youths' socialization experiences and a contradictory component of their emergent identities than to dismiss them out of hand as either irrelevant or only a smoke screen for their other more immediately material demands.

Second, if we are correct, the political content of the youths' demands was part of a confused and contradictory set of desires, reflecting an effort to negotiate a meaningful identity out of the conflicting expectations found in the refugee community and in mainstream consumer society. If part of the three youths' fluid and multiple identity was formed by their identification with the frustrated rightist political aspirations of their father, this casts further doubt on the unsubstantiated claim that the youths were Vietnamese "gangsters." However *noir*, the identities forged by *bui doi* gang members center around felt exclusions, including exclusion from Vietnamese society and culture. Their identities contain no political content whatsoever, let alone a coherent anticommunist political ideology that entails an agenda of return and reconquest. Why, after all, would such *bui doi* youths wish to return to a place where they were discriminated against, excluded as racially inferior, or even forcefully expelled?

Third, none of the four youths involved in the Good Guys hostage taking was a rootless, nomadic gangster. All were longtime residents of Sacramento, currently living with their parents. Therefore, why, other than because of ritualistic application of "standard operating procedures," was the mother of three of the youths not allowed to speak with her children before the siege was terminated by the SWAT team assault and the ensuing killings?

Fourth, we have shown that the "sweep" tactics used by law enforcement officials in Sacramento were inappropriately targeted toward local Vietnamese residents in Sacramento to combat a delocalized, nomadic gang problem. In light of the emergent political climate just described, it is likely that police agencies in Sacramento will be forced by the new circumstances of community mobilization to reconsider blatant violations of the civil liberties of new immigrants in such practices as sweep searches. It remains to be seen, however, whether the emergent coalition of minority groups will be able to institutionalize formal, legal mechanisms capable of preventing police from exercising such sweeping discretion. Since the Vietnamese refugee community is internally divided on this issue, such an outcome is not likely in the near future.

Finally, we have shown that media representations of Vietnamese refugees have been fraught with misunderstandings, exaggerations, and sometimes even clear misrepresentations of the fluid, highly differentiated, and still emergent character of their settlement experiences. At the present historical juncture, the media have been present at the creation of an emergent climate of backlash against Vietnamese refugees. Those involved in "writing culture"—journalists, ethnographers, social and political analysts alike—have a responsibility to look, listen, and write with intelligence, reflection, and care, recognizing that what some have called "the politics of difference" exists as much *within* as between new immigrant groups in their relations with each other and their new society. "Ethnic" experience depends not just on nationality, but also on the differences made by social divisions of gender, class, family structure, and historical and contemporary context.

Law enforcement agencies and the media are key elite shapers of the context of reception through which general public expectations of receptivity or opposition to new immigrant and refugee minorities are socially constructed. Perhaps it is fitting that pressures from below are now being put on these two institutional structures. It is the rhetorical strategies that emerge from the current discourses on the meaning of "new immigrants" and "refugees" that will, in turn, determine the larger meanings of "pluralism" and "democracy." It is these pressures from below that can shift the politics of representation from an elitist game to a democratic contest.

Notes

1. John Cox, "Step-by-Step Walk into a Sacramento Hostage Nightmare," *Sacramento Bee,* April 6, 1991, 1.

2. For a stimulating yet profound mapping of the often hidden workings of the power of the state, the media, and political elites in the narrative constructions of race, class, and gender relations made available to citizens trying to make sense of the Anita Hill–Clarence Thomas hearings, see Wahneema Lubiano, "Black Ladies, Welfare Queens, and State Minstrels: Ideological War by Narrative Means," in *Race-ing Justice, En-gendering Power,* ed. Toni Morrison (New York: Pantheon Books, 1992), 323–64. The classic study of the interplay of power and symbolism is Murray Edelman, *The Symbolic Uses of Politics* (Urbana: University of Illinois Press, 1964).

3. Michael Omi and Howard Winant, *Racial Formation in the United States* (London: Routledge, 1986).

4. Paul Takagi, "The Myth of Assimilation in American Life," *Amerasia Journal,* Fall 1973; Joe Feagin and Nancy Fujitaki, "On the Assimilation of Japanese Americans," *Amerasia Journal,* February 1972; David O'Brien and Stephen Fugita, "Generational Differences in Japanese Americans' Perceptions and Feelings about Social Relationships between Themselves and Caucasian Americans," in *Culture, Ethnicity and Identity,* ed. W. McCready (New York: Academic Press, 1983).

5. Michael Kearney, "Borders and Boundaries of State and Self at the End of Empire," *Journal of Historical Sociology* 4, no. 1 (March 1991): 52–74; Roger Rouse, "Mexican Migration and the Social Space of Postmodernism," *Diaspora* 1, no. 1 (Spring 1991).

6. For a fuller discussion of the research approach deployed in our larger study of new immigrants and refugees in California, see Michael P. Smith, Bernadette Tarallo, and George Kagiwada, "Colouring California: New Asian Immigrant Households, Social Networks, and the Local State," *International Journal of Urban and Regional Research* 15, no. 2 (1991): 250–68.

7. See Michael Peter Smith, "Postmodernism, Urban Ethnography, and the New Social Space of Ethnic Identity," *Theory and Society* 21 (1992): 493–503.

8. For our further elaboration of the questions of cultural accommodation and resistance by Southeast Asian refugees, see Michael Peter Smith and Bernadette Tarallo, "The Postmodern City and the Social Construction of Ethnicity in California," in *Racism, the City*

and the State, ed. Malcolm Cross and Michael Keith (London: Routledge, 1993), 61–76. See also Michael P. Smith and Bernadette Tarallo, "The Unsettling Resettlement of Vietnamese 'Boat People,'" *USA Today Magazine,* March 1993, 27–29.

9. Our original narration of the events in our conference paper, which was delivered six weeks after the shooting, relied more extensively than our current reconstruction on published newspaper accounts of the events. These have been supplemented and interrogated in the present reconstruction by subsequent interviews our research team conducted with Vietnamese community members in South Sacramento, participant observation of community meetings and forums precipitated in the area by the shootings, and our meeting with Sacramento County Sheriff's Department officials. The police and the media are often symbiotic institutions. In this instance, however, viewing us through the lens of the *Bee's* construction of our conference paper as a public report critical of them, SWAT team members called into question some parts of our initial presentation drawn from newspaper accounts. Their critique of the media reporting prompted us to verify selected aspects of the reportage.

10. During the three-hour meeting of our research team with Captain Savage and the other members of his SWAT team, our use of the phrase "new temples of consumer capitalism" was strongly criticized and cited as evidence of an allegedly "Marxist" bias in our analysis. An alternative metaphor was offered by SWAT team members. They constructed the Good Guys store not as a "temple" but as a "fortress." They gave us a blueprint of the layout of the front and back access of the store to show that because of its very limited number of entry points and maze-like arrangement of rooms, the building really *was* a "fortress" that limited their options and increased the danger to SWAT team members in ending the siege. Ironically, the team seemed convinced that their "either-or" logic and the evidence offered to support it was sufficient to demolish our original representation. It did not seem to occur to them that thinking in "and-also" rather than "either-or" terms opens up the possibility that the building's fortresslike design complemented the large array of television, stereo, and electronic equipment put on iconic display in the front of the store and stored in its back. In our view, the back of the building could be viewed as a "fortress" precisely because of the need to guard the commodities of consumer society stored there and, more important, put so prominently on display in its templelike front.

11. Marjie Lundstrom and Steve Wiegand, "Five Die in Store Shootout," *Sacramento Bee,* April 5, 1991, 1, A28.

12. Marjie Lundstrom and David Davila, "Survivors Don't Feel So Lucky," *Sacramento Bee,* April 6, 1991, 1.

13. Chris Bowman and Deb Kollars, "Parents Saw Them as Carefree Youth," *Sacramento Bee,* April 6, 1991, 1, A17.

14. Frank Viviano, "New Era Emerges for Viet Refugees in U.S.," *San Francisco Chronicle,* December 28, 1989, 1, 12.

15. Sam Stanton, "Night of Terror and Death," *Sacramento Bee,* April 6, 1991, 1, A16.

16. Sam Stanton, "Time Had Run Out, Craig Says," *Sacramento Bee,* April 6, 1991.

17. Bowman and Kollars, "Parents Saw Them as Carefree Youth."

18. This does not mean that first-wave Vietnamese have been free of psychic pain following their forced migration and resettlement. For an evocative ethnographic exploration of this question, see James M. Freeman, *Hearts of Sorrow: Vietnamese-American Lives* (Stanford, Calif.: Stanford University Press, 1989).

19. Nazli Kibria, "Adaptive and Coping Strategies of Vietnamese Refugees: A Study of Family and Gender" (Ph.D. dissertation, University of Pennsylvania, 1986).

20. Steven A. Chin and Andy Furillo, "Viet Gangs Growing Threat in State, US," *San Francisco Examiner,* April 28, 1991, 1: emphasis added.

21. Ibid., 10; emphasis added.

22. Frank Viviano, "New Breed of Crooks from Vietnam: Other Refugees Reject Them," *San Francisco Chronicle,* February 20, 1989, 6.

23. Mike Castro, "Report: Asian Gangs Diversify," *Sacramento Bee,* October 21, 1990, B12.

24. This and the overall estimate of *bui doi* gang membership must be viewed with some skepticism, since the principal source of media information about the character and scale of gang activities is police officials who may have an institutional interest in exaggerating the social threat posed by gang activities. For a lucid discussion of the institutional interdependence of police officials and crime reporters in the social construction of "gangs" and the relationship of gangs to "urban violence," see Martín Sánchez Jankowski, *Islands in the Street* (Berkeley and Los Angeles: University of California Press, 1992), chap. 9.

25. Patrick Hoge, "Police Raids Challenged," *Sacramento Bee,* July 2, 1990, 1.

26. Patrick Hoge, "Reaction Split over Raids of Asian Hangouts," *Sacramento Bee,* July 30, 1990, B2.

27. Keiko Ohnuma, "Asians Blast Media, Cops over Sacramento Siege," *Asian Week,* April 12, 1991, 1.

28. Ann Bancroft, "Call for Probe of Shootout at Good Guys," *San Francisco Chronicle,* May 22, 1991, 16.

29. Ibid.

4 / The Rising Significance of Status in U.S. Race Relations

Martín Sánchez Jankowski

The field of race relations in the United States has been dominated by two conceptual frameworks. The first views race relations as involving African Americans and whites. A vast literature has developed that insists on a black-versus-white paradigm. For example, in a recent and penetrating analysis of contemporary U.S. race relations, Andrew Hacker has gone so far as to say that many "other groups find themselves sitting as spectators, while the two prominent players [blacks and whites] try to work out how or whether they can coexist with one another."[1] Despite Hacker's assertion that race relations ought to be defined in terms of African American versus white, the historical experience is anything but dichotomous. There have been numerous racial groups present in the United States, and at least three others (American Indians, Mexicans, and Chinese)[2] have experienced the institutional racism that African Americans have experienced, and they encountered it during the nineteenth and early twentieth centuries when it was in full maturity. Ignoring the historical experience in which a number of racial groups have figured prominently lays the foundation for misunderstanding the entire nature of contemporary race relations.

The second conceptual framework that has dominated recent research has been that which utilizes either race or class as the independent variable to explain contemporary race relations. The recent studies by Hacker, Roy

Brooks, and Douglas Massey and Nancy Denton are examples of those that employ race as the primary variable.[3] On the other hand, the new concern with the impact that shifts in the global economy are having on the development and plight of a growing black "underclass"—a concept used to designate a group so poor and alienated that it poses an impediment to amicable race relations more broadly—exemplifies the use of class as the most salient variable.[4] However, there are several problems with the race-versus-class framework. First, such a framework is ahistorical in that it makes race relations static, failing to appreciate the changing character of racial stratification and the evolutionary process in U.S. race relations. Race has been the dominant factor governing relations between groups, but the caste character of such relationships has broken down. Many of those who employ a class conceptual framework (whether Marxist or not) have recognized that change, but they have not fully grasped that class too has not persisted, that it dominated race relations for a very brief period and is no longer the primary dynamic governing race relations. The new dynamic that has emerged is that of status. By status, I mean the subjective bestowal of honor, by those who monopolize a society's material wealth and power, on the various groups that compose that society, honor bestowed independent of the group's economic situation. Therefore, as Max Weber has noted, a status group can be composed of both propertied and propertyless people. A status system is the rank order of honor that has been bestowed on the various groups.[5] In regard to contemporary U.S. race relations, the dominance of status relations means that groups are at war with other groups.

In this chapter I examine the evolutionary process that has made relations among status groups the primary dynamic governing race relations. I argue that race relations in the United States have involved and continue to involve a number of groups, and that it is impossible to understand either the relations between African Americans and whites or those among other groups without understanding the developmental process that has created a complicated dynamic of racial interaction.

The Dynamics of Social Orders

In order for groups to function as a society, they must establish what Jon Elster has called the "cement of society," that is, some type of social order.[6] A social order is required to preserve the level of stability necessary to sustain the rate of economic activity essential for the society's growth or maintenance. The establishment of a social order, difficult for every society, is particularly problematic in those societies with a number of racial and ethnic groups because in those societies a number of distinct groups compete for available resources.

Races come into relationship when groups occupy a common geographic place. More often than not, groups find themselves interacting as a result of economic forces. This was particularly true in the United States, where race relations began with the interaction of Europeans and American Indians.[7] Because most North American Indian groups either resisted or were not wanted for labor, they continued as long as they could to pursue a nomadic hunting and gathering existence. Everyday contact was minimal, with race relations occurring primarily through trade and through contending interests in land use,[8] so there was not the need to create a structural social order to govern everyday interaction. The most prevalent institutionalized social order was a form of physical separation that would reduce interaction to a small number of geographic places such as the trading post or the Indian village itself.[9] It was what the apartheid theorists in South Africa had hoped to achieve.[10]

This was not the case for the three other racial groups that would have to interact with Europeans. For Africans, Mexicans, and Chinese, contact with Europeans required a social order. That was because these groups provided labor for the developing economic enterprises of white Europeans. Africans were used primarily as forced labor for agribusiness in the South, Mexicans for agribusiness and mining in the Southwest, and the Chinese for railroad construction from the Midwest to the West Coast. Because of the nature of the work and the development of towns around these economic enterprises, interaction between white and nonwhite populations could not be controlled simply by physically isolating the nonwhite populations. Social control, therefore, required the establishment of a formal social order. The initial social order developed in the eighteenth and nineteenth centuries to regulate the interactions of all these groups (including whites) was one predicated on the principles of *caste*—a stratification system based on phenotype; rationalized through a set of beliefs about the intellectual, physical, and moral superiority of some groups over others; and maintained through state law and policy.

There has been some debate about whether African Americans actually experienced a caste system like that found in India rather than some other system of subjugation.[11] Weber's work has allowed us to consider caste relations as a more general phenomenon than that specifically present in India. Caste is present, for Weber, where "status distinctions are ... guaranteed not merely by conventions and laws, but also by *rituals* [Weber's emphasis]" and where "this occurs in such a way that every physical contact with a member of any caste that is considered to be 'lower' by the members of a 'higher' caste is considered as making for a ritualistic impurity and to be a stigma which must be expiated by a religious act."[12] Although Weber's specifications are of an "ideal-type" caste system, the historical experience in the United States of African Americans, Mexicans, and Chinese more or less approximates a caste situation.

In the socioeconomic confinement that each of these three groups experienced, convention, law, and ritual — namely a caste system — regulated the interaction with whites. The caste position of each of these groups began with their legal status. In those regions where the dominant economic activity necessitated their labor, their citizenship and concomitant legal status were used to control the interaction they had with white Europeans. For Africans working in the plantation economy of the South, slavery prohibited citizenship and the rights associated with it and thereby established the political and legal foundations to establish laws governing slave and nonslave relations. Mexicans and Chinese were also denied citizenship status, producing the same type of political climate where laws controlled their behavior.[13]

The "conventions" that Weber talks about in referring to caste relations can also be seen in the social histories of the Africans, Mexicans, and Chinese. These conventions (that is, social mores) were closely associated with Europeans developing an ideology of cultural and genetic superiority to the other groups. Nothing was more critical to the establishment and maintenance of the caste system than the development of the myths of African, Mexican, Indian, and Chinese inferiority. Such conventions excluded peoples of color from intimate contact with each other and with the dominant European white society. Caste norms governed the appropriate (and inappropriate) behavior regarding interracial and interethnic relations and regulated the proper sanctions for those who violated them.[14] Most strikingly, the "conventions" of racial superiority and inferiority associated with a caste social order survived the dissolution of caste, to persist in the new social orders that supplanted it.

For African Americans, Mexicans, and Chinese the rituals of caste were played out in establishing separate practices for eating, sleeping, schooling, worship, and of course sexual activities.[15] A double standard created the rituals necessary to maintain separateness. The rituals associated with the caste system included the punitive actions intended to maintain it; for example, the acts of the authorities to enforce Jim Crow laws toward each of the groups and the acts of groups like the Ku Klux Klan to burn crosses and maim and murder members of these groups.[16]

The origins of the caste system lay in slavery, manifest destiny, and forced Chinese labor, but caste was carried forward in the form of the Jim Crow laws that emerged after the end of slavery and the failure of reconstruction. Jim Crow laws, thought likely to apply to African Americans, also affected (in certain regions) the other two groups, as well. When anti-Chinese racial laws were avoided because white employers wanted Chinese labor, a movement started, supported by white workers, to legally exclude the Chinese. Such a law was passed in 1882, and, along with labor market discrimination, it forced the Chinese to withdraw to circumscribed geographic areas and engage in segregated occupations unwanted by white workers. Deprived of new members and forced back to their Chinatowns, the Chinese remained in their lower caste position. Until after 1965, they had a marginal impact on nationwide race relations. For each group, exclusionary laws, and the customs and rituals associated with them, effectively maintained the social caste system of the nineteenth century well into the twentieth.

Ironically, the need for cheap labor that established the caste system eventually eroded it. Two factors undermined caste relations. First, beginning in World War I, African Americans started to move north, where they could express themselves (especially their political beliefs) with less fear of physical and psychological reprisal.[17] In addition, a number of northern business leaders, in an effort to lower wages and/or cripple the organizing efforts of various unions, were attempting to recruit both African Americans and Mexican origin people for their factories.[18] Along with African Americans from the South, Mexicans from Texas and New Mexico (as well as Mexico itself) migrated to the northern, midwestern, and western cities in large numbers.[19]

This migration caused immense changes within the communities they settled in, most notably in the area of race relations.[20] These groups were moving from caste areas, whose labor markets were governed by a system that had jobs for whites and others for nonwhites, to areas where the market increasingly determined who got what jobs. The societies of the North and East were organized around class stratification.[21] Yet two factors were important in maintaining a significant number of the caste-type relations that were associated with the South. The first was that while northern and eastern cities were accustomed to new European immigrant (that is, white) groups competing with previously arriving groups in the labor market, European immigrant workers, many of whom were on the bottom themselves, did not want to be associated (through living situations or competing occupationally) with groups that were identified with a caste system. Second, white workers, already conditioned to view nonwhites (primarily African Americans) pejoratively and responding to the importation of many African Americans and Mexicans to undermine organized labor's attempts to unionize workers, became increasingly hostile.[22] In fact, white workers established some of the social control practices of the caste-oriented South and Southwest. Thus, the racial discrimination imposed in the job and housing markets had the effect of maintaining, albeit in a muted and somewhat weakened condition, caste-type relations between groups through World War II and into the 1950s. Despite the hostilities faced by these groups, their numbers would steadily increase as the demand for labor increased in preparation for World War II.

As William Julius Wilson noted in his study of the changing character of race relations, World War II was a turning point.[23] First, great numbers of African American and Mexican origin industrial workers moved from rural areas to cities where war-effort jobs were increasing. Second, the fact that African American, Mexican origin, and Asian origin (primarily Japanese) men fought in the war, although sometimes in separate military units, provided these groups with the symbolic resource necessary to push for full citizenship. Because they were willing to die for the country, they were morally entitled to those rights and opportunities offered to others. This significantly weakened the moral principles supporting the legal obstacles to full participation and equal opportunity that had been developed to protect caste relationships. Their military service also emboldened African Americans to demand the end of armed forces segregation and to threaten to refuse military service in a Jim Crow army. The result was President Truman's directive to end armed forces segregation. Nothing would be more important than this act because it showed that African Americans could fight alongside whites and could be trusted to act honorably and competently in a job that was critical to the well-being of the country.

The legal battles to guarantee civil rights and equal opportunity now proceeded in a more favorable position. There seems little doubt that the various cases that were subsumed under the *Brown v. the Board of Education of Topeka* case could not have been won without the moral predicament that was posed by the contributions made by African Americans and other nonwhite groups during the war, along with the increasing numbers of

African Americans, racially blocked from gaining socioeconomic mobility, who were experiencing urban poverty in northern cities. *Brown* also set the stage for the full mobilization of the civil rights movement. The movement, critically influencing subsequent court cases and the force behind the Civil Rights Act of 1965, ushered in a social order driven by a new dynamic.[24] The civil rights period further eradicated the legal basis of the caste system. It would now be very difficult to use caste, and its argument of racial inferiority, to justify racial stratification ideologically. This is not to say that race and racial prejudice did not play an important part in defining subordinate groups. Racial prejudice continued to prohibit African Americans, Mexicans, and Chinese (and other Asian groups, as well) from gaining access to housing and employment opportunities, but the ideological basis had ceased to be "race" as in caste. Rather, because racial prejudice was now against the law, the only way discrimination could be legitimized was through social class standing. Class is the lifeblood of capitalist societies. For without losers, there is no way to know winners. With race overturned as a legitimate method of discrimination, class became central.

Because the state no longer formally supported racial discrimination, more opportunities presented themselves to African Americans, Mexicans, and Asian Americans. Socioeconomic mobility for the groups proceeded more quickly than at any other time.[25] There had already been a middle class among both African and Mexican Americans, but the number of those who were becoming middle class was increasing.[26] Most Americans (white and nonwhite) believed that the solution to the "race problem" was simply what the law now guaranteed, equal access to opportunities. This was of course wrong, but it effectively made social class the primary mechanism to govern stratification.

The new conditions governed by social-class mobility continued to perpetuate racial inequality. To begin, socioeconomic mobility neither occurred at a fast enough rate nor spread wide enough in scope to effect positively the vast majority of African Americans, Mexicans, or Puerto Ricans.[27] This was due to a variety of factors. First, there was some mismatch in the level of skills that many of the farm-oriented migrants (African Americans from the South, Puerto Ricans, and Mexican migrant laborers from Texas and California) possessed as compared with those desired by industry. Second, the number of jobs being created in the host cities was not increasing at a rate that could keep up with the number of new migrants looking for employment. Third, because there was not an unlimited number of industrial jobs, nonwhite ethnics found themselves again in competition with white workers. In this situation, white workers' discontent was successful in pressuring white bureaucrats to hire and promote them over the other nonwhite workers.[28]

In addition to the slow rate of socioeconomic mobility discussed above,[29] during the late 1960s and 1970s, when social class governed race relations, there emerged a second significant outcome, intensification of class discrimination. Class discrimination had always been an important part of American culture, but the growth of a nonwhite industrial working class intensified the fear and disdain felt by the white middle and upper class toward the lower class. This produced among the white population a dichotomous view of the nonwhite population. There was the "acceptable" nonwhite middle class, which included those who had been highly educated and were professionals. For middle-class nonwhites, many of the racial barriers (by no means all) that had affected their groups were removed. An extraordinary number of this group were able to buy homes in previously all-white areas and live without disdain or massive "white flight."[30] However, a significant number of other nonwhites who were middle class were not acceptable to whites. This group was composed of people who had gotten factory jobs of one kind or another, saved their money, and decided to buy homes in middle-class areas. These people were perceived as middle-class impostors by white society. They had the money to be middle class, but their values and behaviors were working class; that is, they were working-class people with money. This caused many lower-middle-class whites (themselves one step removed from the working class) to be fearful that the quality of their lives would deteriorate.[31] The three greatest sources of anxiety for the white middle class (and there was some fear among the nonwhite middle class, as well) were (1) the financial status of their investments in their residential property, (2) the quality of the schools in their neighborhood, and (3) physical harm.[32] This anxiety was predicated on the belief that most of the newly arriving people with lower-class values would bring rowdiness, violence, crime, and sloppiness to their neighborhoods and schools. This, in turn, would negatively affect their property values, as well as their children's education and chances for mobility.[33]

Now some may feel that the argument about the salience of class discrimination is exaggerated in light of the racial barriers that were present. The present argument accepts the fact that racial prejudice did not disappear; the point being advanced is that it assumed a new look. There had always been extreme prejudice against the lower classes. This prejudice always had an ethnic slant to it, because America was a country in which the lower class was constantly being revitalized with new ethnic peoples. Thus, in the past, class discrimination could be facilitated by using ethnic cues such as language usage or language accents attributable to non-English-speaking groups, or some forms of dress (such as that of Orthodox Jews). However, in the case of African Americans, Mexican Americans, Puerto Ricans, and Chinese Americans, physical features could be used as class cues. Conceptually speaking, this established physical characteristics as an overlay to the dynamics of social class.

Ultimately, the fear of lower-class people, who in this case happened to be nonwhite, produced enormous amounts of discrimination in the housing markets. When discrimination (that is, exclusionary tactics) was unsuccessful, massive panic selling occurred. The upshot of this pattern of panic selling and white flight was urban decay and de facto segregation.

In the "class period," some disadvantages associated with a class stratification system were experienced by nonwhites. Yet the significance of this period was that it allowed (however briefly) people of color to be economically mobile and in the process to shed some of the race stigma associated with the caste-stratification system of the past period. Thus, in this period more class solidarity across racial lines was experienced, corresponding to the views of the integrationist theorists. In the group-status system that emerged in the next period, economic mobility for a minority of people of color persisted, but escaping racial stigma through class disappeared.

The Emerging Significance of Status

During this period (from the late 1950s to the early 1970s), housing discrimination produced a racially stratified housing market, segregated schools, and geographic areas where a large number of people were poor. These conditions ushered in a new period (from the mid-1970s to the present) where race relations were no longer governed by class standing, but by the concept of group status. It was no longer the case that the dominant belief among white Americans was that African Americans, Mexican Americans, or Puerto Ricans were genetically inferior; rather white Americans preferred to work or live with some ethnic groups over others. This preference was based on both economic and cultural issues. For example, because the socioeconomic system was unable, and the political system was unwilling, to radically intervene and produce more jobs and opportunities for the mobility of larger numbers of nonwhite minorities, a social pressure-cooker effect was produced for African, Mexican, and Chinese Americans (and for some other groups, as well), and a number of social problems worsened. More crime occurred in these areas, more disciplinary problems in schools, more rundown housing. Many whites believed that the worsening of conditions for African Americans, Mexicans, and Puerto Ricans was due to their own irresponsibility. However, for other white Americans (most notably the white middle class), such conditions could be explained by blocked mobility. Yet, these same middle-class people were unable to determine who among the disadvantaged racial groups posed a problem for them. Thus, despite some understanding that not all African Americans and Latinos committed crimes or were bad students or were irresponsible in maintaining their homes, these same people were not willing to take any risks with their real estate investment, their children's future through education, or their families' bodily safety from crime. Ironically, the prejudice that had been slowly discredited from its exalted position within the caste-oriented systems reemerged as a vital element in protecting individual and group interests within the newly developing status system.

As Weber noted, status systems do not miraculously emerge from some arbitrary process in which the groups involved agree as to which group assumes what status. Rather those who monopolize the resources are in the strategic position to bestow "honor" and the privileges thereby associated with such a status to those groups they choose.[34] It is white Americans that continue to monopolize the resources, and they have been responsible for the emergence of a social order based on status. At present, there are three status categories that ethnic groups find themselves in. First are those ethnic groups that white society finds "desirable," which would include most of those who are white. Second, there are those that are regarded as "acceptable," which would include Jews, as well as a number of Asian groups such as Japanese, Korean, and Chinese. Ironically, the Jews, who faced stiff anti-Semitism, and the Japanese, who were forced to suffer in internment camps during World War II, have regrouped to be considered "model ethnics" by white society. So too have the Chinese, who in the last century and well into this one were portrayed as the "heathen Chinee" and forced to endure racial discrimination and segregation.[35] They have been joined principally (although not exclusively) by the Koreans.

Lastly, there are the groups to be avoided. These groups are on the lowest rung of the status hierarchy and would include a number of African origin groups (African Americans, Jamaicans, West Indians, Haitians) and various Latino groups (Puerto Rican, Mexican, Nicaraguan, and Salvadoran). What is striking about this list is that it includes both old groups of African and Latino origin and new ones. This may strike one as indicating that race, as in the caste-oriented system, is what determines the status categories. Race is a factor, but the new dynamic of race is that of status. Thus, while the actual basis of white discrimination is lower-class behavior (as opposed to feeling that nonwhite peoples are genetically inferior), it is the stigma of physical features that is used to identify someone of the lower class. White Americans (and many Asians they have designated as "acceptable") simply do not want to have much interaction with nonwhites because they do not want to take a chance that members of these lower-status groups will pose an economic or physical threat.

Status and Race Relations Today

Although issues of race and class are still present, it is the issue of group status that has insidiously infected race relations in the four critical areas of housing, education, crime, and employment. Ultimately, status will have moved the focus of race relations from that of the individual to that of the group. Whereas in the previous period, social class emphasized the characteristics of the individual (whether he or she had middle- or lower-class traits), the emphasis in the new period has been on the perceived and labeled traits of the group to which the individual is identified.

Housing and Schools

There is probably no area where status has been more present than in the housing market. For many years, it has been believed that racial discrimination in both the real estate and the home lending industry has been the primary cause for the segregation that has continued to affect the relations between racial groups.[36] However, although some banks and real estate agents have been involved in creating segregated areas through overt racial discrimination, much more often they have merely aided and abetted their clients in doing so.[37] Status has always been a central part of the housing market, but in relation to racial integration, it has been the governing factor in recent years. Realtors nearly always counsel clients that the resale of their homes is dictated by three factors: neighborhood, neighborhood, neighborhood. While there are many criteria that are involved in determining the quality of a neighborhood, none is more important than racial-ethnic composition and schools (which are affected by the district clientele).[38] Since where one chooses to live is for the most part subjective, the status of the area will be of great importance to the client. Many whites either will not buy in an integrated neighborhood or will decide to sell when the neighborhood they are living in appears to be headed toward integration. Most do this because of their overwhelming fear that their property values will be lowered, not necessarily because they loathe the idea of living with people of color. The alarming fact is that they are correct, and while their actions will not cause that to happen, they will greatly facilitate it. Racially integrated areas do not on the whole command the values that housing in all-white areas does. This is because neighborhood stability (that is, remaining integrated and not becoming nonwhite) is questionable and thus the status of the neighborhood is lower. For example, African, Mexican, and Asian American middle-class neighborhoods that are physically separated from the ghetto or barrio (the lower class of their group), with the same type of housing stock as a white middle-class neighborhood, have their homes assessed at an average that is considerably less than those in the comparable white area. This price differential is solely attributable to the status of the area, which in turn is directly related to the status of the groups that reside there. Whites are reluctant to live in an area with large numbers of African Americans or Latinos because they worry about whether they will be able to gain equity in their housing investment, or if they already live in a place and someone of color is planning to move in, they will worry that the value of their property may even deteriorate below the purchase price.[39]

One way the value of a neighborhood increases is if members of an ethnic group that is ranked higher than those who now presently occupy the area begin to buy homes there. The Southeast Asians and Chinese who have recently moved into Los Angeles' Lincoln Heights and Monterey Park (which had been predominantly Mexican American) are good examples of this phenomenon. On the other hand, when groups that are on the lower rung of the status hierarchy are involved in integrating an area, such as Latinos in Los Angeles' African American–dominated South Central area, there is no significant change in housing values.

As racial-group status (as opposed to class status) has assumed a more dominant position in the housing market, it has eradicated many of the gains (albeit small) that the nonwhite populations had achieved in integrating neighborhoods in the 1960s and 1970s. It has especially pulled much of the nonwhite middle class (especially although not exclusively the African American middle class) back into all nonwhite areas. In essence, it has strengthened the segregation associated with the ghetto and barrio.[40] The recent work of Massey and Denton has vividly shown this pattern, but their reliance on "race prejudice" as the main explanatory variable for this trend suggests the old racism found in the caste-oriented social orders rather than the new stratification based on *group*-status.[41] In fact, their use of the concept "prejudice" to explain segregation is better understood as the exercise of my concept of "preference" based on status and not race or class alone.[42]

As is evident to most people who study race relations, social changes in neighborhoods produce social changes in schools. The status of a particular school is influenced by its reputation. When the ethnic composition of schools changes, the status of these schools also changes. Thus, schools that experience ethnic change can maintain an outstanding staff and produce outstanding students, but if the school has become predominantly African American or Latino its status will have been lowered. Conversely, if an African American or Latino school becomes predominantly Asian or white, its status more often than not will have improved. The status of a particular school will be determined by the status of the group (based on class and race criteria) that dominates its student body. Most whites will assume that a school composed of African Americans or Latinos has disciplinary problems and poorer students than one composed of other ethnic groups. This view is primarily based on class behavioral criteria with race as the identifier of the class composition of a particular school. In other words, it is not that whites believe that the African American and Latino middle-class students are genetically inferior and cannot perform as well as other students; rather, it is too difficult for them to determine the number of nonwhite middle-class students in a particular school in order to assess the quality. As a result, white parents who imagine they will otherwise risk their children's educational opportunities withdraw them from the school. This dynamic places African American and Latino middle-class students in schools with large numbers of their lower classes and forces them to endure environments based on lower-class behaviors — less teaching time because of teachers attending to disciplinary problems, violence in the schools, and poor institutional support — that make learning difficult.[43] This of course makes competition with whites and Asians more difficult because when the competition begins in higher education and the job market, the quality of education has not been even. Ultimately, any poor showing by middle-class African Americans and Latinos in head-to-head competition with whites and Asians will reinforce the status position that these groups hold.

Interestingly, the Chinese, who had been placed in a caste-type position in the nineteenth century and legally excluded from immigrating to the United States from 1882 to 1965, have emerged from this position to excel in education. In fact they have been such a great model of success that they are now overtaking whites in educational performance.[44] The question that remains is how white society will react. Will whites allow the ideology of meritocracy to prevail, or will they impose (as they did for Jews) some type of structural parameters to regulate their success?[45]

Employment Patterns

In the past period, when social class was the primary dynamic affecting the social order of various cities and regions, employment opportunities did affect inter- and intrarace relations. During this period, significant numbers of those African Americans and Latinos who had gained middle-class occupations were for the most part accepted by whites (especially middle-class whites) as neighbors, friends, and co-workers because they were thought to be substantially different from their lower-class compatriots. However, in the present period, group status is playing an increasingly significant role in inhibiting access to high-paying jobs. This in turn has had a negative impact on the group members' abilities to improve the general quality of their lives.

As many social scientists have pointed out, shifts in the global economy have limited the opportunities for African Americans and Latinos in the labor market, but the status of these groups within the social-standing hierarchy has played a far more nefarious role.[46] There are three aspects to the status dynamic causing occupational inequality. First, there exist various stereotypes about the work characteristics of certain racial groups. These stereotypes have emerged from various sources (for example, the jealousies of other ethnic competitors, the socioeconomic conditions of some groups, and the actual behavioral characteristics of some, but not all, workers of a particular group), but their net consequence is to have created a racial status hierarchy within the labor market that has affected the attractiveness or unattractiveness of various racial groups for certain jobs. Thus, if a group has been stereotyped (unfairly or not) as being shiftless, poorly educated, not motivated, and crime and drug prone, employers will avoid hiring members of this group.[47] For example, in the status hierarchy in some areas of the country, white workers are the best to hire, followed by Mexicans, then Puerto Ricans, and then African Americans.[48] In other parts of the country where the ethnic mixture is different, the hierarchy would be white workers, Asian workers, Mexican workers, Central American workers, and then African Americans. These different status hierarchies in different sections of the country indicate that any effect that the global economy has on certain ethnic groups gets mediated through the local economy and its concomitant social structure.

The overriding motive for employers acting on the status of the group rather than on the individual is the same: they want to reduce any risk of disrupting their business operations.[49] However, the reasoning supporting their decisions may differ. For example, some employers who do not believe that differences in work ethics exist among ethnic groups discriminate in hiring anyway because they know some members of their workforce believe there are differences, and these employers want to reduce on-the-job conflict by keeping their workforce ethnically homogeneous. Other employers who don't believe there are differences between ethnic groups still refuse to hire a particular group because they believe that their clientele does not want to interact with a certain group.[50] In essence, it is the status of the racial group, more than any other factor, that influences the probability of whether a person will be hired for a specific job or not.

Group Crime as a Contributor to Group Status

The issue of crime both reflects and effectuates the status hierarchy among various racial groups in the United States. It is no secret that, compared with other groups, a disproportionate number of African Americans, Mexicans, and Puerto Ricans are incarcerated. While some have tried to explain this occurrence using heredity, most believe that it is a consequence of inequality in the labor market.[51] Even among the general public the prevailing wisdom is that inequality plays a major role in explaining why certain groups are more involved in crime than others. However, most people acknowledge that not all poor people commit crime and, even more important, not all groups who are experiencing socioeconomic hardship commit crime. Thus, their understanding of the importance of inequality in influencing people to commit crime does not deter them from using stereotypes to predict which racial group will pose the highest risk to their property or themselves. Most often, African American and Latino racial groups who have been placed at the lower end of the status hierarchy are thought to have a propensity toward crime.[52] This has caused many white people to (1) avoid traveling in primarily African American and Latino neighborhoods; (2) refrain from investing in these areas because they are viewed as being gang and crime infested;[53] (3) refrain from hiring African Americans and Latinos for fear that they will pilfer property or do their jobs incompetently because they are consuming illegal drugs; and (4) be wary and constantly vigilant of African Americans and Latinos when they are in a store shopping or even in a public space because they represent potential robbers or assailants.[54]

The prejudice that does occur toward African Americans and Latinos is driven by social-class bias and racial identification. Most people believe that the lower class of these groups is primarily responsible for crime, but since they also believe that the majority of the group is lower class and they have no quick way to determine whether a member of this group is middle class or not, they prejudge anyone who looks like a member of the group as a potential threat. The result is a stereotype that works itself into the employment, housing, and schooling markets, and eventually solidifies the status hierarchy.

The Ascendancy of Status

I have argued that race relations in the United States cannot be understood only as white versus black; they involve a number of groups that influence each other's situation. I have also suggested that contemporary race relations cannot be understood within the race-versus-class debate. Such debates, unintentionally, treat race relations as static.[55]

I have further argued that race relations are increasingly governed by a new dynamic — that of "group status." This dynamic must be seen as part of an evolutionary process that has incorporated both race discrimination (prejudice on the basis of physical features that were associated with the caste-oriented systems of the nineteenth and early twentieth centuries) and class discrimination, which involves a prejudice toward lower-class culture and behavior that has always been present to a greater or lesser degree throughout American history. This combination of "race effects" and "class effects" produced a group-status system whereby white Americans rank various racial and ethnic groups along a status continuum. Finally, this continuum is so strong that it constitutes a social order.

From the argument advanced here, it is also fair to assume that while global restructuring may have an impact on race relations throughout the United States, its total impact will be filtered through the dynamics governing specific local environments. This is because social relations, contrary to pure economic relations, form the principle structure of social orders, and social orders are the products of a long process of conflict and accommodation among groups. Therefore, even if a new dynamic (such as status) has emerged on the national scene, local conditions could either manifest it in ways that are slightly different from the national norm or still be operating under the influence of past dynamics (such as class or caste). This is precisely why I used the words "increasing significance of status." It suggests that change is in process and not complete, and therefore it is quite possible to observe elements associated with the prior social orders as well. Because changes in social orders nearly always involve a lengthy process, there will always be uneven development.[56]

The theoretical scenario that I have outlined here suggests that the rules governing relations between individuals of different racial groups are based less on the attributes identified with any particular individual and more on the identified attributes of the group. Society is moving from a concept of "individual entitlements" to that of "group entitlements." Given this, what are we likely to see in race relations in the future? There will no doubt be enormous competition among various racial and ethnic groups for the resources that exist. Because whites control most of the resources, racial-ethnic groups will attempt to avoid being associated with those groups that whites have identified as low in status. This will be done in the hope that whites will recognize that they are both different and in some way "better" than the other groups, improving their access to resources. For example, it will not be unusual to see Mexicans distance themselves from Central Americans (as they did immediately after the 1992 Los Angeles riot) because Central Americans (who are predominantly poor immigrants) command less status than Mexicans in Los Angeles. Or some Asian groups like the Koreans and Chinese will be distancing themselves (physically, socially, and politically) from the more recent Southeast Asian groups; or Haitians and West Indians will distance themselves from African Americans; or Cubans from Puerto Ricans and Dominicans; or African Americans from the various immigrant populations from Latin America.

We are also likely to see greater competition between Latinos (primarily Mexican, Puerto Rican, and Cuban) and African Americans for government resources and political power. For years, Mexicans and Puerto Ricans have felt that African Americans have been given more than their fair share of federal programmatic support at the expense of their communities. They have attributed this condition to three factors: (1) The African American population is distributed throughout the United States, whereas each of these groups is more regionally based; (2) African Americans have been politically organized for a longer period of time; and (3) organized efforts by African Americans have not only put on pressure at the national level, they have also produced representation in Washington, as well. Yet as the demographics change, as they do quickly in places like California, Texas, and New York, there are likely to be fewer coalitions between Latinos and African Americans and more political competition and conflict for political positions and resources. Witness the recent criticism by Mexicans in Los Angeles over the appointment of an African American to replace a white as police chief. Despite the Rodney King incident, the prevailing Mexican view was that since Mexicans greatly outnumber African Americans in Los Angeles, the police chief should have been a Mexican. Also witness the recent conflict over the appointment of Lani Guinier to be in charge of civil rights enforcement in the Justice Department. Her writings reflect an understanding of the group-status predicament facing various racial minorities in the United States, and that was the reason she was deemed unacceptable for the job—because her group-entitlement prescriptions for such a predicament were considered too threatening to the fictitious individualist ideology that has governed American political culture.[57]

By way of concluding, it is important to draw attention to one rather ominous proposition in the argument I've advanced. Ultimately the value judgments about the subjective hierarchies in social standing (status) among racial-ethnic groups in the United States has produced a resilient system of group queuing. It is unlikely that state intervention will have a significant effect on improving race relations in the foreseeable future. Since the status-oriented system is based on "preference," it is virtually impossible for a liberal democratic state to legislate (dictate) "preference" for its citizens. It is for this reason that policy solutions that rest on legislating greater access for African Americans and Latinos (or any group at the bottom of the status hierarchy) to better employment, housing, and schooling will be ineffectual.[58] This is likely to produce more segregation, which in turn will produce more inward-looking, Balkanized exclusionary racial communities, with more possibilities for intense conflict and social unrest.

Notes

1. Andrew Hacker, *Two Nations* (New York: Scribner, 1992), xii.

2. Although Africans can be considered part of the Negroid "race," and Chinese and Indians part of the Mongoloid "race," Mexicans technically constitute a mixed-race group (a combination of European and Indian groups). Mexicans were racialized when Europeans, in an effort to maximize their interests in the Southwest, went through a process of socially constructing "whiteness" and "otherness."

3. Hacker, *Two Nations*; Roy L. Brooks, *Rethinking the Race Problem* (Berkeley: University of California Press, 1990); Douglas Massey and Nancy Denton, *American Apartheid* (Cambridge, Mass.: Harvard University Press, 1993).

4. While the term *underclass* was first used by the famous Swedish sociologist Gunnar Myrdal in his book *The Challenge of Affluence* (Garden City, N.Y.: Doubleday, 1963), it was William Julius Wilson who raised it to its present importance in his book, *The Truly Disadvantaged* (Chicago: University of Chicago Press, 1987). There have been an enormous number of studies on the African American urban underclass; see, for example, William Julius Wilson, special editor, *Annals of the American Academy of Political and Social Science* 501 (January 1989), special edition on the underclass. For the impact of economic shifts in the global economy, see John D. Kasarda, "Urban Industrial Transition and the Underclass," in the *Annals* volume. Other important studies of the underclass include Christopher Jencks and Paul Peterson, eds., *The Urban Underclass* (Washington, D.C.: Brookings Institution, 1991); Michael B. Katz, ed., *The "Underclass" Debate* (Princeton, N.J.: Princeton University Press, 1993); Christopher Jencks, *Rethinking Social Policy* (Cambridge, Mass.: Harvard University Press, 1992); and Massey and Denton, *American Apartheid*.

5. Although my definition of *status* is not identical to Weber's, it draws heavily from his discussion of status and status groups; see Max Weber, "Class, Status, Party," in *From Max Weber,* ed. Hans Gerth and C. Wright Mills (New York: Oxford University Press, 1958), 186–94.

6. See Jon Elster, *The Cement of Society* (Cambridge: Cambridge University Press, 1989).

7. Just as subjects of the British, French, and Dutch Crowns began race relations through their interactions with the Native Americans of the northern, eastern, and southern sections of the continental United States, subjects of the Spanish Crown were doing the same in the southwestern and western sections of the continental United States; see Ramón A. Gutiérrez, *When Jesus Came, the Corn Mothers Went Away* (Stanford, Calif.: Stanford University Press, 1991).

8. The conflicts are too numerous to recount, but they did involve most of the tribes; see Stephen Cornell, *Return of the Native* (New York: Oxford University Press, 1988). In fact, the U.S. government's first use of biological warfare was in the conflict with American Indians; see William T. Hagan, *American Indians,* rev. ed. (Chicago: University of Chicago Press, 1979), 25.

9. The organizational seeds for the Bureau of Indian Affairs, which would become the colonial office of the United States, were planted in 1824. Most of the treaties that were signed with the Indians were made in an effort to regulate the rate at which whites confiscated Indian land.

10. For studies on the racist views of white Europeans toward the American Indian and how they worked to inform policy, see Michael Paul Rogin, *Fathers and Children* (New York: Random House, 1975); Ronald T. Takaki, *Iron Cages* (Seattle: University of Washington Press, 1982), 80–108.

11. Consult the work of Oliver Cromwell Cox, *Caste, Class and Race* (New York: Monthly Review, 1970), who argued that African Americans did not experience a caste system, and the work of John Dollard, *Caste and Class in a Southern Town* (Garden City, N. Y.: Doubleday, 1949), who found that they did.

12. Gerth and Mills, eds., *From Max Weber,* 188–89.

13. Mexicans were considered citizens of Mexico, and Chinese, citizens of China. For the relationship of Mexicans and Chinese to their respective social environments, see David Montejano, *Anglos and Mexicans in the Making of Texas, 1840–1986* (Austin: University of Texas Press, 1988); Andrés E. Jiménez, "The Political Formation of a Mexican Working Class in the Arizona Copper Industry, 1870–1917," *Review 4,* no. 3 (Winter 1981): 535–69; Mario Barrera, *Race and Class in the Southwest* (South Bend, Ind.: University of Notre Dame Press, 1976); Arnoldo De Leon, *They Called Them Greasers* (Austin: University of Texas Press, 1983); for Chinese, see Ronald Takaki, *Strangers from a Different Shore* (New York: Penguin, 1989), 79–131.

14. For Africans, see Winthrop Jordan, *White over Black* (New York: Norton, 1977); for Mexicans, see *They Called Them Greasers;* De Leon, and for the Chinese, see Takaki, *Iron Cages*, 215–49.

15. For sexual activities, see Takaki, *Strangers from a Distant Shore*, 114–20; George M. Fredrickson, *White Supremacy* (New York: Oxford University Press, 1981), 96–99.

16. For Mexicans, see Montejano, *Anglos and Mexicans*, 146–47; for blacks, see C. Van Woodward, *The Strange Career of Jim Crow* (New York: Oxford University Press, 1955); and for Chinese, see Takaki, *Iron Cages*, 215–49.

17. See Ira Katznelson, *Black Men, White Cities* (Chicago: University of Chicago Press, 1976).

18. Henry Ford is the best known for this maneuver, but other businesses also attempted the same tactic; see Edna Bonacinch, "A Theory of Ethnic Antagonism: The Split Market," *American Sociological Review* 37 (October 1972): 547–59; Fredrikson, *White Supremacy*, 221–27; Sterling D. Spero and Abram L. Harris, *Black Worker* (New York: Atheneum, 1968; originally published in 1931), 128–46. For Mexicans (which also included agribusiness in the Midwest), see Montejano, *Anglos and Mexicans*, 208–12. The Chinese were already tried for this purpose and were eliminated by the Exclusionary Act of 1882.

19. For the Mexican migration to the Midwest, see Julian Samora and Richard Lamanna, "Mexican Americans in a Midwest Metropolis: A Study of East Chicago Indiana" (Los Angeles: UCLA Mexican American Study Project Advance Report no. 8, 1967).

20. For a discussion of the migration process affecting African Americans, see Neil Fligstein, *Going North* (New York: Academic Press, 1981), and Nicholas Lehmann, *The Promised Land* (New York: Vintage, 1992).

21. See Olivier Zunz, *The Changing Face of Inequality* (Chicago: University of Chicago Press, 1982).

22. See ibid., 373–78. On the establishment and perpetuation of racial myths, see David Roediger, *The Wages of Whiteness* (London: Verso Press, 1991); and Michael P. Rogin's analysis of D. W. Griffith's motion picture *Birth of a Nation* in his *Ronald Reagan, the Movie and Other Episodes in Political Demonology* (Berkeley: University of California Press, 1988).

23. William Julius Wilson, *The Declining Significance of Race* (Chicago: University of Chicago Press, 1980), 88–92.

24. See Doug McAdam, *Political Process and the Development of Black Insurgency, 1930–1970* (Chicago: University of Chicago Press, 1982), 178.

25. Wilson, *The Declining Significance of Race.*

26. See Michael Hout, "Occupational Mobility of Black Men," *American Sociological Review* 49, no. 3 (June 1984): 308–22.

27. Puerto Ricans replaced many of the Asian groups in the American racial consciousness. They had been around since the Spanish American War, when Puerto Rico became a protectorate of the United States, but their social significance gained as their numbers and poverty rates increased in the East and the Midwest.

28. A very good example of this was in the Detroit auto industry, where few nonwhite workers were promoted from the shop floor to foreman. This was a primary cause of the wildcat strike (primarily African American, although Mexicans and Arabs were allowed to join) being started by the wildcat union DRUM (Dodge Revolutionary Union Movement). Ultimately, it was successful in closing down Chrysler Corporation and reducing this form of discrimination; see Dan Georgagas and Marvin Surkin, *Detroit, I Do Mind Dying* (New York: St. Martin's Press, 1975), and James A. Gerschwendinger, *Class, Race and Worker Insurgency* (Cambridge: Cambridge University Press, 1977).

29. See Gerald David Jaynes and Robin M. Williams Jr., eds., *A Common Destiny* (Washington, D.C.: National Academy Press, 1989), 312–13.

30. The position I am advancing here is at odds with a position taken in a recent study by Joe Feagin, who found that middle-class blacks remained discriminated against because whites saw them as racially inferior; see Joe R. Feagin, "The Continuing Significance of Race: Antiblack Discrimination in Public Places," *American Sociological Review* 56, no. 1 (February 1991): 101–17. I am reluctant to accept the evidence Feagin uses because it asks blacks about why white people act the way they do, but does not ask whites why they acted the way they did. In brief, it samples the wrong group to answer the question of whether there has been a change or not in white attitudes toward the racial inferiority or acceptability of middle-class blacks.

31. See Hillel Levine and Lawrence Harmon, *The Destruction of an American Jewish Community* (New York: Free Press, 1992).

32. Yona Ginsberg, *Jews in a Changing Neighborhood* (New York: Free Press, 1975), 114–30.

33. The opposition to the policy of busing for educational equality incorporated the fear that those blacks who were being bused would be from the lower class with lower-class traits. This middle-class fear of lower-class behavior in their children's schools was not confined to the black lower class; it also involved the white lower class; see Lilian Rubin, *Busing and Backlash* (Berkeley: University of California Press, 1972); see also Richard P. Coleman, "Attitudes toward Neighborhoods: How Americans Choose to Live," working paper no. 49, Joint Center for Urban Studies of M.I.T. and Harvard University, 1978.

34. See Gerth and Mills, eds., *From Max Weber*, 190–91.

35. It was not until 1965 that the exclusionary act that was passed in the last century to stop the Chinese from immigrating to this country was overturned.

36. Although hard evidence explicitly showing racial discrimination has been difficult to obtain, two studies that have shown racial discrimination are Rose Helper, *Racial Policies and Practices of Real Estate Brokers* (Minneapolis: University of Minnesota Press, 1969), and Robert Schafer, "Mortgage Lending Decisions: Criteria and Constraints," Cambridge, Mass: Joint Center for Urban Studies of MIT and Harvard University, 1979. Much of the literature on this topic is reviewed in Massey and Denton, *American Apartheid*.

37. Some new studies have shown that race discrimination is not the sole factor causing segregation between groups; see William V. Clark, "Measuring Racial Discrimination in the Housing Market," *Urban Affairs Quarterly* 28, no. 4 (June 1993): 641–49.

38. Coleman, "Attitudes toward Neighborhoods."

39. This has certainly happened in both Detroit, Michigan, and Gary, Indiana.

40. Douglas Massey, "Effects of Socioeconomic Factors on the Residential Segregation of Blacks and Spanish Americans in United States Urbanized Areas," *American Sociological Review* 44, no. 6 (December 1979): 1015–22.

41. Massey and Denton, *American Apartheid*.

42. See Clark, "Measuring Racial Discrimination," who found that racial discrimination was not the sole factor affecting housing segregation.

43. See Jonathan Kozol, *Savage Inequalities* (New York: Crown, 1991); Hacker, *Two Nations*, 147–60.

44. See the case of the University of California, where Asians constitute a higher percentage of the incoming students than any other group.

45. Structural parameters (quotas) were (and in some cases, continue to be) used for Jews in many of the elite universities; see Jerome Karabel, "Status-Group Struggle, Organizational Interests, and the Limits of Institutional Autonomy: The Transformation of Harvard, Yale, and Princeton, 1918–1940," *Theory and Society* 13 (January 1984), 1–40.

46. A significant number of studies bear this out; two examples are John D. Kasarda, "Urban Industrial Transition and the Underclass," *Annals of the American Academy of Political and Social Sciences* 501 (January 1989): 26–47, and Wilson, *The Truly Disadvantaged*.

47. This is especially true if prospective employees reside in an area that the employer has identified as being of a certain racial group and poverty-stricken; see Robert E. Cole and Donald R. Deskins Jr., "Racial Factors in Site Location and Employment Patterns of Japanese Auto Firms in America," *California Management Review* 31, no. 1 (Fall 1988); Joleen Kirschenman and Kathryn M. Neckerman, "'We'd Love to Hire Them, But ...'': The Meaning of Race for Employers," in *The Urban Underclass,* ed. Christopher Jencks and Paul E. Peterson (Washington, D.C.: Brookings Institution, 1991), 215–17.

48. Joleen Kirschenman and Kathryn Neckerman, "'We'd Love to Hire Them.'"

49. The Japanese companies have been excellent examples; see Cole and Deskins, "Racial Factors."

50. See Kirschenman and Neckerman, "'We'd Love to Hire Them,'" 211–25.

51. For the use of heredity as the primary explanatory variable, see James Q. Wilson and Richard Herrnstein, *Crime and Human Nature* (New York: Simon and Schuster, 1985). For those who blame inequality, see Elliot Currie, *Confronting Crime* (New York: Pantheon, 1986), and Jencks, *Rethinking Social Policy,* 118. Such authors argue that although inequality does not cause crime, it sets the stage whereby people respond to inequality in either a legal or an illegal manner. Also see Hacker, *Two Nations,* 179–98.

52. African Americans are involved in a significantly larger number of robberies. However, for homicides the number of incidents involving both groups are quite close (46.1 percent of the murder assailants are white and 53.9 percent are black), and rapes are perpetrated much more by whites than by African Americans; see Hacker, *Two Nations,* 183. In the case of Asian Americans, although they may have the reputation of being "law-abiding," they are also involved in a good deal of crime. With the exception of Japanese Americans, most other Asian communities have large numbers of gangs, and those communities have the fastest growth in organized crime in the entire country; see James Diego Vigil, "Vietnamese Youth Gangs in Southern California," and Ko-Lin Chin, "Chinese Gangs and Extortion," in *Gangs in America,* ed. C. Ronald Huff (Newberry Park, Calif.: Sage Publications, 1990).

53. For a discussion of the effects of crime on community development, see Wesley Skogan, *Disorder and Decline* (Berkeley: University of California Press, 1990).

54. See Elijah Anderson, *Streetwise* (Chicago: University of Chicago Press, 1990), chap. 6, "The Black Man in Public."

55. Of course the work of Wilson, particularly his *Declining Significance of Race,* is a partial exception to this assertion, because he has attempted to specify the historical dynamics of change in these relations over time. The problem with his analysis is that it moves from "race" as the cornerstone of race relations to "class" and then stops.

56. For an example of this uneven development as it relates to Chicanos (Mexican Americans), see Martín Sánchez Jankowski, *City Bound* (Albuquerque: University of New Mexico Press, 1986).

57. For an example of her ideas, see Lani Guinier, "The Triumph of Tokenism: The Voting Rights Act and the Theory of Black Electoral Success," *Michigan Law Review* 89 (March 1991): 1077–1154.

58. Such policy proposals are called for in a variety of works. Two notable ones are Brooks, *Rethinking the Race Problem,* and Massey and Denton, *American Apartheid.* It should be said that the Brooks argument does contain an understanding of the problem I just discussed and includes the government's more actively involvement in funding African American "self-help" projects.

5 / African American Entrepreneurship and Racial Discrimination

A Southern Metropolitan Case

Michael Hodge and Joe R. Feagin

The Ethnic Entrepreneurship Literature

Ethnic entrepreneurship has become a major topic for research among social scientists in a number of different disciplines. Central to this research is the argument that ownership of small businesses is a major avenue of social and economic mobility for immigrant Americans and for Americans in historically oppressed groups. Especially in light of the many problems faced by large-scale industries in the United States, the small-entrepreneur sector has been seen as a source of economic growth for Americans in all racial and ethnic groups.[1] Most writing about ethnic entrepreneurs has used data on immigrant-ethnic groups to develop conceptual frameworks to explain the role of ethnic businesses in ethnic group mobility. Racial or ethnic discrimination by white Americans is noted but rarely.[2]

Significantly, ethnic entrepreneurship researchers rarely discuss African American entrepreneurs except as examples of *lack of success* in developing a business economy facilitating group mobility. There has been much speculation about the alleged failure of African Americans to develop business economies. For example, Ivan Light has suggested that African Americans are too individualistic and do not have the necessary level of solidarity, as compared with ethnic communities such as those of Asian Americans.[3] A major flaw in this ethnic entrepreneurship literature is the neglect of in-depth analysis of structural contexts, including political support (as in the case of Cuban Americans) and racial discrimination.

It is also significant that major ethnic entrepreneurship scholars often argue that black Americans have no important business tradition. This argument has been refuted by the historical research of John Butler.[4] There is indeed a substantial, centuries-long tradition of African Americans, like whites and immigrant groups, creating new businesses in an attempt to rise in economic terms. From the eighteenth century to the late twentieth century many African Americans have worked hard to establish small businesses. Black entrepreneurship is part of an oppositional culture, that set of values, coping responses, and collective experiences that enables people of color to resist or survive oppression. Those oppressed by white Americans have often drawn on their own rich cultural resources to provide a powerful ideological critique of mainstream society. The historical evidence is in: since the 1700s African Americans have seen independent businesses as a source of empowerment and community survival.

Today, as in the past, African Americans view a small business as a way of maintaining independence of white employers and supervisors, as in corporate America. In every part of the country black Americans still start many businesses. The number of African American enterprises had grown to more than 424,000, at the beginning of the 1990s. African Americans have the largest absolute number of businesses among all minority groups; yet they (along with Puerto Ricans) have the lowest ownership percentage.[5] Moreover, black businesses garner far less than 1 percent of the total receipts garnered by all U.S. businesses.[6] In spite of the many business failures and the low average profits, however, the concept of starting a personal business continues to be part of the American dream for African Americans. Moreover, since the civil rights revolution of the 1960s this desire has extended to creating a successful business in the historically white business sectors.

What is it like to be a black business owner trying to make it in business sectors that have long been white dominated? For many African American entrepreneurs this is an extraordinarily difficult undertaking. They face racial discrimination everywhere: from creditors, suppliers, government officials, and fellow white entrepreneurs. A critical problem is their exclusion from the informal social networks that are the heart of business sectors across this nation. Long ago W. E. B. Du Bois wrote about the odds that face African Americans generally and black business owners in particular. He wrote, "The worlds I longed for, and all their dazzling opportunities, were theirs, not mine."[7]

Today entrepreneurship is one of the cornerstones of this capitalistic society. Business ownership is held by many to be the ultimate attainment of the American dream.[8] The satisfaction of the desire of owning a business signifies a certain feeling of freedom and of being in control of one's own destiny. African Americans share these same feelings and these same desires for success and happiness in society. Like other Americans, African Americans seek to satisfy these desires through business ownership. Many African Americans hold fast to this view of business ownership as a means toward social as well as financial stability and independence. However, the path toward these goals is often marred by racism and discrimination. Manning Marable points out that the one thing that is often overlooked in talking about the economics of American business is the fact that the "U.S. is not simply a capitalist state, but a racist state."[9]

This chapter examines the experiences and perspectives of an important group of African American entrepreneurs in one of the larger metropolitan areas in the United States.[10] The participants in this study are in the supplies and services business as "vendors" who sell products and services to government offices as well as to private businesses. These business owners supply communications expertise, cleaning services, materials supplies, office supplies, and landscaping and grounds maintenance, among many others. We attempted to interview all the black supply and services businesses that were certified to do business under a county government set-aside program providing contracts for black businesses. We succeeded in interviewing most of those still in business at the time of our interviews in the summer and fall of 1990. Sixty business owners were interviewed about their business experiences in this large metropolitan area.

Struggling against Discrimination and Exclusion

The Enterprise Spirit

The combined experiences of our respondents indicate that despite great discrimination and many setbacks, these African American businesspeople believe in entrepreneurial capitalism as a means to financial and social stability. What motivates a few African Americans to fight against the greatest of odds, the widespread discrimination, to establish a viable business? One respondent notes the lack of African American entrepreneurs:

> There aren't a lot of us entrepreneurs, and it's probably for the same reason that I am a health care provider; when I got ready to go to school, then I only knew of a few areas that I could do that would allow me to be my own boss, and that was my objective, was to be able to own my own business.

This "spirit of enterprise" has significant foundations in the historical tradition of survivorship of African Americans in the United States. Our data indicate that the incentive is not just making a profit, creating a useful product, or providing a needed service. Although these goals are important, the motivation is much deeper. We will discover that the inspiration to own a business is fueled by the goal of personal and group empowerment in a racist society.

The Racialized Business Climate

The idea of African Americans doing business on a significant scale is sometimes presented as new and unusual, yet in the United States many blacks have engaged in entrepreneurial activity, often against great odds, since the eighteenth century. Black business ventures began when free blacks created enterprises before the Civil War. Many of the best smithies and tanneries, for example, were owned and operated by blacks.[11] As we noted above, sociologist John Butler has clearly shown that there were many significant black businesses by the 1770s and that between that time and the present, numerous black business communities were developed in several northern and southern cities. In the first half of the twentieth century, blatant discrimination by white Americans in these cities, including racial attacks on black businesses in the 1920s and 1930s; the Great Depression; and the decline of black-owned banks were major reasons for the slump in black business activity that occurred prior to the 1940s.

Since World War II there has been strong support among African Americans for going into business. Today in every part of the country they work hard trying to start new businesses, even though most of these newly created firms face not only normal business obstacles but also documented racial discrimination. One of our respondents, in a construction supplies business, opened his interview with this soulful response to a question about what it's like being a black businessperson: "It's a struggle every day." Racial discrimination against African Americans in business is an old problem that even took violent and terrorist forms before civil rights legislation was enacted in the 1960s. These laws were the beginning of serious attempts to eliminate blatant, de jure discrimination. However, today the attitudes and practices of many white Americans remain antiblack. As we will see, some discriminatory actions are covert, while others are quite overt. In either case the results are the same — black businesses facing major barriers to entrepreneurial success. In the supplies and service industry represented by our respondents, discrimination is experienced in areas such as business start-up loans, the bidding process, bonding and insurance, and receiving timely payments for completed work.

Most of these business owners started with little capital and often depend on business set-aside and goals programs provided by local and regional governmental agencies to break into the local contract business. However, programs designed to increase the representation of black owned and operated businesses on government-sponsored programs have been beleaguered by false claims of "reverse discrimination." These claims by whites threaten the livelihoods of small black businesses in many U.S. cities today.

In the rest of this chapter we expose the racial discrimination that African Americans face when doing business in the supply and service industry. Even with set-asides and goals programs attempting to improve the opportunities for doing business, African Americans face inordinate barriers to business success. Our commentaries demonstrate the pervasiveness of racism and discrimination in the supply and service industry.

The Importance of Government Set-Aside Programs

Affirmative action policies were enacted in an attempt to "level the playing field" for African Americans so that the historically oppressed groups within the society would have comparable chances of success. Specifically, the passage of Title VII of the Civil Rights Act of 1964 established the Equal Employment Opportunity Commission (EEOC). This agency marked a significant advancement in civil rights activity. Prior to the establishment of Title VII, African Americans had no effective remedy to their allegations of employment discrimination. This executive agency was given the authority to investigate such allegations. In 1972, Title VII was amended and the EEOC was now able to bring charges and bring federal court action to remedy cases of employment discrimination.[12] In addition, during the first Richard

Nixon administration (1969–72) new federal programs were started to foster "black capitalism," including some encouraging local governments to
"set aside" a portion of contracts for minority contractors. In numerous cities
these local set-aside programs have expanded the number of black businesses.
The threat of federal court action has pressured local governments to implement strategies to increase black and other minority representation in
getting local government contracts. In our southern city, many black complaints about discrimination pressured the country commission to adopt a
black business utilization program in the early 1980s.

Set-aside programs refer to the practice of allocating a certain proportion of government contracts to minority owned and operated businesses.
Many of these set-asides established levels that approximated the targeted
minority's proportion in the general population. Government "goals" programs differ from set-asides (although they are often called "set-asides" by
the uninitiated) in that private companies that do business with government
agencies must meet certain minority representation criteria in the selection
of their subcontractors. If a white-owned company cannot demonstrate a
"good faith intent" to recruit black subcontractors, for a government job,
for example, the contract is not awarded. The results of affirmative action
of this type can be seen in the growth in number of black businesses, which
increased from 380,000 in 1982 to 424,000 in 1987, an increase of 38 percent in the critical decade of the 1980s. Gross receipts also increased 100 percent over the same period.[13]

The intent of such programs seems noble enough—making up for
past discrimination toward black and other minority businesses. The success of many programs seems to add credibility to stated intentions. However, these programs have not gone unchallenged. In various cities white
businesspeople have joined together to file lawsuits and declare these programs to be "reverse discrimination." One damaging suit was the 1989 *City
of Richmond, Virginia v. J. A. Croson* case. In this case, J. A. Croson Company, a
construction company, alleged that the city contracts being set aside for
blacks and other minorities violated the white owner's constitutional rights,
and the Supreme Court ruled that there was not enough evidence showing
that minorities had suffered discrimination in Richmond's business contracts.
The court seemed to require proof of intent to discriminate; solid evidence
of racial discrimination's effects was not enough. The *Croson* ruling was a
major setback, "forcing states and municipalities to suspend or at least review thousands of minority set-aside programs."[14]

In the city we researched the set-aside and goals program is critical for black businesses. For example, in a study of black construction contractors in the same city, Joe Feagin and Nikitah Imani found numerous contractors commenting on the program as did this electrical subcontractor:[15]

> I don't think I would be in business without it, okay.... It gives you an avenue to the world, so to speak. Okay, open up the gate and then you can, your record is being set, okay, automatically.... You're now established.

The importance of governments "seeding" minority businesses is critical to the survival and success of these businesses. As a consequence of county-forced utilization, black firms can build reputations and financial bases that result in future contracts. Another black construction contractor in the same study put it even more strongly: "If all of those programs was cut out, I would be out of business *tomorrow*. Because you can't do enough business with the private sector to sustain the business."

Among the black owners of the service and supply businesses we heard a similar view, as in the following comment by an owner to the question "How do you feel about the attitudes of white ... businesspeople in this area?"

> A lot of them don't want to deal with you. And if they don't *have* to deal with you, they *won't* deal with you. Yeah, that goes for the, any of the big companies also.... They have to have that mandate to say you have to work with them, and then they *will* work with you. But other than that, they would prefer not to do it, you know, not to do it at all.

Drawing on his substantial experience, this businessperson notes that most white businesses would rather not have any dealings with him or other black service and supplies businesses unless forced to use them because the contract or a government affirmative action program mandates it. Note too that most service and supply contracts in this city are private and do not have to meet any county government guidelines for blacks and minorities; as a result, most whites can exclude black and other minority participation in the private sector.

We can now turn to the experiences of black businesses directly affected by such programs and policies. There are many problems that affect black entrepreneurship. Our concerns here are the general conditions experienced in starting and maintaining a small black business. We now explore the travails that these tenacious businesspeople overcome to make a living and success out of their enterprise.

Starting a Business

There are many difficulties associated with starting a business whether one is black or white. There are problems of capitalization, inventory, and employee wages. These are normal obstacles that tend to distinguish the spirit of enterprise in particular individuals. Leaping these hurdles and avoiding the common pitfalls of business development can mean successful ventures. African American business owners face these obstacles and like whites use their savvy and acumen to overcome them. However, the U.S. economy does not operate on capitalist principles alone; racism is embedded deeply in its business principles.[16] It is this racism that adds nearly insurmountable barriers to the task of the African American business enterprise.

Many African American businesspeople report accumulating instances of racial discrimination in starting their businesses. Racism is usually not a matter of a few isolated incidents. For example, when the owner of a cleaning services company was asked about discrimination in starting her business, she described a subtle type of racism that still has potentially devastating results on the success of a business venture. She says that she has not openly been confronted with racial discrimination, but

> we've been on some job interviews where I would call on the phone for an estimate, and they'll talk to me and they'll say, "Okay. That sounds good." And you come in and look around and, you know. Like, I'll go in, sometimes I'll even act like an average private buyer, to see what it costs. And then we would go in, and the moment my husband, who is very dark, he goes in and they say, "Oh!" Then they say, "Oh. Well, we're sorry, you know. We just gave it . . . somebody else got the job." This is within, when you're talking, like, an hour afterwards. And I know, I know that it's because of race. A lot of times I speak with these people on the phone and I just know right away from, you know, whether it's from the accent or whatever, that I'm not going to get this job. . . . This has happened quite a few times, and I never really even let it bother me very much. I just know that it has happened quite a number of times.

This dedicated businesswoman and her husband attempt to conduct legitimate business in this particular city. They note that this differential treatment by whites has happened often. Here is a clear example of covert racial discrimination; their racial status is the only added variable in such inter-personal contact situations.

In the next excerpt another service company owner finds difficulty in obtaining start-up and operating capital. He is denied even small loans from the lending institution he has dealt with for several years:

> As far as getting money to get started, yes I did find a tremendous amount of that [racism] with the bank and other lending institu-tions. [What types of the problems have you faced in terms of bank-ing?] Well, I find, I [have] been banking with one particular institu-tion for over seven years and, you know, my funds have steadily grown with them and whenever I try to get a loan, a small loan say even a thousand dollars, from five hundred to say five thousand dollars, I find that they don't respond because of your, they are saying that your taxes is not compatible to the amount of money that you would like to borrow. I personally think that's ludicrous, you know.[17]

Drawing on his experience and noting his business success and good finan-cial standing, this businessperson points out the flimsy excuse the bank uses to disqualify him from obtaining even very small amounts as loans. This is a common experience among black businesspeople. Some white readers of accounts like this have raised the issue of whether their problem might not be one of institutionalized racism, of the fact that the black business does not have the business record, collateral, or liquidity to secure loans. While these can be factors, in cases like this one the problem is not these conditions but rather blatant discrimination, because the loans are quite small and the black business is successful. In addition, some respondents report a white business in similar circumstances that got a loan. One of the major qualities of racial discrimination is that it operates independently of the individual. In his in-terview this respondent points out that he deals with many different indi-viduals and the results are the same.

Another respondent, in a landscaping business, connected his problems of banks and bonding companies:

> These days it's been pretty much seesaw, up and down. And it's kind of tough being black doing business in this town, you know, being that you don't get the same treatment at the banks and the bonding companies.

The racial barrier system includes all white-dominated institutions that play a role in establishing and maintaining a viable business enterprise.

Such institutions include banks and associated lending agencies, insurance or bonding companies, and potential clients, the usually larger, white-owned general contractors and government agencies. Financial institutions have been implicated in creating unnecessary barriers to African American business ventures by denying loans. Shelley Green and Paul Pryde have recently confirmed Gunnar Myrdal's earlier findings that black businesses have long faced greater difficulties in securing commercial credit.[18] A rather routine and covert practice that results in negative and differential impact on African American business involves the bank practice of requesting excessive collateral for development capital as well as start-up financing. The owner of a repair service company details the difficulties:

> Well, when I went to borrow money, first of all, banks wanted the mortgage on my house. At the time I had a Mercedes Benz, they wanted ... papers on that. At the time I had a Chevy van, they wanted papers on that, too. I mean, and which everything was mine, that I paid for, which was collateral. Plus my house, you know, which is collateral. And for some reason, after they realized it was a loan for a business-orientation type loan, for some reason they find ways not to give me the money, so. [How can you decide or how do you feel that it was really a racial, or another reason?] Well, whether it was racial or not, it's hard for me to say whether it was racial or not, but I figure if you ask me for all the requirements that's needed to make a loan, and if I bring everything in the presence of you that you ask me for, okay, and everything was satisfied to that point, there should be a reason why you didn't give me the loan. Now, whether or not I would say it was racially motivated or not, and this didn't happen with just one bank, you know what I mean, this happened with maybe a few banks.

Again the institutionalization of discrimination is suggested. In the experience of our respondents, higher collateral standards are used for black businesses than for similar white businesses, probably because of the perception that African Americans in business have a higher risk of failure than white businesses. Bankers' prejudice is made self-fulfilling when the racial barriers are erected that contribute to business failure. Here too we see that the black businesspeople sometimes cannot be certain that a series of barriers are racial, but that seems likely because they keep hitting the same barriers at each turn. Green and Pryde have shown that significant racial barriers to black entrepreneurial success remain in place in the contemporary United States.[19] The current conditions that face African American entrepreneurs are often different than those of an earlier segregation era. The face of racism has many disguises, some overt and some subtle or covert. Our respondents indicated that while racial discrimination is sometimes more difficult to pinpoint, the results of its institutionalized, systemic nature remain destructive, if not devastating.

Consider the comments of this service company owner, who explains why she feels some of her loan denials have been racially motivated. This respondent indicates that there was a white person in a similar situation that received start-up capital.

> Well, almost the same situation.... I've known people — this is something I know, this is something that happened with a guy that I know that came by the school, ... and he got a franchise with [a major computer company], almost a couple of years ago, way back. And you know, he was fresh out of college, but for some — well, maybe, I don't know, it's hard to say. Maybe he had collaterals or maybe they had collaterals, so I don't know. You know, when a man is fresh out of college and can go in and start a franchise, you know, that's telling you something.... I mean, I've been in my line of work now ... since 1968, and I have a lot of experience, plus I've got a lot of work experience. And from the previous job that I was working on, which was [XYZ Company], I got a lot of business experience, because ... the electronic department was run and controlled by me. So over the past, from 1979 or 1980 up until 1985, I can say to myself, I controlled the electronic department. Or everything that was needed for the electronic department as far as parts and everything else was concerned; parts and accessories. I was the one that did most of the ordering. The only thing I didn't order was the main equipment, which was the computers and other type of stuff, which sales and purchasing already had the rights to do that.

Black qualifications — in this case service as a manager in a large computer firm — are often not counted as much toward business loans as for comparable white applicants. Like other of our respondents, this businessperson indicates the twisted set of conditions that allows a young, fresh-out-of-college white person to obtain enough money to buy into a computer franchise while she cannot get money to start a small business even with her collateral and great experience. Moreover, if the young white man here did happen to have better collateral (that is unclear), perhaps even some family wealth, that would suggest the background reality of 370 years of racial discrimination, the condition that has retarded and still retards the ability of African Americans to create wealth.

Underlying this pervasive and destructive racism is the deeply ingrained attitude that African Americans cannot be skilled and sophisticated enough to operate a business and provide quality services. The owner of an office supplies company adeptly summarizes the foundation of the negativity toward African American business. When asked what it is like doing business as an African American in his urban community, he responds:

> It is really, really, really rough. [Give me a little historical background on your business.] Well, I basically started out in marketing and selling data processing services, i.e., bookkeeping services, payroll processing, oh, in the early 1980s. And at that time, in this community, which is where I started the business, the people in the community, be they black, white, Spanish, does not matter, did not perceive me as being a serious businessperson, in that they did not think that I had the wherewithal to handle an automated accounting system and to actually do their bookkeeping, be able to process their payroll checks on a weekly, timely basis. And also at that time, which is one of the services I was offering, have the ability to provide them with all the necessary IRS-type reports that go along with it, i.e., the 940s, 941s, W2s, and all that. They, for whatever reason, and THEY, I say the whole community — when I say "they" I'm talking about the entire community — just ... did not perceive that I, being a black person, would have a handle, a grasp of what all of that was and be able to do it correctly. Although I came through the industry with over twenty years of computer background. [Laughs.] They had no idea, they did not think about this. Whatever, they just didn't think that was something I could do.

The perception that many whites hold of blacks in business is one of incompetence. A reading of the ethnic entrepreneurship literature, as well as E. Franklin Frazier's *Negro in the United States,* will find references to what some scholars call a lack of black business sophistication. Indeed, Frazier suggests that racism and prejudice are not causes of black enterprises' shortcomings; rather it is some flaw in the "black business culture."[20] While some "mom and pop" operations lacked the business sophistication when Frazier wrote his treatise, many African American businesspeople, like the last owner quoted, are today educated and skilled entrepreneurs.

Fighting Discrimination in Everyday Business

Starting a business is only one aspect of the problems African American entrepreneurs face. Discrimination is a real adversary in many other spheres, as well. The motivation to triumph over racial deterrents is demonstrated in more than the creation of a useful product or of needed services. Addressing a general question on what is it like being a black businessperson in this metropolitan county, a food service company owner notes:

> It's not much better than it was some years ago. The only difference is that you don't see the racism up front now, as it used to be. It's more simmered down, but nevertheless *we* are one-third, black, in the total population of this county, and we do not get one-third of the trades here.

Much confrontation of racism in everyday business takes the form of covert discrimination, that which takes place behind the scenes. Addressing the same question, a lawn services company owner speaks of the double effort it takes to overcome everyday discrimination:

> Well, it's almost dirt, in a manner of speaking, because you got to do twice as much as the other man. You've got to do it three or four times better than the other man, and then you still get slapped in the face.

Also answering the same general question, the owner of a business supplies firm notes how difficult being a black in business in this country is:

> Tough. Unbelievably tough. It really can be. It's tough, it's really tough because you're not taken seriously. People tend not to notice you or give credence to some of the things that you may say or do, as it relates to getting and running a business in this county.

One way discriminatory whites react to black competition is not to take black businesspeople seriously, to wave them off, as it were.

Successful entrepreneurship means the ability to make decisions in one's best interest within the relevant institutional frameworks. There is a critical political aspect to this. "Political" is taken here in the broad sense of the *empowering* of interconnectedness with certain individuals and groups, the networks, formal and informal, that are crucial for a successful venture. These African American entrepreneurs want to be able to exert influence in these empowering social arenas so that their interests and needs are made part of the agenda at both the governmental and corporate levels. These

African American businesspeople see value in being socially and politically active. It is imperative to be socially and politically "connected." African American businesspeople are often shut out of the critical social and political networks, making it virtually impossible to run a business successfully. Setting the agenda for empowerment is one of the strong motivations for black business ownership. The owner of one service company describes the political workings that enable white firms in his community to be prosperous:

> It's a very, very ephemeral thing that you can't really prove, you know what I mean? And it's their word against ours.... And it's very difficult to deal with someone, and then that someone goes out there and goes back up to the other person that happens to be the president of this multimillion-dollar firm, you know, and then they go back here and then they go into a deal with the commissioners directly, because this is who they deal with. And then the commissioners come back down to you and say, "Oh, hold on, lay off" or whatever, whatever.... I mean, not that the commissioners are corrupt or anything like that, but you've got to understand that it's also politically based. If you got all these firms together, okay, and you have these people that deal with each other, and then the person, you know. So you know that there's a lot of votes in there, too, so it's political also, obviously.

Similarly, a grocery store owner describes how people are discriminated against by being outside of crucial networks. When you are on the outside, the benefits go to those who are connected:

> And I feel that what they did, they discriminated against poor people who were not connected with the county, and by so doing, they hurt people, hurt the homeless out there. And there was no organization out here in this community now that is providing the services for the tenants. And they did it, I feel, because of the fact that they wanted a program for the county. They took all the money and channeled it to HUD, or channeled it to whatever organization they felt was politically expedient for their further need.

And a lawn service company owner expresses his concern to become connected to opportunities for larger contracts:

> Some of the divisions, you know, like departments on the small minority business there. There's some questions I've asked and I never got answers, you know, from the phone. You know, it's like, as to, say, when is a good time to go down and talk to someone

about securing a small business loan or a small business contract. Matter of fact, I really, I'm not concerned about a loan, I'm concerned about connections as to how to get larger business, like through the governments. And the only ones that I have made direct contacts with was through the federal government, which is HUD.

It is well recognized that much of the business that is transacted is done at informal, social events. The people who are well connected will reap the greater benefits. This sometimes subtle, sometimes blatant, form of discrimination is referred to as the "good-ole-boy network" or the "buddy-buddy" system. This black entrepreneur explains how a bid was acquired that excluded any chance of any other company or firm competing:

> I think that probably the person that they wanted to do the job was privy to the information and the particulars well before we were, so therefore they had better time to prepare. [Why do you suppose they do that?] Again, as I pointed to the old boy network, good buddy system. That's why.

The owner of a carpeting company responds to the question of what it is like owning a business by discussing the difficulties of finding opportunities without those networks and associations being in place:

> I think it's kind of difficult to find a lot of opportunities, or opportunities that, from a minority businessperson's standpoint, you can compete effectively and go through the bid process effectively in terms of having lower costs. I think that some of the barriers that minority businesses face in general are because they cannot, they don't have the connections to the mills or to the vendors or to the suppliers. They don't have lines of credit to guarantee payment.

A construction materials supplier discusses the informal networking that goes on to get government agency bids:

> There's this informal rules networking that's going on in some government agencies that whoever gets the formal contract bid also gets some more on the side that's not bid work.

Each of the last several businesspeople understand the value of a social network of associates helping to stimulate business and helping to keep a business viable. Being connected to the larger community of businesses is seen as critical for black business survival in the long run.

Discrimination and Empowerment in Business

The orientations and actions of these business owners reveal a drive toward personal, familial, and community empowerment. Manning Marable has suggested four interrelated components of this attempt at African American empowerment. He writes that empowerment is simultaneously economic, social, political, and psychological.[21] Each of these components can be viewed as a process. Together, these processes create a complex of activity by which African Americans strive for success in the U.S. political-economic system.

The attempt at business empowerment can be significant economically. Through business ownership, African Americans can gain a sense of controlling their own economic destinies. A private business consultant joyously expresses what it is like to be empowered:

> I love it! I love it because I don't have to share my accomplishments with anybody.... It gives you a sense of accomplishment ... because success is how you define it, the person, the individual, not how Mary Jane over here defines success.... I like it because I have a sense of control of something. What it is I have yet to define it, but I have a little sense of control of my life. And I can make some decisions on my own, be they right or wrong I'm able to do that ... and I kinda like being able to control my own destiny.

This control involves African American entrepreneurs having direct input into decisions.

Even working within the local government set-aside program, many of our respondents feel a lack of input into the program and, thus, a lack of control over their businesses, as suggested by this small business owner:

> Black businesses and minorities as a whole should have a direct input in what is set up, and so it would be set up based on the needs, not based on what someone feels that need might be or might not be. Because in my opinion, I believe that what has been happening is that those needs have not been met. It's simple.... I think personally, based on my experience with these programs, I really feel it's inadequate and it's set up for failure, in my estimation. It's a program that is not meeting the needs of any entrepreneur as far as for ... minority or black persons in this area. And from that setting, I think it's an injustice.

Many programs that are intended to provide assistance for minority businesses are devoid of input from those directly affected. Real empowerment in this sense means having a part in the decision-making process. For African Americans this sense of control is even more important than it is for white Americans also seeking the classical American dream in starting a small business. Significantly, racism in the larger society gives black Americans a sense of powerlessness that no white American feels. Being one's own boss thus has a double significance for African Americans.

Another aspect of empowerment is the sense of freedom from white domination. This psychoemotional sphere is pointed out by the following respondent's wish that whites would treat minorities differently, as equals. She says:

> They're just going to have to stop telling us what's best for us and giving us what's best for us, and we're going to have to start making what's best for us and taking what's best for us.

Another aspect of this drive for empowerment is the effect it has on whites. Gaining money and capital gives black businesspeople the ability to become independent and self-sufficient in ways that most whites in the same economic and social spheres are not accustomed to. When African American businesses become competitive in white arenas, whites may become jealous. Some whites, including businesspeople, may become envious or covetous as they lose some control and as racial exclusiveness begins to crumble. For African American entrepreneurs there is indeed empowerment vis-à-vis white competitors through business ownership and success:

> One example would be with the contract that I had with the school board, in that it's a pretty healthy contract and some of the innuendoes that I get when I go to get my check is, "You're sure making a lot of money" or "Are you going to be around?" or "Are you going on your yacht?" And the other one is with the first year contracting we had at the Aviation Department, where the general contractor always alluded to I was making so much money that he couldn't understand why I always cried broke. And my subtle feeling is that there is a fear that if we make money, then we understand that the power base is money, and that once you have the ability to do the things that you need to do in your business, that you don't have to beg for the crumbs, that you can be competitive.

A security company owner explains the fear and resistance whites exhibit when black businesses become competitive:

> The potentiality of making money is there, and like I told you, I've been staffing right now. My billing rate is killing me; they don't want me to have that type of money. It's like they're still controlling what should go to him, that's what he [a white man] said. "We don't want you to have everything." [Laughs].

This black vendor expresses the concern he feels when he notes that whites still want to control the amount of business his company can do. The final statement is powerful and is punctuated with laughter — but laughter with an ominous ring.

Empowerment through business ownership also means improving the quality of life and educational opportunities for one's children. Despite institutional racism and discrimination, African Americans seek success in business in part to advance the standing of their children, as this business owner made clear:

> I think my primary concern right now is the education of my children. I think that, more than anything else, is my primary concern. I think it drives me more than anything else, and if I were to list my priorities, I would say that the first thing I would like to do is to get them an above-average education so that they can compete in the workforce, in a workforce that I believe … does not totally accept them. So I still believe in operating under the philosophy that they must be better.

As Marable points out, these varying processes of empowerment are interconnected. The economic, social, and political facets penetrate the psychoemotional effects of striving toward entrepreneurial success. Exclusion from political agendas that have an impact on business growth and development and exclusion from informal, as well as official, networks are part of the plight that African Americans in business constantly struggle to overcome. One respondent lucidly describes the interconnectedness of several facets of empowerment.

> That's the name of the game; you have to network. I have control over the things that I have control over, whether it's a job that I have, okay, there are a certain amount of controls that I have. If we're to achieve the goal talked about and to network, then we have control over a certain element and exercise that control, and as you exercise that control and you build up networking, that increases

the probability of success and also control, which is the bottom line, translating to political and other infrastructure, or the inroads to the other infrastructures within that world or community.

Conclusion: Entrepreneurship as Independence and Resistance

The American dream is very much alive among these black entrepreneurs. African Americans who have been endowed with the entrepreneurial spirit seek the opportunity to earn financial and social security and stability through independent business ownership. In the racialized environment that is still endemic to the business world, this is very difficult. Entrepreneurship among African Americans is part of a continuing struggle for legitimation and empowerment in a racist social, economic, and political system. The experiences that the businesspeople cited in this study relate demonstrate a type of resistance to racial categorization and individual and institutional discrimination. African Americans have long made use of many tactics and strategies to overcome oppressive, discriminating white-racist regimes. Business ownership is a component of this general resistance, a resistance that is both cultural and organizational. In our interviews are reported the experiences of black businesspeople seeking social, economic, and political empowerment through owning and running their own businesses. Most soon recognize the racial barriers and difficulties and have thought through strategies to overcome them.

John Butler has suggested the resistance idea in what he calls the "truncated Afro-American middleman."[22] There is much discussion in the racial and ethnic relations literature of certain immigrant groups in the United States and elsewhere becoming "middlemen" in the economic system. For example, Edna Bonacich has explored the in-between position, in terms of power and resources, that certain ethnic groups have occupied in stratified societies.[23] Some groups develop small-scale business economies as a way of moving up the economic ladder. Thus many first-generation Jewish Americans, excluded from mainstream employment by white Protestants, became small-scale merchants, tailors, and restaurant operators. Significantly, African Americans have attempted to develop a business economy that could operate in this middleman fashion, but they have faced much greater opposition than other groups.

African Americans have a long historical tradition of business interest and experience that contradicts the notions of some writers in the ethnic entrepreneurship literature, as well as the ideas of the prominent sociologist E. Franklin Frazier.[24] By their commitment to a philosophy of self-help and business, African Americans have, at least since the 1700s, developed businesses in numerous cities against tremendous odds. African American entrepreneurship is part of an oppositional or resistance culture. As our respondents make clear, business action is taken even when it appears very difficult. Reviewing the black business record from the 1770s to the early 1900s, Butler highlights this resistance in the face of oppression in the defining characteristics of the African American "truncated middleman" group, which

> (1) adjusted to hostility by turning inward and developing economic and community institutions; (2) developed a strong tradition of family stability and excellent quality of life through housing, health care, and other means, and . . . (3) began a very strong emphasis on the importance of higher education for their offspring.

Contrary to Milton Gordon's assessment of the black middle class as totally assimilating,[25] Butler argues that cultural values, both African and American, are part of a black middle-class view not reducible to a whitewashed middle-class-ness. Circumstances created, and still create, a black entrepreneurial group within the black middle class—one responding to continuing racial barriers to inclusion in the U.S. economy, society, and polity.

Resistance to economic oppression and a commitment to personal, familial, and community empowerment are still aspects of African American entrepreneurship. They are the driving forces attempting to make life in America the dream that it is touted to be. Business ownership is seen as a way to financial and social independence for African American entrepreneurs. Despite continual negative racial attitudes from whites in private businesses as well as in government agencies, these vendors, like the one quoted below, understand that they "have to keep on going":

> I have to keep on going, if I'm going to develop my business and eventually be independent to the point where I don't have to work for another person.

Yet it is also quite clear from our interviews that active federal and local government intervention in the form of set-aside and goals programs is essential, for decades to come, to overcome persisting racial discrimination in all areas of business life. As Theodore Cross has noted:

> Policies that expressly set aside government contracts for minority bidding provide blacks with much broader economic opportunities, including the chance, long denied them through law and custom,

of significant capital formation. . . . Whatever racial stigma may attach to specifically assigned privileges based on race is overcome manyfold by the huge expansion in black powers and opportunities that these laws deliver.[26]

While there is much white opposition to past and current affirmative action strategies such as the set-aside and goals programs, this opposition often comes most aggressively from white businesspeople competing for the same business and contracts as the new black-owned businesses. In part, it is because of this competition that white businesspersons react negatively to set-aside programs. Many white detractors of equal opportunity policies argue that the so-called free market or free enterprise must be given full reign to operate. Yet it is the *racialized market* that is the ongoing problem. There is not now, nor has there ever been, such a thing as a free market. Among other limiting factors, racial discrimination today makes sure that economic markets are biased in favor of those (whites) with greater power and resources. Even critical business networks are often off limits to African American entrepreneurs.

Without addressing the festering anger that racial discrimination brings in business and the workplace, we as a nation may well face more of the violent racial unrest and upheaval for which the American cities have become infamous in the last three decades. A key issue for local, state, and federal government policy in the late twentieth century, and into the twenty-first century, is whether the U.S. economy can be reshaped to provide truly equal and fair business opportunities for African Americans. A level playing ground, over the long term, is all the black businesspeople are asking for, as a repair business owner made clear:

> Because I don't want nobody to give me nothing, because in my vocabulary there ain't no such thing as "give." I don't want nobody to give me nothing. Not a penny. I don't want nothing from nobody. Give me, give me a hundred percent opportunity, as you would give everybody else, and let's go at it, the best man win. All right? That's the way I feel, that's the way I see the whole deal, you know what I mean. Don't give me nothing, . . . let me work for it. Let me work for it.

The drive for economic, political, and familial empowerment is a major motivating force for entrepreneurial activity in the African American community. The resistance to a sense of helplessness and a lack of control of one's destiny and the desire for social and financial stability are key factors in the spirit of entrepreneurship of African Americans.

Notes

1. Roger Waldinger et al., *Ethnic Entrepreneurs: Immigrant Business in Industrial Societies* (Newberry Park, Calif.: Sage, 1990), 19–21.

2. See Ivan Light, *Ethnic Enterprise in America* (Berkeley, Calif.: University of California Press, 1972); Waldinger et al., *Ethnic Entrepreneurs,* 44–46.

3. Light, *Ethnic Enterprise.*

4. John S. Butler, *Entrepreneurship and Self-Help among Black Americans: A Reconstruction of Race and Economics* (Albany: State University of New York Press, 1991), 245.

5. Waldinger et al., *Ethnic Entrepreneurs,* 56.

6. David H. Swinton, "Economic Status of Black Americans during the 1980s," in *The State of Black America 1990,* ed. Janet Dewart (New York: National Urban League, 1990), 42–43.

7. W. E. B. Du Bois, *The Souls of Black Folk* (New York: Avon Books, 1903).

8. See Robert N. Bellah, Richard Madsen, William M. Sullivan, Ann Swidler, and Steven M. Tipton, *Habits of the Heart: Individualism and Commitment in American Life* (New York: Harper and Row, 1985), 35–51.

9. Manning Marable, *How Capitalism Underdeveloped Black America: Problems in Race, Political Economy and Society* (Boston, Mass.: South End Press, 1983), 166.

10. We keep the city anonymous to protect the respondents from retaliation.

11. John Hope Franklin and A. A. Moss Jr., *From Slavery to Freedom: A History of Negro Americans,* 6th ed. (New York: McGraw-Hill, 1989).

12. Derrick Bell, *Race, Racism and American Law,* 3rd ed. (Boston, Mass: Little, Brown, 1992), 880–88.

13. See *Black Enterprise,* 1992 annual edition of the "Top 100 Black Businesses" (New York: Graves, 1992).

14. Alphonso Pinkney, *Black Americans,* 4th ed. (Englewood Cliffs, N.J.: Prentice-Hall, 1993), 72.

15. Joe R. Feagin and Nikitah Imani, "Racial Barriers to African American Entrepreneurship: An Exploratory Study," *Social Problems* 41 (November 1994): 562–84.

16. See Immanuel Wallerstein, *Historical Capitalism* (London: Verso, 1983).

17. The names of specific banks and other institutions were removed to protect the confidentiality of the respondents in all of the excerpts in this report.

18. Shelley Green and Paul Pryde, *Black Entrepreneurship in America* (New Brunswick, N.J.: Transaction, 1990); Gunnar Myrdal, *An American Dilemma* (New York: Harper and Brothers, 1944).

19. Green and Pryde, *Black Entrepreneurship in America.*

20. E. Franklin Frazier, *The Negro in the United States* (New York: Macmillan, 1949).

21. Manning Marable, *The Crisis of Color and Democracy: Essays on Race, Class and Power* (Monroe, Maine: Common Courage Press, 1992), 68–73.

22. Butler, *Entrepreneurship and Self-Help among Black Americans.*

23. Edna Bonacich, "Class Approaches to Ethnicity and Race," *Insurgent Sociologist,* Fall 1980, 11–15.

24. E. Franklin Frazier, *Black Bourgeoisie* (New York: Free Press, 1954).

25. Milton Gordon, *Assimilation in American Life: The Role of Race, Religion, and National Origin* (New York: Oxford University Press, 1964).

26. Theodore Cross, *The Black Power Imperative* (New York: Faulkner, 1984), 769.

Part III

Race, Segregation, and the State

6 / Black Ghettoization and Social Mobility

Norman Fainstein

Some images about race confront us every day when we turn on our television sets: teenage mothers on welfare, crack addicts, drive-by shootings, run-down neighborhoods, children dying in tenement-house fires, the MTV rap world of fast girls and violent boys. Such images reflect and reinforce popular identification of African Americans with the worst-off and the most socially "deviant" segments of the black poor—the members of the so-called underclass—and with the places where they live—the black ghetto.

The prominent black sociologist, William Julius Wilson, minces no words as he describes the "underclass" in his influential book, *The Truly Disadvantaged*:

> Today's ghetto neighborhoods are populated almost exclusively by the most disadvantaged segments of the black urban community, that heterogeneous grouping of families and individuals who are out of the mainstream of the American occupational system. Included in this group are individuals who lack training and skills and either experience long-term unemployment or are not members of the labor force, individuals who are engaged in street crime and other forms of aberrant behavior, and families that experience long-term spells of poverty and/or welfare dependency. These are

the populations to which I refer when I speak of the *underclass.* I use this term to depict a reality not captured in the more standard designation *lower class.*[1]

Thanks to Wilson—and a host of other scholars, journalists, foundations, and government agencies—the study of the underclass has provided a raison d'être for refocusing attention on race and poverty.[2] But it has also reproduced in academic jargon, buttressed by powerful statistical tools, the very image that it has sought to clarify and explain, if not dispel. While the literature on the subject is too vast to review here in any detail, it is worth outlining the basic feature of the underclass interpretation of how race and economics intersect.[3]

The "underclass" comprises people who used to be called down and out, individuals who for various reasons do not work and apparently behave "antisocially" in other respects, as well. By focusing on the rather small core of people perennially disattached from the official labor market, researchers inevitably ignore the majority of low-income people who do work, although at wages that keep them in economic deprivation.[4] Rather than offering a theory of the labor market, of how and why it seems to be generating more and more low-wage and underground jobs, rather than examining the continual movement in and out of work at the bottom of our economy, underclass theory tries to explain the personal and environmental attributes of the permanently unemployed. Correlated with the joblessness of such people are a host of the other characteristics of the urban poor that are readily visible in the television picture of "the ghetto."

Depending on the politics of the analyst, the blame for the underclass is lodged either with government programs that have bred dependency and corrupted the morals of the poor or with an economy that has literally left the poor behind: some combination of suburbanization of new jobs and deindustrialization has created a spatial mismatch and brought skill levels up beyond the educational attainment of inner-city residents (thereby effecting a skills mismatch).[5]

All sides downplay race as a factor, even though the underclass seems to be mainly African American, and most attention is focused on central-city, lower-class black neighborhoods. These neighborhoods are increasingly "isolated" from mainstream society and economy, with their inhabitants ever more "concentrated" in a pathological environment. To students of social history, the imagery of the underclass inhabiting its packed ghettos is quite familiar: it resonates almost perfectly with previous models of the undeserving poor and their disease-laden districts, of the slum (which needed to be cleared), and of the pathological immigrant ghetto.[6]

There is, however, an important twist to the idea of the underclass as it is played out these days by social scientists, one that did not exist in past theories of slum life. The argument is now made that the very pathology of the "ghetto" and its impoverished, isolated residents has been produced, in good part, by the success of upwardly and outwardly mobile black households. Thus, many scholars have detailed the growth of a black middle class as well as the exodus of such families from the worst — "ghetto" — neighborhoods. Increasing class inequality among blacks has, in this view, combined with residential mobility to leave "behind" the large residuum that is the "ghetto poor," deprived of the "better elements" who used to provide role models and institutional ballast.[7]

By an unstated logic, therefore, the underclass not only results from the increasing bifurcation of black society, but reaffirms by its existence the reality of black success. It would not be too much to say, in fact, that the sociology of the underclass tells whites that working and middle-class blacks, including, of course, black professionals, are *not* the underclass, that the appropriate lens with which to examine the economic situation of African Americans is class, not race.

But that lens distorts: race has not gone away. It remains a biting reality for African Americans, perhaps especially for those who have achieved some economic success. To see this, we need to free our minds from the television and social science equation of racial and economic stratification with the impoverished ghetto and the underclass. Instead of imagining dilapidated black neighborhoods and their downtrodden and sometimes "dangerous" inhabitants, we might think of another picture, this one drawn by the 1990 census of a city known for its large black working and middle class: Washington, D.C. A century ago W. E. B. Du Bois spoke of the "color line" that divided the races, in the North as well as the South, regardless of income and occupation. Washington's neighborhoods today remain divided by that same color line. While few cities are so perfectly bisected by a single racial fault line, most are just as segregated as the nation's capital. Moreover, residential segregation is no mere remnant of a racist past. It is a glaring sign of the continued racial segmentation of our society today. As I will show, segregation plays a critical role in redefining class for African Americans and in reducing their prospects for upward economic mobility.

The Realities of Continued Economic Deprivation and Residential Segregation

The economic success of any social group, in this case African Americans, over an extended period of time can best be understood, on the one hand, in terms of a changing structure of economic opportunity and, on the other hand, in terms of the resources possessed by group members as they compete with others for economic advantage. Both within their lifetimes and between generations, some members of a group will experience upward mobility in a changing opportunity structure, and others downward mobility. Group success is a reflection, on balance, of net upward mobility. The same applies to a particular stratum, like the black poor. Poverty will decrease if the resources possessed by lower-income blacks provide them with sufficient advantages to be upwardly mobile on average in relation to other low-income groups. By thinking of poverty, or any other status, as an instantaneous picture of dynamic processes centrally rooted in the economy, we will not just better understand the reasons for continued black poverty, but also better explain the competitive situation of all African Americans.

The American economy has traversed two distinct periods since the depression. The first, which extended from 1940 to 1973, witnessed steady improvement in the economic condition of the typical American, with a general reduction in overall inequality along the way. The second, through which we have now suffered for two decades, has been associated with real overall growth as measured by GNP and related indicators (although at a much slower rate than earlier), yet with no improvement for the typical American because economic inequality increased sharply and the wealthiest households reaped all the benefits of such growth as there has been.[8]

In this kind of situation, African Americans, who were disadvantaged at the start, could not be expected to make much economic progress along the way. So it is unremarkable that black median household income increased by less than $100 between 1973 and 1991, with the typical black household remaining at only 59–60 percent of the income of a typical white household (see table 6.1). The black middle class, those with incomes of $25,000–50,000, *contracted* slightly during the period, as did the white. And while upper-middle-class and elite black households grew in these eighteen years, they still composed but 12 percent of all black households, compared with more than 27 percent of white households. By contrast, the percentage of blacks in poverty has *not* increased since 1973, but it remains very high, at more than two-fifths of all black households. These data explain why it is

Table 6.1. Race and income structure, 1967–91:
Annual household income in constant (1991) dollars

	Poverty ≤14,999	Marginal 15–24,999	Middle 25–49,999	Upper Middle 50–99,999	Elite ≥100,000	Median
Black Distribution						
1967	46.7	24.9	23.3	4.7	0.5	16,228
1973	42.0	21.7	28.1	7.7	0.6	18,713
1979	42.4	20.4	26.6	10.0	0.5	18,650
1985	44.0	20.3	25.5	9.5	0.8	18,758
1991	42.4	19.1	26.6	10.8	1.1	18,807
White Distribution						
1967	24.4	19.8	40.5	13.5	1.8	27,949
1973	22.2	16.6	38.1	20.2	2.9	31,791
1979	21.9	17.4	36.1	21.3	3.3	31,766
1985	22.3	17.3	34.4	21.9	4.1	31,529
1991	21.9	17.3	33.3	22.7	4.8	31,569

Note: The median income of all U.S. households was $26,801 in 1967, $30,333 in 1973,
$30,297 in 1979, $29,896 in 1985, and $30,126 in 1991.
Source: U.S. Bureau of the Census, *Current Population Reports,* Series P-60, no. 180 (1992),
Table B-2.

so important to examine the economic situation of all African Americans,
not just to concentrate obsessively on the nonworking poor. The reality is
that the entire black income structure has remained relatively unchanged in
shape and unimproved relative to that of whites.

It should be noted, however, that even during the period of most rapid
economic growth, the gap between blacks and whites was closed mainly
because of the transformation of the southern economy from semifeudal to
industrial. A good indicator is provided by the ratio of black to white median family income between 1950 and 1990. Over these forty years there
was no gain for the median black family; the improvement in the 1960s
was lost by 1974. What is more, outside of the South the *relative* position of
black families actually deteriorated between the early fifties and the early
nineties. Of course, real median family income was much higher in 1990
than in 1950, so the typical family, whether black or white, saw its standard
of living improve. Only in these "absolute" terms were blacks *on average* socially mobile.

Popular images—and the more sophisticated discussion of the underclass—have managed to avoid confrontation with evidence about income
distribution and economic reorganization, even in the face of an abun-
dance of empirical and theoretical work in these areas. The same may be

said about the most omnipresent and long-standing reality about African Americans — their residential segregation. The color line that bisects Washington may be seen everywhere in America by those who care to look. In fact, throughout most of the twentieth century blacks have stood alone in the extent of their physical separation, regardless of time, place, or class attributes.[9]

The 1990 census shows that blacks remain highly segregated, particularly in the large metropolitan areas where most are concentrated (see table 6.2). Even the small declines in some places are probably an artifact of the expansion of black neighborhoods into adjacent areas, which appear to be racially integrated at the moment of the census count.[10] Particularly disquieting for people who believe that the black middle class has become integrated are the figures in the lower panel of table 6.2. These show that blacks in New York City with household incomes of at least $100,000 a year are as highly segregated as blacks in poverty. While findings from the 1990 census are just now appearing, extensive analyses of the 1980 and 1970 censuses show that blacks throughout America were residentially segregated whatever their social class.

In table 6.3 we look at evidence of black-white segregation using both income and education as indicators of social class. The first column shows the degree of segregation of blacks at specified income or education levels from whites of any incomes or education. For example, the index number is .79 for blacks with incomes of $50,000 or more in 1980. This means that 79 percent of these black persons would have had to move from their census tracts in order to match the distribution of whites as a whole within their metropolitan area. It is apparent from the data that blacks at every class are equally isolated from white society. In the second column, we look at segregation with class controlled for both blacks and whites, in other words, at the level of interracial segregation of blacks and whites with the same incomes or educations. Again, race overwhelms class. Middle-class blacks, working-class blacks, and poor blacks are equally segregated from their white class counterparts. Clearly, higher class standing does little to buy African Americans a racially integrated environment. When better-off African Americans move out of the most impoverished black neighborhoods, nearly all move into other segregated areas.

Blacks are ghettoized through political and economic processes that establish residential segregation as a sign of, and basis for, group subordination. The black ghetto — like the Jewish ghetto of the Middle Ages — encompasses the entire population bearing an ascriptive attribute, in this case

Table 6.2. Racial segregation in 1980 and 1990:
Index of segregation (D) of blacks from all other groups

	1990	1980	Difference
Ten largest metropolitan areas in 1990			
New York	.82	.82	.00
Los Angeles-Long Beach	.73	.76	.03
Chicago	.86	.89	.03
Philadelphia	.77	.77	.00
Detroit	.88	.90	.02
Washington, D.C.	.66	.66	.00
Houston	.67	.74	.07
Nassau-Suffolk County	.76	.76	.00
Boston	.68	.71	.03
Atlanta	.68	.75	.07
Metropolitan Statistical Areas (MSAs) by size			
All	.69	.74	.05
Large MSAs	.74	.78	.04
Medium MSAs	.64	.69	.05
Small MSAs	.58	.61	.03
New York City			
All black households	.84	.84	.00
Incomes below $15,000	.86	.87	.01
Incomes above $100,000	.88	.88	.00

Note: Figures for metropolitan areas are values of the index of dissimilarity (D), a measure of residential segregation. The index shows the proportion of black households that would have to change census tracts within a metropolitan area in order to be distributed in the same manner as the comparative nonblack population. D ranges between zero and 1.00. In the distribution of D, 0–.30 is considered low, .30–.60 moderate, and .60–1.00 high. Thus, all values of D in this table are, in fact, in the high range.

For New York City, D is again the measure of segregation, but in this case with block groups rather than census tracts as the unit of area. Since block groups are smaller and therefore more homogeneous than census tracts, D is likely to be slightly higher. The subcategories for New York City measure, respectively, the segregation of blacks in poverty and those with elite incomes from all other groups. Incomes are expressed in constant (1990) dollars. The categories used for comparison between 1990 and 1980 are not perfectly identical, however, so changes in D for specific income groups are approximations, while comparisons between categories in either 1980 or 1990 are exact.

Source: Roderick J. Harrison and Daniel H. Weinberg, "Racial and Ethnic Residential Segregation in 1990," Table 1; and "Changes in Racial and Ethnic Segregation, 1980–1990," Tables 1, 2, and 12; U.S. Bureau of the Census, 1992. Andrew A. Beveridge and Hyun Sook Kim, "Patterns of Residential Segregation in New York City, 1980 to 1990: Preliminary Analysis," New York Metropolitan Area Demographics Laboratory, Queens College, 1992.

Table 6.3. Segregation of African Americans from whites:
Index of racial residential segregation (D) in Standard Metropolitan
Areas (SMAs) with largest black populations, 1980

	Index of Segregation from White Persons	
	Regardless of income or education of white persons	White persons with same income or education
Black persons		
Family income		
Under $10,000	.79	.76
$15,000–19,999	.76	.75
$25,000–34,999	.77	.76
$50,000 or more	.79	.79
Education		
9–11 years	.83	.77
High-school graduate	.78	.76
Some college	.75	.74
College graduate	.72	.71

Note: Both columns exhibit values of the index of dissimilarity (D), a measure of residential segregation. It measures the number of black households that would have to change census tracts within a metropolitan area in order to be distributed in the same manner as the comparative white population. D ranges between zero and 1.000. (In this table, D is rounded off to 100ths and ranges between zero and 1.00.) For the distribution of D, 0–.300 is considered low, .300–.600 moderate, and .600–1.000 high. Thus, all values of D in this table are, in fact, in the high range.

The columns are drawn from two somewhat different but overlapping samples. The first comprises the 10 metropolitan areas with the largest black populations in 1980. Here D shows how many black persons with a particular characteristic of famility income or personal education would have to be redistributed to match the distribution of *all* whites among census tracts in each SMA. The final number is a weighted average of D for all ten SMAs. The second column uses the same methodology for the 16 SMAs with the largest black populations. But here D measures the redistribution of black persons required to match the distribution of white persons with the *same* characteristic. For example, the number .71 in the lower right-hand corner of the table means that 71 percent of college-educated black persons would need to change census tracts in order to match the distribution of college-educated white persons.

Source: (First column) Nancy A. Denton and Douglas S. Massey, "Residential Segregation of Blacks, Hispanics, and Asians by Socioeconomic Status and Generation," *Social Science Quarterly* 69 (1988): Table 1; (second column) Reynolds Farley and Walter R. Allen, *The Color Line and the Quality of Life in America* (New York: Russel Sage Foundation, 1987), Table 5.10.

skin color, which signifies a deeply rooted set of historical and contemporary relations. The black ghetto is continually and mainly intentionally reproduced by white Americans and the institutions that they dominate. Earlier in the century, the black ghettos were established through a combination of violent white communal resistance to integration and a host of well-known governmental processes, including legal restrictions on interracial sales, explicit policies by the Federal Housing and the Veterans Administrations, and the activities of municipal governments in zoning, urban redevelopment, and public housing construction. Banks, realtors, and rental agents all played their parts.[11]

They continue to do so today, even when official government policy supports integration. While a majority of whites claim to oppose discrimination, most also would not want to live in an integrated neighborhood.[12] White behavior—buttressed by an institutional system of governmental fragmentation and decentralization of political power[13]—seems hardly to have changed at all:

> Two decades after the passage of the Fair Housing Act, levels of black segregation remain exceedingly high in large urban areas.... This high level of segregation cannot be explained by blacks' objective socioeconomic characteristics, their housing preferences, or their limited knowledge of white housing markets. Rather, it is linked empirically to the persistence of discrimination in housing markets and to continuing antiblack prejudice.[14]

Segregation, as we have seen, is hardly limited to just the most impoverished neighborhoods that some now call the "ghetto," thereby usurping the term, implicitly and quite innocently suggesting that other black neighborhoods are not ghettoized.[15]

William Julius Wilson was right when he emphasized the intersection of race and poverty in his 1990 presidential address to the American Sociological Association, arguing that we should stop speaking about the underclass and instead use the term *ghetto poor*.[16] His explanation of black poverty would have been much improved, however, if he had also considered the significance of the ghettoized working class, the ghettoized middle class, and yes, the ghettoized rich.

Racial Segregation and Social Mobility

Whatever advantages blacks have gleaned from ghettoization—mainly in political representation—constitute a silver lining in an otherwise dark cloud that has negatively affected communal life, economic success, and, most generally, the political situation of blacks and whites alike. For ghettoization is not compatible with racial equality; separation, as it has been established in the American system, reflects and supports subordination.

At least since the depression, numerous studies have recognized the inherent evil of ghettoization in isolating blacks of *every* social class, in breeding black resentment and feelings of inferiority, in contributing to social pathology and to white prejudice. A pathbreaking postwar national study committed to integration by Robert Weaver, who would go on to become the first African American cabinet officer as secretary of the nascent Department of Housing and Urban Development, concluded:

> The modern American ghetto is a Black Belt from which the occupants can escape only if they move into another well-defined Negro community.... This ghetto has all incomes and social classes. Its inhabitants are better prepared and more anxious than ever before to enter the mainstream of American life. Residential segregation, more than any other single institution, is an impediment to their realization of the American dream.[17]

Two decades later St. Claire Drake could stress that "the spatial isolation" of Negroes from whites "increased consciousness of their separate subordinate position, for no whites were available to them as neighbors, schoolmates, or friends"; rather, blacks encountered whites in the superordinate positions of landlords and street-level bureaucrats such as police officers and school officials.[18] Indeed, it was this situation of continuing subordination across the class structure that helped precipitate the movement for "community control" of black neighborhoods in the sixties and seventies.[19]

Over the years there has been much social science research that has attempted to identify the immediate effects of segregation and its long-term consequences for black well-being. With regard to the former, there is clear and relatively unambiguous evidence. Blacks face a highly segmented housing market that poorly fits the standard economic model. In that market, they are the victims of continual racial discrimination by sellers, realtors, landlords, and lending institutions. Two results follow: compared with whites at similar income levels, they get less housing for the money in whatever jurisdictions they find themselves, and they are excluded from jurisdictions with higher levels of public services and better-quality schools.[20]

Another immediate consequence of segregation that has been much examined in the case of the black poor is that blacks are concentrated in central cities at a level far beyond what one might expect from their incomes relative to that of whites. Given the decentralization of jobs over the last several decades, analysts at least since the days of the 1968 Kerner Commission Report have identified a spatial mismatch between residence and employment opportunities. The validity of this argument is supported more by repetition than by evidence, however. That there is a mismatch is without doubt, but in a time when everyone drives to work, the consequences of disproportionate concentration of black residences within the *centers* of decentralized metropolitan labor markets is unclear, whether with regard to unemployment or wages.[21]

Racial segregation has also been indicted — correctly I think — as the main cause of an increase of concentrated, inner-city black poverty.[22] But the further claim that such poverty can be explained by increasing spatial separation of social classes within the ghetto (understood simply as the black part of metropolitan areas) needs to be scrutinized. For it suggests that there has been a heightening of *class* segregation among blacks, and that the effect has been mainly to isolate the black poor. What does the evidence show about class separation among blacks and about trends in those figures?

The answer depends upon how we think about class separation. If we employ the same kind of indicator as we commonly do in measuring overall *racial* separation, the index of dissimilarity that reflects the *unevenness* of a spatial distribution, then we discover that blacks and whites have quite similar scores; in each case, indexes typically are at the low or moderate levels. Researchers in the fifties and sixties were surprised at this finding because they had expected much less spatial separation among blacks.[23] But the fact remains that by measures of unevenness, blacks and whites have had similar patterns at least since 1940, and nothing much has changed recently.[24]

Measures of unevenness in the distribution of classes within racial groups tell us only part of what we want to know about spatial contact or isolation of classes. The problem with these measures is that they are *not* sensitive to the relative sizes of different groups. Actual spatial contact (or isolation) depends not just upon the unevenness of a distribution but also upon the relative size of groups. Let me give a concrete example. Suppose that poor and nonpoor blacks were distributed in the 1940s within northern cities in more or less the same way as they are now; the index of dissimilarity between these classes would not have changed. But fifty years ago roughly 60 percent of that black population was poor, while today's figure is closer to 30 percent. Accordingly, the chances of a poor black having contact with nonpoor blacks would have *increased* substantially over the period, simply as a result of the changing proportions of the poor and nonpoor. Of course, if *both* the evenness of the distribution and the proportions of each group changed over the years, one would have no way of knowing a priori how much change there had been in contact. For this reason, we need a measure of contact that is sensitive to how a population is distributed spatially as well as to its relative size. Such a measure is P★, which reflects the percentage of individuals of one group — say poor blacks — living in the same census tract as the average individual of another group — say nonpoor blacks.

Unfortunately, there have been very few studies over the years that have utilized a measure of probable contact like P★, in part because until recently nobody much cared about class contact and isolation within races. The only large-scale study that looked at several measures of class and examined class contact among blacks and among whites was carried out for the Chicago metropolitan area in 1970.[25] It showed, as we would expect, that while black and white occupational and income groups were spatially distributed in a similar way, patterns of class contact were quite different within each race. Compared with blacks, whites were more likely to be in higher occupational categories. For that reason, the average white at the upper end of the class scale was likely to have much less contact with lower-class whites than would blacks of similar class standing with lower-class blacks. The converse was also true. Poor blacks — being relatively much more numerous than poor whites — were less likely to have contact with better-off blacks than were poor whites with better-off whites. For example, the average black unskilled manual worker lived in a census tract in which 8 percent of the black population was employed in professional or managerial occupations; the average white unskilled manual worker lived in tracts where 23 percent of his white neighbors were professionals or managers. The same kinds of results were found when class was measured by income or education.

While we would like more comparative and longitudinal data, these findings are likely to be quite generally true in other places and after 1970, as well.[26] For they are almost inevitable. So long as levels of racial segregation remain little changed, and so long as the black economic structure remains depressed compared with the white — and we have seen hardly any change in either dimension since 1970 — then this pattern of class contact among blacks will remain. As we saw, upper-income blacks were no more likely to live near whites than were low-income blacks. But the proportion of blacks who are lower income is much greater than the proportion of whites at those levels. Therefore, the typical better-off black household, unable to move into an integrated or white neighborhood at its own class level, is forced to live in a black neighborhood in which many lower-class blacks also live. Put another way, the spatial payoffs of upward mobility are lower for blacks than for whites because of racial segregation.

These are exactly the findings of a second study that analyzes class contact among blacks and whites.[27] Douglas Massey and his colleagues present evidence from Philadelphia, a city with black neighborhoods at every class level. Using several different indicators of social class, they show that middle-class whites are much less likely than middle-class blacks to encounter people with so-called underclass attributes in their neighborhoods. For example, a middle-income black family is about three times as likely as a similar white family to have neighbors who are on welfare. Equally important, the study examines in great detail other measures of the quality of life in neighborhoods occupied by working-class and middle-class blacks versus those occupied by whites of similar class. It finds that class simply does not buy blacks the environment that it buys whites in a society where class stratification is expressed spatially:

> High status blacks, like whites, seek to convert past socioeconomic attainments into improved residential circumstances. However, very few blacks are successful in achieving these locational outcomes. The vast majority live in segregated neighborhoods where blacks have long been, or are rapidly becoming, the majority, areas characterized by high crime, poor schools, economic dependency, unstable families, dilapidated housing, and poor health. All evidence indicates that blacks are no different than whites in trying to escape such an environment, when they are able. They are just less able.[28]

The authors suggest that the relative social heterogeneity of middle-income black neighborhoods reduces the ability of the black middle class to reproduce itself through cultural capital transmission:

> Because of residential segregation, middle class blacks must send their children to public schools with children far below their own class standing, children with more limited cognitive, linguistic, and social skills. Given the strong effect of peer influences and environment on aspirations, motivation, and achievement, it is hardly surprising that so many young black people, even those from middle class families, fail to achieve high test scores or educational distinction.[29]

But do the reduced spatial payoffs of black social mobility actually reduce black mobility itself? In a vicious cycle, does racial segregation contribute to the high proportion of blacks in poverty and thereby to the costs for better-off black households of not being able to move into more class-homogeneous neighborhoods? This question points in almost the opposite direction from the problematic posed in many studies of the underclass, where the supposed absence of better-off households is advanced as an explanation of poverty.

The contemporary social science argument according to which "solid" working- and middle-class families will uplift the poor recapitulates the rationale of the settlement house. But popular opinion tends toward a very different metaphor, that of the bad apples that spoil the barrel. In this image too many lower-class households intrude upon the lives of those African Americans who might otherwise be socially mobile. Particularly in the critical years of adolescence, when undesirable school and street environments can pull children down, better-off black households cannot sufficiently distance themselves at any point in time from impoverished ones. Among the poor as well, those making the first moves toward mobility are forced by the segregation of all blacks to live in a spatially and culturally compressed environment, one that cannot possibly facilitate mobility. In this way, racial residential segregation rests as a critical—but of course, not the sole—cause of inadequate black social mobility, and thereby of continued poverty among a large lower class.

Nearly every black and white family in America assumes that inferior neighbors will drag them down and tries to distance itself from those beneath it. Social scientists, however, have failed to demonstrate that bad apples do spoil the barrel. Thus, Christopher Jencks and Susan Mayer have conducted an exhaustive review of all of the sociological evidence compiled in the seventies and eighties.[30] In trying to determine the social consequences of growing up in a poor neighborhood they conclude—not surprisingly—that neighborhoods matter, although how they matter is highly dependent on particular institutional settings. The most unambiguous evidence, which extends back a quarter century to the Coleman Report,[31] is that a child does better if he or she attends a school where classmates are predominantly of a higher social class. Beyond that, however, the sociological picture of schooling becomes quite fuzzy, even though nearly everyone concerned about the education of their *own* children tries to keep them away from kids with poor performance or behavior—both correlated with a lower social class. As to other "social consequences," Jencks and Mayer come to conclusions that are laden with qualifiers.

One body of evidence that has so far pointed clearly toward the effect of a "good" environment derives from the so-called Gautreaux decision, which required that federally subsidized housing be made available to low-income people in the suburbs of Chicago.[32] It appears that, other things being equal, poor black and Latino families who moved from inner-city neighborhoods have done better in school and in the labor market than those like them who stayed behind.[33] But it is a long step from this and similar studies to a convincing demonstration of just how ghettoization affects social mobility.

The Social Construction of Black "Otherness"

Beyond the technical reasons I have enumerated for the weakness of social science evidence, I would argue that ghettoization has produced a political atmosphere and a mentality in both races that affect a host of other factors, from motivation on the part of black children to discrimination by white employers to the whole character of American social policy. This atmosphere gums up nearly all empirical social science research, even while it cannot itself be demonstrated "scientifically."

For African Americans, ghettoization makes a daily symbolic statement of group subordination. Blacks are contained, separated, isolated—and their "otherness" is derived from the immutable physical attribute of skin color. The ghetto is at once the reflection, the reminder, and the component of the larger construction in American history, that of race itself as a "natural" social category. The inescapability of race and of the likelihood of racial subordination results, for many, in alienation from American institutions and thereby contributes to individual self-fulfilling prophesies of academic and economic failure. Collectively, Afrocentrism, even to the point of some advocates demanding all-black schools, has both widened the racial divide and played into the hands of white segregationists.

For whites, the physical ghettoization of nearly all blacks, along with the media focus on the "worst" black neighborhoods and the most socially deviant elements in them, has reinforced a stereotyped image of black people. By blurring or eliminating class differences among blacks, and by equating blacks with criminals and welfare mothers, whites are freed from guilt or even sympathy. In the white mentality, the social problems of race and economic inequality become reduced to a single, colored, televisioned image of the black "ghetto," at once a dangerous place and an undeserving population.

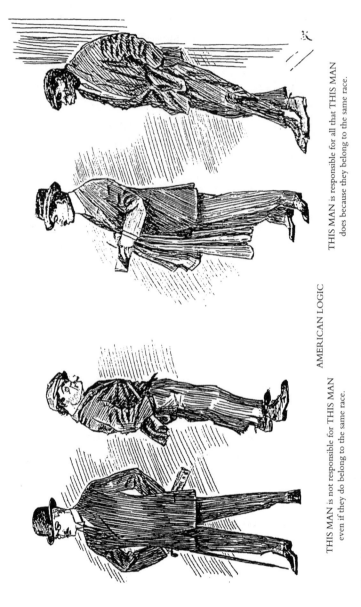

AMERICAN LOGIC

THIS MAN is not responsible for THIS MAN even if they do belong to the same race.

THIS MAN is responsible for all that THIS MAN does because they belong to the same race.

Figure 6.1. American logic. (Source: *The Crisis*, June 1913).

The encapsulation of the black lower classes in our central cities functions very effectively not only to obscure more general processes of spatial and social stratification — to reify them into categories like "inner city" and "the poor" — but to reduce a much larger issue of the place of African Americans in America to a single question: What are we to do about the black poor — that is, about welfare, crime, and idleness? I do not know if there is a way out of this impasse. Yet I remain convinced that residential segregation is simultaneously cause and effect of the segmentation of our society. In Gramsci's terms, the ghetto is the basis for a social trench, a physical arrangement transformed into a sociopolitical boundary and barrier. Blacks under attack from superior white power are defined, homogenized, and ultimately demoralized by their containment behind that trench, one that whites built and some blacks now maintain. The 1913 illustration of the color line found in *The Crisis* (figure 6.1) reminds us of the frightening continuity of the American racial pattern.

Notes

1. William Julius Wilson, *The Truly Disadvataged* (Chicago: University of Chicago Press, 1987), 7–8.

2. See Carole Marks, "The Urban Underclass," *Annual Review of Sociology* 17 (1991): 445–66.

3. See Norman Fainstein, "Race, Class, and Segregation: Discourses about African Americans," *International Journal of Urban and Regional Research* 17, no. 3 (1993).

4. By the time the various qualifiers are attached to individuals that make them members of the underclass, as opposed to just suffering from low income, the "real" underclass shrinks to less than 2 percent of the "poor" (Erol Ricketts, "The Nature and Dimensions of the Underclass," in *The Metropolis in Black and White*, ed. George Galster and Edward Hill [New Brunswick, N.J.: Rutgers University Center for Urban Policy Research, 1992], 51).

5. For an exposition of mismatch theory, see John Kasarda, "Urban Industrial Transformation and the Underclass," in "The Ghetto Underclass: Social Science Perspectives," *Annals* 501, ed. Willliam Julius Wilson (January 1989): 33–57. I offer a detailed critique in Norman Fainstein, "The Underclass/Mismatch Hypothesis as Explanation for Black Economic Deprivation," *Politics and Society* 15, no. 4 (1986): 403–51.

6. See David Ward, *Poverty, Ethnicity, and the American City* (New York: Cambridge University Press, 1989), and Michael Katz, ed., *The Underclass Debate — Views from History* (Princeton, N.J.: Princeton University Press, 1993).

7. See Elijah Anderson, *Streetwise* (Chicago: University of Chicago Press, 1989), 58–59.

8. U.S. House of Representatives, Committee on Ways and Means, *Overviews of Entitlement Programs* (Washington, D.C., 1991), appendix J, table 23; Bennett Harrison and Lucy Gorham, "What Happened to African American Wages in the 1980s?" in *Metropolis in Black and White,* ed. Galster and Hill, 56–71.

9. Reynolds Farley and Walter Allen, *The Color Line and the Quality of Life in America* (New York: Sage, 1987); Douglas S. Massey and Nancy A. Denton, *American Apartheid* (Cam-

bridge, Mass.: Harvard University Press, 1993).

10. Roderick J. Harrison and Daniel H. Weinberg, "Changes in Racial and Ethnic Segregation, 1980–1990," U.S. Bureau of the Census (Washington, D.C., 1992), 17.

11. See Massey and Denton, *American Apartheid,* chap. 4, and G. Thomas Kingsley and Margery Austin Turner, eds., *Housing Markets and Residential Mobility* (Washington, D.C.: Urban Institute Press, 1993).

12. Reynolds Farley, "Neighborhood Preferences and Aspirations among Blacks and Whites," in *Housing Markets and Residential Mobility,* ed. Kingsley and Turner, 161–92.

13. Gregory Weiher, *The Fractured Metropolis: Political Fragmentation and Metropolitan Segregation* (Albany: SUNY Press, 1991).

14. Douglas Massey, "American Apartheid: Segregation and the Making of the Underclass," *American Journal of Sociology* 96, no. 2 (1990): 354. Massey supports his conclusion with numerous references that I cannot detail here.

15. Until the terms of discourse were turned by the underclass school, the word *ghetto* was used to characterize segregated black neighborhoods encompassing a variety of class strata, and residential segregation was viewed as distorting the whole range of black-white relations. It was in this sense that Kenneth Clark called Harlem in the fifties and sixties a "dark ghetto," which he identified with "institutionalized pathology" as he excoriated Harlem's institutions and leaders, not least of all its black politicians and community elites (Kenneth Clark, *Dark Ghetto* [New York: Harper and Row, 1965], 81).

16. William Julius Wilson, "Studying Inner-City Social Dislocations," *American Sociological Review* 56 (February 1991): 1–14.

17. Robert Weaver, *The Negro Ghetto* (New York: Harcourt, Brace, 1948), 7.

18. St. Claire Drake, "The Social and Economic Status of the Negro in the United States," in *The Negro American,* ed. Talcott Parsons and Kenneth B. Clark (Boston: Houghton Mifflin, 1966), 7–8.

19. Norman Fainstein and Susan Fainstein, *Urban Political Movements* (Englewood Cliffs, N.J.: Prentice-Hall, 1974).

20. Besides the work cited earlier, see Gary Orfield and Carole Ashkinaze, who show just how segregation in the Atlanta region works to reduce the quality of schooling, housing, and public services for African Americans, including those of the middle class (Gary Orfield and Carole Ashkinaze, *The Closing Door* [Chicago: University of Chicago Press, 1991]). An excellent analysis of data from the seventies is provided by Mark Schneider and John Logan, "Suburban Racial Segregation and Black Access to Public Resources," *Social Science Quarterly* 63 (1982): 762–70.

21. An extensive review of evidence on spatial mismatch is provided by Harry J. Holzer, "The Spatial Mismatch Hypothesis: What Has the Evidence Shown?" *Urban Studies* 28, no. 1 (1991): 105–22. Also see the discussion in Susan Fainstein and Norman Fainstein, "The Racial Dimension in Urban Political Economy," *Urban Affairs Quarterly* 25 (December 1989): 187–99.

22. Douglas S. Massey and Mitchell L. Eggers, "The Ecology of Inequality: Minorities and the Concentration of Poverty, 1970–1980," *American Journal of Sociology* 95, no. 5 (1990): 1153–88.

23. Karl E. Taeuber and Alma F. Taeuber, *Negroes in Cities* (Chicago: Aldine, 1965); Nathan Kantrowitz, *Ethnic and Racial Segregation in the New York Metropolis* (New York: Praeger, 1973).

24. Reynolds Farley, "Residential Segregation of Social and Economic Groups among Blacks, 1970–1980," in *The Urban Underclass,* ed. Christopher Jencks and Paul E. Peterson (Washington, D.C.: Brookings Institution, 1991), 274–98. Preliminary analyses by Andrew Beveridge of the 1990 data for the New York metropolis show little change from the 1980 patterns (Sam Roberts, "Shifts in Eighties Failed to Ease Segregation," *New York Times,* July

15, 1992, B1.

25. Bridgette Mach Erbe, "Race and Socioeconomic Segregation," *American Sociological Review* 40 (December 1975): 801–12.

26. Using individual data from the neighborhood files of the 1970 census, Wayne Villemez found that at a given income level, blacks are less able to achieve class segregation than whites (Wayne Villemez, "Race, Class, and Neighborhood: Differences in the Residential Return on Individual Resources," *Social Forces* 59, no. 2 [1980]: 414–30).

27. Douglas S. Massey, Gretchen A. Condron, and Nancy A. Denton, "The Effects of Residential Segregation on Black Social and Economic Well-Being," *Social Forces* 66 (September 1987): 29–56.

28. Ibid., 52.

29. Ibid., 54.

30. Christopher Jencks and Susan Mayer, "The Social Consequences of Growing Up in a Poor Neighborhood," in National Resource Council, *Inner-City Poverty in the United States* (Washington, D.C.: National Academy Press, 1990), 111–86.

31. James S. Coleman et al., *Equality of Educational Opportunity* (Washington, D.C.: GPO, 1966).

32. Mary Davis, "The Gautreaux Assisted Housing Program," in *Housing Markets and Residential Mobility,* ed. Kingsley and Turner, 243–54.

33. James E. Rosenbaum, "Black Pioneers—Do Their Moves to the Suburbs Increase Economic Opportunity for Mothers and Children?" *Housing Policy Debate* 2, no. 4 (1991): 1179–1213; James E. Rosenbaum and Susan J. Popkin, "Employment and Earnings of Low-Income Blacks Who Move to Middle-Class Suburbs," in *The Urban Underclass,* ed. Jencks and Peterson, 342–56.

7 / Historical Footprints

The Legacy of the School Desegregation Pioneers

Leslie Baham Inniss

Almost forty years after the Supreme Court struck down "separate but equal" schools, we are now witnessing a trend away from the original school desegregation process and toward implicit and explicit resegregation in America's school systems. In many cities "a substantial proportion of black pupils continue to attend segregated (and unequal) schools."[1] In some cities, such as New York and Milwaukee, separate schools for black males are being established. In those schools that are still "desegregated," white and minority students are separated spatially or through other subtle mechanisms such as tracking.[2] This current state of affairs, along with early school desegregation experiences, have many blacks beginning to question the high opportunity costs of school desegregation and the desirability of one-way assimilation.[3] In calculating these costs, many who went through the desegregation process are now concluding that school desegregation has included the forced assimilation of blacks into a white world where they were not wanted or welcomed, along with the ultimate dismantling of black school systems and communities.[4] Today, some black leaders, including Benjamin Hooks, former executive director of the NAACP, and Harold Cruse, professor emeritus of the University of Michigan, are calling for a movement away from the goal of integration.[5]

But what does this new ideological stance among blacks mean for the current racial scene? Does this push away from the goals of integration indicate a growing consensus among blacks that the implementation of school desegregation policy has failed and indicate as well a reassessment of their commitment to desegregation?[6] If so, why has there been such a dramatic ideological shift and how does that shift influence urban education today?

Certainly one reason for this new African American stance is the previously described disillusionment with the idea of "integration at any cost." Moreover, those blacks who were among the school desegregation "pioneers," the first of their race to have the opportunity to attend previously all-white schools,[7] now report psychological and emotional damage from those experiences. Those who were the first to attend desegregated schools are now challenging the idea that all that was necessary for improving race relations, minority achievement, and minority self-esteem was for the "door to be opened." Instead, they are currently describing many of the negative experiences that occurred when black children first entered those doors and are comparing those past experiences with similar ones being felt by many of today's minority students.[8] Their arguments suggest a belief that integration was a good idea but the school desegregation policies have been and continue to be poorly implemented—that is, sending a few black children into a hostile white environment where they have to fend for themselves and where the teachers, administrators, other students, and surrounding community are all white and mostly unwelcoming is not the ideal means of attaining an integrated society. According to these desegregation pioneers, only one small aspect of institutionalized discrimination is being addressed, and further, school desegregation has, by design, been incomplete. The tentative conclusion that can be drawn from their experiences and current perceptions is that the goals of the civil rights movement for full political, economic, cultural, social, and educational equality were probably never meant to be, and could never be, fulfilled by one-way assimilation or through counterfeit integration.[9] Thus, many blacks today, including school desegregation pioneers, are abandoning the dream that desegregated schools would eventually lead to a truly integrated society, and are now calling for separate schools for black children, for multiculturalism as a social policy, and for a separate, Afrocentric curriculum.[10]

This ideological shift is accompanied by current demographic and economic changes in urban communities. These changes in population numbers have affected the cultural composition and residential patterns of the urban school population. There is more cultural diversity, with Hispanic and Asian students increasing in number.[11] These new students, particularly Hispanics and their families, seem less willing to accept forced assimilation into the dominant culture and more determined to maintain most of their cultural identities, particularly language.[12] This is compounded by the fact that today large central cities are seeing "greater isolation of the minority students who are unable to move to the suburbs."[13] Thus, in terms of education, today's racial scene includes more and more segregated schools, either by race or ability grouping; a proliferation of bilingual education; and a louder call for a multicultural curriculum.[14] These trends, coupled with the fact that the school desegregation policy was originally designed to resolve a black/white racial problem, makes the policy obsolete for dealing with the new demographic profile of the United States today.[15]

Thus, emerging scholarship and recent recollections are beginning to illustrate that even after almost forty years, far from being the culmination of a dream, school desegregation today remains incomplete; that the personal experiences of its pioneers have had an impact on their adult lives and racial outlooks; and that history should be combined with current circumstances in order to better understand the current racial scene and to improve race relations scholarship.

This chapter represents an ongoing effort to update the history of black education to include the perceptions and subsequent race relations adjustments of those most closely affected by racial educational policies. In this chapter I employ the findings from an exploratory study of school desegregation "pioneers" to examine the ways in which black adults' negative experiences with school desegregation as children have affected their current thinking on that radical educational policy and how this new way of thinking has led them to conclude that what was a very good idea — that learning to live and work together at an early age would lead to improved race relations — was one that was poorly implemented. I will undertake such an examination by first presenting a brief history of the segregation era and then by focusing on the findings from the aforementioned school desegregation project, one that examines the school experiences of pioneers as well as their current attitudes about school desegregation and contemporary race relations. Using quotes from these school desegregation pioneers, I will demonstrate that they believe they have experienced long-term negative consequences from the school desegregation process and are today counting themselves among those calling for a different way of achieving black integration into American society. Following that, I will indicate how their thoughts and experiences have implications for educational policy. Finally, in conclusion, I will argue that policies such as Afrocentric curriculum and separate schools for black males should be an interim response to failed desegregation.

The Segregation Era

Before the Supreme Court's 1954 *Brown* decision, there was de facto school segregation in the North and de jure school segregation in the South. Under both systems black and white children, for the most part, attended separate schools. Unfortunately, African Americans had no legal way of protesting these and other injustices. The legacy of slavery, which forbade the education of black children, and the Supreme Court's 1896 *Plessy vs. Ferguson* decision had fostered a social policy of "separate but equal" schools.[16] However, the main problem was that the black schools were not on a par with the white schools, neither in facilities like school buildings, science labs, or libraries nor in supplies like textbooks, library books, or lab equipment. These obvious inequalities led NAACP lawyers, who were beginning to wage legal battles and who already had developed an integrationist orientation,[17] to challenge the *Plessy* decision. Using the testimonies of social scientists, these lawyers argued against school segregation by claiming that separate schools were inherently unequal and that segregation itself violated the equal protection under the laws guaranteed by the Fourteenth Amendment. Thurgood Marshall, the chief counsel for the NAACP's case, stated that there can be no separate equality because "segregation represented a badge of inferiority" for black children.[18] Implicit in all of the social scientists' arguments were the three main goals of school desegregation: (1) an increase in self-esteem for minority children, (2) an increase in social integration leading to a reduction of prejudice, and (3) an improvement in minority group achievement.[19] While these were lofty goals that were decided on and argued for by adult leaders, the actual implementation involved placing the burden of dismantling an entrenched system of structural inequality on the backs of powerless little children. Of course, the assumption was that these three goals were most likely to be achieved if intergroup contact began at a young age. Unfortunately, history has shown this to be an erroneous assumption. As we'll see in the next section, what is even more ironic is that some of the words used by the social scientists to describe the detrimental effects of school segregation on black children are the same words used by desegregation "pioneers" to describe the detrimental effects they felt by being among the first desegregators.

School Desegregation

Background

School desegregation was a federal policy designed to favorably alter ma-
jority-minority relations in American society while also improving the social status and mental health of African Americans. It was believed that having black and white children attend school together, "opening the doors,"
so to speak, would change black and white prejudiced attitudes, in turn
changing discriminatory behavior in society. In order to test these assumptions, I recently completed a study of the attitudes, experiences, and feelings
of school desegregation participants (administrators, teachers, and pioneers).
The findings from this study suggest that this was an erroneous starting assumption and one that has produced long-term negative consequences for
the children who were the pioneers in this great social experiment. Opening the doors without monitoring what went on behind them appears to
have been a grave social injustice to school desegregation's first participants.
Other recent scholarship documents how poorly implemented desegregation plans have produced negative unintended consequences.[20]

Methodology

Although there have been numerous large-scale quantitative studies of the
impact of school desegregation, there is a paucity of research on the actual
experiences of those who participated in the process and what they believe
are the long-term consequences of those experiences. A more intensive, qualitative look at these desegregation "pioneers" is called for as researchers try
to explain current trends in race relations. With these factors in mind, I conducted in-depth interviews with twenty-five African American adults who
were among the first to have the opportunity to desegregate high schools
in the South. In these interviews the respondents talked at length about their
personal experiences and feelings.

Starting with class lists and parental addresses and phone numbers supplied by administrators at the formerly segregated elementary schools that
served as feeder schools to the newly desegregating high schools in one
southern city, I tracked respondents through a snowballing technique. Potential respondents were contacted by phone and follow-up postcards in a
closely administered process.[21] Subsequently, as the project progressed, "pioneers" from other cities volunteered their own experiences. The final sample

included eleven males (four who attended desegregated schools) and fourteen females (seven who attended desegregated schools). Other relevant demographic characteristics, obtained through self-administered questionnaires, are shown in table 7.1.

The semistructured interviews were conducted during the fall of 1991 and spring of 1992 by the author. Nineteen took place in the respondents'

Table 7.1. Demographic characteristics of desegregation "pioneers"

Gender	
Males	11
Females	14
Religion	
Catholic	25
Social class (self-ascribed)	
Working	10
Middle	15
Education	
High school	6
Some college	8
Bachelor's degree	7
Master's degree	3
Doctorate	1
Current occupation	
Blue collar	3
White collar	17
Housewife	4
Disabled	1
Income in 1990	
$10,000–$14,999	2
$15,000–$19,999	2
$20,000–$24,999	5
$25,000–$29,999	4
$30,000 or more	12
Marital status	
Single, never married	2
Separated	3
Widowed	0
Divorced	7
Married	13

homes and/or places of business; the remainder (six) were conducted by telephone. Because the interviewer had gone to school with most of the respondents, the interview usually began with the following prompt: "Do you remember when we were in eighth grade and it was announced that the high schools would desegregate the next year?" Generally, most of the needed information followed this prompt, but among the questions important for this chapter are the following: "What do you remember about that time?" "Did you attend a desegregated high school?" If yes, "Tell me about your experiences there?" "What do you see as some of the positive and negative effects?" If no, "How did you feel about those who did attend the desegregated schools?" "What were your own high-school experiences?" "What is your opinion of school desegregation now?" "What do you think school desegregation has meant for the black community?" "What is your current outlook on the relations between blacks and whites?" This chapter investigates the major features of the school desegregation's pioneers' experiences and how those experiences have affected their current views of school desegregation. This is done by focusing on the perceptions, thoughts, and feelings of the pioneers.

Findings

Overview / As it was implemented, school desegregation policy involved using powerless children as a catalyst for changing entrenched racist attitudes and discriminatory practices. Most of the pioneers feel this was done without regard for the high emotional and psychological price these children would eventually have to pay as adults. Unfortunately, these psychological pressures have apparently destroyed two of the pioneers from a larger potential sample: one male who suffered a nervous breakdown in his junior year at a desegregated school and who, according to his father, "has never been the same since" and one female who, according to family members, "has never gotten over the [name of school] experience" and who is now "strung out on drugs." Among those who survived the experience, the consensus seems to be that survival came from being focused; as one male put it, "You just maintain and say, 'Look my goal is to get out of here and make my grades and to get out of here, and you start getting focused on that and you know it's a transition period, there is a beginning and there is an end and when it's over you'll be out of there and you will have accomplished your goal and you go on and that's what I did and you know it had an end." One consistent response that came from the question about the experiences in the desegregated schools centered around the experiences with whites, whether it was other students, teachers, or administrators. Concerning any long-term effects, among those mentioned were emotional, psychological, and physical effects. There were also reports of positive effects. The following section will outline each of these findings and then look at responses concerning the hoped-for effects of school desegregation: an increase in minority achievement, improvement in race relations, and better self-esteem.

Experiences with White Students / The experiences with white students were both positive and negative; there were tormentors but there were also supporters. Several respondents made distinctions among the white students, such as, "There was one group that seemed to be that this was their mission in life to harass us and then there was another group who just kind of went their merry way and didn't bother with us one way or the other, and the group of kids who went through flack because they tried to be friendly and so on like that." Similarly, "So I mean there were just a few things that stood out and I think otherwise most of the kids just kinda minded their own business. They were into their little clubs and football team and student government, and you know, whatever else these people get involved in. Most of them were pretty removed from us but there was a group that sort of viewed it as their duty to, you know, to see that our stay was as miserable as possible."

One male desegregator described the sequence of events that led up to the tormentor students "doing their duty." According to him, "The first couple of days it was very quiet, it was extremely quiet. We were—you know how you feel like you are in a zoo and these kids they had never been close to black kids and they really didn't know how to react. It was like what do we do; they're here now, they bring a lot of attention to the school but they're not really bothering anybody, just going to class and just kind of like other kids you know, so they didn't quite know how to react. But after a while all hell broke loose and they really started harassing us. It seemed like they said, 'Well, these are Negroes you know ... these are more than just students, these are black students and we are supposed to do something because we're white."

Most of the descriptions of the white tormentors and their actions were similar. "Well, we had a little group that would meet us every morning, I mean they would say little ditties to us, it was sort of like it became entertainment. After a while I mean you kind of expected them to be at the door greeting us with little songs." Or, "You would only have a problem if there was a real crowd in the hall and people kind of jarred you a little bit.... One incident I remember I was going to class one morning and somebody squirted me with a water pistol. So I went the same way the next day and somebody squirted me again.... Well, yeah, students would know because there is only so many classes you can take in school so they know you go the same route every day."

According to a few of the respondents the torment went beyond the school day; for example, "We would all get these phone calls and sometimes we would hear our parents getting in these cussing matches on the phone." Or even worse, "So somebody shot in our house one time but that was about the only major incidence."

As in any situation, there was also a more supportive group of students; as one respondent said, "And there were kids who withstood the ostracism to be friendly and those people to me they were courageous. I mean, it took a lot of courage for them to buck their peer pressure, their peer group and be friendly to us."

Finally, as an illustration of the desegregators' view that the tormenting continued throughout their high-school years, a couple of respondents talked about their graduation experiences. "The day we were to graduate we had to march in pairs and you were paired alphabetically and the person who was paired with me would not walk beside me at graduation. I remember thinking, girl you don't want to walk next to me, that's fine, I'll be out of here in a couple of hours forever so I don't care." Another reported, "I remember at graduation time, they started playing this song, "It's So Hard to Say Goodbye to Yesterday," and that became the theme song of the senior class. And they played it at all the senior year functions and all the white girls would start crying because they were leaving and we were crying because we couldn't wait to leave."

Experiences with White Teachers / From the desegregators' responses about the white teachers, they fell into two camps: "There were some teachers who were really nice and who tried to make us feel welcome and there were some who made you feel like you couldn't do as well as the other students." The more positive teachers also seemed to be protective: "Sometimes teachers would station themselves in the hallway so that they could follow us. In other words they would be out there to see us go to class. . . . I mean they knew there were kids who were problems and they would just kind of shove those kids along, 'all right, get to your class' or 'now stop showing off and go to class' and they would be out there, they would do their jobs."

The more negative teachers seemed to align themselves with the tormentor students. "I can remember one teacher who was the tenth grade social studies teacher of American history or something like that and she would actually be with those kids who were harassing us, egging them on to do stuff. They would crack jokes in class and she'd be involved with them. I remember one day in class a white student said to me, 'Why did ya'll have to come to our school and mess it up?' and this teacher told me to answer the question."

Experiences with White Administrators / In musing about why the administration didn't do more to prepare for desegregation, one respondent discussed her experiences and conclusion:

> See, remember this was all new to everybody and they didn't know what to tell anybody. They didn't want to put too much emphasis on it. It was almost expected that the white kids would react negatively so they were taking the approach of downplaying it to them, "We don't want to embarrass our school so let's be sensible" or "This ain't the end of the world, let them come and you go about your business." So that was the attitude they took. They had no base line to start from to know that you say this or this is what you're supposed to do and this is what we will do in reaction to this so let's plan this. They were reactive rather than proactive because they had no way of knowing what to do. This was the first time this had been done so they didn't have any plan in mind, other than to keep the lid on it and so they only reacted to precise incidents.

Another respondent decided about the administrators that "all in all they did a pretty good job of it but for the wrong reasons, not to protect us but just to not embarrass the school."

Those were some of the remembered experiences, but the respondents also reported on what they perceived to be long-term effects of those experiences. Again, as previously mentioned, many report a belief that they have paid too high an emotional price, have lost opportunities, and have experienced psychological damage and even long-term physical effects.

Emotional Prices / Looking back on these experiences, one desegregated school attendee reported, almost in a counterfactual analysis, that she often wonders "what I would have thought like and been like before all those people impinged what they think and are on me." Another female laments that "we gave up so much and got so little in return." Finally, an extremely angry and bitter male states that "forced integration was the worst thing that happened to our race." He goes on to explain that during school desegregation, "we were forced to play their game by their rules but now my goal is to extract all their knowledge and use it to beat them at their own game. My job is not to help white folks but to educate my son so that he is prepared and he is able to compete with those people at a very early age and that's what I'm trying to teach him."

Lost Opportunities / Along with these cited emotional prices were the lost opportunities. One teacher who once taught at a newly desegregated school recounts how "I always worried about the talents that the black students were not allowed to use and the many opportunities they were forced to give up in their role as pioneers." She went on to describe her most vivid memory as one involving "a black girl who said all her life she always wanted to be a cheerleader, but who cried inconsolably because she knew she would never be a cheerleader at this school because no one would elect her."

This recollection is particularly poignant when juxtaposed with a comment by one of the desegregation pioneers: "In our segregated neighborhoods and schools we didn't feel deprived, we didn't even know that we lacked self-esteem, we were happy and secure in our all-black neighborhoods and our all-black schools. We felt that we belonged, hell, we did belong. There was no fear of trying to join the band or the drill team, or of trying out for cheerleader." This same woman described going from a segregated school where she was "into everything" extracurricular to a desegregated school where she was "afraid to go out for anything."

Psychological Damage / Another teacher says she often wonders "why there wasn't any counseling or work on the foolishness (protest signs outside the school as well as phone calls to the principal) going on in the community surrounding the school." Laughing, she described an incident in which she always felt "God intervened." It was one of the first few days after the school desegregated, a day when school picketers were especially vicious in the things they were shouting. The school administrators had originally decided that they were going to "keep things as close to normal as possible," and one stated school policy was that the school doors were not opened until a certain time even if students were milling outside. On the day in question, there were swarms of mosquitoes like "locusts from hell" and the administrators were able to use that as an excuse to open the doors early and allow students into the building and away from the hecklers.

This humorous incident aside, the total disregard for school desegregation's damage to blacks is today being perceived by these pioneers as a subtle mechanism that was used for perpetuating inequality, even among blacks. As adults, these minority pioneers are handicapped by the long-term emotional consequences of either having been desegregation's self-described "guinea pigs" or self-described "rejects." The guinea pigs were the students who were chosen to go to the newly desegregated schools and the rejects were the ones who were not chosen and who were very aware of not being chosen. Contrary to popular belief, during the first few years of school desegregation, self-selection to attend desegregated schools was the exception rather than the rule. For the most part, school administrators, principals, or teachers usually chose the students who would attend, and the criteria used were, generally, high academic ability and easy-going, docile personalities. The first quality was needed to ensure success, the second to endure hostility.

Ironically, to not have been among the "chosen" appears to have had as detrimental an effect in adult life as to have been one of those selected to attend a desegregated school. One woman painfully recounts her memories of the selection process: "It was bad enough being in the last row [the class was seated according to overall average, with the first person in the first row having the highest average and the last person in the last row having the lowest average], but then when they started asking people to attend the white schools, I knew they wouldn't even consider us (in the last row)." This painful recollection illustrates the divisiveness even of the desegregation pioneer selection process, a divisiveness that later caused attendees to be shunned by former friends from their previously all-black schools. One desegregated school attendee recalls the first football game for the all-black school she had originally planned to attend: "People who had been my friends wouldn't even talk to me. They acted like I wasn't even there. It hurt worse than what happened at [name of school]. I expected the whites to treat me that way, but the blacks ... that really hurt." Another recalls: "We caught as much flack from the black kids as we did from the white kids. I mean they would say, 'You think you better than we are' or 'What's wrong with [the all-black school]?' and 'Oh, you think you're special.' That was the most hurting part." Finally a third attendee gives more explanation: "If it was anything that really hurt me it was the way the black kids treated us. That hurt because in a sense you did understand that part of your mission was to integrate the schools, you did understand that in the back of your mind. And you did kind of feel that it was a benefit to them and they took it totally wrong. They were saying, like 'what are you doing over there with those folks?' and 'you just think you are better than us,' but it was just sort of somebody had to open the gate and we just happened to be first at the gate and that was it. I was just a kid trying to get into a biology class where I could share a microscope with one other student rather than thirty other students. I mean it was no more complicated in my mind than that."

Many of the desegregation pioneers' comments are particularly telling when contrasted with the social scientists' testimonies used to argue for the *Brown* decision to eliminate segregated schools. Kluger cites some of this testimony: "Segregation [has] definitely detrimental effects on the personality development of the Negro child." Or, "... basic feelings of inferiority, conflict, confusion in his self-image, resentment, hostility toward himself, and hostility toward whites." And finally, "A child who expects to be rejected, who sees his group held in low self-esteem is not going to function well, is not going to be a fully developed child."[22] Contrast these testimonies with the words of a few desegregation pioneers: "Desegregation left me with feelings of alienation and incompetence." Or, "We had to learn their way of doing things — acting, talking, dressing — their way of being, but nobody was interested in our way. We wanted so badly to be accepted, we tried to do and be all they wanted and we were still rejected. Even today, I have a really big problem with rejection of any kind." And finally, "At our schools, the buildings and books might not have been as good, but at least the teachers cared whether or not you learned. At their schools, the teachers didn't think we could learn."

Physical Effects / Along with the above long-term psychological and emotional effects, one male reports on a physical effect, "To this day, this morning, I never eat breakfast and I don't miss it and I don't think about it. But when I do, I know it's because for those four years my stomach was so much in knots I couldn't eat before I went to school and then I couldn't eat lunch. I wouldn't sit down in the lunchroom because of the things they would do and I knew I couldn't go to the bathroom. It was a very uncomfortable time and maybe to some extent you block that stuff, I mean you just sort of say it's stuff that you don't want to revisit but deep down you know that it's stuff that still affects you."

All of these comments suggest that, in the eyes of its participants, the way in which school desegregation was implemented was not as well thought out as it could have been, and, because of that, it took an enormous toll on the subsequent mental (and in some cases physical) health of its pioneers. "I just don't have a lot of great warm feelings about it and usually don't want to relive it or bring it up or you don't even want to think about it. Like I say, it's just something you live with and you have to kind of keep a lid on it intellectually in your head just to survive and I've kept a lid on it for twenty-five years or so, so, you know . . ."

Of course, to concentrate on only negative effects would overlook the fact that there were several positive effects as perceived by the "pioneers."

Positive Effects / One woman talked about the life-long white friends she eventually acquired from those girls who befriended her in spite of the peer pressure not to do so. She told me about one in particular who was a bridesmaid in her wedding and is the godmother of her oldest child. They still keep in touch and periodically travel across country to see one another. As a group, they also overwhelmingly agree that they received an incredible education. Many feel that they were exposed to courses and facilities that were unavailable at the all-black schools of the time. One pioneer reported:

> Also, because the gods were smiling on me, the thirty-year reunion was held last summer. Participating in that was like closing the loop and one other woman called it a catharsis. Because of the project, we shared some of our feelings about that time and many of the women who as young girls were particularly mean expressed remorse for having done so. Several apologized for the hell they put us through. One woman who I remember being nice at the time said she felt guilty about not being more courageous about it. In other words, she was one of those, she was sort of like the silent majority type, you know she was a very bright student and I think she in retrospect just sort of looked back on it and just felt she could have done more than just not be negative.

Many of the misperceptions came out at this cathartic reunion. After the reunion one of the black respondents reported the following: "One woman told me that the white kids thought we were getting special treatment because they would never see us in the bathrooms. Well, they didn't know I was just simply holding my bladder all day. The faculty had their own bathroom with a key and they thought since they didn't see us using the student restrooms, well, the rumor was the reason you didn't see the black students in the bathrooms was because we had a key to the faculty bathrooms ... so there was this big to-do about bathrooms." Another re-called: "One of the most rewarding experiences from the reunion weekend was attending a cocktail party at one white female's house, one who had been among the group that pretty much ignored us. When we entered her living room, she had her son's prom picture prominently displayed and his date was black."

Thus, many of the pioneers cited both positive and negative long-term effects. But what about desegregation's explicit goals of higher achieve-ment, better self-esteem, and improved race relations? As adults, are school desegregators any different from those who attended segregated schools?

Effects on Achievement / In terms of objective social-status criteria such as education, occupation, and income, both groups have some extremely suc-cessful and some not-so-successful members. Thus, the school desegrega-tion goal of improved minority achievement for those who attend desegre-gated schools appears not to have been reached any better for those who did than for those who didn't attend. The one exception was a Ph.D. level of education among the attendees, a level unmatched among the nonatten-dees. Other than that one exception, both groups had an education range from high-school diploma through master's degree and occupational posi-tions including lawyers, teachers, small business owners, accountants, clerks, and manual laborers. However, members of both groups report that if they are successful in white organizations, their credentials are considered ques-tionable possibly because of the current stigma surrounding affirmative ac-tion. It seems to be the current way of thinking that any successful African American is an "affirmative action baby,"[23] and the school desegregation pioneers are no exception. Many also report feeling that they're being mea-sured by a "different yardstick" than the one used for their white colleagues, and they feel that there is a pervasive and perverse expectation that they will never measure up and will somehow fail. However, if they do "beat the stick," then they are considered "special" or somehow "different" from other blacks. Conversely, if unsuccessful, several report being accused of "not having made the best of a golden opportunity" or of "not having taken ad-vantage of all that was given to ya'll." Thus, we see what appears to be a damned-if-you-do and damned-if-you-don't paradox surrounding black achievement among these pioneers.

Self-Esteem Effects / In terms of desegregation's goal of enhanced minority self-esteem, most of the pioneers who were attendees of desegregated schools report just the opposite, a decreased sense of self-esteem. One objectively successful female states that the desegregation "experience had the most profound effect on my self-confidence. I constantly question myself and my abilities." She goes on to say, "What makes this so difficult is that my parents had always made me believe that I could do and be anything I wanted." It is her contention that "the desegregation process destroyed my whole foundation of self-worth." Another female, now heavily involved in Eastern religions, recalls her high-school experiences as "extremely traumatic at the most vulnerable period of my life." She also reported that she is grossly overweight and attributes her obesity to "the psychic pain that I still carry around from the desegregation experience." A male attendee was reluctant to recall his desegregation experiences because when he does "I feel like I'm in no-man's land" and because "I'm still trying to forgive all those guys who were so abusive to me."

Effects on Race Relations / Regarding desegregation's argument that an increase in social interaction among schoolchildren would lead to a reduction in prejudice, many of the pioneers describe feelings of "dread" and "anxiety" whenever they know they are about to enter a predominantly white situation or environment. "No matter how much I prepare myself, there's still that gut feeling that something bad might happen." When asked to describe this dread, one woman called it "a fear that someone will be openly rude or ugly or hostile and will make it very clear that I am not welcome." This fear is then followed by "feelings of foolishness because no one acts like that anymore no matter what they're thinking or feeling." But, then there's a feeling of "maybe I better prepare yourself, just in case it happens anyway." Of course, all this is going on internally; as one male put it, "Never let them see you sweat." Perhaps the most telling evidence that this goal has not been reached is a woman who reported that after her school desegregation experiences she "would never even consider sending my children to an integrated school."

Discussion

Given that conclusion, how are the school desegregation pioneers' experiences and subsequent feelings related to the current racial scene? Can findings based on experiences from the early 1960s be useful for understanding the realities of race relations today? Or have circumstances changed so dramatically that this study can only be of historical interest? I believe that the findings from this study have significance for the present because the current racial scene is beginning to mirror those trends that were apparent during the height of the original civil rights revolution and thus can speak to another that appears to be looming in the immediate future. This contemporary mirroring of the past is well illustrated by the current trend among African Americans away from integration and toward separatism accompanied by a renewed call for black nationalism. The flourishing popularity of Malcolm X and any X paraphernalia and quotes from national black leaders such as Benjamin Hooks and Harold Cruse show the gaining popularity of this ideology. The angry male previously cited describes this new mood best: "We have to do it by ourselves, for ourselves. Only we can regain all that we lost from before when we were separated."

A second and related trend is the call for separate schools for young black males and for Afrocentric education and curricula. The woman who would not even consider sending her children to integrated schools is a staunch advocate of an Afrocentric curriculum. According to her, "We tried it their way, now it's time to do it our way." These comments reflect a new interracial mood reminiscent of the 1960s call for blacks to control their own communities.

It would seem from these interviews and from contemporary events that from the point of view of school desegregation pioneers and of many other blacks today, the whole premise of integration through one-way assimilation has been too costly for the black community. Therefore, it may now be time for a new educational policy to be considered. I would suggest that perhaps this new policy could be equalitarian pluralism. Martin Marger defines equalitarian pluralism as a society where, through mainly voluntary separation, "groups maintain cultural and structural autonomy but remain relatively equal in political and economic power."[24] This seems to be what many African-Americans, particularly desegregation pioneers, are calling for and, in fact, what many school districts are beginning to implement. This "structural autonomy" suggests that schools would again be separate but this time they would also be equal in all important aspects: buildings, facilities, books, and personnel. Of course, the other part of the definition, "relatively equal in political and economic power," has not yet occurred. The call for black nationalism and separatism may be a step in that direction. Before becoming sidetracked and silenced by the civil rights movement, many black intellectuals were suggesting that changing structures was more important than changing attitudes.[25] Toward that end, they saw the separatist phase as the first step in minority group advancement. My concern is that, at least in education, many are seeing this trend toward separatism as the end rather than as the means to a more desirable end. The only way to a genuine equalitarian pluralism is through affirming the principle of coequality.[26] Coequality means that all views are represented and respected. When applied to the school system, this would mean pluralistic multiculturalism in multicultural institutions. Separate schools for blacks (and I would advocate that these schools allow both males and females to attend), particularistic multiculturalism, and Afrocentricity all have positive points and certain inherent advantages,[27] but they are an inadequate policy response to failed desegregation.

Perhaps separate schools (for both black males and females) and Afrocentricity could be considered an interim step in that direction, and as such they have merit. Certainly, the words of the desegregation pioneers suggest that, as they are currently set up, mixed schools have a detrimental impact on minority student mental health, and until we can change what goes on in these schools, separate black schools may be one solution. However, I would have to say that these schools should be open to both black males and females and not exclusively to black males.

By the same token, a curriculum that places Africa at the center in the development of civilization and that attempts to amend traditional history by including the contributions made by African people is certainly a long-overdue curricular improvement. Moreover, if, as Asante suggests, "it is difficult to create freely when you use someone else's motifs, styles, images, and perspectives," then an Afrocentric curriculum might enhance the mental health of black students. But in order to live in a multicultural world, black children also need to learn to value the history, culture, and perspectives of other ethnic groups, as well. This is truly affirming the norm of coequality.

Thus, the best conception of integration must be as a two-way exchange rather than as the one-way conformity to the dominant group that occurred during school desegregation. Certainly, the most basic lesson from the desegregation pioneers is that it wasn't the idea of integration or the goals of the *Brown* decision that were a failure, it was the manner in which school desegregation policy was implemented that made the goals unattainable. Instead of discarding the idea of integration, we need to broaden its scope to mean coequality between all groups by including the interests of the new minority groups, and thus we need to come up with better ways of reaching the goals of the *Brown* decision: improvement in race and ethnic relations, minority group achievement, and minority group self-esteem.

Conclusion

Prior analyses of school desegregation have been severely limited by the lack of knowledge about the personal experiences and feelings, thoughts, and perceptions of those who were among the first to go through the desegregation process. The exploratory study presented in this chapter has attempted to fill that gap and thus has provided insights into the reasons that many blacks are now part of a trend away from the original school desegregation policies and toward a search for new ways of educating inner-city minority youth.

There are also other factors fueling this new trend. Today, our urban schools are no longer simply black and white but, rather, reflect the demographic changes that are taking place. The inclusion of Hispanic and Asian students, who also suffer prejudice and discrimination, means that today's debate over the value of assimilation versus separatism will affect these groups, as well. There are other societal changes that signal a need for a new policy regarding urban education. The demographic changes are not only causing a shift in numbers of students, but also are fostering more cultural diversity within the school population. Both the home and the family are being redefined. We're becoming an information-based economy with a significant number of transactions being done from the home. At the same time there's an increase in "nontraditional" families, which include mothers working outside of the home. Finally, our society now features an aging population with less commitment to the education of young people. This changing social context, along with black disillusionment with desegregation as it was implemented, calls for a school social policy that is able to address the many issues fostered by these changes.

If, as suggested by negative experiences and perceptions of the school desegregation pioneers, the implementation of the social policy known as desegregation was a failure, what new policy can be used to resolve the problems of urban education, particularly for minority students? One answer is a multicultural curriculum. Multiculturalism, if set up so that every point of view is represented as part of the mix, if implemented so that individuals are exposed to the variety of cultures represented in the U.S. population, could be an improved method of implementing genuine coequal integration and a giant step toward equalitarian pluralism. Any other type of curriculum or structure, particularly one that fails to affirm the principle of coequality, one that in essence attempts to set up a new hierarchy in the form of an ethnocentric curriculum, is unfortunately doomed to the same failure as the desegregation policy of the 1950s. The school desegregation policy, and its assimilationist implementation, was a direct result of the belief that a "Western" education was superior because white culture was superior and other cultures had no value. Thus, Afrocentric education would have to be one aspect of this new social policy of multicultural education because it helps to restore the culture and history that African Americans lost during slavery. But an Afrocentrism that attempts to make African culture superior simply shifts the weight to favor a different culture instead of instilling balance and stability to our urban educational system.

Given the historical legacy documented by this study's pioneers, it is difficult to argue against segregated schooling. But we cannot allow the perceived stigma of integration to permit us to return to a system of segregated schools, even if it is self-imposed segregation. The changing social context calls for an equalitarian new school policy for resolving the problems of urban education: multiculturalism.

Notes

1. Alphonso Pinkney, *Black Americans,* 4th ed. (Englewood Cliffs, N.J.: Prentice-Hall, 1993), 65.

2. D. Stanley Eitzen and Maxine Baca Zinn, *Social Problems,* 5th ed. (Boston: Allyn and Bacon, 1992); James E. Blackwell, *The Black Community: Diversity and Unity,* 3rd ed. (New York: Harper-Collins, 1991); Janet Ward Schofield, "The Review of Research on School Desegregation's Impact on Black Americans" (paper commissioned for the Committee on the Status of Black Americans of the National Research Council, April 27, 1987).

3. Pinkney, *Black Americans.*

4. Kalamu ya Salaam, "The Failure of Integration," *Utne Reader,* May/June 1991, 38–41; *Sojourners* 19, no. 2 (August/September 1990): 4–26, special issue titled "What's Wrong with Integration?" featuring the following articles: Jim Wallis, "From Integration to Transformation"; Anthony A. Parker, "Whose America Is It? A New Generation Reconsiders Integration"; Manning Marable, "The Rhetoric of Racial Harmony"; Delores S. Williams, "Exposing False Distinctions"; and Harold W. Cruse, "Stalled Out in History: The Past and Future of Integration."

5. *Sojourners* 19, no. 2 (August/September 1990).

6. David G. Carter, "Second-generation School Integration Problems for Blacks," *Journal of Black Studies* 13, no. 2 (1982): 175–88.

7. I am using the word *pioneer* to indicate the first blacks who were eligible to attend previously all-white schools, whether they did so or not. Because the first wave of attendees were chosen by teachers and administrators, those who were not chosen report their own

feelings of rejection or of somehow having been stigmatized as "not good enough" to be among the first to attend the desegregated schools. Both pioneer attendees and nonattendees perceive desegregation as a poorly implemented policy.

8. Carter, "Second-generation School Integration Problems for Blacks"; Glenn R. Smith, "Desegregation and Assignment in Classes for the Mildly Retarded and Learning Disabled," *Integrated Education* 21, no. 6 (1983): 208–11; Daniel J. Monti, " 'Brown's Velvet Cushion: Metropolitan Desegregation and the Politics of Illusion," *Metropolitan Education* 1 (1986): 52–61; William A. Sampson, "Desegregation and Racial Tolerance in Academia," *Journal of Negro Education* 55, no. 2 (1986): 171–91.

9. William R. Jones, and Loretta Jones, "Coping with the Four R's: Reading, 'Riting, 'Rithmetic, and Racism," in *Liberation Theory: North American Style* (New York: Vertizon, 1987).

10. Leslie B. Inniss, "Surviving Desegregation: Blacks Assess the Price of Pioneering" (unpublished manuscript, Department of Sociology, Florida State University, 1992).

11. Gary Orfield, *Status of School Desegregation: The Next Generation* (Alexandria, Va: National School Boards Association, 1992).

12. Joe R. Feagin and Clairece Booher Feagin, *Racial and Ethnic Relations,* 4th ed. (Englewood Cliffs, N.J.: Prentice-Hall 1993); Jennifer L. Hochshield, *The New American Dilemma* (New Haven, Conn.: Yale University Press, 1984), 169.

13. Orfield, *Status of School Desegregation,* 16.

14. Eitzen and Zinn, *Social Problems.*

15. Harold Cruse, *Plural but Equal: Blacks and Minorities in America's Plural Society* (New York: William Morrow, 1987).

16. Walter G. Stephan, "A Brief History of School Desegregation," in *School Desegregation,* ed. Walter G. Stephan and Joe R. Feagin (New York: Plenum Press, 1980), 3–23.

17. Cruse, *Plural but Equal.*

18. Stephan, "A Brief History," 11.

19. Richard Kluger, *Simple Justice: The History of Brown v Board of Education and Black America's Struggle for Equality* (New York: Vintage Books, 1976).

20. See Hochschield, *New American Dilemma,* 162–69 for an overview of these studies.

21. Don A. Dillman, *Mail and Telephone Surveys: The Total Design Method* (New York: Wiley, 1978).

22. Kluger, *Simple Justice,* 353.

23. Stephen Carter, *Reflections of an Affirmative Action Baby* (New York: Basic Books, 1991).

24. Martin N. Marger, *Race and Ethnic Relations: American and Global Perspectives,* 2nd ed. (Belmont, Calif.: Wadsworth, 1991), 13.

25. Barbara A. Sizemore, "The Politics of Curriculum, Race, and Class," *Journal of Negro Education* 59, no. 1 (1990): 77–85.

26. William Jones, address to Florida State University Fall Convocation, 1993.

27. Diane Ravitch, "Multiculturalism: E Pluribus Plures," *American Scholar* 59, no. 3 (1990); Molefi Kete Asante, *Afrocentricity* (Trenton, N.J.: Africa World Press, 1989).

8 / Retreat from Equal Opportunity?

The Case of Affirmative Action

Cedric Herring and Sharon M. Collins

Introduction and Overview

Affirmative action policies have generated widespread opposition among Americans. Results from a 1991 *New York Times*–CBS News poll reveal that only 28 percent of Americans "believe that where there has been job discrimination against women in the past, preference in hiring should be given to women today."[1] When a similar question is asked about opportunities for African Americans, only 20 percent "believe that where there has been job discrimination against blacks in the past, preference in hiring should be given to blacks today."[2]

White Americans see altering the rules as tantamount to letting disadvantaged groups win unfairly. And as the competition for education and jobs that secure middle-class lifestyles has become stiffer, equal opportunity (affirmative action) programs find little support even among those whites who concede the persistence of discrimination.

The increased lack of public support for affirmative action has broad implications. When support for affirmative action among white Americans erodes, the political mandate to continue these programs may also weaken. In turn, a new public mandate to dismantle or weaken existing affirmative action programs may have consequences for the future of city life. Because economic factors such as poverty and long-term unemployment are powerful predictors of crime and urban violence, overturning the policy of affirmative action may have devastating effects on the already high levels of racial tensions found in most major cities. Indeed, despite affirmative action efforts, nonwhite minorities remain disproportionately at the bottom and most vulnerable rungs of the urban economic ladder.

In this chapter, we provide provisional evidence concerning some of the empirical questions raised by the objections to affirmative action. We use data from the 1990 General Social Survey and a 1992 survey of Chicago adults to provide tests of arguments about the effectiveness of affirmative action as a strategy for bringing about more racial and gender equality. In particular, we examine the degree to which affirmative action practices redistribute life chances, nurture negative stereotypes of minority workers, and erode the economic well-being of white male workers. We explore these claims by examining the relationship between the presence of affirmative action programs and the income, proportional representations, occupational rankings, and work-related interracial perceptions and attitudes of minority and nonminority workers.

Definition of Affirmative Action

Affirmative action is a government mandated or voluntary program that consists of activities specifically to identify, recruit, promote, and/or retain qualified members of disadvantaged minority groups in order to overcome the result of past discrimination and to deter employers from engaging in discriminatory practices in the present. It has come to mean several different things to the public, and we will discuss the reality of the program in more detail below. Affirmative action is based on the argument that simply removing existing impediments is not sufficient for changing the relative positions of women and people of color.[3] And it is based on the premise that to be truly effective in altering the unequal distribution of life chances, it is essential that employers take specific steps to remedy the consequences of discrimination.

Affirmative Action in Historical Context

It is well documented that prior to the 1960s, women and various people of color were the victims of employment discrimination.[4] In the effort to curtail such discrimination, since at least the 1940s, executive orders have been issued and federal legislation enacted to prohibit discrimination against minorities and women workers.[5]

In the early 1940s, President Roosevelt issued executive orders declaring an end to discrimination in the federal civil service and creating the Fair Employment Practices Committee. The federal effort to prohibit discrimination continued during the 1950s when President Truman issued two executive orders to establish fair employment procedures within the federal government structure, to abolish discrimination in the armed forces, and to establish compliance procedures for government contractors.

In 1965, President Johnson expanded equal opportunity efforts by issuing Executive Order 11246 to improve the economic and social statuses of protected-class individuals (women and racial minorities). This order was essentially the same as its immediate predecessor issued by President Kennedy in 1961, which required government contractors and subcontractors to take "affirmative action" to insure that applicants and employees were not discriminated against.[6]

Given the entrenched nature of discriminatory employment patterns on the one hand and the escalation of black protest on the other, it is not surprising that the concept of equal employment opportunity evolved into a more aggressive stance both in approach and in implementation between the 1940s and 1960s. In the 1940s, the approach was voluntary "nondiscrimination." In 1955, the broader term "equal opportunity" was used by President Dwight D. Eisenhower in Executive Order 10590. In 1961, under President Kennedy, and again in 1965, under President Johnson, the concept of "affirmative action" was used to guide the policy of the federal government. Affirmative action evolved when compliance efforts that relied on "good faith" and "equal opportunity" proved to be an ineffectual and inadequate approach to eliminating deep-rooted discriminatory employment processes.

Enforcement of Affirmative Action Policies

By the time Title VII was debated in Congress it had become increasingly evident that meaningful enforcement of a fair employment law would require active intervention, namely affirmative action, in hiring. Moreover, it would require virtually all major business enterprises to be covered by the law. Toward these goals, the regulatory sphere of Title VII includes a vast array of employment settings and almost every area in which the federal government has responsibilities.

Title VII provided for the establishment of the Equal Employment Opportunity Commission (EEOC) as the law's administrative agency. The commission is, perhaps, the most visible federal enforcement agency, yet its effectiveness as an instrument for affirmative action has been constrained by a lack of enforcement power.[7] Business interests adamantly resisted the idea of government oversight in hiring practices despite the obvious patterns of employment discrimination that existed in the private sector. As a result, Congress limited the commission's role to investigation, persuasion, and conciliation at its inception in 1965, although Congress later granted the commission the power to initiate litigation in district courts.

The EEOC may be more visible to the public, but the Office of Federal Contract Compliance Programs (OFCCP) is arguably the more powerful of the two instruments of affirmative action. The OFCCP was created to enforce requirements that federal contractors identify, hire, and promote minorities and women in numbers roughly proportional to their availability in the labor market. The underlying premise of this requirement is that if employers acted in a nondiscriminatory fashion, their workforce would at some point reflect the composition of the populace that surrounded their establishments. Thus, the OFCCP was vested with the authority to withhold or withdraw federal funds from federal contractors, giving it the ability to compel equal employment opportunity in the nation's major employers.

Hiring criteria to guide the employment efforts of government contractors make up the concrete standards and procedures that underpin the concept of affirmative action. The OFCCP first issued Order No. 4 requiring contractors to make detailed and extensive efforts to increase the employment of underrepresented minorities. Revised Order No. 4 added goals and timetables for women and specified in detail how contractors should analyze the utilization of minorities and women in order to comply with hiring obligations. Under Revised Order No. 4, federal contractors also are to submit a written "affirmative action plan" with numerical goals and timetables for achieving these goals for hiring and promoting women, blacks, and other designated minority groups. Thus, the OFCCP transformed the concept of affirmative action into a specific and accountable employment practice.

Challenges to Affirmative Action

Since it first emerged on the national scene the policy of affirmative action has been surrounded by controversy and opposition. Between 1965 and 1973, government contractors made good faith efforts to employ minorities and women.[8] In some cases, however, good faith effort resulted in "quotas" and the use of minorities and women as "tokens" to meet affirmative action requirements.[9]

In 1974, affirmative action programs came under legal challenge (in *De-Funis v. The University of Washington Law School*) at the U.S. Supreme Court level. In the next few years, as more lawsuits over the issue of "reverse discrimination" were filed, white support for affirmative action began to decline.

In 1978, the U.S. Supreme Court issued a landmark affirmative action decision in *University of California Regents v. Bakke.* In *Bakke,* a special affirmative action admission program of the University of California at Davis Medical School was challenged. The Supreme Court, in a narrow decision, held that the special program was not constitutional but that race could be taken into account in the admission program; however, race could not be the only criterion for admission.

In 1979, Brian Weber, a white employee of Kaiser Aluminum, brought suit alleging the company's affirmative action efforts to increase the proportion of blacks in a company training program violated Title VII. The Supreme Court held that Kaiser's affirmative action was legal and permissible under the law and did not violate Title VII, even if some qualified whites were disadvantaged.

In the 1980s, the Reagan administration promoted a major reversal in equal employment opportunity and affirmative action policies.[10] The administration took the position that it "oppose[d] court-ordered and court-sanctioned racial preferences for non-victims of discrimination."[11] Indeed, it actively argued against the use of preferential treatment and quotas in employment practices. Some adversaries of affirmative action went so far as to suggest that employers who tried to implement equal opportunity programs would find themselves in trouble if they established programs that utilized set-asides or racial preferences.[12]

If anything, anti-affirmative-action policies were pursued even more vigorously during the Bush administration. President Bush vetoed a new version of the Civil Rights Act on the grounds that it would require employers to establish quotas. Proponents of the legislation argued that it simply restored the legal framework of the workplace to what it had been prior to a series of Supreme Court decisions in the late 1980s.[13]

Today, affirmative action programs currently are the subject of a great deal of contention and discord. The objections are numerous, and the explanations of such opposition are plentiful. In some instances, opposition to affirmative action is part of an effort to shift attention to macroeconomic and human capital characteristics that limit the labor market chances of disadvantaged black Americans. In other instances, these viewpoints are part of a neoconservative ideology that denies the weight of racism and discrimination against women and nonwhite minorities to justify dismantling affirmative action programs. In either instance, these challenges are components in a larger justification of the retreat since 1980 from a national policy of protective legislation and race-based reparations.

Objections to Affirmative Action

Affirmative action has come under siege not only for being politically unpopular, but also for being ineffective as a policy for reducing levels of inequality for targeted groups.[14] Some have challenged affirmative action because it purportedly helps those members of minority groups who need assistance least at the same time that it does little for those who are among the "truly disadvantaged."[15] Others have criticized such programs for unfairly stigmatizing qualified minority candidates who must endure the perception that they were selected or promoted only because of their institutions' needs for minority representation.[16] And still others have derided affirmative action policies as "reverse discrimination" that benefits minority groups at the expense of equally or more qualified white men.[17]

Affirmative Action is Ineffective

Objections to affirmative action programs often incorporate the idea that such programs are politically unpopular because they are not effective. Variations of this view suggest that affirmative action policies simply have had no noticeable effect on the economic standing and representation of minority group members.[18] For these opponents, affirmative action constitutes just another example of costly but ineffective government regulation. Given that such programs are expensive but unsuccessful in enhancing the positions of women and people of color, they should be dismantled.

Other variants of this argument suggest that affirmative action leads to a situation in which the wrong victims and the wrong beneficiaries are identified. These opponents argue that well-off minorities are likely to be preferred over poor minorities since poor minorities are less likely to qualify for skilled employment. William Julius Wilson explicitly argues that "race-specific" policies such as affirmative action cannot succeed in helping the "underclass" or in reducing inequality.[19] Such policies, he argues, while beneficial to more advantaged minorities, do little for those who are "truly disadvantaged" inasmuch as the effects of race and class subordination passed from generation to generation are disproportionately present among the poor. These people lack the resources and skills to compete effectively in the labor market. Thus, policies based on preferential treatment of minorities linked to group outcomes are insufficient precisely because the relatively advantaged members of racial minority communities will be selected and will reap the benefits to the detriment of poor minorities. Moreover, those whites who are rejected due to preferential programs might be the most disadvantaged whites whose qualifications are marginal precisely because of their disadvantages.

Affirmative Action Stigmatizes Minorities

A second kind of objection raised by opponents of affirmative action is that because whites often believe women and people of color are less qualified than white men (or even that no qualified candidates from those groups exist), it will stigmatize all minority workers. Those minorities and women who are qualified and can make it in society will be looked down on as having been favorites of the law who did not really make it on their own. In addition, this could have the effect of a self-fulfilling prophecy: Because employers believe that minority workers are less likely than are white male workers to be qualified for employment, they set lower standards in order to satisfy affirmative action requirements. In turn, minority workers have less incentive to perform at higher levels, as better performance will do little to enhance their chances of meeting company standards that have been lowered. Performances by minority workers that do not exceed the employers' lowered expectations serve to confirm the employers' initial beliefs about minority workers' lower levels of preparation and qualification. In other words, legally preferred groups realize that less is expected of them and, therefore, perform at a lower standard. This lower accomplishment, in turn, substantiates the stereotypes that reluctant employers and co-workers held initially.[20]

Affirmative Action Is Reverse Discrimination

Another kind of objection to affirmative action is that it is tantamount to "reverse discrimination."[21] To the degree that affirmative action seeks to provide compensatory justice for past wrongs, it is laudable. Some critics would argue, however, that affirmative action programs are zero-sum undertakings: Under such plans, to the degree that minorities and women make economic progress, white men will suffer. Moreover, they would argue, some innocent white men who have never discriminated against minorities or women might be punished unfairly while some chauvinists and bigots might be spared. This objection to affirmative action makes the judgment (as an empirical fact) that whites lose to minorities. This empirical fact, per se, should disallow affirmative action according to these critics.

Below, we provide provisional evidence concerning some of the empirical questions raised by these objections to affirmative action. In particular, we examine the degree to which affirmative action practices are ineffective in redistributing life chances, culpable for negative stereotypes of minority workers, and deleterious to the economic well-being of white male workers. Before we test these claims, we provide some basic information about our data sources and operationalizations.

Samples and Indicators

The first data set that we used in the analysis comes from the 862 respondents in the 1990 General Social Survey who answered questions about affirmative action programs at their place of employment.[22] We used these data to operationalize affirmative action programs, racial minority status (blacks and Latinos), sex, occupational prestige, family income when growing up, and beliefs about blacks' work efforts.

Because indicators about the composition of respondents' place of employment were not available in the General Social Survey, we also used data from a 1992 survey of Chicago adults. These data on 763 respondents come from a random-digit dialing telephone social survey conducted by the University of Illinois Institute of Government and Public Affairs. These data were used to operationalize personal income, size of firm, proportion of black workers at respondent's place of employment, and proportion of female workers at respondent's place of employment.

In both surveys, for the affirmative action indicator, respondents were asked: "Does the place where you work have an affirmative action program or make any special effort to hire and promote minorities?" These self-reports provide a means of distinguishing between those who believed they worked where affirmative action programs were in place and others. It also, in effect, furnishes a method of examining the effects and effectiveness of affirmative action on several work-related outcomes. For race, respondents were classified as either white or as having racial minority status, that is, as nonwhite. Sex was divided between men and women.

Does Affirmative Action Make a Difference to Economic and Employment Outcomes?

How valid are the objections to affirmative action programs raised by opponents of such policies? Do such programs increase incomes of racial minorities? Do they reduce the incomes of whites? Figure 8.1 presents the mean incomes of workers employed by affirmative action and non–affirmative-action firms for whites and nonwhites by firm size. This graph shows that when people of color work for affirmative action firms, their average incomes are higher. This holds true regardless of the size of the firm. Nonwhites working for small firms receive over $1,200 more if their firms are affirmative action employers. Racial minorities in medium-sized affirmative action firms earn $7,000 more than nonwhites in comparable non–affirmative-action companies. And in large firms, people of color with affirmative action companies earn more than $6,000 more than do racial minorities in non–affirmative-action settings.

For white workers, the picture is a bit more complicated: Whites in small and medium-sized firms earn between $2,400 and $5,900 more on average if they are not employed by affirmative action firms. Whites with large firms, however, earn more than $2,800 more when working for affirmative action employers. Again, because more than six times as many white workers with larger (higher-paying) employers are with affirmative action firms and because nearly 60 percent of whites in affirmative action firms are with larger firms, on average the presence of affirmative action programs corresponds to boosts in their average incomes of more than $3,000.

The income increments associated with affirmative action employment are substantial, especially for racial minorities. Does this, then, mean that affirmative action provides reverse discrimination? On this point, we should point out that the incomes of racial minorities do not eclipse those of whites. This holds true for all sizes of firms and irrespective of the presence or absence of affirmative action programs. Indeed, it is only in the case of large firms that people of color approach parity with whites in comparable settings.

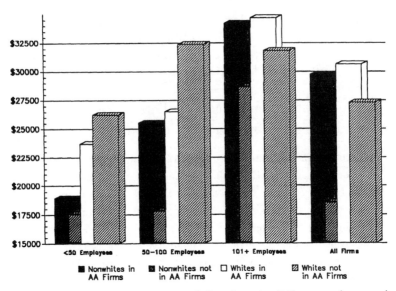

Figure 8.1. Mean incomes by the presence of affirmative action (AA) programs by race and size of firm

Figure 8.2 illustrates similar patterns with respect to the relationship between affirmative action employment and income by sex and firm size. For women, employment in an affirmative action setting is associated with an increase in income for firms of all sizes. These gains range from a little more than $500 in medium-sized firms to over $2,500 in small firms. For men, affirmative action employment is associated with higher incomes only in large firms. In these cases, however, the income differences exceed $11,000. Again, for both men and women, the overall income differences are substantial. Only in large non-affirmative-action firms do women earn incomes that are comparable to or higher than those of men.

Is affirmative action related to higher proportions of blacks and women working in companies? Figures 8.3 and 8.4 present some answers to this question. Figure 8.3 shows that only 7 percent of workers employed by affirmative action companies say that their firms employ no blacks. This compares with 33 percent of those employed by non-affirmative-action firms. Similarly, while 16 percent of those working in affirmative action companies say their companies employ few blacks, 26 percent of those in non-affirmative-action companies report that their companies employ few blacks. Almost half of those working for affirmative action companies report that their firms have workforces that are at least 50 percent black. In contrast,

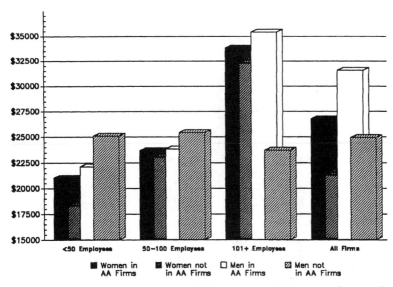

Figure 8.2. Mean incomes by the presence of affirmative action (AA) programs by sex and size of firm

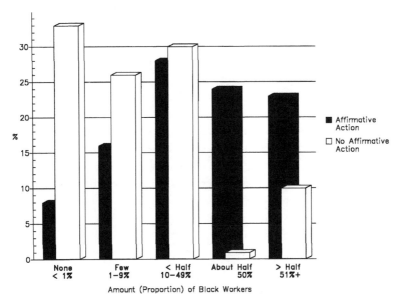

Figure 8.3. Percentage working for companies with given amounts (proportions) of black workers by the presence of affirmative action (AA) programs

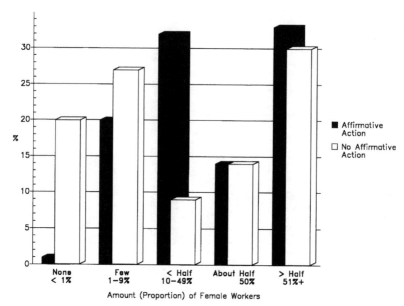

Figure 8.4. Percentage working for companies with given amounts (proportions) of female workers by the presence of affirmative action (AA) programs

less than 12 percent of those in non-affirmative-action companies say their companies' workforce has 50 percent or more black workers.[23]

Figure 8.4 depicts similar patterns with respect to the proportion of female workers employed by affirmative action and non-affirmative-action companies. This chart shows that fewer than 2 percent of people working for affirmative action companies report that their companies employ no women, and 20 percent of them report that their companies hire few women. In contrast, 20 percent of those in non-affirmative-action settings report that their companies have no female employees, and 27 percent report few female employees. Again, these patterns for affirmative action and non-affirmative-action companies reverse when the proportion of female workers approaches or exceeds half.

Is affirmative action associated with higher-level employment for people of color and women? Figure 8.5 illustrates that affirmative action employment is associated with higher occupational prestige. On average, racial minorities, women, people who grew up poor, and white men all have more prestigious occupations in settings that have affirmative action programs. These groups gain about four occupational prestige points under affirmative

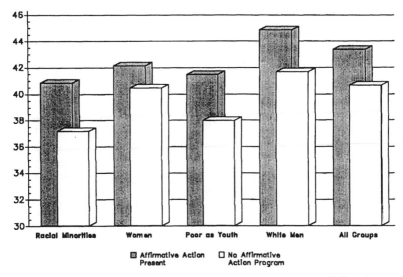

Figure 8.5. Mean occupational prestige of selected groups by the presence of affirmative action programs

action. This is about the difference between a plumber and an insurance agent, or between a public school teacher and a banker. The gains are greatest among those who were poor as youths and among racial minority workers. This chart shows, however, that women and white men in affirmative action firms also hold an advantage over women and white men who work for employers without affirmative action policies.

So the results suggest that affirmative action is associated with higher incomes for people of color and women. Also, such programs are related to higher proportions of women and minorities in companies, as well as higher occupational prestige. Moreover, the findings indicate that whites and men are not greatly penalized by the existence of such programs. But what about perceptions and attitudes? Are affirmative action programs correlated with any work-relevant beliefs? Figure 8.6 suggests that despite evidence showing that groups other than racial minorities also benefit from affirmative action programs and despite previous research suggesting that few cases of "reverse discrimination" actually occur,[24] the presence of affirmative action programs is associated with the expectation that "reverse discrimination" is likely to occur. This pattern is in keeping with the prediction that the qualifications of racial minority workers who occupy affirmative action positions would become suspect.[25] Not surprisingly, this wariness is more

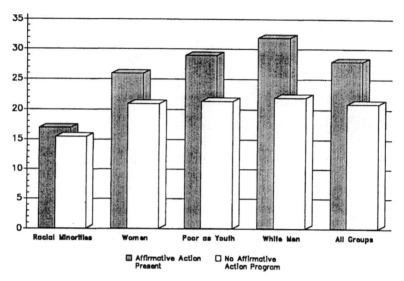

Figure 8.6. Percentage of selected groups who believe that "reverse discrimination" is very likely to occur these days

pronounced among white men than among other groups. However, affirmative action is related to anticipation of reverse discrimination among racial minorities, women, and people who grew up poor.

Is affirmative action associated with less positive impressions of minority workers, as some scholars suspect?[26] Figure 8.7 shows that there is a slight tendency for racial minorities and women in affirmative action settings to have lower appraisals of black workers' work efforts. At the same time, the presence of affirmative action corresponds with the tendency for white men and those who were poor as youths to hold more favorable images of blacks' work efforts. It should be noted that white men who work where there are no provisions for affirmative action are the least favorable in their impressions of blacks' work efforts.

Discussion

We began this chapter by noting that dismantling affirmative action policies could have consequences for urban life. If the federal government reins in the commitment to affirmative action, the efforts of private sector employers to maintain equal employment opportunity could erode. Our findings indicate that, under these conditions, the economic status of blacks may

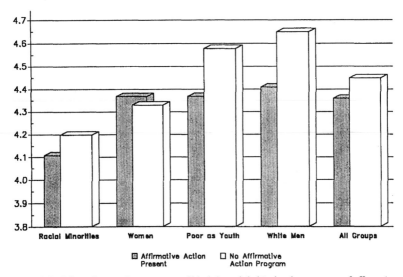

Figure 8.7. Selected groups' assessments of blacks' work habits by the presence of affirmative action programs (1 = hard working; 7 = lazy)

shrink dramatically in Chicago. First, the results showed that the presence of affirmative action is associated with higher incomes for racial minorities and women. Moreover, because more than ten times as many people of color who work for large, higher-paying firms are with affirmative action employers, and more than 65 percent of all nonwhite affirmative action employees are in large firms, the overall earnings differences between racial minorities in affirmative action companies and other nonwhites exceed eleven thousand dollars per year! Needless to say, affirmative action has a substantial impact on the earnings of nonwhite workers.

Similar patterns emerged with respect to the relationship between affirmative action and proportional representation, as well as affirmative action and occupational prestige. That is, the presence of affirmative action improves the chances of nonwhite minorities to be employed in Chicago's private sector and, moreover, to be employed in a higher-status job. This last point is particularly true for those nonwhite workers who grew up poor. Overall, our findings argue that the economic status of blacks is elevated a considerable amount by the presence of affirmative action.

We also noted earlier that economic characteristics are powerful predictors of crime in urban environments and social upheaval. In the 1960s, for example, blacks acted out their sense of deprivation through civil disorder that disrupted the social and the business environments of major cities across the country. Thus, from the perspective of "enlightened self-interest," affirmative action is simply a good business practice. Better minority representation in corporations can enhance marketing savvy vis-à-vis minority consumers and can help companies compete for the increased disposable income that results from better job opportunities due to affirmative action. Better minority representation also helps to pacify minority challenges to the policy decisions of predominantly white male governments or agencies. It helps, finally, to alleviate problems associated with poverty and unemployment and, in general, to keep a lid on the volatile bubbling cauldron known as the inner city.

Urban policies aimed at economic expansion, development, and job training are far more politically popular than programs that involve direct government intervention in the hiring and promotion practices of employers. Such programs do not, however, provide real solutions to sex and race inequality. They are of limited use when there are recessions and a growing scarcity of jobs. And in the face of economic downturns, these policies will do little to prevent women and people of color from being the "last hired and the first fired" or to guarantee that these groups will make progress.

As for the various objections to affirmative action raised by opponents of such polices, our data clearly show that most of these claims are not substantiated. We have shown that affirmative action does indeed elevate the life chances of historically excluded groups and, particularly, those who were raised in impoverished circumstances. Moreover, the elevation of the status of racial minorities does not detract from the chances of white men. Rather than being a zero-sum game, there are more winners than losers. Along with minorities and women, white men also benefit when affirmative action is present. Interesting enough, these benefits to white men accrue socially — in the reduction of stereotypes — as well as in economic terms.

We find the notion of "reverse discrimination" to be more myth than fact. Yet the myth that affirmative action policies benefit minorities at the expense of qualified white men stubbornly prevails. We suspect that such a myth is founded in a tradition in which wealth, power, and prestige are acquired by severely limiting nonwhite and nonmale competition. It may be that white men who object to affirmative action are less interested in social justice than in protecting their monopoly over these valuable social advantages.

If public leaders are sincere in their concerns about helping women and people of color realize equal opportunity, they will need the courage to push for strategies that are effective. Affirmative action is one such strategy.

Appendix

For respondents in the General Social Survey, occupational prestige refers to the social standing of their occupations as measured by the score received on the Hodge-Siegel-Rossi measure. Family income when growing up was measured by asking respondents the following: "Thinking about the time when you were 16 years old, compared with American families in general then, would you say your family income was far below average, below average, average, above average, or far above average?" Respondents who reported their family incomes as being "below average" or "far below average" were coded as having been poor as youths.

To tap beliefs about "reverse discrimination," respondents were asked, "What do you think the chances are these days that a white person won't get a job or promotion while an equally or less qualified black person gets one instead?" Answers were dichotomized into "likely" = 1 and "not likely" = 0.

To measure firm size, respondents in the Chicago survey were asked, "About how many people in total work for your employer at the location where you work?" Responses were collapsed into three categories: (1) small (fewer than 50 employees), (2) medium-sized (50 to 100 employees), or (3) large (more than 100 employees). In addition, to measure proportion of black workers at respondent's place of employment, respondents were asked, "Think about the people you work with each day on your job. About how many (what percentage) of them are black or African American?" Responses were collapsed into (virtually) none (less than 1 percent), few (between 1 percent and 9 percent), some but less than half (between 10 percent and 49 percent), about half (50 percent), and more than half (over 50 percent). Similarly, to measure proportion of female workers at respondent's place of employment, respondents were asked, "About how many (what percentage) of them are women?" These responses were also collapsed into (virtually) none (less than 1 percent), few (between 1 percent and 9 percent), some but less than half (between 10 percent and 49 percent), about half (50 percent), and more than half (over 50 percent). To measure beliefs about blacks' work efforts, respondents were asked to indicate on a seven-point Likert scale whether blacks (and other groups) "tend to be (7) hard working or . . . tend to be (1) lazy." Finally, personal income was assigned a score that corresponded to the midpoint of the respondent's income category, ranging from less than $1,000 (assigned a value of $500) to more than $75,000 (assigned a value of $90,000).

Notes

1. Results are from a September 1991 *New York Times*–CBS poll reported in the *New York Times Pollwatcher Letter,* May 12, 1992.

2. Ibid.

3. Paul Burstein, *Discrimination, Jobs, and Politics: The Struggle for Equal Employment Opportunity in the United States since the New Deal* (Chicago: University of Chicago Press, 1985).

4. Burstein, *Discrimination, Jobs, and Politics*; Reynolds Farley, *Blacks and Whites: Narrowing the Gap?* (Cambridge, Mass.: Harvard University Press, 1984); Reynolds Farley and Walter R. Allen, *The Color Line and the Quality of Life in America* (New York: Russell Sage Foundation, 1987); Gerald David Jaynes and Robin M. Williams, eds., *A Common Destiny: Blacks and American Society* (Washington, D.C.: National Academy Press, 1989); William Julius Wilson, *The Declining Significance of Race* (Chicago: University of Chicago Press, 1978).

5. For comprehensive discussions of affirmative action and equal employment opportunity programs, see Nijole V. Benokraitis and Joe R. Feagin, *Affirmative Action and Equal Opportunity: Action, Inaction, Reaction* (Boulder, Colo.: Westview Press, 1978); Leonard Hausman, Orley Ashenfelter, Bayard Rustin, Richard F. Schubert, and Donald Slaiman, eds., *Equal Rights and Industrial Relations* (Madison, Wis.: Industrial Relations Research Association, 1977); and Richard P. Nathan, *Jobs and Civil Rights: The Role of the Federal Government in Promoting Equal Opportunity in Employment and Training* (Washington, D.C.: Brookings Institution, 1969).

6. A federal contractor is any company (or any of its establishments) that has a primary contract or a first-tier subcontract to provide goods or services to a federal government agency.

7. For an extensive discussion of the history of the EEOC, see Herbert Hill, "The Equal Employment Opportunity Acts of 1964 and 1972: A Critical Analysis of the Legislative History and Administration of the Law," *Industrial Relations Law Journal* 11 (1977): 1–96.

8. Floyd D. Weatherspoon, *Equal Employment Opportunity and Affirmative Action* (New York: Garland, 1985).

9. James A. Belohlav and Eugene Ayton, "Equal Opportunity Law: Some Common Problems," *Personnel Journal* 61 (1982): 282–85.

10. William T. Hudson and Walter D. Broadnax, "Equal Employment Opportunity as Public Policy," *Public Personnel Management* 11 (1982): 268–76.

11. William Bradford Reynolds, "The Justice Department's Enforcement of Title VII," *Labor Law Journal* 34 (1983): 259–65.

12. Orrin G. Hatch, "Senator Hatch Wrestles with Affirmative Action," *Personnel Administrator* 25 (1980): 78.

13. Cynthia A. Wilson, James H. Lewis, and Cedric Herring, *The 1991 Civil Rights Act: Restoring Basic Protections* (Chicago: Urban League, 1991).

14. Oscar A. Ornati and Anthony Pisano, "Affirmative Action: Why It Isn't Working," *Personnel Administration,* September 1972, 50–52; Craig W. Cole, "Affirmative Action: Change It or Lose It," *EEO Today* 8 (1981): 262–71; James P. Smith and Finis Welch, "Affirmative Action and Labor Markets," *Journal of Labor Economics* 2 (1984): 269–99; William Julius Wilson, *The Truly Disadvantaged: The Inner City, the Underclass, and Public Policy* (Chicago: University of Chicago Press, 1987).

15. Wilson, *The Truly Disadvantaged.*

16. Stephen L. Carter, *Reflections of an Affirmative Action Baby* (New York: Basic Books, 1991); Glenn C. Loury, "Affirmative Action as a Remedy for Statistical Discrimination" (paper presented at a colloquium at the University of Illinois, Chicago, 1991).

17. Cole, "Affirmative Action"; Nathan Glazer, *Affirmative Discrimination: Ethnic Inequality and Public Policy* (New York: Basic Books, 1975); Barry R. Gross, *Discrimination in Reverse:*

Is Turnabout Fair Play? (New York: New York University Press, 1978); George Sher, "Justifying Reverse Discrimination in Employment," *Philosophy and Public Affairs* 4 (1975): 1159–70.

18. Smith and Welch, "Affirmative Action and Labor Markets."

19. Wilson, *The Truly Disadvantaged.*

20. Loury, "Affirmative Action as a Remedy."

21. Glazer, *Affirmative Discrimination.*

22. James A. Davis and Tom W. Smith, *General Social Surveys, 1972–1990 Cumulative Codebook* (Chicago: National Opinion Research Center, 1990).

23. Readers should keep in mind that these data are specific to Chicago. According to the 1990 census, Chicago is a city that has more black residents than white ones.

24. Paul Burstein, "'Reverse Discrimination' Cases in the Federal Courts: Legal Mobilization by a Countermovement," *Sociological Quarterly* 32 (1991): 511–28.

25. See Loury, "Affirmative Action as a Remedy."

26. Ibid.

9 / Demobilization in the New Black Political Regime

Ideological Capitulation and Radical Failure in the Postsegregation Era

Adolph Reed Jr.

It is ironic that the exponential increases in black public-office holding since the 1970s have been accompanied by a deterioration of the material circumstances of large segments of the black citizenry. Comment on that irony comes both from those on the Left who underscore the insufficiency of capturing public office and from those on the Right who disparage the pursuit of public action on behalf of blacks or push oblique claims about black incompetence. In the middle are liberal social scientists and journalists who construe this inverse association as a puzzling deviation from the orthodox narrative of American interest-group pluralism. The liberal and conservative tendencies especially are often elaborated through a rhetoric that juxtaposes black political power and white economic power, treating them almost as naturalized racial properties, rather than as contingent products of social and political institutions.

At the same time, a different anomaly bedevils those on the Left who presume that oppression breeds political resistance to power relations enforced through the state apparatus. The intensification of oppression over the 1980s — seen, for example, in worsening of material conditions and an expanding regime of social repression — has not produced serious oppositional political mobilization. This is the key problem for articulation of a progressive black urban politics in the 1990s.

Making sense of these anomalies requires examining critical characteristics of post-segregation-era black politics. Although the disparate fortunes of black officialdom and its constituents are not causally linked, their relation sheds light on popular demobilization. This relation connects with each of the three features of the contemporary political landscape that hinder progressive black mobilization: (1) political incorporation and its limits, (2) the hegemony of underclass discourse as a frame for discussing racial inequality and poverty, and (3) the Left's failure to think carefully and critically about black politics and the ways that it connects with the role of race in the American stratification system.

The Limits of Incorporation

Systemic incorporation along four dimensions has been the most significant development in black urban politics since the 1960s. First, enforcement of the Voting Rights Act has increased the efficacy of black electoral participation; invalidation of cruder forms of racial gerrymandering and biased electoral systems, as well as redress against intimidation, have made it easier for black voters to elect candidates.[1]

Second, a corollary of that electoral efficacy, has been the dramatic increase of black elected officials. Their existence has become a fact of life in U.S. politics and has shaped the modalities of race relations management. Black elected officials tend to operate within already existing governing coalitions at the local level and within the imperatives of the Democratic party's internal politics, as well as with an eye to their constituents. The logic of incumbency, moreover, is race-blind and favors reelection above all else. Not surprisingly, black officeholders tend to be disposed to articulate their black constituents' interests in ways that are compatible with those other commitments.

Third, black people have increasingly assumed administrative control of the institutions of urban governance. Housing authorities, welfare departments, school systems, even public safety departments are ever more likely to be run by black officials, and black functionaries are likely to be prominent at all levels within those organizations.[2] Those agencies have their own attentive constituencies within the black electorate, radiating out into the family and friendship networks of personnel. And a substratum of professional, often geographically mobile public functionaries with commitments to public management ideologies may now constitute a relatively autonomous interest configuration within black politics. This dimension of incorporation short-circuits critiques of those agencies' operations crafted within the racially inflected language most familiar to black insurgency. A critique that pivots on racial legitimacy as a standard for evaluating institutional behavior cannot be effective—as a basis for either organizing opposition or stimulating critical public debate—in a situation in which blacks conspicuously run the institutions. Because they have their own black constituencies and greater access to resources for shaping public opinion, public officials have the advantage in any debate that rests simplistically on determining racial authenticity.

A fourth and related dimension of incorporation is the integration of private civil rights and uplift organizations into a regime of race relations management driven by incrementalist, insider negotiation.[3] The tracings of this process could be seen dramatically at the national level during the Jimmy Carter administration with the inclusion of Jesse Jackson's Operation Push and the National Urban League as line item accounts in Department of Labor budgets. The boundaries between state agendas and elites and those of black nongovernment organizations may even be more porous at the local level, where personnel commonly move back and forth from one payroll system to another and where close coordination with local interest groupings is woven more seamlessly into the texture of everyday life.

An effect has arguably been further to skew the black politically attentive public toward the new regime of race relations management. On the one hand, generation of a professional world of public/private race relations engineers drawn from politically attentive elements of the black population channels issue-articulation and agenda-formation processes in black politics in ways reflecting the regime's common sense. On the other hand, insofar as the nongovernmental organizations and their elites carry the historical sediment of adversarial, protest politics, their integration into the new regime further ratifies its protocols as the only thinkable politics.

These trajectories of incorporation have yielded real benefits for the black citizenry. They have enhanced income and employment opportunity and have injected a greater measure of fairness into the distribution of public benefits in large and small ways. Black citizens have greater access now to the informal networks through which ordinary people use government to get things done—find summer jobs for their children, obtain zoning variances and building permits, get people out of jail, remove neighborhood nuisances, or site parks and libraries. Objectives that not long ago required storming city council meetings now can be met through routine processes. These accomplishments often are dismissed in some quarters on the Left as trivial and evidence of co-optation. Certainly, such characterizations are true "in the last analysis," but we don't live and can't do effective politics "in the last analysis." For them to function effectively as co-optation, for example, the fruits of incorporation cannot be trivial for those who partake or expect to be able to partake of them. The inclination to dismiss them reflects instead problematic tendencies within the Left to trivialize and simultaneously to demonize the exercise of public authority.

The new regime of race relations management as realized through the four-pronged dynamic of incorporation has exerted a *demobilizing* effect on black politics precisely by virtue of its capacities for delivering benefits and for defining what benefits political action can legitimately be used to pursue. Ease in voting and in producing desired electoral outcomes legitimizes that form as the primary means of political participation, which naturally seems attractive compared with others that require more extensive and intensive commitment of attention and effort. A result is to narrow the operative conception of political engagement to one form, and the most passive one at that.

Incumbent public officials generically have an interest in dampening the possibilities for new or widespread mobilization because of its intrinsic volatility. Uncontrolled participation can produce unpleasant electoral surprises and equally can interfere with the reigning protocols through which public agencies discharge their functions. As popular participation narrows, the inertial logic of incumbency operates to constrict the field of political discourse. Incumbents respond to durable interests, and they seek predictability, continuity, and a shared common sense. This translates into a preference for a brokered "politics as usual" that limits the number and range of claims on the policy agenda. Such a politics preserves the thrust of inherited policy regimes and reinforces existing patterns of systemic advantage by limiting the boundaries of the politically reasonable.[4] The same is true for the insider-negotiation processes through which the nongovernmental organizations now define their roles, and those organizations often earn their insider status by providing a convincing alternative to popular political mobilization.

Underclass Rhetoric and the Disappearance of Politics

Fueled largely by sensationalist journalism and supposedly tough-minded, policy-oriented social scientists, underclass rhetoric became over the 1980s the main frame within which to discuss inner-city poverty and inequality.

The pundits and scholars who created this "underclass" define the stratum's membership in a variety of slightly differing ways; however, they all circle around a basic characterization that roots it among inner-city blacks and Hispanics, and they share a consensual assessment that the underclass makes up about 20 percent of the impoverished population in inner cities.[5]

The underclass notion is a contemporary extrapolation from a Victorian petit bourgeois fantasy world, and it is almost invariably harnessed to arguments for reactionary and punitive social policy. Even at its best—that is, when it is connected with some agenda other than pure stigmatization and denial of public responsibility—this rhetoric is depoliticizing and thus demobilizing in at least three ways.

First, the underclass frame does not direct attention to the political-economic dynamics that produce and reproduce dispossession and its entailments but focuses instead on behavioral characteristics alleged to exist among the victims of those dynamics. The result is to immerse discussion of inequality, poverty, and racial stratification in often overlapping rhetorics of individual or collective pathogenesis and knee-jerk moral evaluation. Conservatives bask in the simplicity of a discourse that revolves around racialized stigmatization of people as good, bad, or defective.[6] Even those versions propounded by liberals, like that offered by William Julius Wilson, which purport to provide structurally grounded accounts of inner-city inequality, describe the "underclass" in primarily behavioral terms.[7]

In both conservative and putatively liberal versions, the underclass rhetoric reinforces tendencies to demobilization by situating debate about poverty and inequality not in the public realm of politics—which would warrant examination of the role of public action in the reproduction of an unequal distribution of material costs and benefits (for example, federal and local housing and redevelopment policies that feed ghettoization and favor suburbs over inner cities, that favor homeowners over renters in the face of widespread and blatant racial discrimination in access to mortgages, and subsidies for urban deindustrialization and disinvestment)—but on the ostensibly private realm of individual values and behavior, pivoting specifically on images of male criminality and female slovenliness and irresponsible sexuality. The specter of drugs and gangs is omnipresent as well, underscoring the composite image of a wanton, depraved Other and automatically justifying any extreme of official repression and brutality. Even when acknowledged as unfounded, invocation of suspicion of the presence of drugs and gangs exculpates arbitrary violation of civil liberties in inner cities and police brutality to the extent of homicide.

Insofar as this focus opens to public policy at all, it tilts toward social and police repression, as in ubiquitous proposals for draconian "welfare reform" that seek only to codify the punitive moralism propelling the underclass narrative. That essentially racialized agenda is not likely to fuel broad political mobilization among black Americans, not in service to progressive agendas, at any rate.

Second, the underclass rhetoric reinforces demobilization because of its very nature as a third-person discourse. As a rhetoric of stigmatization, it is deployed about rather than by any real population. No one self-identifies as a member of the underclass. To that extent, as well as because the rhetoric presumes their incompetence, exhortations of the stigmatized population to undertake any concerted political action on their own behalf are unthinkable.

Its association with "self-help" ideology is in fact the third way that the underclass narrative undercuts popular mobilization. Because behavioral pathology appears in that narrative as at least the proximate source of poverty, inequality, and even contemporary racial discrimination, the programmatic responses that arise most naturally within its purview are those geared to correcting the supposed defects of the target population. This biases programmatic discussion toward bootstrap initiatives that claim moral rehabilitation of impoverished individuals and communities as part of their mission.

In this context two apparently different streams of neo-Jeffersonian romanticism—those associated respectively with the 1960s' New Left and Reaganism—converge on an orientation that eschews government action on principle in favor of voluntarist, "community-based" initiatives. Particularly when steeped in a language of "empowerment," this antistatist convergence overlaps current manifestations of a conservative, bootstrap tendency among black elites that stretches back at least through Booker T. Washington at the turn of the century. Indeed, it was the Reagan administration's evil genius to appeal to that tendency by shifting from a first-term tactic that projected combative black voices, like Thomas Sowell and Clarence Pendleton, to a more conciliatory style exemplified by Glenn Loury. In Reagan's second term the administration apparently opted for a different posture as a new group of its black supporters, led by Loury and Robert Woodson of the National Center for Neighborhood Enterprise, stepped into the spotlight. Although this wave of black Reaganauts could be pugnacious with adversaries, they were far more inclined than their predecessors to make overtures to the entrenched race relations elite. Those overtures

disarmed partisan skepticism by emphasizing the black middle class's supposedly special responsibility for correcting the underclass and the problems associated with it.[8]

Underwriting this version of self-help are three interlocked claims: (1)
that black inner cities are beset by grave and self-regenerative problems of
social breakdown and pathology that have undermined the possibility of
normal civic life, (2) that these problems are beyond the reach of positive
state action, and (3) that they can be addressed only by private, voluntarist
black action led by the middle class. Over the late 1980s and early 1990s
these three claims—each dubious enough on its own, all justified at most
by appeal to lurid anecdotes, self-righteous prejudices, and crackerbarrel
social theory—congealed into hegemonic wisdom. Black public figures
supposedly identified with the Left, like Jesse Jackson, Roger Wilkins, and
Cornel West, have become as devout proselytizers of this catechistic orthodoxy as are rightists like Woodson, Loury, and Clarence Thomas.[9]

The rise and consolidation of the Democratic Leadership Council and
the "New Liberalism" as dominant within the Democratic party no doubt
reinforced and were reinforced by black self-help bromides' elevation to
the status of conventional wisdom. On the one hand, black self-help rhetoric
historically has been associated with presumptions that blacks have no hope
for allies in pursuit of justice through public policy, and the successful of-
fensive of Democratic "centrists" and neoliberals—predicated in large part
on flight from identification with both perceived black interests and down-
wardly redistributive social policy—certainly lends credence to the impression that the federal government is not a dependable ally of black objectives.
Even the celebrated declamations by New Liberal consciences Bill Bradley
and John Kerry for racial justice and tolerance were mainly, after brief statements against bigotry, extended characterizations of impoverished inner cities
as savage hearts of darkness, saturated in self-destructive violence and pathology; the speeches carried no particular warrant for action addressing inequality and its effects except calls for moral uplift.

Despite its foundation on notions of grassroots activism, the self-help
regime is best seen as community mobilization for political demobilization.
Each attempt by a neighborhood or church group to scrounge around the
philanthropic world and the interstices of the federal system for funds to
build low-income housing or day-care or neighborhood centers or to organize programs that compensate for inadequate school funding, public safety,
or trash pickup, simultaneously concedes the point that black citizens cannot legitimately pursue those benefits through government. This is a very

dangerous concession in an ideological context defined largely by a logic that, like that in the post-Reconstruction era of the last century, could extend to an almost genocidal expulsion of black citizens toward a bantustanized periphery of society.

We cannot concede the important ground of black people's equal proprietorship of public institutions with all other citizens; affirming the legitimacy of black Americans' demands on the state—on an equal basis with those who receive defense contracts, homeownership subsidies, investment tax credits, flood protection, and a host of other benefits from government—is also affirming black Americans' equal membership in the polity. The more ground we give on this front, the more the latter-day versions of the Southern Redeemers will take. Frederick Douglass put it succinctly, "The limits of tyrants are prescribed by the endurance of those whom they oppress."

The problem with self-help ideology is that it reifies community initiative, freighting it with an ideological burden that reduces to political quietism and a programmatic mission it is ill equipped to fulfill. It is absurd to present neighborhood and church initiatives as appropriate responses to the effects of government-supported disinvestment, labor market segmentation, widespread and well-documented patterns of discrimination in employment and housing as well as in the trajectory of direct and indirect public spending, and an all-out corporate assault on the social wage.

Its endorsement by public officials is a particularly ironic aspect of the self-help rhetoric. That endorsement amounts to an admission of failure, an acknowledgment that the problems afflicting their constituents are indeed beyond the scope of the institutional apparatus under their control, that black officials are in fact powerless to provide services to inner-city citizens effectively through those institutions.

A key to overcoming the demobilizing effects of self-help ideology, as well as those of underclass rhetoric more generally, lies in stimulation of strategic debate—grounded in the relation between social conditions affecting the black population and public policy and the larger political-economic tendencies to which it responds—within and about black political activity. This in turn requires attending to the complex dynamics of interest and ideological differentiation that operate within black politics, taking into account the who-gets-what-when-where-how dimension of politics as it appears among black political agents and interest configurations. In principle, the Left should be intimately engaged in this project, which is the stock-in-trade of Left political analysis.

The Left and Black Politics

By outlawing official segregation and discriminatory restrictions on political participation, the Voting Rights Act and the 1964 Civil Rights Act ren-
dered obsolete the least common denominator—opposition to Jim Crow—
that for more than a half-century had given black political activity coherence
and a pragmatic agenda plausibly understood to be shared uniformly among
the black citizenry.[10] (This effect no doubt is a factor—along with the
spread of self-help ideology and the aging of the population that can recall
the ancien régime—driving contemporary nostalgia for the sense of community that supposedly flourished under segregation. That perception was
always more apparent than real; the coherence and cohesiveness were most
of all artifacts of the imperatives of the Jim Crow system and the struggle
against it. In black politics as elsewhere, what appears as political cohesiveness has been the assertion of one tendency over others coexisting and
competing with it—in this case, first, white elites' successful projection of
Booker T. Washington's capitulationist program and then, for the half-century after Washington's death, the primacy of the focus on attacking codified segregation.) The Voting Rights Act, additionally, ensued in opening
new possibilities, concrete objectives and incentives for political action, and
new, more complex relations with mainstream political institutions, particularly government and the Democratic party at all levels.

In the decade after 1965 black political activity came increasingly to re-
volve around gaining, enhancing, or maintaining official representation in
public institutions and the distribution of associated material and symbolic
benefits. The greatest increases in black elective-office holding occurred
during those years. That period also saw the rise of black urban governance,
both in black-led municipal regimes and in growing black authority in the
urban administrative apparatus.

At the same time this shift exposed a long-standing tension in black
political discourse between narrower and broader constructions of the practical agenda for realizing racially democratic interests. The narrower view
has focused political objectives on singular pursuit of racial inclusion, either
accepting the structure and performance of political and economic institutions as given or presuming that black representation is an adequate basis
for correcting what might be unsatisfactory about them. The essence of this
view was distilled, appropriately, in two pithy formulations in the late 1960s:
the slogan demanding "black faces in previously all-white places" and the
proposition that, as an ideal, black Americans should make up 12 percent

of corporate executives, 12 percent of the unemployed, and 12 percent of everything in between.[11] The broader tendency is perhaps best seen as an ensemble of views joined by inclination toward structural critique. This tendency sees simple racial inclusion as inadequate and argues for tying political action to insurgent programs that seek either to transform existing institutions or to reject them altogether in favor of race nationalist or social revolutionary alternatives.

The tension between these two views has been a recurring issue in black politics, overlapping and crosscutting—and, arguably, being mistaken for—other fault lines that appear more commonly in the historiography of black political debate (for example, the militant/moderate, protest/accommodationist, and integrationist/nationalist dichotomies).[12] In the 1960s, however, the combination of broad popular mobilization and heightened prospects for victory against legally enforced exclusion made this tension more prominent than at any prior time except during the 1930s and early 1940s, when Ralph Bunche and other Young Turks pushed sharp, Marxist-inspired critiques into the main lines of black debate.

Black accession to responsible positions in the apparatus of public management enabled for the first time—save for fleeting moments in Reconstruction—a discourse focused on the concrete, nuts-and-bolts, incrementalist exercise of public authority. Three factors compel the new pragmatic orientation toward incrementalism. First, the inclusionist program had developed largely as an insider politics, seeking legitimacy in part through emphasis of loyalty, particularly in the cold war context, to prevailing political and economic arrangements except insofar as those were racially exclusionary. To that extent it has been predisposed to take existing systemic and institutional imperatives as given. Second, experience in War on Poverty and Great Society programs socialized the pool of potential black officials into the public management system's entrenched protocols and operating logic, initiating them into existing policy processes. This socialization spurred articulation of a rhetoric exalting realpolitik and keying strategic consideration only to advancement of black representation among beneficiaries within existing institutional regimes.[13] This notion of political pragmatism not only reinforces incrementalism; it also requires a shifting construction of "black" interests to conform to options set in a received policy and issue framework. For instance, Mayor Maynard Jackson strained to define one of the alternatives in a developers' fight over siting a new Atlanta airport as the black choice, although building a second airport on either location would have had no discernibly positive impact on black Atlantans; public

192 / Adolph Reed Jr.

support for the project on any site, moreover, would amount to a redistribution of fiscal resources away from the city's black population to developers
and remote, generally hostile metropolitan economic interests.[14] Finally, inclusionist politics affords no larger vision around which to orient a critical
perspective on either the operations and general functions of political institutions or the general thrust of public policy. This characteristic, which
might appear as political myopia, is rationalizable as pragmatic; in any event,
it further reinforces incrementalism by screening out broader issues and
concerns.

The hegemony of incrementalism has facilitated elaboration of a political discourse that sidesteps a critical problem at the core of post-segregation-era black politics: the tension between black officials' institutional legitimation and their popular electoral legitimation. The institutions that
black officials administer are driven by the imperatives of managing systemic racial subordination, but the expectations they cultivate among their
constituents define the role of black administrative representation in those
institutions as a de facto challenge to racial subordination.

So by the 1990s it was commonplace to see black housing authority
directors' policy innovations run to advocating lockdowns and random police sweeps, black school superintendents discussing their duties principally
through a rhetoric of discipline and calling for punishment of parents of
transgressors in their charge, black mayors and legislators locked into a victim-blaming interpretive frame accenting drug abuse and criminality as the
only actionable social problems—and all falling back on the bromides
about family breakdown and moral crisis among their constituents to explain the inadequacy of public services. This rhetoric obscures their capitu-
lation to business-led programs of regressive redistribution—tax breaks
and other subsidies, as well as general subservience to development interests in planning and policy formulation—that contribute further to fiscal
strain, thus justifying still further service cuts, which increase pressure for
giving more to development interests to stimulate "growth" that supposedly will build the tax base, and so on. From this perspective, Sharon Pratt
Kelly's Washington, D.C., mayoralty is emblematic; her tenure was distinguished only by repeated service and personnel cuts and her 1993 call for
the National Guard to buttress municipal police efforts—even as the District of Columbia already has one of the highest police-to-citizen ratios in
the United States. There could hardly be a more striking illustration of the
extent to which minority public officials are the equivalent of Bantustan

administrators. Incrementalism serves as blinders, sword, and shield. It blocks alternative courses from view, delegitimizes criticism with incantations of realpolitik, and provides a Pontius Pilate defense of any action by characterizing officials as incapable of acting on their circumstances.[15]

Continued debate with the oppositional tendency in black politics could have mitigated the corrosive effects of incrementalist hegemony. Such debate might have broadened somewhat the perspective from which black officials themselves define pragmatic agendas. It might have stimulated among black citizens a practical, policy-oriented public discourse that would either have supported black officials in the articulation of bold initiatives and/or held them accountable to autonomously generated programmatic agendas and concerns.

Yet few would dispute the argument that radicalism has been routed in postsegregation black politics. Some fit that fact into a naturalistic reading of incorporation: radicalism automatically wanes as avenues open for regular political participation. Others concede incrementalist, petit bourgeois hegemony in electoral politics but claim that radicalism's social base has not been destroyed but only displaced to other domains — dormant mass anger, Louis Farrakhan's apparent popularity, rap music and other extrusions of youth culture, literary production, and the like — suggesting a need to reconceptualize politics to reflect the significance of such phenomena. Both sorts of response, however, evade giving an account of how the radical tendency was expunged from the black political mainstream, which is critically important for making sense of the limitations of inherited forms of black radicalism and for the task of constructing a progressive black politics in the present.

The oppositional tendency in postsegregation black politics was hampered by an aspect of its origin in black power ideology. Radicals — all along the spectrum, ranging from cultural nationalist to Stalinoid Marxist — began from a stance that took the "black community" as the central configuration of political interest and the source of critical agency. This stance grew from black power rhetoric's emphasis on "community control" and its projection of the "community" as touchstone of legitimacy and insurgent authenticity. This formulation is a presumptive claim for the existence of a racial population that is organically integrated and that operates as a collective subject in pursuit of unitary interests. That claim, which persists as a grounding principle in black strategic discourse, is problematic in two linked ways that bear on elaboration of a critical politics.

First, positing a black collectivity as an organic political agent preempts questions of interest differentiation. If the "community" operates with a single will and a single agenda, then there is neither need nor basis for evaluating political programs or policies with respect to their impact on differing elements of the black population. Any initiative enjoying conspicuous support from any group of black people can be said plausibly to reflect the community's preference or interest; the metaphorical organicism that drives the "black community" formulation presumes that what is good for one is good for all.

Similarly, because the organic black community is construed as naturalistic, the notion precludes discussion of both criteria of political representation and the definition of constituencies. Those issues become matters for concern when the relevant polity is perceived to be made up of diverse and not necessarily compatible interests and/or when the relation between representatives and represented is seen as contingent and mediated rather than cellular or isomorphic. By contrast, in the black community construct those who appear as leaders or spokespersons are not so much representatives as pure embodiments of collective aspirations.

As the stratum of black public officials emerged, black power radicalism's limitations became visible. Blacks' accession to prominence within the institutional apparatus of urban administration did not appreciably alter the mission or official practices of the institutions in their charge. Putting black faces in previously all-white places was not sufficient for those who identified with institutional transformation along populist lines or who otherwise rejected the status quo of race relations management. Yet, because black power's communitarian premises reified group identity and could not accommodate structural differentiation among Afro-Americans, the only critical frame on which radicals could draw consensually was the language of racial authenticity.

By the end of the 1960s, black power's inadequacy as a basis for concrete political judgment had begun to fuel radicals' self-conscious turn to creation and adoption of "ideologies" — global political narratives encompassing alternative vision, norms, and strategic programs — that promised to provide definite standpoints for critical judgment and platforms for political mobilization. This development underwrote a logic of sectarianism that embedded a cleavage between Marxists and cultural nationalists as the pivotal tension in black oppositional politics.

Ironically, the impetus propelling the ideological turn — the need to compensate for the inadequacies of black power's simplistic communitarianism—was thwarted by failure to break with the essential flaw, the stance positing the "black community" as the source of political legitimation and its attendant rhetoric of authenticity. Indeed, the turn to ideology may have reinforced propensities to rely on communitarian mystification because the flight into theoreticism made the need to claim connections with popular action all the more urgent.

The quandary faced by the oppositional politics that evolved from black power produced two main organizational responses: the National Black Political Assembly (NBPA) and the African Liberation Support Committee (ALSC).[16] The NBPA, which grew from the 1972 National Black Political Convention at Gary, was spearheaded by the cultural nationalist camp and was an attempt to unite activists and elected officials in support of a common, generically black agenda. Reflecting the view that there is a racial political interest that transcends other affiliations or commitments, the NBPA was organized on Imamu Amiri Baraka's principle of "unity without uniformity." ALSC was the outgrowth of an ad hoc African Liberation Day Coordinating Committee that had organized the first African Liberation Day national mobilization, also in 1972. Creation of ALSC reflected a concern to formalize a presence to act in support of African liberation movements, particularly in the Portugese colonies, Rhodesia, South Africa, and southwest Africa. Like the NBPA, ALSC was in principle ecumenically black. ALSC differed, however, in its focus on popular mobilization; its agenda centered on mass political education and agitation, largely in concert with organizing an annual African Liberation Day demonstration, as well as fund-raising for annual allocations to designated liberation movements. To that extent ALSC was more an activist organization and was somewhat less oriented to building formal relationships with mainstream politicians. Both organizations represented radicals' desire to define a space for oppositional politics in the postsegregation context; both were attempts to create organizational bases that could institutionalize racially autonomous radicalism in the new Afro-American political culture and facilitate pursuit of practical agendas consonant with black power ideological positions. There was also substantial overlap in radicals' participation in the two organizations.

Even with their best intentions, however, the radicals in ALSC failed to connect with an effective social base. Efforts to create a popular constituency by perfecting and propagating one or another abstract ideology required that people disengage from their worlds of lived experience and undergo a process of ontological change not unlike conversion. Neither Marxists nor nationalists offered programs with demonstrable payoffs comparable to those promised by mainstream politicians; more important, neither radical camp provided concretely persuasive or inspiring critiques of mainstream agendas. To that extent, they held out no reason to compel the leap of faith for which they called. In those circumstances radicals were incapable of braking or modifying mainstream politicians' assertion of hegemony, and ALSC collapsed entirely into sectarian infighting. By 1977 all that remained was a squabble over the organization's carcass, as three factions simultaneously held competing "national" African Liberation Day demonstrations in Washington.

In both Marxist and nationalist camps the ideological turn was an imposition on rather than a product of analysis of the forces animating black American politics. As a consequence, radicals were never moved to confront the ideal of effective political agency that they had brought forward from black power rhetoric—the reified notion of the "black community" and the language of racial authenticity attendant to it. Because the black community idea is a mystification, it gives no solid standpoint from which to situate policies or political programs.

So expired the last gasp of the autonomous black radicalism spawned in the 1960s. Paroxysms continued here and there. The Communist Workers party's 1979 shootout with the Ku Klux Klan in Greensboro, North Carolina, for instance, was the culmination of a sectarian spiral that reached back through ALSC to a pan-Africanist and black power activism rooted in dynamic labor and poor people's organizations. Individuals and networks adjusted to the new regime and attempted to advance progressive interests within it; some simply were incorporated. Nevertheless, by the time Jimmy Carter was elected president no signs of institutionalized opposition were visible in black political life except on a sectarian fringe; all traces of alternatives to the incrementalist program of black officialdom had been expunged from Afro-American civic discourse. In 1977, for example, Mayor Maynard Jackson was able to fire two thousand striking black Atlanta sanitation workers without significant dissent; he won reelection in the same year with over three-fourths of the vote.[17] The victory of the new regime was so complete that in the early 1980s liberal social scientists ratified it in whiggish accounts that represented the contemporary status quo as the precise goal toward which the previous generation of black activism had unfolded smoothly, willfully, and ineluctably. This fundamentally Orwellian victor's narrative canonized as the only thinkable reality—the teleological fulfillment of black political aspiration—what was in fact the outcome of contingency and contestation, thus denying space for radical critique in both present and past.

The purblindness that has omitted post-black-power radicalism from accounts of the transition "from protest to politics" partly reflects a perspective that derives from either prior commitment to incrementalist politics or premises that apprehend black political activity in relation to a simple inclusion/exclusion axis. From either vantage point it seems natural and automatic that the mainstream, incrementalist agenda would become hegemonic upon removal of fetters blocking regular, systemically conventional forms of political participation. Omission occurs also, however, because the radical tendencies that emerged from black power sensibilities were purely endogenous to black politics. Consonant with their black power origins, radicals actively sought to maintain a racially exclusive universe of critical political discourse; they generally neither pursued interaction with whites nor were centrally concerned with interracialism as an issue. Therefore, those strains of autonomous black radicalism were largely invisible to white observers, who as a rule do not attend closely to machinations internal to black politics.

Whites' failure to discern endogenous tendencies among Afro-Americans extends across the political spectrum and has clearly undermined the Left's ability to generate an appropriate strategic approach to black political activity. At least since the Students for a Democratic Society's 1969 proclamation of the Black Panther party as the "vanguard of the black revolution" two problematic features have organized white Left discourse about Afro-American politics: (1) a reluctance to see black political interests and activity as internally differentiated in ways that are grounded in social structure and (2) a converging focus on willingness to align with whites as the primary criterion for making judgments about individuals or currents in black politics. The first problem stems from and reinforces the familiar assumption of the existence of an organic "black community." In white strategic discourse this notion not only has the same evasive and counterproductive qualities as it does in black political rhetoric; it also implies that black life is opaque to those outside it. Knowledge appears to require identifying individuals or groups who reflect the authentic mood, sentiments, will, or preferences of the reified community. This impulse places a premium on articulate black spokespersons to act as emissaries to the white Left. By definition, such emissaries—even if they adopt a different posture—satisfy the interracialism criterion, and the operative premises and biases leave no space for interrogating the claims to authentic- ity or popular legitimacy that underlie the role of racial emissary.

This circumstance led to the irony that in the 1980s—thanks in part to the consolidation of Democratic Socialists of America, which provided a national forum—the institutional apparatus of the white Left began desig- nating and projecting one black figure after another as the voice of black radical activism, long after the last embers of organized oppositional ac- tivism had been expunged. In the absence of independent knowledge or nuanced insight regarding black politics, assessment of claims to authentic- ity ultimately relies on the appeal that a given claimant's persona or stance offers to white auditors. Critical evaluation tends toward designation of good and bad, true and false black leaders. This failing has underwritten in one venue after another—as, for example, in the case of former New York City mayor, David Dinkins—a cycle of exaggerated estimation of the pro- gressive commitments of black mainstream politicians followed by crashing disillusionment when they fail to live up to expectations. This cycle not only impedes practical strategic analysis; it has also greased the skids of this generation's "god-that-failed" rightward political slide. Treatment of blacks as bearers of a deeper humanity and higher morality opens to a rhetoric of betrayal, and the imagery shifts to venality and immorality—thus synec- dochically justifying resistance to black political aspirations.

The costly and dangerous entailments of the white Left's approach to black politics reached a national apotheosis in the knee-jerk embrace of Jesse Jackson's campaign of self-promotion. In 1984 Jackson, who had been a consummate insider for at least a decade, proclaimed himself an outsider, parlaying a well-publicized southern speaking tour into a Potemkin move- ment. He traded precisely on gullibility about the organic black community to project himself as the literal embodiment of a popular black insurgency.

The Left generally—black and white—accepted Jackson's propaganda on face value, in part through simple wish fulfillment but in part also out of opportunistic attempts to ride on his coattails. Black activists' hopes to co-opt Jackson's initiative demonstrated naiveté regarding their ability to manipu- late politicians to advance their ends. Having established himself as the sup- posed champion of a Rainbow Coalition of the "locked out," between 1984 and 1988 Jackson abandoned his outsider posture and tightened his links with black regular Democrats. He had pried open a space for himself, momentar- ily at least, as primus inter pares in the national black political elite and had attained a quasi official status in the Democratic hierarchy—both mainly on the strength of his claim to represent a popular black constituency. This claim was legitimized by the enthusiastic assent of his activist supporters, who sought through his cachet to create just such a constituency.

As it had for the NBPA and ALSC in the mid-1970s, this gambit backfired for the Rainbow Coalition activists. Radicals hardly succeeded in using Jackson to gain access to a popular base; instead, he used and discarded them. Significantly, skepticism in the white Left about the Jackson phenomenon revolved primarily around the extent to which he would attempt to fashion a multiracial constituency. There was no significant effort to undertake critique of Jackson's essentially personalistic appeal to black voters or to make sense of his role in black politics. From this perspective, for instance, Jackson's move between 1984 and 1988 boosted his progressive credentials because of his elaborate, if pro forma and symbolic, multiracialist gestures in the latter campaign—even though those gestures were crafted to project his image as a responsible insider.[18]

The combination of opportunism and evasive romanticism that blocked critical evaluation of Jackson's enterprise also left both black and white insurgents without effective response to its denouement. After all the symbolic rhetoric, photo ops with striking workers, and canned leftist position papers, Jackson bargained at the Democratic convention for an airplane to use in campaigning for nominee Michael Dukakis and payoffs for cronies—benefits even skimpier and more narrowly personal than the ornamental fruits of his brokerage in 1984. Between 1988 and 1994 he provided ample evidence of his self-aggrandizing and conservative agenda—launch of a talk show career, quixotic definition of statehood for the District of Columbia as the most important civil rights issue of our time, the "Shadow Senator" farce, pouting refusal to commit to or dissent from any candidate in the 1992 Democratic nominating process, and worst of all his proclamation that black criminality is the central problem in contemporary Afro-American life.

In both of his campaigns radicals endorsed Jackson's rhetoric of hope and inspiration as a way to sidestep grappling with empirically dubious claims about his impact on black voter registration and turnout and his candidacy's electoral coattail effects. In the process these evasions obscured the possibility that, despite his constant allegations that the Democratic party takes black voters for granted, Jackson's campaign facilitated just such an outcome. Especially in 1988, when it was clear from the beginning that Jackson would have nearly unanimous black support, the other contenders for the nomination made only perfunctory appeals to black voters during the primaries. Without Jackson's presence in the field at least some of the other candidates may have courted black Democrats, if only to gain a comparative electoral advantage in the South. With the black primary vote—and that of the party's left wing as well—conceded to Jackson, however, the others simply could avoid addressing black interests until the convention, at which point the eventual winner could broker some concessions to Jackson in the name of Afro-American and progressive concerns.

In this regard also, Jackson's campaign may well have strengthened the party's rightist faction, formalized as the Democratic Leadership Council (DLC) in the aftermath of Mondale's defeat.[19] The two Jackson campaigns were arguably purely beneficial for the Democratic Right. Jackson's insurgency maximized black visibility yet posed no genuine threat programmatically, because at the same time it demobilized blacks' participation in the debate over the party's future substantively and strategically. It demobilized black Democrats substantively by defining their interests solely in relation to Jackson's personal fortunes and strategically by funneling black action through his insider's style of brokerage politics. By 1992 the rightist narrative had become nearly hegemonic in the Democratic party and in the society at large, thanks principally to its continual, virtually unchallenged repetition as fact by sympathetic journalists and academics.

Of course, the Jackson insurgency did not generate the DLC camp, which would have sought to stigmatize blacks and the Left anyway. The critical problem is that Jackson's radical supporters reproduced the pattern of opportunism and abstract purism that has consistently evaded tough-minded analysis of the practical forces driving American politics and black politics in particular. As a result, they were unable to respond frankly and forthrightly to Jackson's increasingly crude, personalistic maneuverings after 1988. In acquiescing to a frame that designates Jackson ascriptively as the embodiment of progressive interests, leftists and black activists sacrificed the political distance that would give a critical foundation from which to assess his behavior.

Certainly, by the time the 1992 Democratic field was set, there was no real Left option; Kerry, Clinton, and Tsongas all operated entirely within the new rightist conventions, and even the short-lived Harkin candidacy—perhaps the last gasp of the party's labor-Left wing—was ambivalent in practice if not rhetoric about catering to the white middle class. In this environment no challenge appeared when the well-organized Clinton forces swept through, remonstrating with black elites to support their candidate without questions because his nomination was a fait accompli. The Clinton campaign exploited a long-standing problem in black political life, the tendency to conflate descriptive representation and representation of substantive interests. By defining representation among campaign leadership and prospective appointments as the key shorthand expression of openness to black concerns, Clinton and his black supporters manipulated this tendency—which Jackson's insistent personalism had ensconced as the coin of militant black critique—to avoid confronting the material implications of his rightist "New Democrat" agenda for black Americans.

Considering a counterfactual may highlight the limits of the Jackson phenomenon more clearly. What forms could an effective Left insurgent Democratic candidacy have taken? In the first place it would have had to proceed from an institutional base within the party's left wing and from a coherent, well-articulated programmatic agenda—not the whim of a random individual. Any such insurgency most likely would have little chance of actually winning the nomination; its objectives would have to be gaining specific programmatic concessions, exerting a leftward pull on political debate, and perhaps strengthening and building progressive networks within the party and outside. And those objectives require relative clarity of political vision and concreteness of strategy. The focus would have to be on advancing a specific program or critique rather than an individual. The candidate-centered bias in U.S. electoral politics creates openings to co-optation for which an insurgent movement would have to compensate by fastening the candidacy as much as possible to a concrete agenda. The Jackson candidacies met none of these criteria.

In the current situation black (and white) radicalism has retreated ever more hermetically into the university, and the unaddressed tendency to wish fulfillment has reached new extremes, so that oppositional politics becomes little more than a pose livening up the march through the tenure ranks. The context of desperation and utter defeat enveloping activist politics outside the academy has not only reinforced the retreat to the campus; it has also removed practical fetters on the compensatory imagination guiding the creation of intentionally oppositional academic discourses. In this context the notion of radicalism is increasingly removed from critique and substantive action directed toward altering entrenched patterns of subordination and inequality mediated through public policy.

The characteristics of this dynamic are mainly crystallized in the turn to a rhetoric pivoting on an idea of "cultural politics." The discourse of cultural politics does not differentiate between public, collective activity explicitly challenging patterns of political and socioeconomic hierarchy and the typically surreptitious, often privatistic practices of "everyday resistance"—the mechanisms through which subordinates construct moments of dignity and autonomy and enhance their options within relations of oppression without attacking them head on. The failure to make any such distinction—or making and then eliding it—dramatizes the fate that befalls black radicalism's separation of abstract theorizing from concrete political action when academic hermeticism eliminates the imperative to think about identifying and mobilizing a popular constituency. Participating in youth fads, maintaining fraternal organizations, vesting hopes in prayer or root doctors, and even quilt making thus become indistinguishable from slave revolts, activism in Reconstruction governments, the Montgomery bus boycott, grassroots campaigns for voter registration, and labor union or welfare rights agitation as politically meaningful forms of "resistance."[20]

Conclusion

The collapse of popularly based radicalism in the 1970s underlies the failure of a critical politics to develop as a significant force, even in response to the Reagan-Bush years' heavy-handed assault on the interests of racial equality. The demise of that autonomous radical strain has had important and extensive consequences. For instance, the absence of a populist activism has eliminated a constraint on the incrementalist, demobilizing tendencies of systemic incorporation. To that extent, it has distorted the development of what might have been, as some thought, a functional division of labor or, what was more likely, a creative tension between the new black public officialdom and attentive black constituencies. That tension could well have broadened processes of interest articulation and differentiation in black politics and brought them into the realm of public debate.

Contrary to the communitarian reflex on which Afro-American political discourse has pivoted for a generation, stimulation of overt interest-group dynamics—organized on the basis of neighborhood, class, gender, occupation, or other aspects of social status, as well as a variety of interest groups whose memberships overlapped and other coalitional activity—could enrich democratic participation by encouraging controversy among black Americans over the concrete, tangible implications of policy issues. A sharply focused civic discourse grounded on the interplay of clearly articulated interests could feed political mobilization, both electoral and otherwise, by highlighting the human impact of government action and the stakes of political activity in general. Elaboration of a political discourse based explicitly on a consideration of the differential allocation of costs and benefits of public policy within an attentive, relatively mobilizable polity could also increase public officials' accountability to the black constituencies they purportedly represent.

It certainly seems possible that systemic incorporation might have occurred on terms that embedded more seriously progressive vision and momentum in black politics than has been the case. Either because electoral processes may have produced individuals independently more attuned to progressive black agendas or because of the need to respond to popular pressure, an outcome could have been a stratum of mainstream politicians and officials at least marginally more inclined to press aggressively against the Left boundaries of dominant policy streams and to use the visibility of office as a bully pulpit from which to help shape the contours of black action and discourse in a leftward direction.

A sophisticated, sharp, and popularly grounded progressive black presence in the national Democratic coalition also could have exerted a more effectively countervailing force against the "retreat from McGovernism" narrative and program as they developed from Carter forward. A coherent black response along social democratic lines could have helped both to discredit the conservative Democrats' initiative on substantive grounds and to galvanize a broader, class-based counterattack.

The keys to generation of such a politics, now as then, include breaking with the mystification of an organic black community. Recognition that all black people are not affected in the same ways by public policy and government practice is central to construction of a civic discourse that revolves tough-mindedly around determining who benefits and who loses from public action.

Breaking with the communitarian mythology also means rejecting a first-person/third-person rhetoric concerning black Americans' relation to the institutions of public authority. The perception of black people as passive recipients of the actions of a government fundamentally alien to them reflected a material reasonableness during most of the Jim Crow era; it has been superseded by full enfranchisement and systemic incorporation since passage of the initial Voting Rights Act. In fact, as the history of black mobilization for governance during Reconstruction shows, the segregation era marked a shift—expressing the realities of systematic expulsion from civic life—from a presumption that the Thirteenth, Fourteenth, and Fifteenth Amendments authenticated Afro-Americans' claims to equal proprietorship of American political institutions. In positing a reified "we," however, the black community formulation sets up "America"—and, therefore, official institutions—as a "they" to which black people relate most authentically as a collectivity, not as individual citizens.

With regard to specific foci for political action that could support progressive mobilization, a critical task is transcendence of a simplistic inclusion/exclusion axis for strategic thinking, with respect to both positive programs and critical responses to dominant initiatives. This implies recognition that vigorous pursuit of an affirmative action/set-aside agenda is necessary but not sufficient for advancing the interests of racial democracy. Progressives' strategic thinking in black politics should be based more than it is on public policy and government institutions, with specific attention given to actual and potential effects of each on black Americans. Examples of pertinent issues and policy areas are the relation of government action to deindustrialization and its roots in global capitalist reorganization; the racially and intraracially differential impact of federal and local housing, transportation, redevelopment, and revenue policy; and the racist, anti-civil-libertarian programmatic rhetoric and presumptions undergirding the criminal justice system. Similarly important initiatives could include the fight against privatization of public services, the fight for equalization of school funding, stimulation of open discussion, where appropriate, of metropolitan tax base sharing, and metropolitanization of functions on an equitable basis, in ways that ensure minority constituents' capacities to participate effectively by electing representatives of their choice.

The interests of constituents and incumbents are not always identical on issues like reapportionment and packing of legislative districts. Progressives' mandate should be to expand the electorate, an objective in which incumbents often have little interest. In addition, efforts to register new voters have begun to yield diminishing returns in recent years, suggesting that conventional methods may have nearly exhausted the population of the unregistered who might be added to the rolls with relative ease.

In relation to a political strategy focused on issues of policy and governance, black academic radicals' romance of inner-city youth seems mistaken. Although politicizing young people certainly is important, making them the central point of strategic discourse amounts to leading from a position of weakness. They are among the most alienated and the least connected segments of the black population, with the least practical understanding of how the world works, the thinnest commitments, the greatest volatility, and the most transient social status. Their energy and openness to experimentation only partially offset these limitations.

A more efficacious strategy would center on segments of the population that are already politically attentive, people who presume efficacy in political action. To that extent, a more rational and effective course would be to undertake a struggle for the hearts and minds of the black working and lower middle classes who attend to political affairs. These are in a way the most centrally placed strata of the Afro-American population. They overlap — through family, friendship, and neighborhood networks, as well as in their own life courses — the ranks of the unemployed and recipients of those forms of public assistance designated for the poor. These are also the people who actively reproduce the character of black political discourse by trying to make sense of the world and constructing their own interests within the inadequate and self-defeating frames of underclass and self-help rhetoric, with which they are bombarded and on which they confer legitimacy by use in the absence of better alternatives. A crucial objective must be to provide such alternatives.

Similarly, a practical Left agenda might profitably include cultivation of such progressive or even guild consciousness as can be identified among the stratum of minority public functionaries and service providers. This is perhaps the most politically sophisticated element of the Afro-American population, the most knowledgeable regarding the real workings of political institutions. Yet they also, by and large, operate without an adequate alternative to the reactionary and victim-blaming frames that presently prevail. Many of them, of course, do so quite happily and will not be susceptible to Left critique; the stratum is, after all, petit bourgeois. Some fraction of them, perhaps mainly among staff-level professionals, however, are committed to ideals of public service and use of government for progressively redistributive purposes. Their pragmatic understanding of government and policy processes could also significantly benefit elaboration of a credible, systematic, and practicable Left program. One approach to undercutting the effects of the current rightist hegemony among them, moreover, might be to attempt to organize coalitions of service providers and constituents of their institutions' services. It should prove less difficult to reach alienated young people in an adult environment characterized by political debate and mobilization.

An approach of this sort provides the best possibility for transcending a simplistic politics that offers as critical touchstones only an abstract, disembodied racism or the victim-blaming self-help line. "Racism" has become too often an empty reification, an alternative to unraveling the complex, frequently indirect processes through which racial inequality is reproduced. Racial stratification is not enacted simply in the indignity of a black professor's inability to get a cab in Manhattan or being mistaken for a parking lot attendant, in discrimination in access to employment, business loans, mortgages, rental housing, or consumer discounts, or even in the demonization of black and brown poor people and the police terror routinely visited upon minority citizens. These problems—from the more petty to the more grave—must be attacked, of course. But racial inequality is also built into the "natural" logic of labor and real estate markets; it inheres, for example, in culturally constructed and politically enforced notions of the appropriate prices for different units of labor power and in the ways that parcels of land are valorized. Racial inequality has been a central organizing premise of federal, state, and local public policy for at least a century, as housing, development, tax, defense, and social welfare policymaking have almost unfailingly reproduced and reinforced it.

The deeper structures of racial stratification are not accessible to the hortatory and demobilizing style of insider negotiation and communitarian mythology around which black political activity has been organized. What is required is the aggressive mobilization of black citizens to pursue specific interests in concert with articulation of a larger programmatic agenda centered in the use of public power—the state apparatus—to realize and enforce concrete visions of social justice. This in turn requires resuscitation of a climate of popular debate in black politics, proceeding from an assumption of civic entitlement and ownership of the society's public institutions.

This is the combined opportunity and challenge presented by the successes of the civil rights movement; it has so far not been met in black politics. Especially now, as the forces of horrible reaction—both black and white—gather steam once again precisely around such premises, it is vitally important to reject emphatically all explicit or tacit claims that black Americans are somehow citizens with an asterisk. Rejection must proceed not only by argument but most of all through the matter-of-fact acting out of black citizenship—through struggling, that is, to use and shape public institutions to advance black interests.

Notes

1. See Frank Parker, *Black Votes Count* (Chapel Hill: University of North Carolina Press, 1990); James W. Button, *Blacks and Social Change* (Princeton, N.J.: Princeton Univer-

sity Press, 1989); and Chandler Davidson and Bernard Grofman, eds., *Quiet Revolution in the South* (Princeton, N.J.: Princeton University Press, 1994).

2. Peter Eisinger, "Black Mayors and the Politics of Racial Economic Advancement," in *Readings in Urban Politics: Past, Present and Future,* ed. Harlan Hahn and Charles Levine (New York: Longman, 1984); Eisinger, "Black Empowerment in Municipal Jobs: The Impact of Black Political Power," *American Political Science Review* 76 (June 1982): 380–92.

3. Earl Picard, "New Black Economic Development Strategy," *Telos,* Summer 1984, 53–64.

4. See Clarence N. Stone, "Social Stratification, Nondecision–Making, and the Study of Community Power," *American Politics Quarterly* 10 (July 1982): 275–302.

5. For a critique, see Adolph Reed Jr., "The 'Underclass' as Myth and Symbol: The Poverty of Discourse about Poverty," *Radical America* 24 (Winter 1991/92): 21–40; Brett Williams, "Poverty among African Americans in the Urban United States," *Human Organization* 51 (Summer 1992): 164–74; Leslie Innis and Joe R. Feagin, "The Black 'Underclass' Ideology in Race Relations Analysis," *Social Justice* 16 (Winter 1989): 13–33.

6. See Lawrence Mead, *Beyond Entitlement: The Social Obligations of Citizenship* (New York: Free Press, 1986).

7. William Julius Wilson, *The Truly Disadvantaged: The Inner City, The Underclass, and Public Policy* (Chicago: University of Chicago Press, 1987).

8. See, for example, Murray Friedman, "The New Black Intellectuals," *Commentary* 69 (June 1980): 46–52; Glenn Loury, "Who Speaks for Black Americans?" *Commentary* 83 (January 1987): 34–38.

9. See Joint Center for Political Studies, *Black Initiative and Governmental Responsibility* (Washington, D.C.: JCPS, 1987); Eugene Rivers, "On the Responsibility of Intellectuals in the Age of Crack," *Boston Review,* September/October 1992; Anthony Appiah, Eugene Rivers, Cornel West, bell hooks, Henry Louis Gates Jr., Margaret Burnham, and special expert Glenn Loury, "On the Responsibility of Intellectuals, (in the Age of Crack)," *Boston Review,* January/February 1993.

10. Bayard Rustin's famous essay, "From Protest to Politics," *Commentary* 39 (February 1965): 25–31, noted at the time the challenge that the civil rights movement's successes posed for progressive black interests.

11. See Nathan Wright, *Black Power and Urban Unrest* (New York: Hawthorn, 1967).

12. See Howard Brotz, *Negro Social and Political Thought, 1850–1920* (New York: Basic Books, 1966), 1–33.

13. Robert J. Kerstein and Dennis R. Judd, "Achieving Less Influence with More Democracy: The Permanent Legacy of the War on Poverty," *Social Science Quarterly* 61 (September 1980): 208–20.

14. Adolph Reed Jr., "A Critique of Neo–Progressivism in Theorizing about Development Policy: A Case from Atlanta," in *The Politics of Urban Development,* ed. Clarence N. Stone and Heywood Sanders (Lawrence: University of Kansas Press, 1987).

15. See "Murder Capital: A Mayor's Call for Help," *Newsweek,* November 1, 1993; Don Terry, "A Graver Jackson's Cry: Overcome the Violence," *New York Times,* November 13, 1993; William Raspberry, "Jesse Jackson Calls on Nation's Blacks to 'Tell It' Like It Is," *Chicago Tribune,* October 11, 1993.

16. The Black Panther party's absence from this account may seem curious. It is nonetheless justified. The BPP was in effect the creature of a transitional moment between simple black power rhetoric and the clearly articulated formation of incrementalist mainstream and radical wings. The BPP crested as an autonomous black political organization in the late 1960s, before the institutional entailments of systemic incorporation had begun to take their

ultimate forms. By the time the practical outlines of the new regime were clearly discernible, the party was in disarray practically everywhere except Oakland, California.

17. Clarence N. Stone, *Regime Politics: Governing Atlanta, 1946–1988* (Lawrence: University of Kansas Press, 1989), 93, 166; Mack H. Jones, "Black Political Empowerment in Atlanta: Myth and Reality," *Annals of the American Academy of Political and Social Science* 439 (September 1978): 90–117.

18. See Leslie Cagan, "Rainbow Realignment," *Zeta*, May 1989; Thulani Davis and James Ridgeway, "Jesse Jackson's New Math: Does It Add Up to a Winner?" *Village Voice*, December 22, 1987.

19. Thomas Byrne Edsall and Mary D. Edsall, *Chain Reaction: The Impact of Race, Rights and Taxes on American Politics* (New York: Norton, 1991); William Crotty, "Who Needs Two Republican Parties?" in *The Democrats Must Lead: The Case for a Progressive Democratic Party*, ed. James MacGregor Burns, William Crotty, Lois Lovelace Duke, and Lawrence D. Lovejoy (Boulder, Colo.: Westview Press, 1992).

20. See, for example, George Lipsitz, "The Mardi Gras Indians: Carnival and Counter-Narrative in Black New Orleans," *Cultural Critique*, Fall 1988, 99–121; Elsa Barkley–Brown, "African–American Women's Quilting: A Framework for Conceptualizing and Teaching African–American Women's History," *Signs* 14 (Summer 1989): 921–29; and Michelle Wallace and Gina Dent, eds., *Black Popular Culture* (Seattle, Wash.: Bay Press, 1992).

Part IV

Globalization and the New Boundaries of Race and Ethnicity

10 / The Real "New World Order"

The Globalization of Racial and Ethnic Relations in the Late Twentieth Century

Néstor P. Rodríguez

Introduction

The late twentieth century has witnessed an increasing globalization of racial and ethnic relations in the United States. Since the mid-1960s, world developments, transnational migration, and the emergence of binational immigrant communities have significantly affected the character of intergroup relations in U.S. society. Perhaps not since the initial European colonization of the Americas has the global context been such a prominent macrostructural background for evolving racial and ethnic relations in the United States. Domestic and foreign capitalist expansion, technological advances in communication and transport, antisystematic movements and counterinsurgency campaigns abroad, and growing global strategies in the structuration of everyday life among third-world working classes have been major social forces affecting the globalization of intergroup relations in the United States and in other Western capitalist societies.

Increasing Globalization of Racial and Ethnic Relations

Since its inception in the "long" sixteenth century, capitalist world development has influenced relations—especially power relations—among racial and ethnic populations in many world regions. The subjugation of indigenous

211

populations in the Americas, the harnessing of African slave labor in the West Indies, and the subordination of immigrant labor in Western industrial societies are examples of the historical capitalist influence on intergroup relations. The state has played a crucial role in the formation and maintenance of racial-ethnic structures in contexts of capitalist development. In the United States, the state has played an important function in the racial formation of society through such means as designating racial categories (for example, "white," "Negro," and "Indian" in the nineteenth century), implementing racial policies (for example, "separate but equal" education), and equilibrating the racial order (for example, through civil rights acts).[1] Through their institutional capacities, including religious positions, northern European white males were the primary architects of the initial structures of capitalist-related domination, that is, the intertwined structures of race, class, and state relations. To a considerable extent, the racist ideological foundations laid by northern European white males continue to frame issues of race relations today.

Given the historical continuance of world-capitalist influence on evolving racial and ethnic relations, what has to be explained are the present era's different relational dimensions between global capitalist development and evolving intergroup relations. To the extent that new dimensions evolve out of fundamental changes in the global structuration of capitalism, they represent discontinuities, and thus new moments of advanced capitalism. As I will argue later, human agency among working-class peoples in less-developed regions, and not just the impersonal structural growth of capital, is very much at the root of this development.

Global Diasporas

One dimension is the massive movements of people between different regions of the world. While earlier periods of the capitalist world system involved the voluntary and forced movement of populations, in the late twentieth century international migration reached a watershed in the massive numbers of migrants and in the great diversity of sending and receiving communities. Another major characteristic, and one prefigured by the nineteenth-century Irish emigration, is the migration from peripheral regions (Africa, Asia, and Latin America) to core societies of the capitalist world system. Starting in the age of industrial capitalism and accelerating in the era of advanced capitalism, this migration significantly affects racial and ethnic relations in Western societies.

In the United States, by the mid-1970s undocumented Mexicans alone reached the high mark of 1.3 million immigrants per year recorded in 1907, during a decade of heavy European influxes.[2] Affected by a change in U.S. immigration law, the period from the 1960s through the 1980s saw a dramatic shift in the origin of legally arriving immigrants: the number of legally arriving European immigrants decreased by 52.1 percent, while the number of legally arriving Asians and Latinos increased by 456.7 percent and 88.4 percent, respectively.[3] While European immigrants came from a number of different cultural backgrounds, together Asian and Latino immigrants represented a much broader cultural spectrum. Equally important, some Asian and Latino immigrants (for example, Hmong, Montagnard, Garifuna, and Maya) represented cultural backgrounds new to U.S. society.

Global Urban Contextualization

A second world development affecting today's racial and ethnic relations is the increasing global-urban context of racial and ethnic intergroup relations. As major urban centers become increasingly incorporated into the world economy, relations among racial and ethnic populations in these centers become increasingly sensitive to international developments. Since the beginning of the capitalist world system, major urban centers in core societies have played various roles in providing resources for world economic exchange and development. In specific historical periods, some cities have owed much of their population growth to their specialization as financial or production centers in the global economy.[4] Often the growth of these specialized cities has included substantial immigration as investment or work opportunities attract foreigners.[5] This pattern has accelerated in the present era of high-tech communications and rapid travel.

In the United States, world cities have substantial foreign-born populations. For example, 28.4 percent of New York City's population and 38.4 percent of Los Angeles' population was foreign-born in 1990.[6] Miami, a banking center and entrepôt for the Caribbean and Latin America, had a 1990 foreign-born rate of 59.7 percent.[7]

International developments can quickly affect racial and ethnic relations in U.S. world cities strongly linked to a global system. Problems abroad that reduce markets or in other ways constrain industrial growth in the metropolises of world cities can lead to tensions among economically stressed racial and ethnic groups in these areas. For example, when dropping world oil prices paralyzed Houston's economy in the mid-1980s, anti-Latino and antiblack sentiments increased among many white homeowners in the city's west side. Settling by the thousands in west-side apartments vacated by unemployed white office workers, Latino immigrants and black in-migrants dramatically changed the character of many previously all-white neighborhoods, which were also experiencing shrinking property values with the collapse of the city's real estate market.[8]

The international stimulus of evolving intergroup relations in urban areas may also be political. For instance, Central American refugee influxes during the 1980s created new Latino-Anglo relations in U.S. cities through the sanctuary movement. Latino and Anglo activists crossed ethnic and class lines in many urban localities to weld political alliances in community-based organizations that fed, housed, and transported Central Americans on the run from U.S. government agents. The story of this Anglo-Latino alliance has yet to be written, but its development can be traced in the newspapers, newsletters, and other documents of community-based organizations working with Central American newcomers.

In a second example, supportive relations between the Cuban government and the African National Congress (ANC) strained relations between African Americans and Cuban Americans in Miami. During a visit by Nelson Mandela, the city's Latino mayor refused to meet the African leader because of his praises for Fidel Castro's support for the ANC—a definite taboo among the city's Cuban-origin population. Offended by this Latino ostracism of Mandela, some African American leaders called for a boycott of the city by outsiders. This was but an additional case in a lengthy series of problematic developments between African Americans and Latinos (Cuban Americans) in Miami.[9] The killing of black men by Latino police officers precipitated three major riots in the 1980s in the city's poor black areas. A mayoral election in the 1980s demonstrated the souring of Miami's black-Cuban relations: 95 percent of black voters voted against the Cuban American candidate.[10]

Binational Immigrant Communities

A third global factor presently affecting U.S. racial and ethnic relations is the growth of binational Latino immigrant communities. Taking advantage of modern technology, many Latino immigrants have a binational existence, enjoying social reproduction in their new settlements *and* in their communities of origin.[11] Some Central American families have evolved trinational households as members exist and interact across Central America, the United States, and Canada. Transcending spatial barriers with rapid communication and transportation, Latino immigrant families evolve transnational households that concentrate income-earning activities in the United States and maintain considerable social and cultural nurturing in their communities of origin.

From the East Coast to the West Coast, the binational social reproduction of Latino immigrants is highly evident. The constant crisscrossing of the country in immigrant journeys between U.S. settlement areas and hometowns in Mexico and Central America, the rapid growth of Latino satellite communication businesses and fast-courier companies that reach even remote village areas in Central America, the high-wattage beaming by Mexican AM stations to the United States, the proliferation of Latino-international television and newspaper media in U.S. cities—all are part of the immigrants' binational reproduction. Latino bus and van businesses have emerged to transport immigrants to localities in Mexico and the United States. In the same neighborhoods where these transport businesses are located can be found courier services to take letters and packages to immigrant communities of origin in Mexico and Central America. Some of these businesses also offer telephone service directly to many communities in Mexico and Central America. La Ranchera de Monterrey, a high-wattage radio station (1050 AM) in Monterrey, Mexico, transmits nightly throughout Mexico and many parts of the United States. The station plays songs dedicated across the U.S.-Mexico border and sends messages concerning family emergencies to Mexican immigrants in the United States.

Binational existence affects intergroup relations in immigrant settlement areas by reinforcing the immigrants' internal social and cultural infrastructure, reducing dependency on mainstream social resources. Indeed, the binational residency of many Latino immigrants has helped foster a new set of intergroup dynamics: *intra*group relations between long-term residents and new immigrants.[12] Especially among first-generation immigrants, incorporation into the mainstream or into established ethnic groups of English-speaking Latinos becomes optional in the presence of a highly viable binational social structure.

Recent Impact of Globalization on U.S. Racial and Ethnic Relations

In *The Disuniting of America,* noted historian Arthur M. Schlesinger Jr. bemoans the loss of the vision of America (the United States) as a melting pot creating a people with a unifying American identity.[13] According to Schlesinger, a number of recent developments — for example, the end of the cold war, mass migrations, and faster modes of communication and transport — have brought changes, especially the "cult of ethnicity," that threaten to segment, resegregate, and retribalize U.S. society. Resurgent ethnicity, according to Schlesinger, is disintegrating nations across the world: "What happens when people of different ethnic origins, speaking different languages and professing different religions, settle in the same geographical locality and live under the same political sovereignty? Unless a common purpose binds them together, tribal hostilities will drive them apart. Racial and ethnic conflict, it seems evident, will now replace the conflict of ideologies as the explosive issue of our times."[14] The future of U.S. intergroup relations in the next century thus "lies darkly ahead," according to Schlesinger.[15]

My own view is that the ethnic dynamics that Schlesinger perceives to be decomposing the United States are but one subprocess of a multitude related to the increasing global contextualization of U.S. intergroup relations. Many of the major patterns of presently evolving racial and ethnic relations can be grouped into the following three categories: intergroup competition and conflict, intergroup incorporation, and intergroup labor replacement. These intergroup processes can transpire at two levels: between established racial and ethnic groups (for example, between African Americans and Anglos), and between established and new-immigrant groups (for example, between Mexican Americans and new Mexican immigrants).

Intergroup Competition and Conflict

On a daily basis newspapers in large U.S. cities carry stories of intergroup competition and conflict. The reconfiguration of political districts, elections for single-district representatives, the redrawing of neighborhood-school boundaries, physical assaults by hate groups, police brutality in minority neighborhoods, outbreaks in the inner city — all are contemporary instances of problematic intergroup relations. The long history of racial and ethnic conflict in our society, as well as in other societies, suggests that it is a basic mode of societal organization, especially in determining the distributions of societal resources (educational, health, and the like) among groups differentiated by power.[16]

White racism, the original and still central racism in the United States, for example, flourished in the post–Civil War era when blacks started to make social, economic, and political gains. In southern cities, for instance, when black workers made sizable percentage gains in the building trades in the late 1800s, white racism in trade unions acted to systematically eliminate blacks from skilled jobs. In an August 1906 diatribe against blacks who were used by Chicago employers to replace striking white workers, trade union leader Samuel Gompers referred to the black workers as "hordes of ignorant blacks … possessing but few of those attributes we have learned to revere and love … huge strapping fellows, ignorant and vicious, whose predominant trade was animalism."[17] By 1950, black workers accounted for only 1 percent to 3 percent of the workforces in building trade occupations.[18]

The history of capitalist development is replete with the use of ethnic divisions to structure economic activity. This practice continues in the present era. As a multicultural society, the United States is an exaggerated case of this structuration. U.S. industrialists and other business owners frequently segmented or replaced workforces by recruiting ethnics, especially immigrants.[19] Needless to say, this fostered tensions between U.S.-born and immigrant workers.[20]

In the recessive times of the late twentieth century, large and small capitalists have seized upon immigrant labor with special vigor. Economic restructuring strategies contained in the great U-turn of the U.S. economy have given immigrant labor critical status in some cases. Sociologist Rebecca Morales has shown how employers in Los Angeles' automobile manufacturing industry used Mexican immigrant workers in the late 1970s to restructure production.[21] In the 1980s, the Houston area showed a novel immigrant role in capitalist recomposition strategies: using immigrants to restructure consumption.[22] Facing a sharp decline of middle-class tenants during the city's recession, apartment complex owners turned to newly arriving immigrants, mostly undocumented Latinos, to rebuild their tenant populations. This initially nondivisive strategy had the latent effect of antagonizing many white homeowners in surrounding neighborhoods.

Obviously, capitalist economic strategies do not account for all intergroup tensions. As illustrated above, political developments also may lead to racial-ethnic tension. In addition, in settlement communities, intergroup relations at times lapse into sharp competition or conflict as the arrival of new groups leads to the redefinition of sociospatial boundaries.

Intergroup Incorporation

In many cases throughout the United States, settlement communities that have witnessed intergroup tensions have also witnessed efforts to enhance intergroup incorporation, often simultaneously. A host of sources (educational, political, religious) promote the incorporation of ethnically and racially different groups.[23] This is especially true concerning recently arrived immigrants. Perhaps more than before, attempts to incorporate newcomers sometimes include measures to maintain their culture and integrate part of it into the mainstream, semiotic structure.

Across many U.S. localities, formal activities currently undertaken to promote the value of diversity and the goal of intergroup incorporation include Diversity Week on university campuses, Unity conferences, cultural-awareness training seminars in private and public organizations, International Day in places of worship, and ethnic commemoration months in grade schools. Two concerns drive participants in formal, incorporating activities. One concern is that society's growing diversity must be managed to ensure constructive results; the second concern is that racial minority groups must learn to work together as they ascend politically in the inner city.[24]

The promotion of intergroup incorporation through informal activities (for example, family celebrations, sandlot games, and ganging) no doubt has a much greater impact, as neighbors, co-workers, and friends spin intergroup webs with primary relationships, forming interpersonal bonds across group boundaries. Especially among ordinary people, commonality is an important stimulus for informal social interaction that promotes intergroup incorporation. For example, the Changing Relations Project, which investigated relations between established residents and newcomers in the late 1980s, found that common social space (such as apartment complexes and workplaces) sometimes created opportunities for informal intergroup interaction.[25]

What is different about intergroup incorporation in the present era is that the process can be multidirectional, in contrast to the mostly Anglo-conformity trends of earlier times. Across social, cultural, economic, and political dimensions, mainstream actors (business owners, elected officials, religious organizations, and so on) can be found incorporating the interests of newcomers, helping to maintain the newcomers' cultural distinctiveness.[26] For many business owners in large cities, multidirectional, intergroup relations create new markets and strategies. In a Houston case, for example, Korean investors opened a restaurant and hired Mexican immigrant workers to cook Chinese food for mainly African American customers. In California and Texas cities, Asian investors have ventured into Mexican businesses, learning Spanish better than English in some cases.

Intergroup Labor Replacement

U.S. race and ethnic relations have involved a long history of intergroup labor replacements. Capitalists in a variety of industries (agricultural, construction, manufacturing, and so forth) have constantly replaced groups of workers with different groups of workers. The growth of agribusiness on the West Coast, the founding of manufacturing on the East Coast, and the building of the country's railroad system involved a multitude of cases where capitalists reconstituted their workforces with ethnically or racially different workers.[27] In particular, new immigrant groups replaced established labor groups as employers found special qualities among newcomer workers, such as self-recruitment, less work resistance, and the acceptance of lower pay.

Intergroup replacement in the labor force is not a matter of job competition. It is not a situation in which newcomers compete with, and take jobs away from, U.S. workers. It is a racial-ethnic structural recomposition of the labor market, *eliminating* intergroup job competition. In time, certain job sectors become visibly immigrant, and U.S. workers do not even bother to look for work in those sectors' industries, creating a sort of reserved labor market for immigrant workers.[28] Things can quickly turn around, however. For example, when office-cleaning Central American crews voted to unionize in downtown Houston, their corporate employer called in the Immigration and Naturalization Service and turned to U.S. workers to rebuild its workforce.

In many urban and rural labor markets throughout the United States today, new Latino immigrant workers (men and women) have replaced established black and Latino workers as the preferred workforce in low-skilled, low-wage industries. Especially in the most labor-intensive industries of the service sector, many employers have turned to new Latino immigrant workers to fill their labor needs. In some cases, employer racism against blacks is at the root of the newfound preference for immigrant labor, while in other cases new-immigrant labor is just too good a bargain to pass up, even in the face of employer sanctions.[29]

As employers find new immigrant labor more attractive, the work opportunity structure of unskilled, low-wage U.S. workers suffers a relative decline, if not an absolute one.[30] The impact of intergroup labor replacement is especially severe in inner cities with large poverty concentrations, settings in which the center of gravity of the labor market keeps moving farther and farther away from the masses of unemployed and underemployed people.

The plurality of racial-ethnic relations (competition and conflict, incorporation, labor replacement) reflects the increasing diversity of influencing sources, which at times contradict each other. Within capital, for example, employers in workplaces may promote intergroup tension as a strategy to divide and control workers, while corporate executives in city growth machines may promote intergroup harmony as a strategy to attract and settle businesses. Moreover, while economic segmentation (for example, stratified labor markets) may keep groups apart, noneconomic institutions (for example, places of worship) may bring them together.[31] The multiplicity of existent intergroup scenarios reflects not an indeterminacy of racial and ethnic relations, but highly dynamic matrices of classes, institutions, subcultures, networks, and individuals.

A large volume of immigration has contributed significantly to the dynamism of intergroup relations in U.S. society. In the following section, I will discuss how growing globalization of everyday life in peripheral regions of the capitalist world system has affected this change.

The Globalization of Everyday Life

A factor influencing the globalization of U.S. racial and ethnic relations is a growing globalization of everyday life in less-developed countries. For many families in the bottom socioeconomic strata of these countries, the fulfillment of everyday-life activities (such as housing, schooling, clothing, eating) has become dependent on the transnational income-producing strategy of international migration.[32] In the late twentieth century, guest workers in Western Europe and Latino immigrant workers in the United States illustrate this development.

Global Structural Context

Structural developments of the capitalist world system have given rise to conditions that promote international income-producing strategies in many less-developed regions. Periodic economic crises resulting from increased national integration into the world market, austere social policies dictated by foreign financial agencies, insurgent movements against economic and political elites, and counterinsurgency programs are examples of developments that severely constrain masses of urban and rural workers in less-developed regions and lead many of them to seek global survival strategies.

My observations in one Mayan *municipio* in the western highlands of

Guatemala exemplify this development.[33] Facing increasing economic hardships—for example, rising food prices, unemployment, and reduced artisan marketplaces—and almost no viable economic alternatives in a national context of severe economic recession and civil war, over two thousand of the *municipio's* fourteen thousand inhabitants left during the 1980s to look for work in the United States. Having grown up in the *municipio's* small town or in its surrounding villages, only a few of the undocumented Mayan migrants had traveled long distances prior to their migration. After finding work in the United States, many of the Mayan immigrants remitted wage earnings to their families back home, helping them to survive and even prosper in some cases. Remittances from the United States have affected the *municipio's* social structure by creating degrees of social mobility, village-to-town migration, and land price inflation.

Decades of intervention by the United States, the World Bank, and other international financial organizations have laid the transnational structural context that restricts the capacity of many Maya and other Guatemalans to survive economically. Since the U.S.-planned coup against the democratically elected government of Jacobo Arbenz in 1954, the United States has supported (if not actually organized) political and economic activities in Guatemala to ensure the country's openness to foreign investors. The United States has supported Guatemalan government actions against popular movements and has obtained international funding for Guatemalan infrastructural projects to attract private investors into the country's export sector.[34] As part of a project to convert the Central American Pacific Coast into an export zone, the World Bank provided millions of dollars for highway construction in Guatemala's coastal areas at a time when many of the country's rural population (the majority of the population) lived in isolated communities lacking adequate road linkages.[35] Opening up roads in the Mayan highlands would have created a potential for growth in the area's farming and artisan economy, a family-centered economy where economic health depends on travel to marketplaces.

Structural developments in Western core societies of the capitalist world system also promote international income-producing strategies among working-class families in less-developed regions. In the United States, the institutionalized use of immigrant labor throughout the lower echelons of the labor market created a permanent attraction for foreign workers, including the undocumented. Through several programs (student and temporary visas, green cards, H-2 certifications, braceros, amnesty and legalization, temporary

protective status, and so on), the U.S. government has directly and indirectly assisted the creation and reproduction of foreign-worker labor markets, which help sustain families in less-developed regions.

Human Agency

Systemic, structural developments create the need to migrate, but it is reflective and willful human action that organizes and carries out the migration. In the Guatemalan *municipio* described above, arguments pro and con
illustrate the reflective assessment of migration as an income-producing strategy. Indeed, many economically stressed households in the *municipio* refuse
to adopt this strategy, or show only minimal and sporadic interest in migrating. In some cases, immigrants return to their *municipio,* disappointed
with immigrant life or eager to restart their artisan businesses. Some of these
migrate again to the United States after reconsidering their decision to return or after suffering new economic setbacks.

The enormous surge of undocumented immigrants in the United States
in the late twentieth century demonstrates a growing popular autonomy
among working-class peoples in the sending communities.[36] The autonomy
consists of implementing transnational, sustaining strategies (organized from
the individual to the community level) independent of intergovernmental
migrant-labor programs. As a class act, the state-free movement of undocumented migrants challenges the U.S. border's legitimacy as a sociopolitical
boundary, not by seeking to redefine it, but by making it irrelevant. In
many U.S. urban areas the results of this autonomous human action has
been the formation of binational communities. This autonomous, transnational development has been nothing short of remarkable, with millions of
undocumented men and women significantly reshaping social structures
across national boundaries completely independent of direct state support.

Within the larger framework of global capitalism, much like the worker
organizing that attempted to overcome capital's divisions in industrial societies, the autonomous migration of millions of undocumented workers represents a popular struggle to overcome capital's divisions in the world economy. The struggle is not to escape capitalism, but to relocate in its prosperous,
core areas.

Conclusion

The globalization of U.S. racial and ethnic relations seriously challenges intergroup relational theories that fail to address transnational contexts. Social

scientists need to wake to evolving intergroup changes in the 1990s affected by global events and contrasting sharply with assumed prevailing patterns of intergroup convergence. For example, more attention should be given to how immigration in the past decade and a half created conditions of intergroup divergence, as newcomers developed alternative social structures or as established residents responded with resistance and withdrawal. The latter occurrence raises a crucial question of how new social divisions affect a society still riddled by racism and other forms of subordination against peoples of color and women.

Bringing the global into sociological research is always a challenge. It is an especially important challenge in intergroup research at a time when large proportions, the majority in some cases, of residents in racial and ethnic concentrations are foreign-born and maintain social-reproductive ties to communities abroad.

Incorporating a global perspective into intergroup research requires reexamining conceptualizations derived mainly from a national or local unit of analysis and searching for their global significance. For example, it requires going beyond conceptualizing the ethnic enclave as an alternative, economic opportunity structure and seeing its interstitial role of globalizing the local and the familiar in immigrant settlement areas. The global perspective also requires a more comparative and relative research approach, one that explores and compares the diverse, and at times competing, views of different actors involved in intergroup activities. The task here is to understand how different worldviews generate intentions that aggregate into the visible social order. This is a crucial task in further understanding the ancillary capacity of the globalized social to transform heterogeneous ambiences into homogeneous experiences or into organic pluralities.

By far the biggest conceptual challenge of the global perspective is to reconcile the global with the local. This challenge is more than providing a global contextualization or a global causal factor for local developments. The challenge is to explore the capillary agencies (formal and informal institutions, communities, households, networks, individuals, etc.) transforming the local and the global into each other.

Notes

1. Michael Omi and Howard Winant, *Racial Formation in the United States* (New York: Routledge and Kegan Paul, 1986), chap. 5.
2. In 1975 the U.S. Border Patrol apprehended 579,400 "deportable" Mexicans. If we assume that at least two or three Mexicans entered successfully for every one apprehended,

then over 1.4 million undocumented Mexicans entered in 1975. For the 1975 number of apprehended Mexicans, see U.S. Bureau of the Census, *Statistical Abstract of the United States, 1989,* 109th ed. (Washington, D.C.: GPO, 1989), table 297.

3. U.S. Bureau of the Census, *Statistical Abstract of the United States: 1992,* 112th ed. (Washington, D.C.: GPO, 1992), table 8.

4. Néstor P. Rodríguez and Joe R. Feagin, "Urban Specialization in the World-System," *Urban Affairs Quarterly* 22, no. 2 (December 1986): 187–220.

5. Ibid., 194–211; Japanese cities with banking and manufacturing international activities are an obvious exception to this historical pattern.

6. U. S. Bureau of the Census, *1990 Census of Population and Housing Summary,* CPH-5-1 (Washington, D.C.: GPO, 1992), table 1.

7. Ibid.

8. Néstor P. Rodríguez and Jacqueline Maria Hagan, "Apartment Restructuring and Latino Immigrant Tenant Struggles," *Comparative Urban and Community Research* 4 (1992): 175–76.

9. Joe R. Feagin and Clairece Booher Feagin, *Racial and Ethnic Relations,* 4th ed. (Englewood Cliffs, N.J.: Prentice-Hall, 1993), 324–26.

10. Ibid., 325.

11. Leo R. Chavez, *Shadowed Lives* (New York: Harcourt Brace Jovanovich, 1992), chap. 7; Reynaldo Baca and Dexter Bryan, "Mexican Undocumented Workers in the Binational Community," *International Migration Review* 15, no. 4 (1980): 737–48.

12. Louise Lamphere, ed., *Structuring Diversity* (Chicago: University of Chicago Press, 1992). Also see Robert L. Bach, *Changing Relations* (New York: Ford Foundation, 1993).

13. Arthur M. Schlesinger Jr., *The Disuniting of America* (New York: Norton, 1992).

14. Ibid., 10.

15. Ibid., 10.

16. Feagin and Feagin, *Racial and Ethnic Relations;* Anthony H. Richmond, *Immigration and Ethnic Conflict* (New York: St. Martin's Press, 1988).

17. Quoted in Philip S. Foner, *History of the Labor Movement in the United States,* vol. 3 (New York: International, 1975), 242.

18. Ibid., 238.

19. For example, see David M. Gordon, Richard Edwards, and Michael Reich, *Segmenting Work, Divided Workers* (Cambridge: Cambridge University Press, 1982).

20. Foner, *History of the Labor Movement in the United States,* vol. 1.

21. Rebecca Morales, "Transnational Labor," *International Migration Review* 21 (1987): 4–26.

22. Rodríguez and Hagan, "Apartment Restructuring," 167–69.

23. Lamphere, *Structuring Diversity;* Bach, *Changing Relations,* chaps. 2 and 4.

24. Some Latino established leaders have yet to see the value of working together in the political ascension of minority groups in Houston's inner city; see Rob Gurwitt, "Collision in Brown and Black," *Governing* 6, no. 4 (January 1993): 32–36.

25. Bach, *Changing Relations,* chaps. 2 and 4.

26. Ibid., chap. 4.

27. Carey McWilliams, *Factories in the Fields* (Hamden, Conn.: Archon Books, 1969); Foner, *History of the Labor Movement,* vol. 2; Stanley Feldstein and Lawrence Costello, eds., *The Ordeal of Assimilation* (Garden City, N.Y.: Anchor Press, 1974).

28. For a case study discussion of this situation, see Néstor P. Rodríguez, "Undocumented Central Americans in Houston," *International Migration Review* 21, no. 1 (Spring 1987): 4–26.

29. The Immigration Reform and Control Act of 1986 made the hiring of undocumented workers a federal criminal offense for the first time in the country's history.

30. Vernon M. Briggs Jr., *Mass Immigration and the National Interest* (Armonk, N.Y.: Sharpe, 1992), chap. 7.

31. Bach, *Changing Relations,* chap. 4.

32. For example, see Chavez, *Shadowed Lives,* 72, and Douglas S. Massey, Rafael Alarcón, Jorge Durand, and Humberto Gonzales, *Return to Aztlan* (Berkeley: University of California Press, 1987). In visits in the late 1980s and early 1990s to a *municipio* in the western highlands of Guatemala, I have also witnessed this transnational income strategy.

33. From 1988 to 1992 I made yearly visits with migrants who return to the *municipio* during its annual patron saint fiesta in late July. The *municipio* is located in the department of Totonicapan.

34. David Landes with Patricia Flynn, "Dollars for Dictators," in *The Politics of Intervention,* ed. Roger Burbach and Patricia Flynn (New York: Monthly Review Press, 1984), 133–61.

35. Ibid.

36. "Autonomy" is a central concept in some Marxist analyses of working-class struggles; see Harry Cleaver, *Reading Capital Politically* (Austin, Tex.: University of Texas Press, 1979), 45–66.

11 / The Effects of Transnational Culture, Economy, and Migration on Mixtec Identity in Oaxacalifornia

Michael Kearney

One of the prototypical social identities of anthropology is "the peasant," defined as a small agriculturist making autonomous decisions about production primarily for autoconsumption.[1] In the classic images of peasants they live in small "rural" communities and are bearers of "traditional" culture. Indigenous communities of Mesoamerica are often taken as iconic examples of peasant societies. This paper is based on work with Mixtec communities whose homeland is in the state of Oaxaca in southern Mexico. Taken in their local context Mixtec communities appear classically "peasant" with respect to their technology and social and symbolic forms. But a different impression of them is obtained when they are regarded in California, where tens of thousands of them work as seasonal migrant farm workers.[2] Whereas previous work examines the emergence of Mixtec ethnicity as a consequence of migration,[3] my focus in this chapter is on the transnational context within which Mixtecs migrate and within which their identity is shaped. Indeed, the social, cultural, and economic identity of Mixtecs is only understandable when seen within this space, which is increasingly being referred to as Oaxacalifornia.

Scene 1

I am sitting at my kitchen table in Southern California drinking coffee with a committee of men appointed by the authorities of San Jeronimo Progreso, a Mixtec town in Oaxaca. Most of the members of the committee are currently part-time migrant farm workers in the San Joaquin Valley of Central California. Their assignment is to assess heads of families from San Jeronimo residing in California 80 dollars toward the purchase of a television satellite dish and transmitter to bring television reception to San Jeronimo. They have come to me, an honorary member of the community, to collect my contribution. I realize that we are participating in the fusion of the San Jeronimo migrant network with global media networks.[4]

Anthropological studies of migration have been overwhelmingly framed within issues of development and underdevelopment of rural communities, but for the most part have not been linked to debates over the status of peasants as a social identity.[5] Recent theoretical advances in the anthropology of migration are, however, relevant to reconceptualization of the peasantry. As originally formalized, the basic assumptions of migration theory were predicated on a thoroughly dualist structuring, the clearest and most comprehensive expression of which was spelled out over a hundred years ago in Ravenstein's "laws of migration."[6] Basic to this thinking is the assumption that migration is the movement of populations through geographic space organized by polar nodes that "push" and "pull" migrants. Thus migrants may be pushed from "sending" areas and/or pulled by "receiving" ones. This imagery is one of a bipolar force field in which individuals move and are distributed much like iron filings in a magnetic field. This model was also used to conceptualize subsequent anthropological studies of rural-urban migration, similarly conceived in "bipolar terms."[7] Largely a reflection of the massive one-way movements of emigrants from Europe to the Americas in the nineteenth and early twentieth centuries, this bipolar model is an inadequate representation of much contemporary migration, which reconfigures the spatial constitution of communities and has implications for how we conceptualize social types such as "peasants," "workers," and indeed "migrants." Two developments are relevant. One is increased attention to the cultural dimensions of migration and to the identity of migrants as opposed to a previous preoccupation with migration seen primarily as a demographic process. The other development in migration studies is the emergence of nonbinary theoretical perspectives, which in effect deconstruct the dualism inherent in the classic models. Notable here are concepts such as "transnational socio-cultural system,"[8] the "transnational community,"[9] "transmigrants" and the "deterritorialized nation-state,"[10] and "transnational grassroots politics."[11] All of these concepts shift thinking about migration from a primary concern with demographic questions of individuals moving through bipolar spaces in a time frame assumed to be progressive to other ways of conceiving migration that are not predicated on modernist assumptions about time, space, and social identity. Indeed, change in any one of these dimensions implies and is implied by changes in any other.[12]

To a great extent the reconceptualization of migration has been stimulated by an increased awareness of the multidirectionality of movement. "Rural" to "urban" movement is often accompanied by comparable flows in the opposite direction, as is often true with transnational migration. Furthermore, considerable movement occurs among multiple sites, not just two. The most common fields of migration are thus not bipolar and unidirectional, but instead multipolar, with complex flows among the poles. Such new images of migration imply a reconceptualization of the identity and consciousness of migrants as historical subjects. Briefly, take the case of so-called peasants who engage in circular migration in and out of peasant agriculture, wage labor in commercial agriculture, and urban activities. When considered by dualist thinking, they are conceptualized as hyphenated types, such as the "peasant-worker." But in their lived reality they share structural features with the commuters who every day jam expressways, trains, and buses. But such migrants differ from commuters in that they travel farther and stay over longer at their destinations. Moreover, they are unlike most commuters in their frequent participation in different spheres of production (for example, farm work, services, self-employment), which may be located in two or more nations (for example, some Mixtec migrants now work in Mexico, the United States, and Canada).

Migration is significant for the reconstitution of identities not only because it permits migrants to move through multiple social fields in which identity is formed, but also because it allows migrants to escape the official categories that contain subject identity. Thus migration allows partial escape from subject identity that is constructed and contained by the state, with its laws and literatures that limit the identities and movements of people and keep them in their place, as was the purpose of internal passports and residency requirements in South Africa and the Soviet Union, and still is in China. Escape from such constraints on freedom of movement and the removal of constraints on identity that such freedom implies is most true of "illegal" transnational migrants and especially illegal migrants working in the informal economy, who thus doubly defy the state. Indeed, to the high degree that global migration is associated with movement into informal economies, such migration erodes standard identities, such as that of "the peasant." Similarly, at the international level, much migration erodes the spatial structure of neocolonialism—which depends on a separation of colonial self and colonized other—and intersperses the self and the other in interpenetrating spaces.[13]

Reconsideration of the identity of peasants as migrating persons implies similar rethinking of their communities. In modernist anthropological imagery, peasants are mainly located in bounded "little communities"[14] and "closed corporate communities."[15] But recent ethnographic research on transnational migration has come to appreciate the great degree to which such communities have become unbounded[16] and as such require novel imagery that represents the complexity of their spatial distributions and sociocultural dynamics.

From Articulation to Networks

The first major appreciation of the ways in which the lives of peasant migrants defied the assumptions of bipolar spatiality and unilineal history inexorably moving from tradition to modernity was that body of literature known as articulation theory.[17] The experiences of anthropologist Claude Meillassoux are typical. He notes that "it was through our acquaintance with the world of the African migrant workers in France that the problem of their exploitation was posed in a critical way. Our research, which had begun in African villages, led us to the squalid and overcrowded dormitories of Paris suburbs where the very same men that we met in their places as proud peasants were converted into anonymous proletarians."[18] Meillassoux was faced with the task of interpreting the lives of those migrants from rural African communities whom he found working in Paris to earn remittances to send back to Africa. Articulation became the metaphor of choice to depict such relationships since, in anatomical terms, bones—hip and femur, for example—remain structurally and functionally distinct by virtue of being articulated.[19] Similarly, the noncapitalist remains such by virtue of being joined with the capitalist. Another application of articulation theory closer to the case at hand was Michael Burawoy's comparison of the structure of apartheid in South Africa with Mexican farm labor in California.[20] In the former case the tribal "homelands" were artificially created and maintained as sites for the reproduction of labor absorbed in distant industries and services. In the latter case, circular migrant farm workers in California are produced in and retired back onto rural Mexican communities. In both cases participation in "modern, capitalist" spheres allowed for the social and cultural reproduction of the "traditional noncapitalist."[21]

Central to the development of articulation theory was the growing awareness among field anthropologists of the economic importance of migrant wage labor in the reproduction of ostensibly peasant households and communities. In case after case it was demonstrated that what at first glance appeared to be very traditional local rural communities were in fact maintained in great measure by migrant remittances, often earned in a different nation.[22] Whereas articulation theory, like the variants of dependency theory that preceded it, was largely discussed and debated in the abstract, field anthropologists like Meillassoux were confronted with the task of making sense of not only the complex productive relations in which peasant migrant workers engaged, but also their solutions to cultural reproduction under such complex regimes. Out of this work came an appreciation of the diverse patterns of production and consumption in these communities. But upon closer ethnographic inspection, the multifaceted lives of members of such communities were not adequately represented by the still-residual dualist terminology of articulation theory, which predisposed us to posit hyphenated types such as the "peasant-worker."[23]

Movement beyond such lingering conceptual dualism is made possible by consideration of identity formation in the theoretical space of the transnational community. Several ideas are basic to this concept. First, in contrast to the articulation of modes of *production* model, which grew out of various peasantist and proletarianist positions of which it was a fusion, the idea of the transnational community gives equal weight to *consumption* broadly defined to include cultural consumption. Such consumption takes place via networks that are, to mix metaphors, the nerves and vessels of the transnational community. Things flow through these networks, namely persons, things, values, signs, and information. Communities conceived as networks in the microsociological sense are not of much use for the issues with which we are here concerned. Of more value is "network" in the sense of a communication network, as a medium of communication. The human component of the social network, namely face-to-face communication, is now augmented in most places by electronic communication, which more than face-to-face communication dissolves the spatial boundaries of rural communities. To the degree that personal identity is constructed from the consumption of information, the consumption of information as generated and channeled by extensive networks shapes the identity of its members in correspondingly distinctive ways. The networks that structure persons in transnational communities thus quite literally in-form their members in a manner that differs from the shaping power of, for example, a closed corporate community.

Similar in conception to the transnational network is Roger Rouse's notion of "migrant circuits."[24] Like *network, circuit* connotes the flow of things through it. But network is arguably a preferable metaphor because of its resonance with "communication networks" through which information flows, which in turn inform subjects who are in the network. Moreover, "transnational networks" contrast with the usual meaning of social networks in network theory, which emphasizes links between persons, as opposed to the idea that people move—migrate—through spaces inflated by the networks. The ethnography of such transnational networks defines spaces and forms of production and consumption that belie the neat dualist distinction of spatially separated but articulated modes. Thus, whereas the imagery of articulation supports a distinction between "rural" and "urban," reconsideration of migration as occurring within transnational communities that are formed of social and communication networks carries forward the conceptual dismantling of the rural-urban distinction and also advances migration theory from a concern with the migration of bodies to include migration and transmigration of signs and other values that move through and are transformed within networks. Furthermore, the ethnographic subjects who inhabit and are constituted within such networks are powerfully deconstructive of the opposition between peasant and proletarian, which are the primary social types associated with the standard spaces.

The network is also an image that enables theorizing transnational subjects as complex internally differentiated identities. The difference between a theory of internal and external differentiation is that in the latter the subject is the node in a network of relationships. In contrast, in the case of the internally differentiated subject the nodes of networks are internal to the subject and constitute it. To the degree that these nodes result from informal networking on the part of the subject, such networking constitutes subjects' identities as distinct from those that are officially constructed. It is to such transcendence of the official construction of community that *transnational,* in the second sense, refers—that is, the construction of subaltern identity autonomous of the official categories of the nation-state and its disciplines.[25]

And in addition to adequately representing complex migratory subjects, the network concept well represents communities of such subjects. There is first of all the limitless capacity of networks to extend themselves spatially. Migrant networks, for example, may have their historical origin in some "traditional" spatially localized and socially bounded corporate community, but as they spread, daughter communities condense that are spatially distant from the original mother community, yet are components of a larger transnational community that subsumes mother and daughter communities.[26] These networks are without spatial beginnings and ends that might correspond, for example, to head or tail. Furthermore, they have little internal formal structure. Thus, the social morphology of networks is like an amoeba, a creature with complex internal differentiation, but without distinct cells and organs that correspond to the social components of corporate communities. Also, unlike official communities that are bound to delimited spaces, amoebas can extend themselves in any and all directions.

"Network" also points to an active process of self-differentiation: as a verb it suggests a creative, ad hoc sociality in which persons tactically articulate facets of their identity with complementary facets of other persons — they network. Networking thus allows the person to escape the "mechanical solidarity" of traditional communities. But the networks so formed are not instances of that modernist polar opposite of traditional social organization, namely, "organic solidarity." Quite to the contrary, the complex internally differentiated subjects of these networks have escaped the individualized monochrome identities of the modern subject — the butcher, the baker, and the candlestick maker.

Regarding electronic communication, much attention has been given to the effect of the penetration of electronic mass media into the countryside and their influence on local and national culture. The working assumption of theories of modernization is that such consumption of mass culture erodes local traditional society and facilitates the spread of modernity. But there is somewhat of an internal contradiction in these assumptions of the effects of mass culture; it resides in the difference between electronic and print media. Theories of literateness, in opposing two qualitatively different kinds of society — the oral versus the literate — are variations of the unilinear, dualist master narrative.[27] But with respect to literateness, which is a major indicator of "modernity," cultural processes in subaltern communities appear to be leading not to greater literateness, but instead to access to electronically mediated non-print-based information located in global spaces, information that implodes into rural communities. Ease of access to these means of communication, which do not require the user to be literate, is thus enabling peasantoid communities to segue from a literate modernity and oral-based tradition to a third sociocultural space not envisioned by theories of literateness and modernization.

Also comparable to the effect of mass media on rural communities is that of user-friendly recording and transmission devices — camcorders, video-cassette players, tape recorders, telephones, teleconferencing, money orders, electronic banking, faxes, electronic mail, cameras — all of which extend networks spatially while also compressing their social density.[28] Furthermore, as communication systems, networks channel not only the flow of persons and information, but also value. As migrants travel through their networks from various sites of economic, social, and cultural production, consumption, and reproduction, they often carry cash on their persons or they may transmit money electronically or by mail. And, of course, as workers they carry within them embodied labor power, which for the most part is reproduced within the networks and sold outside of them. Indeed, the direct generation, transmission, and consumption of signs, symbols, and value via these media are variations of the communication dynamics of networks of which the migration of persons is a primary form.

For ease of exposition we may, as above, distinguish internally generated signs, symbols, values, and migrants that flow through transnational communities from the contents of mass media. But it must be understood that no such distinction between internal and mass culture is made when members of transnational communities consume the cultural materials made available to them within their networks. Such omnivorous consumption affects social differentiation within the transnational community and between it and the social fields in which it is located in ways quite different from the consumption of "traditional culture" within closed peasant communities and also from their consumption of "modern culture" within national spaces. It is in this third type of space, which is more or less synonymous with the global space of nonprint media noted above, that transnational migrants produce and consume, and so construct their identities.

The ethnography of transnationalism reveals that heightened consumption of cultural content from the global smorgasbord promotes a homogeneity in certain patterns of consumption and mass culture, but in ways that also challenge the waning hegemonic cultural projects of modern nation-states. Thus Mixtec migrants in California do accept new cultural traits that are seemingly the trappings of modernity, but these traits are likely to have been generated and to circulate within global spaces rather than being distinctive of, say, "American culture" or "Mexican culture" per se. Among the more notable of such counterhegemonic global cultural arti-

234 / Michael Kearney

facts are current styles of youth attire, such as baseball caps worn backward, baggy short pants, and T-shirts. This costume is part of a larger international cultural complex which also includes the sociology of African American and Latino American youth gangs, rap music, and drugs, and which is intentionally oppositional to "mainstream" society and culture. The ascendancy of such oppositional identities give the basis for much immigrant bashing, belying the fact that the vast majority of immigrants and migrants in California are in many ways ideal potential citizens with respect to their work ethic and propensity to save and the high value that they place on education, as has been the case for over a century of migration into the state.

But apart from the consumption of global culture, there is a deeper structural condition underlying the decline in the hegemonic power of dominant national culture, which has to do with a reordering of interethnic relations. Throughout the first half or more of the twentieth century all immigrant national groups coming into California were for the most part received by a dominant European American society, which was their primary point of reference with respect to their construction of identities as immigrants. But for hundreds of thousands of contemporary migrants in California the bipolarity of this former immigrant experience has collapsed into a multipolar field of interethnic relations in which the former dominant European American receiving culture is no longer the primary frame of reference within which immigrant identities are constructed.

Notable in this culturally reconstituted landscape is the recent formation of ethnic enclaves throughout California that reproduce socially and culturally largely outside of European American contexts. Juan Vicente Palerm, for example, identifies 148 communities in the state that are Latino enclaves, 61 of which he classifies as "Chicano and Mexican 'Majority' enclaves."[29] Palerm attributes the ongoing formation and growth of these enclaves in part to structural changes in California agriculture causing shifts from field crops to more labor-intensive fruit and vegetable specialty crops, which have stimulated increased migration of farm workers from Mexico. Although many of the new migrants settle in migrant enclaves, "they continue to attract kin and friends to California as permanent immigrants or seasonal migrants. However this increased and continuous flow of migrants from Mexico, as well as Central America, undermines employment opportunities and working conditions for the domestic, settled and legalized farm labor force."[30] Recent research by Michael Peter Smith and Bernadette Tarallo speaks to the dynamics of cultural identity in such enclaves. They find that the men and women we interviewed are becoming increasingly isolated from the larger U.S. society, adapting more to the existing binational Mexican community in California than to the economic and sociocultural mainstream. They live their daily lives apart from the rest of society in residential enclaves, and have become increasingly marginalized in enclave businesses or in secondary service-sector jobs requiring no use of English-language skills. This tends to breed a vicious cycle of marginality, as the very vitality of their cross-border cultural identity and their difficulty with English mark them as "others" and foster continuing discrimination against them in employment, housing, and basic respect.[31]

Also part of this picture are the numerous other Latin American origin settlement groups, as well as enclaves of Asians, Southeast Asians, Pacific and Caribbean islanders, Iranians, and other settlers from the Middle East who now form a heterogeneous cultural mosaic in California.[32] In addition to the growth of ethnic majority enclaves, this increasing heterogeneity is supported by other demographic trends: a decline in the demographic predominance of European Americans is occurring statewide such that by the first decade of the next century California will be a state of minorities, a condition that has already been reached in Los Angeles.

The combined result of this enclavement and heterogeneity erodes the hegemony of the once dominant European American national cultural project. In the context of the former robust nationalist project centered in European American culture, English-speaking "American" communities were the reference points against which immigrant communities resisted and succumbed to acculturation and incorporation into the national fabric. But with the rise of ethnic enclaves formed in the space of transnationalism, that bipolarity is giving way to a more complex multipolar frame of reference within which accomodation and differentiation occur. Thus in Los Angeles, for example, ethnic tensions between blacks and Koreans rival those between blacks and whites. Similar frictions between Southeast Asians and Latinos are often more salient dimensions of their interethnic relations than either group's relations with whites in this " 'post-Anglo', poly-ethnic Los Angeles of the year 2000."[33]

It is within this mosaic of ethnic communities in California that Mixtec migrants and immigrants form their own enclaves within enclaves.[34] Located mainly in rural areas of the state, Mixtec migrants live and work in social contexts that are essentially Mexican and that insulate them from immersion in European American society and culture. Indeed their main points of contact with non-Mixtecs are most likely to be Mexican and Chicano landlords, merchants, and foremen and Spanish-language radio, television, and movies. An especially important point of non–European American contact is the labor contractor. Within the context of the restructuring of California agriculture noted earlier, labor contracting is tending to replace direct hiring by growers. Although interposing another level of management between workers and employers, the contractor is usually able to deliver labor to capital at costs lower than direct hiring. This reduction of overhead is achieved by price gouging and kickbacks. Thus, the contractor provides not only work, but also a number of "services" — the purchase of which are often requirements of work and quite exploitive — such as housing, transportation, food, drinking water, check cashing, and tools. These practices are often in violation of labor and other laws; notable in this regard is the widespread failure to pay the minimum wage.[35] The resurgence of farm labor contracting in California and the above-noted practices are associated with a general worsening of living and working conditions for farmworkers, providing the context within which Mixtec enclavement takes place within the Mexican and Chicano enclaves.

These trends in farm labor are set within larger structural conditions affecting production in California agriculture that have caused deterioration of living and working conditions for farmworkers in general and Mixtec farmworkers in particular. In this context urban sprawl causes the price of land and irrigation water to rise, in turn putting downward pressures on wages. Also, California growers are increasingly competing in global markets with respect to both the export of their products and the penetration of foreign produce into domestic markets. Recent drought and heavy freezes of fruit trees are also part of this picture, causing growers to seek an ever cheaper workforce. It is within this context that Mixtecs are recruited in large numbers, often in preference to mestizo Mexican workers. Coming from Oaxaca, one of the poorest states in Mexico, they typically arrive in California desperate for work, and in supersaturated labor markets they are vulnerable to the exploitive practices noted above. The necessity to remit money to family in Oaxaca and the often dubious legal status of migrants also reinforce the conditions promoting enclavement.

Community

But what concerns us here is the decomposition of the correspondence between anthropological and official constructions of community. As in Mexico, the bounded local communities in Guatemala that anthropologists wrote about and in part invented have become transnationalized by the migration to California, Mexico, and Florida of tens of thousands of refugees, that is, survivors, from the recent and still smoldering Guatemalan civil war. As with transnational "peasant" communities in general, this demographic, social, and cultural reproduction occurs primarily outside of the original national space.

Studies dealing with the decomposition of Mesoamerican peasant communities have tended to focus on proletarianization.[36] But when the work histories of persons within transnational networks and circuits are examined, it is apparent that many of them participate heavily in so-called informal economies. In productionist terms this is a nebulous social world populated with ambiguous types who are not engaged on a full-time basis in either peasant production or wage labor, but who are nevertheless economically active most of their waking hours. People so engaged earn money in many diverse ways limited only by their ingenuity. A partial list might include such activities as street vending, shoe shining, washing windshields of cars stopped at intersections, babysitting, sewing, ragpicking, street music, making crafts and gadgets, maid work, gardening, day labor, hauling cargo, prostitution, loan sharking, production and sale of narcotics, and so forth. In some directions these "informal activities" fade into criminality as defined by the state, while in others they slide into another conceptual morass summed up variously as "lumpen," "homeless," or "derelict." Examination of the lives of persons and families who work in the informal economy also often as not lead us back into the "peasantry" and "working class." But in doing so these lives invariably mock such categories. For rather than being essential identities, they are rather like hats that one puts on or takes off according to the job of the moment. These varied ways of making a living are tactics in more complex economic strategies that nullify attempts to classify subjects and their communities on the basis of the standard productionist types.

The transnational community is spatially unbounded and composed of social and communications networks that include, in addition to face-to-face communication, electronic and other media. One additional aspect of such communities bears mentioning: the ways in which productive activities in them become partially or completely cognitively detached from geographic space and reconstituted in hyperspaces.[37] As I use the term, a hyperspace is culturally constructed, it is not anchored permanently in a specific locale, and it is inhabited mainly by strangers. Furthermore, it has a certain universal quality to it that is detached from and independent of any specific locale in which it might occur. International airports are one example, as are shopping malls, the facilities of international hotel and fast food chains, and housing subdivisions. Agroindustrial production throughout northwest Mexico, California, and Washington is another hyperspace marked by a uniformity that is imposed onto and obliterates local landscapes and communities as distinct locales. Such a free-floating "global field,"[38] so detached from permanent local place, has a sameness to it comparable to the sameness of its chemical fertilizers, pesticides, and uniform, genetically engineered crops. Referring to Mixtec migrant workers in California corporate agriculture, Federico Besserer notes that for them spatial referents are based not on local geography but on the hyperspaces of production. Thus one worker told him, "Yes, well I don't know where we could have been because we were working in tomatoes"; asked where his sons were, another man said, "They went to the oranges."[39]

In order to do research and political work it is necessary to bracket social fields and to enter them in search of social identities that reside and reproduce therein. Transnational corporate agriculture appears to be a field that can be justifiably bracketed for purposes of research. But the point is that many internally differentiated types come together in this general field of activity. As we dissect it we find that it has no essential core, there is no such individual as the "transnational agriculturist." What we do have is a system of production, distribution, and consumption in which a number of internally differentiated persons, corporations, and agencies come together and articulate facets of their identities, to produce and reproduce in a transnational hyperspace. It is in such hyperspace detached from a bounded geographic place that the transnational community is situated.

Class Identity and Consciousness

In classic political economy the social identity and corresponding consciousness of subjects are shaped by their social location in the mode of production, and it is from this position that they are seen as struggling to retain and to acquire use and/or exchange value. But what are we to make of presumed peasants or proletarians who are displaced from "traditional" sites of production and reproduction and who enter into hyperspaces that are more complex fields of production, reproduction, and struggle for value? A feature of these fields is that the lines of political and social differentiation, which is to say the circuits of exchange and accumulation, that structure them and by which they are structured are not binary. Instead they are complex circuits of equal and unequal exchange within which subalterns are situated and by which they are constituted in correspondingly complex ways; they have the total effect, with respect to the classic conception of the subaltern subject, of de-essentializing that subject. Such repositioning of subjects within much more complex hyperspaces of production and reproduction is most apparent in the ethnography of Mixtec migration, whereby migrants alternate participation in different, spatially separate kinds of production ranging from wage labor to work in the informal economy to subsistence farming. What happens to their identity when they reproduce themselves in these complex fields? Clearly there is now a certain liberation, a certain freeing from the more or less unitary subject position as it was experienced by the nonmigrating subject.

But such internal differentiation also threatens to fragment the subject into a centerless, kaleidoscopic self. The impact of massive migration, occupational diversity, and the consumption and production of mass and popular culture all combine to promote complex social differentiation that erodes any possible single, unitary subject position as a basis of subjective class identity. Indeed, categories such as "the peasant" and "the proletarian" as both analytic categories and subject identities have mostly disappeared as objective identities upon which a self-consciousness of class membership might condense. I have, however, taken this observation not as demonstration of the nonexistence of class as a formative dimension of identity, but rather as demonstration of the impotence of class, as a basic dimension of identity, to inform *subject identity*—in other words, to be reflected in consciousness as class consciousness, as a sense of class membership.

This analysis does not, however, lead to a discarding of class as *the* fundamental dimension for the analysis of subjective identity. On the contrary, this low saliency of class consciousness requires a reconsideration of class as an objective basis of differentiation and the ways in which this differentiation is not so much reflected but rather refracted in consciousness in some cases, such as the Mixtecs, as ethnicity and also as the motive force of some new social movements.[40]

Land, labor power, finance capital, the household, the transnational community, the person are all complexly articulated in transnational hyperspaces that do not correspond to the classic categories. The identity of the transnational migrant in such a space is as complex as the corporate identity of the transnational corporation. Both present conceptual and theoretical problems to the state with respect to their legal definition and control. But of the two, the transnational person is most problematic. States have developed workable definitions of the transnational corporation as a legal entity and indeed have facilitated its growth. But the state encounters a contradiction in the case of transnational persons whom they wish to contain as individuals, as nationals. The contradiction arises from the inconsistency between the actual lived identity of such persons who live and reproduce transnationally and the official identity of citizen. Just as the transnational corporation has since World War II escaped the confines of the nation-state, so, too, to a great extent, have transnational migrants. But legal definitions of personhood have not evolved to a degree comparable to that in the recent evolution of the transnational corporation as a legal person. Such a lack of coincidence between formal legal and other textual definitions of social identity and actual lived identities is what I have defined as containment.[41] Similarly, to the degree that transnational migrants escape the constitutive power of the state, to that degree reconceptualization of their identity is possible.

All civilizations until the twentieth century were based on a structural dichotomy of urban and rural, of city and country. But, as discussed earlier, what we see now in the late twentieth century is the collapse of this primordial structuring. But at a global level, the remnants of this structure linger on as the distinction between developed and de-developed regions and nations. But this difference, too, is being leveled by the combined effects of transnational corporations and transmigrants increasingly moving persons, value, information, and "stuff" around the globe at increased volumes and velocities. Rather than eliminating "underdevelopment" in the periphery, these processes appear to be replicating a heterogeneity in core areas in which ethnic subaltern enclaves have aspects of peripheral de-development. But this "peripheralization at the core"[42] is in large measure a dissolving of the structural and spatial distinctions that defined core and periphery, developed and de-developed, sending and receiving, and other such dualist oppositions so central to the identity and functioning of modern nation-states.

Notes

1. In writing this chapter, which is based in part on my forthcoming book, *Reconceptualizing the Peasantry* (Boulder, Colo.: Westview Press), I have benefited from conversations with Michael Peter Smith and from his editorial assistance.

2. Carol Zabin, Michael Kearney, Anna Garcia, David Runsten, and Carole Nagengast, *Mixtec Migrants in California Agriculture: A New Cycle of Poverty* (Davis: California Institute for Rural Studies, 1993).

3. See Michael Kearney, "Integration of the Mixteca and the Western U.S.-Mexican Border Region via Migratory Wage Labor," in *Regional Impacts of U.S.-Mexican Relations*, ed. Ina Rosenthal Urey (San Diego: Center for U.S.-Mexican Studies, University of California,

1986), 71–102; Michael Kearney, "Mixtec Political Consciousness: From Passive to Active Resistance," in *Rural Revolt in Mexico and U.S. Intervention,* ed. Daniel Nugent (San Diego: Center for U.S.-Mexican Studies, University of California, 1988), 113–24; Michael Kearney, "Borders and Boundaries of State and Self at the End of Empire," *Journal of Historical Sociology* 4, no.1 (1991): 52–74; and Carole Nagengast and Michael Kearney, "Mixtec Ethnicity: Social Identity, Political Consciousness, and Political Activism," *Latin American Research Review* 25, no. 2 (1990): 61–91.

4. Taken from the author's field notes, March 12, 1992.

5. On studies of migration and development, see Michael Kearney, "From the Invisible Hand to Visible Feet: Anthropological Studies of Migration and Development," in *Annual Review of Anthropology,* vol. 15 (Stanford, Calif.: Stanford University Press, 1986), 331–61.

6. Ernest George Ravenstein, *The Laws of Migration* (New York: Arno Press, 1976; first published in 1885).

7. Roger Rouse, "Making Sense of Settlement: Class Transformation, Cultural Struggle, and Transnationalism among Mexican Migrants in the United States," in *Towards a Transnational Perspective on Migration: Race, Class, Ethnicity, and Nationalism Reconsidered,* ed. Nina Glick Schiller, Linda Basch, and Cristina Blanc-Szanton, Annals of the New York Academy of Science, vol. 645 (New York: New York Academy of Science, 1991), 26.

8. Constance Sutton, "The Caribbeanization of New York City and the Emergence of a Transnational Socio-cultural System," in *Caribbean Life in New York City: Sociocultural Dimensions,* ed. Constance Sutton and Elsa Chaney (New York: Center for Migration Studies, 1987), 25–29.

9. Michael Kearney and Carole Nagengast, "Anthropological Perspectives on Transnational Communities in Rural California," working paper no. 3, Institute for Rural Studies, Working Group on Farm Labor and Rural Poverty, Davis, Calif., 1989.

10. Nina Glick Schiller and Linda Basch, "Transnational Projects of Immigrants and Ethnographers, and the Cultural Politics of Nation States" (paper presented at the Annual Meeting of the American Anthropological Association, San Francisco, Calif., December 1992); Linda Basch, Nina Glick Schiller, and Cristina Szanton Blanc, *Nations Unbound: Transnational Projects, Postcolonial Predicaments, and Deterritorialized Nation States* (New York: Gordon and Breach Science, 1994).

11. Michael Peter Smith, "Can You Imagine? Transnational Migration and the Globalization of Grassroots Politics," *Social Text* 39 (Summer 1994): 15–33.

12. See also Kearney, "Integration of the Mixteca" and "From the Invisible Hand to Visible Feet," on migrant "networks"; on "migrant circuits," see Roger Rouse, "Mexican Migration to the United States: Family Relations in the Development of a Transnational Migrant Circuit" (Ph.D. dissertation, Stanford University, 1988), and Rouse, "Mexican Migration and the Social Space of Postmodernism," *Diaspora: A Journal of Transnational Studies* 1, no. 1 (1991): 8–23.

13. See Kearney, "Borders and Boundaries." This postcolonial breakdown of spatial and categorical distinctions between anthropological self and ethnographic other is associated with other blurred boundaries that have provoked the recent so-called crisis of representation in anthropology, in which epistemological and political questions about the authority of anthropologists as authors to speak and write about others is questioned; see James Clifford, "Introduction: Partial Truths," in *Writing Culture: The Poetics and Politics of Ethnography* (Berkeley: University of California Press, 1986), 1–26.

14. Robert Redfield, *The Little Community and Peasant Society and Culture* (Chicago: University of Chicago Press, 1956).

15. Eric R. Wolf, "Closed Corporate Communities in Mesoamerica and Central Java," *Southwestern Journal of Anthropology* 13, no. 1 (1957): 1–18. In Wolf's depiction of the closed

corporate community, it is closed primarily with respect to the penetration of outsiders and to outside culture, which could disrupt the common front that it presents to disruptive forces. It is, however, considerably open with respect to the extraction of value from it, and indeed it was so established as an institution of Spanish colonialism.

16. See Basch et al., *Nations Unbound.*

17. Aiden Foster-Carter, "Can We Articulate Articulation?" *New Left Review* 107 (1977): 47–77.

18. Claude Meillassoux, *Maidens, Meal and Money: Capitalism and the Domestic Economy* (Cambridge and New York: Cambridge University Press, 1981), ix–x.

19. See, for example, Harold Wolpe, ed., *The Articulation of Modes of Production* (London: Routledge and Kegan Paul, 1980).

20. Michael Burawoy, "The Functions and Reproduction of Migrant Labour: Comparative Material from Southern Africa and the United States," *American Journal of Sociology* 81 (1976): 1050–87.

21. See, for example, Kearney, "Integration of the Mixteca."

22. See Kearney, "From the Invisible Hand to Visible Feet."

23. See Kearney, "Integration of the Mixteca," for an application of articulation theory applied to Mixtec migration.

24. See Rouse, "Mexican Migration and the Social Space of Postmodernism," and "Mexican Migration to the United States."

25. See Kearney, "Borders and Boundaries."

26. See Kearney and Nagengast, "Anthropological Perspectives on Transnational Communities."

27. See, for example, Jack Goody, *The Interface between the Written and the Oral* (Cambridge and New York: Cambridge University Press, 1987), and Walter J. Ong, *Orality and Literacy: The Technologizing of the World* (London and New York: Methuen, 1982).

28. For example, Robert Smith describes how the municipal government of a seemingly very traditional Mixtec "peasant" community in the state of Puebla, Mexico, is effectively administered by migrants in New York City who make regular use of teleconferencing and other means of electronic communication to maintain a "presence" in the town even though they do not reside in it (Robert Courtney Smith, " 'Los ausentes siempre presentes': The Imagining, Making, and Politics of a Transnational Community between Ticuani, Puebla, Mexico, and New York City" [Ph.D. dissertation, Columbia University, 1994]).

29. Juan Vicente Palerm, *Farm Labor Needs and Farm Workers in California: 1970 to 1989* (Sacramento, Calif.: Employment Development Department, 1991).

30. Ibid., iii.

31. Michael Peter Smith and Bernadette Tarallo, *California's Changing Faces: New Immigrant Survival Strategies and State Policy* (Berkeley: California Policy Seminar, 1993), ix–x.

32. Currently over eighty languages are used in instruction in the Los Angeles Public School District. Also, there is considerable non-English radio and television programming directed at the various ethnic groups in California.

33. Mike Davis, *City of Quartz: Excavating the Future in Los Angeles* (New York: Vintage, 1992), 328. Although black-Korean tensions were an important dimension of the 1992 Los Angeles riots, black and Korean small business owners have recently joined forces to oppose a current rapid growth in street vending in Los Angeles. Since street vendors are overwhelmingly Mexicans and Central Americans, the black and Korean businesspeople are pitted against "Latinos" ("Life and Times," KCET-TV, Los Angeles, December 10, 1993). For ethnographic and theoretical insight into such situations, see Michael Peter Smith, "Can You Imagine?" and Michael Peter Smith, "Postmodernism, Urban Ethnography, and the New Social Space of Ethnic Identity," *Theory and Society* 21 (1992): 493–531.

34. Zabin et al., *Mixtec Migrants in California Agriculture.*

35. Ibid. For more on Mixtec working and living conditions in Californian and Mexican agriculture, especially with respect to pesticides, see also Angus Wright, *The Death of Ramón González: The Modern Agricultural Dilemma* (Austin: University of Texas Press, 1990).

36. See, for example, Frank Cancian, *The Decline of Community in Zinacantan: Economy, Public Life, and Social Stratification, 1960–1987* (Stanford, Calif.: Stanford University Press, 1992), and Kearney, "Integration of the Mixteca."

37. See Frederick Jameson, *Postmodernism; or, The Cultural Logic of Late Capitalism* (Durham, N.C.: Duke University Press, 1991), 43, 115–18.

38. Federico Besserer, *Los mixtecos en el campo global de producción de vegetales y significados* (paper presented at the 13th International Congress of Anthropological and Ethnological Sciences, Mexico City, August 3, 1993).

39. Ibid., 11, my translation.

40. On the emergence of ethnicity within Mixtec transnational communities, see Nagengast and Kearney, "Mixtec Ethnicity."

41. Kearney, *Reconceptualizing the Peasantry.* At this writing, debate over the recently passed North American Free Trade Agreement (NAFTA) is raging within the context of a virulent antimigrant reaction aimed mainly at Mexican nationals in California. The purpose of NAFTA is to facilitate the transnational flow of products and capital, but it does not address the corresponding transnational movement of people that such increased international integration implies. Restrictive immigration policy is thus necessary to continue this contradiction between capital and labor that results from the reordering of space effected by transnational migration.

42. Saskia Saseen-Koob, "Recomposition and Peripheralization at the Core," *Contemporary Marxism* 5 (1982): 88–100.

12 / Models of Immigrant Integration in France and the United States

Signs of Convergence?

Sophie Body-Gendrot

Two great "models" of social integration are usually put forward when comparing the United States and France.[1] These relate to the historical principles setting social integration in action in both nations, to conceptions of immigration, to perspectives on international relations, and to the centrality of race in the United States. But a closer look at the difficulties experienced by large cities in both countries paradoxically reveals striking convergences, such as growing exclusion of marginalized and heterogeneous minorities; the incapacity of local authorities to deal with "the bubbling cauldron" of ethnic and racial diversity; the inadequacy of institutions such as school to process social integration as they did in the past; the impossible task for rich countries to seal their frontiers against the flow of undocumented migrants. In all these cases, the erosion of the French model of integration is visible. My aim in this chapter is to show that despite different historical constructions, the distance between the processes deriving from the two "models" of social integration is narrowing. The lack of clear vision of national and local decision makers is clearly perceptible as they are confronted by increasingly complex issues.

The French "Model" of Social Integration

Although France and the United States issued from revolutions, the conditions of construction of the respective nations have not led to similar principles. The criteria of entry, selection, and integration have differed in the two countries, one open to immigration and the other a country whose state and nation have been engaged century after century in the conquest of a territory. Moreover, according to historical circumstances and ensuing policies, the myths and principles of incorporation of newcomers in the nations fluctuate, political definitions are not fixed for eternity, and they are submitted to revisions, as seen in the recent German example. The mode of production of a national identity is therefore meaningful only by reference to those who have been selected for admission, and in France and in the United States they do not look alike. These models reveal that the French promote the ethnicization of majorities, and Americans that of minorities.[2]

An Ethnicization of Majorities

For a long time, France was perceived to be an ethnically homogeneous country, deeply anchored in its history of nation building.[3] In contrast to the experience of the American nation ritually celebrating its immigrants, the centrality, continuity, and unitary identity of France, based on a fictitious and reconstructed ethnicity, were emphasized. Yet, by 1931, according to the census, France was the first country of immigration in the world, in relative value.[4] Immigrants came from neighboring countries Belgium, Italy, Switzerland, and Spain and from eastern Europe. Currently, France is still a country of immigration, with over 10 percent of its population foreign-born, a percentage considerably higher than that of any other European country but Germany, and 30 percent higher than the foreign-born population of the United States.[5]

An explanation of this blindness comes from the fact that the French consciousness of a common ancestry started as early as the twelfth century among the elites.[6] During the revolution, the single locus of an indivisible power was then transferred from the monarchy, which had politically and culturally unified France, to "the Nation," moved by a collective and political vision. The nation became the depository of national sovereignty. The social construction of French nationhood became a powerful agency in the melting of differences: a fictitious unitary and linear identity from the Gauls to the revolution was imposed from the top, along with the idea that the French had invented the political notion of citizenship.

The principle of secularization that accompanies this vision is also political. Everyone is equal before the law, despite one's origins, race, and class, and is part of a unitary political community. While Americans enforced freedom over equality and respected national, religious, and racial particularisms in a haphazard manner,[7] the French principles promoted a legal and judicial equality of treatment of all. The state—and the public service that diffuses universalistic principles—is consequently the producer of the social sphere and the major agent of unification of a society composed of atomized individuals.

Along with a strong centralized state between 1870 and 1970, powerful institutions—the school system, the army, the church, welfare agencies, the trade unions, and the political machines—enforced a consensual representation of French society. Schooling is a perfect example. In 1914, fourteen languages, including German, Alsacian, Breton, Basque, Occitan, Catalan, and Corsican, were still spoken in the various regions of France. Through rigidly defined school curriculum and behavior rules, these particularisms were bulldozed. In 1950, the vernacular languages were no longer in use.[8]

The French law of legalization, which the French call naturalization, was the most generous of all European countries. It mixed jus sanguinis (89 percent of children born in France are French through filiation because at least one of their parents is or was French) and a double jus soli (the twenty thousand children born in France who have at least one parent born in France are French). Moreover, until 1993, all individuals born in France from foreign parents automatically became French if they had lived in France for five years before they turned eighteen.[9] This principle was founded on the idea that those who daily share French values and human rights are part of the life of the nation and should be granted nationality with the rights of citizenship. Since 1993, formal acquiescence at eighteen is required to obtain French nationality.

A Political Choice: The Official Denial of Particularisms and the Assertion of Universal Principles

As soon as they become part of the nation, individuals cannot claim for themselves or for their ethnic group any specific treatment that would loosen the links of the implicit contract they have, as individuals, with the French national sovereignty. This ideology is based upon an indissoluble bond between citizenship and nationality, a French specificity. France shelters "aliens," "guest-workers," "immigrés," then recognizes French citizens after their naturalization. Unlike the British or American experiences, once citizenship is obtained, nothing legally and statistically distinguishes the former alien from the old-stock French. All attempts to take advantage of ethnic markers as a resource to exert ethnic pressures lead to a blind alley. The state, in short, does not actively participate in racial or ethnic formation.[10]

This principle poses problems for (comparative) research, as general statistics on the population are based on nationality. Statistics are a product of social life. All questions relative to religious affiliation since 1872 and to national origin are forbidden. No survey attempts to track ancestry via the birthplace of grandparents. Researchers demonstrate that politically, the ignorance of origins and race protect the population from persecution, as occurred for Jews during the Vichy regime (1940–44). They argue that the concepts of race and ethnicity are not rigorous or scientific. Some even exert pressures to have the word *race* removed from the constitution.[11] They explain that constructing concepts of differentialism (minority, community, race) would materialize their existence. In fact, such social scientists, whose research is frequently government funded, simply submit themselves to institutional categories that have influenced public representations. Such exclusions handicap collective struggles against racial and ethnic discrimination. Besides, other researchers "in the field" have found here and there forms of "ethnicization" of immigrant populations in France, especially among the young.

It is fair to say, however, that the French "model" of immigrant integration has been efficient (53 percent of immigrants' children born in France in 1960 are white-collar employees today), but gradually the cleavage between the official unitary space of the state and the processes of definition and redefinition of values, codes, identities, and practices of unsuccessful immigrants has increased.

The American "Model": The Ethnicization of Minorities

By contrast, the origins of the U.S. republic have revealed tensions about the definition of a unitary state. The Constitution has distributed responsibilities between the federal government and the states, a first sign of fragmentation; in the debate between Jefferson and Madison, paralysis was preferred to the tyranny of power. The separation of the three branches of power has given way to different definitions of what policies should be, a second source of fragmentation. As recorded by Lawrence Fuchs, the origins of the population settlement allowed immigrants to organize as they wished, ethnicity and race were recognized as signs of distinction, and it was possible to be an American and to practice one's language and religion and to follow one's traditions.[12]

Nevertheless, American institutions have oscillated between openness, universalism, and the respect of particularisms, on one hand, and protectionist local practices and nativist impulses, on the other. For Lincoln and Jefferson, civil religion and loyalty to the democratic values were the essential conditions of citizenship. Enduring cultures, religions, and habits belonging to the private sphere were for them a secondary political matter. Because of numerous factors, including decentralized political parties, immigrants and their children could develop an ethnic space within the public domain and even appropriate it via the political machines; "ethnics" or "minorities," as American citizens, could lobby to defend their interests, and the pluralist political system frequently has yielded to such forms of pressure. The interaction of disparate cultures has therefore given America a unique feature.

As in France, however, the principles of freedom and equality have been distorted by political necessities. At the end of the nineteenth century, groups hostile to "new" immigrants from eastern and southern Europe brought into question the inclusive principles that had governed the long period of national construction and the values expressed by Thomas Paine. The definition of the political community, of its limits, of acceptable and accepted "races" became a critical issue. The state had to choose and refuse those who could not belong to the club; "no one could become a citizen of the nation without the nation's consent."[13] Efforts were made to reconstitute a nation that never actually existed, to obliterate the tensions of its creation, and to establish a clear line between the in-group and "them." As in France, a fictitious ethnicity with unitary origins became the myth forcing immigrants into Americanization, or rather "Waspification." After 1924, no state any longer granted immigrants voting rights. This conflict between openness and exclusion marks the continuing tension about concerns for national integration and the danger represented by aliens for American society.[14]

In the case of racial minorities, the American cleavage line has not been one of citizenship but of race. Since the 1960s, following the civil rights movement and urban racial disorders, American society has had the difficult task of integrating new pieces into an already complicated ethnic mosaic. One approach of public policymaking has been to integrate "underrepresented" racial and ethnic minorities by creating a new kind of ethnicity. In the way that it counts population, spends public aid, and develops affirmative action programs for minorities, the federal government has produced a three-part classification based on race and has placed in the same categories populations fragmented by class, race, and ethnicity. The concerned groups have been conscious of the advantage of adopting these classifications for their individual and collective interests. As a result, an official multiethnic society acknowledging multiethnic lobbies and minority coalition-building has received legitimacy while the myth of the "melting-pot" has been discarded.

This political process, linking the state with ethnic groups whose structure and organization have been influenced by policy decisions of the state, is poles apart from the French political approach.

Two Converging Models?

Brutal Economic Changes in France

As in most developed European countries, global economic changes inducing an internationalization of processes have put an end in France to what one could call a "national society," culturally integrated by a state imposing a vision legitimized by past political experiences, expectations, and procedures and by more or less homogeneous segments forming the French population.

The internationalization of the economic sphere has had disastrous effects on the social arena that had been structured by this national state. The globalization of production, the defense of the currencies, and international competition give economic agendas a priority. As a consequence of the decline of manufacturing jobs and the growth of the service sector, unemployment has worsened and has hit over 12 percent of the population in 1994. No longer is work an integrative tool into society or an access to modernity. The sociourban sphere is fractured and no longer connected to the economic issue.

Dramatic changes have affected prevailing structures of work, residence, and social interaction in formerly working-class neighborhoods. The decomposition of the Communist party (and then of the Socialist party) and unions due to the erosion of the working class, to fragmentation, to changes in work production, and to a lack of adaptation to mutations caused the collapse of the labor movement in France.

During the greater part of the twentieth century, all segments of French society had been structured and integrated by a major class conflict opposing the dominated to the dominants. The labor movement encompassed civic and neighborhood issues in working-class areas. Today, the departure of highly motivated activists and leftist elected officials from such places has created a vacuum in grassroots and party structures. Atomized, "side-by-side" forms of struggle, where heterogeneous unemployed residents, especially the young, no longer recognize themselves in the labor discourse, have replaced the "face-to-face" movements of former days. No other value has replaced work as a legitimate social and political source validating claims for integration. Groups experiencing social difficulties of all kinds are linked by a new identity emanating from the space where they live and based on a perception of abandon. The conflict is about "ins" and "outs." Fathers are unemployed; older brothers who went to school, received job training, and participated in social movements are also unemployed. Why would the younger ones hope to get hired as manual workers? The new logic today, shared by everyone and transmitted by the media, relates to consumption, easy money, and winners. The development of an underground economy is approved by an increasing portion of the relegated populations sharing a law of silence and physical solidarity against the police.

The Salience of the Local Sphere

What has become new for the French — and this marks a convergence with the United States — is that the political space where conflicts occur and potential solutions arise is increasingly local in France. For a long time, because of centralization, the importance of the state machinery, and the prefects' enforcing Parisian decisions at the levels of *départements,* the subnational levels were too often registry offices, despite the plurality of offices merging various levels of power. Important battles were won in Parliament either by the Right or by the Left via political parties' contentions. Reforms were carried through inside the state apparatus by factions pushing forth new ideas. But with the decentralization laws of 1981–83, extended powers (in terms of land use and social control) have been given to local authorities. The local sphere becomes thus the arena where major social difficulties are revealed, as cities become the mirrors of transnationalization, the loci of urban pauperization, and experimental laboratories for alterations in social processes. Poverty and a diversity of cultural practices and the tensions that they generate are daily visible in the deprived neighborhoods of industrial cities. As a consequence, they become the prime object of solicitude of national politics.

Urban policy, elaborated at the national level and inspired by local experimentations, consists in providing institutional and financial support to five hundred outer fringe areas especially hit by the economic crisis, areas whose populations have multiple handicaps. Newcomers from the third world, that is from Muslim countries; families with numerous children; single-parent families; school dropouts; and, most of all, unemployed workers are increasingly unable to move out of such disqualified spaces. In 1990, a survey by the National Institute of Statistics (INSEE) in these neighborhoods representing three million residents and qualifying as target urban areas, revealed a disenfranchised social landscape.[15] Unemployment in target areas approximates twice the rate of the rest of the country (20 percent), and is 10 percent higher for males and females age 20 to 24 (24 percent and 34 percent). Such areas shelter twice as many foreigners (18 percent) and foreign youth as do other metropolitan areas. These foreigners are 81 percent non-European (in metropolitan France, the 9 percent foreigners comprise 67 percent of non-Europeans). Even if the percentage of households over six persons is small (7.5 percent), it is more than twice that of other metropolitan areas (3.1 percent).

Massive help is thus needed, and all political parties, except the National Front, agree and want to prevent social violence. With the Socialist government, led by Michel Rocard, eager to reduce collective urban violence and promote more social justice, the territorial approach prevailed over the social one at the end of the 1980s. The conversion of the social issue into an urban issue has been an attempt to circumscribe multiple and complex problems in territorializing them, in "overlocalizing the social" issues.[16] Massive funding and human resources were provided. When the government required the tax money from four hundred rich localities to be transferred to the poorest four hundred, it was approved by Parliament. When it gave state representatives the power to seize empty property for social housing to be built in localities that did not provide any, the bill was not defeated. This liberal bill requiring mayors to encourage social mixing in public housing was passed by Parliament in June 1992.[17]

But intellectually, this urban policy presents several problems. First, social problems are reduced to urban dysfunctions, as if a change in the image of degraded neighborhoods and their residents would have the effect of bringing them back into the global matrix. Improvements in the appearance and architecture of poorly maintained projects, in educational services and job training, in cultural integration produce limited effects, however, and they do not convince the residents that they are now part of the mainstream. Second, the approach that tends to concentrate social workers, community police, educators, organization leaders, building janitors, and responsible parents of foreign origin on the solving of local problems of "social pathology" is in contradiction with the organicist policy. Place-oriented policies also have an unintended effect: they favor a logic of "ins" and "outs" and sustain the overdeveloped theme of "exclusion," a spatial metaphor emotionally charged with disciplinary connotations implying setting aside, deporting, rejecting. Such a policy of "inclusion into exclusion" indeed lumps together, in terms of social distress, the victims of racism, the long-term unemployed, the residents of disadvantaged sites, the physically handicapped, young delinquents, and so on.

The other vision expressed by these urban policies relies on an old dream of early-twentiethth-century reformists praising social mixing and the return of the lower middle classes to their former neighborhoods, as defined by the 1992 law. The logic of the law implies that the spatial coexistence of various social classes in the same spaces will produce social links and that the poorer (and dangerous) classes will be "educated" by their contact with upwardly mobile elements (or will be under their surveillance). This myth has given support to the construct of a new term that submerges the current political discourse in France — "the social link," again referring to social cohesion, an organicist vision of society.[18]

Strikingly, the Conservative government after March 1993 has espoused such policies with little change. In France, it is indeed in the interest of all political parties, except the extreme Right, to keep the urban issue alive. First, the symbolic political benefits are important — there is an agreement in the general public that dangerous classes must be under surveillance, that social explosions in deteriorated areas must be prevented, and there is little tolerance of intersocial violence: politicians are always blamed for their inaction. Second, there is still a prevailing ideology according to which citizens must win over taxpayers. Yet an implicit cleavage line defines an in-group that benefits from the historical solidarity of the political community and an out-group made up of immigrants.[19]

All French policymakers agree — as if echoing the "law and order" theme in U.S. politics but also in other European Economic Community

(EEC) countries—to keep the troika security-immigration-nationality on the political agenda: physical safety has to be strengthened and law strictly enforced, and the main culprits in terms of delinquency and drug dealing are deemed to be undocumented immigrants. As a consequence, tougher rules on French citizenship and tighter controls on third-world immigration were approved in 1993 by the Conservative-dominated Parliament, along with sweeping police reforms reinforcing immigration surveillance in airports, along borders, and in the streets. Interior Minister Charles Pasqua pledged "zero immigration" for the years to come, meaning keeping out unskilled third-world immigrants, "for whom," he says, "there are no jobs." Applications for asylum are closely reviewed. Judges have received more power to enforce the twenty thousand annual deportation orders in agreement with other European Union countries.[20] Foreigners must have resided two years in France before being allowed to bring in relatives under reunification programs. Women in polygamous unions are banned.[21] New measures empowering police to stop foreigners and citizens at random in the streets to check their documents have stirred a debate that sidesteps race and culture.[22]

Differences Still . . .

Despite converging phenomena of unemployment, deprivation, and urban marginality, French grimy industrial suburbs differ from American ghettos. First, twenty to thirty nationalities live together in those spaces. Second, old-stock French and naturalized populations are still frequently a majority there and youth is rarely divided by race. Whether they are French or Algerians, the young share the same misery.[23] Felt discriminations are expressed by those of the French and the naturalized who experience a loss of status as they see their neighborhood change and do not feel "at home" any more, and on that point, the same is true in transition zones in the United States.

Third, since the 1970s, state financial subsidies have slowed down social deterioration, and public services have functioned. It is true that bureaucratic procedures have had their costs; grants have frequently been poorly used and clientelism has taken a heavy toll. Yet a control exists from the top about the evolution of such sites, and *laissez-faire* is not an appropriate term to describe the observed processes. This intervention of the state in social integration—welfare and work allowances, whatever the origins of the beneficiaries are; family benefits and pensions, whatever the social class is—still ties French society together. Ninety percent of the French agree with unemployment benefits being allotted to foreign labor, and 89 percent, with foreign children attending public schools. The equivalent of minimum-wage salary given to the unemployed and socially handicapped as a counterpart for economic participation (RMI) has encountered little political opposition, except from workers paid at the minimum-wage level.

Resistance on Political Rights

It is striking to observe that in the presidential elections of 1988 and in the regional elections of 1992, the French residents of stigmatized public housing projects did not vote any differently from those in the other neighborhoods of the same cities. First, local traditions, political configurations, and stakes are more predictive than the sharing of the same social handicaps.[24] Second, as with the "underclass," the collective identity forged on exclusion is a social construct, imposed by those who are not part of it. According to circumstances and interactions, residents emphasize their misery or, on the contrary, demonstrate how attached they are to their neighborhoods. When an interviewee says, "I am not French, I am from Marseille," he expresses his attachment to the city and his lack of identification with French universal values. But abroad he would probably mark his differentiation by emphasizing his French belonging.

The xenophobic vote for Le Pen does not come automatically from deprived zones but from adjacent ones as well, where the fear of insecurity and social disqualification due to the presence of Muslim immigrants is prominent. These syndromes are not different from those experienced in American working-class or lower-middle-class neighborhoods. As described by Jonathan Rieder about Canarsie in Brooklyn, European residents were entangled in a quest for respectability and searched for an upward position in life. They became outraged by the presence of poor racial minorities threatening the value of their property, their norms, and their self-respect. The struggle to protect their turf against black advances looked like one of the many "communal conflicts" led by white mobs in urban neighborhoods of northern or border cities in the 1920s over territoriality, but it was also one over identity emanating from space.

The ethnocentric factor necessary in most wide and rapid mobilizations leads the resistors to violently discredit their perceived invaders with stereotypes.[25] This demonization of the "Other" echoes the words of one of A. Sayad's interviewees, an older French resident living side by side with an Algerian family at the periphery of Paris and unable to accept the changes that have occurred in her neighborhood. Like most residents opposed to "the young" in the neighborhood, she complains first on an intergenerational basis: according to her, Arabic children "are coarse, they are full of hatred, they look at you nastily, they always stare at you, with spite. You always feel they would like to thrash you... and you get scared." But the misunderstanding has deep cultural roots, which in France is a substitute to biological racism: "Nothing is right. Nothing can get right. We cannot get along. We do not have the same tastes, the same behaviors.... We do not see things the same way. So we cannot agree, we agree on ... nothing."[26] Yet, whereas in the American case developed by Rieder the enclave consciousness prevails, leading to a possessive communalism founded on a hierarchical racial system, in France isolated and vulnerable longtime residents, the remnants of an economic disaster, complain about an ineluctable fate that they visualize as blind bureaucratic or vast economic forces (city hall, the state, plant closures) over which they feel disempowered. To avoid being judged as racists by an interlocutor who does not belong to their immediate environment, they displace their malaise on an easy target, the foreign newcomers, complaining about their noisy cats, their smells, the thinness of the walls, and so on. But the grievance emanates from several perspectives: first, the legitimacy of the presence of "*immigrés*" is denied, especially as they are perceived as benefiting from rights or goods that are, according to the former, the privileges of nationals. Second, the perception of an invasion combines with a feeling of abandon and refers to power differentials. Third, the stake is about a personal status endangered by the aliens' proximity or the status of one's residential environment devalued symbolically and physically.

Voting rights are then frequently seen as the symbol marking the cleavage between those who belong to the political community at large and share a common universal destiny and "them"—those who are culturally different. Only 35 percent of the French agree with voting rights for long-term non-EEC residents at the local level. According to the distinction established by T. H. Marshall, they approve social and civic rights for foreigners as a means of integration, but they require naturalization for political rights: they are unwilling to dissociate nationality and citizenship and to depreciate the latter.[27] In the French social imaginary, there is no differentiation between a national vote and a local vote that is massively attended (80 to 85 percent), in part because of the stakes involved and in part because of the overlap between local and national political officeholding. Over 80 percent of

Parliament members in the National Assembly hold local offices at the same time (half of them are mayors who feel that their local problems need to be discussed in the national arena).

The Failure of New Expressions of Cultural Pluralism in France

Cultural transformations have been observed that show an erosion of the rigid assimilationist model. Among the French, 65 percent agree with the teaching of the history of religions in public schools; 62 percent, with the construction of mosques (but not in my backyard).[28] Requirements by immigrant activists that their language of origin be taught in the local public schools to assert the cultural heritage of their group were approved by institutions in 1983. Bilateral agreements with eight countries allowed Arabic, Portuguese, Spanish, Italian, Serbo-Croatian, and Turk to be taught in French public schools during extracurricular activities by selected instructors sent by the home countries. (Yet because of the perception of possible folklorization and stigmatization that are linked in France to special treatments, those languages have remained marginal.)[29] More and more often, *hallal* meat (meat cut according to religious ritual) is served in public schools, in the army, and in prisons. Special spaces in cemeteries are devoted to Muslims who must face Mecca. Such signs mark an openness of institutions, following that of public opinion.

But on the front of the comparatively recently integrated immigrants, forms of resistance to a unitary cultural model have been expressed by groups culturally French yet eager to assert their particularisms and construct a political space of their own. Their attempts are perceived as threatening for French society, and they have failed in large measure, as they marked a wide departure from historical processes of immigrants' integration.

The first episode, that of the Islamic scarf, illustrates French exceptionalism and should be set in contrast with American particularist demands. As a comparison, the Ocean Hill–Brownsville school controversy that I have analyzed at length elsewhere exposed the dilemma of New York local authorities confronted with African American leaders' particularist demands for community control from 1964 to 1969, a demand that appeared as legitimate to liberal political decision makers, granted the disastrous level of education in the ghettos.[30] But it conflicted with universalist values, including due process, and with labor contracts, which, according to teachers' and other employees' unions, were being violated. The escalation of the conflict threatened the mayor's reelection, broke the decades-long progressive alliance of blacks and Jews and left enduring scars. But on the whole, even though the conflict had wide-ranging implications about minorities' rights and prevailing norms, the struggle of the contenders remained confined within New York State, and other cities, such as Detroit, had the capacity to pursue other options.

In contrast, particularist demands appearing as a threat to dominant norms in France (one should remember the Dreyfus Affair) bring violent reactions as a shock wave throughout society and cannot leave national leaders indifferent. In the fall of 1989, three adolescent girls entered their classroom in Creil, their head and neck covered with a scarf (veil or *tchador,* according to interpretations). Secularization in France forbids distinctive signs in the public school space that could be seen as "pressure, provocation, proselytism, or propaganda." In this case, the focal point was the scarf, interpreted as an ostentatious provocation from Islamic fundamentalists. The high-school principal, a national from the French Antilles, required the girls to take their scarves off in the classroom, but they refused, invoking Allah's law. These girls were backed up by movements of re-Islamization aiming to prove that the French public school system is a failure; such minority movements are eager to set up Koranic schools or to keep the girls away from instruction.[31] They assert that religious rules prevail over the laws of the French republic, an unacceptable claim for French secularist culture.

In the Creil case, and with Islamic fundamentalism perceived as a cultural threat since the Iranian revolution, within days the national media, major organizations representing immigrants, and numerous politicians issued violent statements and reinterpreted the incidents in terms of historical church-state conflicts, ethnic pluralism versus integration, and women's rights. Prominent intellectuals evoked "the Munich of the School of the French Republic" and urged teachers "not to surrender." This controversy quickly became the concern of the minister of education and of National Parliament. It symbolized France's uneasy relationship with a growing population of Muslim immigrants perceived as culturally "unmeltable" and backed up by sovereign Islamic countries seeking entry into French affairs. Yet the Council of State's decision to turn the decision back to local educational authorities put too much pressure on them, and they began to be dragged to court by expelled students' parents. Continual confrontations occurred throughout 1993 and 1994, inflaming passions.

A previous form of ethnic political expression—which failed—may explain the current success of re-Islamization. In 1983–85, youth of Arabic origin, mostly from the Lyons region (calling themselves "Beurs"), who were victims of discrimination, decided to launch Marches for Equality throughout France to protest racism and marginalization. In the public political sphere, their motto — "respect my difference" — and their strategy of assertion were innovative. They exposed a reconstructed and hybrid ethnicity and a fluid system of identification revealing the composite origins of the marches' participants. This strategy of culturally integrated political entrepreneurs dramatized the identity and relational construct issue. With the help of the media, their struggle meant to address the highest summits of the state. Their forms of pressure were not different from those of American racial minorities eager to reemphasize the importance of their specific cultural heritage. Before the "politically correct" movement, African Americans attempted to valorize African culture in terms of food, clothes, rites, and language, in order to prove that African Americans had a whole heritage to bring to a multicultural society. The institutional approval of the celebration of Martin Luther King's birthday on the model of Saint Patrick's Day or Columbus Day is a sign that the system is reactive rather than proactive and should be endlessly lobbied by minority groups.

However, in the French case, Beurs were assimilated to French culture; the difference that they looked for referred to a redefinition of integration. The dominants indeed impose an assimilationist conception based on compliance, submissiveness to normative behaviors, and conformity to and interiorization of the models, whereas the Beur residents from degraded spaces demanded the recognition of their hybrid identity, an extension of their fields of intervention, and equal opportunities (based, in fact, on models of historical and democratic freedom developed in French schools, exhibited on the media, and emphasized by the state).

These demands could only add fuel, however, to nationalists on the extreme right. Accused of betraying universal principles with particularist demands, the young marchers soon chose the motto "respect my indifference." In that case, indifference was the demonstration of powerlessness. Subsequently, some of them became co-opted by institutions, others joined Muslim organizations, and a national organization, SOS-Racisme, supported by the majority Socialist party, recaptured the theme with the support of the state before fading away. On the whole, from that moment on, the depoliticization of the issue of integration has been actively pursued by the major established parties.

The threat raised by Islamic fundamentalism is currently omnipresent in the French public's mind, activated by the media, and it delays the full integration of Muslims into French society. During the Gulf War, for instance, the media predicted violent tensions between the four million Arab Muslims in France, some of them openly pro–Saddam Hussein, and segments of the French population, including Jews. According to a poll, 68 percent of Muslims in France, 75 percent of those twenty-five to thirty-four years old, were hostile to the Western military intervention, while 75 percent of the French favored it.[32] However, no violent reaction occurred. Moslems controlled their discourses and practices for fear of retaliation and to preserve the gains they had already made in inserting themselves into French society, since 80 percent of those who were already French citizens and 70 percent of the nonnationals preferred to live in France rather than in their country of origin. A large majority of them who do not side with fundamentalists expressed their fear of more police control (82 percent), more racism (77 percent), more problems in finding work (74 percent), and more deportations (63 percent) (Institut Français d' Opinion Publique [IFOP]) as a consequence of the Gulf War.[33]

Such accounts reveal that French society is torn not only by the most severe economic crisis since World War II but also by a cultural oscillation between the tolerance of differences and withdrawal (as is also the case in the United States). Tools of integration in France (family, religion, school, army) do not function as well as in the past. They no longer correlate national norms and individual motivations. Still, a majority of the French believe in the success of the French "model" of integration. [34]

Conclusion: "We Are All in the Fog"

But did the past French model function as well as it is thought? Are we not producing a myth, and is the present situation as dysfunctional as it is claimed, even if everyone admits that the tools of integration are eroded? Which conception should then inspire public policies of integration? Are there ideas to be drawn from the American "model"?

The major question relates to the role of the state.[35] In the United States, in terms of immigrant integration, it is considered that the state does not have to intervene in the social processes of an "automatic society";[36] the absence of institutional intervention (or its adverse effects) is compensated, it is thought, by the attraction of universal values based on individualistic freedom, equal opportunity, and the consensus about the American Dream. These beliefs may have been efficient for past immigrants from all over the world and even for racial minorities at times of economic expansion. They are not specific to America, and similar processes are observed in all rich democracies. But what about those who do not succeed and who are unable to denounce the exploitation, misery, and discrimination that they experience? Some observers claim that American affirmative action programs for minorities have two unintended effects: they stigmatize and marginalize the beneficiaries and generate the angry disapproval of other groups.[37] However, as shown by Cedric Herring and Sharon Collins in chapter 8, newcomers and minorities need specific protection to compensate for their power differentials. Affirmative action thus makes a difference in terms of economic and employment outcomes for minorities, improves images of minorities' work efforts, and reduces prevailing stereotypes. France, for its part, provides massive public support in terms of housing, education, health, family benefits, and the like, but its refusal to incorporate in its national debates concepts used to analyze problems of racism, discrimination, migration, and minorities may radically marginalize and alienate those who fail to pass the test of integration and assimilation. Such failure explains the limited but growing success of fundamentalists.

The strength of the American ideology comes from the tolerance of the diverging and multicultural identities of those who frequently adopt it voluntarily while preserving at the same time their own interpretation of the world.[38] French political elites do not see what multiculturalism would bring to the country. Yet France is now caught in an international (and European) matrix that may force it eventually to renegotiate its principles of assimilation.

Notes

1. The term *model* is, of course, an oversimplification. It is a social construct the only justification of which is to allow comparisons through the enlargement of certain features deserving attention.

2. Etienne Balibar and Immanuel Wallerstein, *Race, nation, classe* (Paris: La Découverte, 1988), 20.

3. Sophie Body-Gendrot, "Pioneering Moslem Women in France," in *Mobilizing the Community,* ed. Joe Kling and Robert Fisher (Beverly Hills, Calif.: Sage, 1993).

4. Gérard Noiriel. *Le Creuset français* (Paris: Le Seuil, 1988), 21.

5. Sophie Body-Gendrot and Martin Schain, "National Policies, Local Policies: A Comparative Analysis of the Development of Immigration Policies in France and in the U.S.," in *Immigrants in Two Democracies,* ed. Donald L. Horowitz and Gérard Noiriel (New York: New York University Press, 1992), 412.

6. Colette Beaune, *Naissance de la nation France* (Paris: Gallimard, 1985); Suzanne Citron, *Le Mythe national* (Paris: Editions Ouvrières, 1987), chap. 2.

7. Lawrence Fuchs, *The American Kaleidoscope* (Middletown, Conn.: Wesleyan University Press, 1990).

8. Dominique Schnapper, *La France de l'intégration* (Paris: Gallimard, 1991), 108. However, despite this iron law of assimilation, small distortions were tolerated within the secular public school, especially in favor of the Catholic religion. Alsace was granted special treatment. From the 1970s onward, after the repatriation of French Jewish families from North Africa to metropolitan France, Jewish students would frequently wear the yarmulke in public schools.

9. Automatic citizenship was modified by the conservative government of 1993, which required formal acquiescence.

10. For a case a contrario, see Michael Omi and Howard Winant, *Racial Formation in the United States* (New York: Routledge, 1986).

11. See Jean Jacques Israel and Simone Bonnafous, "Sans distinction de ... race," in *Mots* (Paris: FNSP, 1992).

12. Fuchs, *American Kaleidoscope*.

13. *Elk v. Wilkins,* 1884.

14. Sophie Body-Gendrot, *Les Etats-Unis et leurs immigrants* (Paris: La Documentation française, 1991).

15. See *INSEE Première* 234 (December 1992).

16. V. de Rudder, "Housing and Integration of Immigrants in the French Cities," in *Immigrants in Two Democracies,* ed. Horowitz and Noiriel; A. Belbahri, "Les Minguettes ou la surlocalisation du social," *Espaces et sociétés* 45 (July–December 1984).

17. The law is referred to under the name LOV–Loi d'orientation sur la ville.

18. G. Chevalier, "Le Social réduit à l'Urbain," *Le Monde,* July 7, 1993, 2.

19. The government elected in March 1993 tried to reach the widest possible constituency. The Home Ministry emphasized the security issue and repressive approaches while the Ministry of Health, Social Affairs, and City developed humanitarian concerns. The role of the prime minister was ambiguous: while asserting his strong friendship for the home secretary, who emphasized strong policing and immigration restriction, Balladur's rhetoric was frequently Left-oriented: "In our times, it is not less welfare that is required but more.... I would not want the economic crisis to be used as an excuse to destroy the welfare benefiting the most deprived recipients" (television interview, August 12, 1993).

20. According to the Schengen agreement, undocumented immigrants will be sent back to their first-entry European country. However, most of them destroy their IDs, and when they do not, their home countries are reluctant to take them back.

21. Barry James, "France to Act on Immigrants," *International Herald Tribune,* June 18, 1993.

22. On the question of how to recognize foreigners, Pasqua's simple answer—"by asking them for their papers"—has fueled controversy. The 1946 decree still in force states that "persons of foreign nationality must be in a position to present documents on the basis of which they are authorized to travel or reside in France in response to any request by the police." A previous bill would have authorized spot identity checks based "on any evidence other than race that a person is foreign." The formulation "suspected foreigner" has disappeared from the ultimate version of the law to put an end to accusations of discrimination.

23. François Dubet et al., *La galère* (Paris: Le Seuil, 1987); Pierre Bourdieu et al., *La misère du monde* (Paris: Le Seuil, 1993).

24. François Platone and Henri Rey, "La participation politique dans les quartiers en crise," in *L'Engagement politique* (Paris: FNSP, 1993), 953–80.

25. A few Canarsians saw the ghetto as "a jungle infested with dark-skinned 'animals' whose wild sexuality and broken families defied all ideas of civilized conduct.... An Italian utility worker wailed ... 'They live like animals' " (Jonathan Rieder, *Canarsie* [Cambridge, Mass.: Harvard University Press, 1985], 25–26).

26. Abdelmalek Sayad, "Une famille déplacée," in *La misère du monde,* ed. Bourdieu et al., 45–46.

27. Thomas H. Marshall, *Class, Citizenship and Social Development* (Westport, Conn.: Greenwood Press, 1973).

28. SOFRES Survey, *Le Figaro,* November 23, 1985; *Libération,* November 30, 1990.

29. Most parents, nationals or not, prefer their children to learn English or German. Only 7 percent of children of Arabic origin study Arabic in school, especially since it was discovered that some instructors sent by the countries of origin were proselytes encouraging the return of French acculturated children to the home country; see Danielle Boyzon-Fradet, "The French Education System: Springboard or Obstacle to Integration?" in *Immigration and Ethnicity,* ed. Horowitz and Noiriel, 148–66.

30. Sophie Body-Gendrot, *Ville et violence* (Paris: Presses universitaires de France, 1993), chaps. 2 and 3.

31. A public claim for a community identity is still rare in France. In the case of Islam, it started in the mid-1970s, after the war between Egypt and Israel and the first oil shock, when single birds of passage of North African origin turned into sedentary families with numerous children in the low-income outer fringe areas or decayed neighborhoods of French large cities. Family reunification was authorized by the Council of State, France's highest administrative authority, after the immigration gates closed. Islam became the second most common religion in France. I have explained elsewhere what the first collective strikes of Muslims were about; see Sophie Body-Gendrot, "Migration and Racialization of the Postmodern City in France," in *Racism, the City and the State,* ed. M. Cross and M. Keith (New York: Routledge, 1992).

32. Guillaume Malaurie, "Musulmans de France: Ni Bush ni Saddam," *L'Express,* January 31, 1991, 68.

33. On the whole, those fears were not founded, and more than three Muslims out of four declared that they had felt "no change in attitudes toward them" (SOFRES). The IFOP poll was taken between January 29 and February 1, 1991; the SOFRES poll on January 24 and 25.

34. Commission des droits de l'homme, *La Lutte contre le racisme et la xénophobie* (Paris: La Documentation française, 1992).

35. Thedda Skocpol, *Protecting Soldiers and Mothers* (Cambridge, Mass.: Harvard University Press, 1993).

36. Theodore Lowi, *The End of Liberalism* (New York: Norton, 1969).

37. Ony 19 percent of whites in 1991 approved of qualified blacks receiving preference over equally qualified whites in such matters as getting into college or getting jobs; 42 percent of blacks equally oppose special advantage for qualified blacks, even when justified by "past discrimination"; see Seyour Martin Lipset, "Two Americas, Two Value Systems: Blacks and Whites," *Tocqueville Review* 13, no. 1 (1992):137–77.

38. For examples, see Michael Peter Smith, Bernadette Tarallo, and George Kagiwada, "Colouring California: New Asian Immigrant Households, Social Networks, and the Local State," *International Journal of Urban and Regional Research* 15, no. 2 (1991): 250–68.

Part V

Race, Ethnicity, and Community Power

13 / When the Melting Pot Boils Over

The Irish, Jews, Blacks, and Koreans of New York

Roger Waldinger

Assimilation is the grand theme of American immigration research. The classic sociological position provided an optimistic counter to the dim assessments of the new immigrants prevalent at the early part of the century. Notwithstanding the marked differences that impressed contemporaries, Robert Park, Ernest Burgess, W. I. Thomas, and others contended that the new immigrant groups would lose their cultural distinctiveness and move up the occupational hierarchy. Milton Gordon's now classic volume distilled the essence of the sociological view: immigrant-ethnic groups start at the bottom and gradually move up; their mobility takes place through individual advancement, not group collective action; in the process of moving up, ethnic groups lose their distinctive social structure; and as ethnics become like members of the core group, they become part of the core group, joining it in neighborhoods, in friendship, and eventually in marriage.

But the image of immigrants moving onward and upward is hard to reconcile with the darker, conflictual side of American ethnic life. Conflict, often of the fiercest kind, runs like a red thread through the history of American ethnic groups. Certainly New Yorkers evince an extraordinary propensity to come to blows over racial and ethnic differences. The latest conflicts pitting blacks against Hasidim and Koreans in Brooklyn or Chinese against Puerto Ricans in Manhattan are but the latest episodes in a longer saga, extending from the anti-Catholic crusades of the 1850s to the school conflicts of the 1890s, to the controversies engendered by the Coughlinites and the German Bund of the 1930s, to the school integration struggles of the 1960s, right up to this day.

The contradiction between ethnic assimilation and ethnic conflict is more apparent than real. Where the classic sociological model goes wrong is not in its depiction of an upward trajectory, but rather in its individualistic assumptions about the process of ethnic change. The story of ethnic progress in America can be better thought of as a collective search for mobility, in which the succession of one migrant wave after another ensures a continuous competitive conflict over resources. Groups move up from the bottom by specializing in and dominating a particular branch of economic life; that specialization goes unchallenged as long as the newest arrivals are content to work in the bottom-level jobs for which they were initially recruited. This chapter develops the story in the form of brief episodes from the New York experience of four ethnic groups—Irish, Jews, African Americans, and Koreans. Each group is associated with the four successive waves of migration that have swept over New York in the past two hundred years.

The Irish

Nearly one and a half million Irish flocked to the United States between 1846 and 1855 in flight from famine; they converged on the eastern port cities of Boston, Philadelphia, and New York, where, lacking resources, about a quarter stayed. Low levels of education, lack of exposure to industrial or craft work, and lack of capital led the Irish into the lower ranges of manual work, with women taking domestic work and men engaging in insecure, low-paid itinerant employment, especially in construction. Irish progress from the bottom proceeded at a slow pace.

By 1900, however, the Irish had already established themselves in public employment. At the time, the public sector provided relatively few jobs, but this was soon to change. Irish employment in New York City government almost quadrupled between 1900 and 1930, increasing from just under 20,000 to 77,000, while the total number of city workers climbed from 54,000 to 148,000, less than a factor of three.[1]

Irish penetration into the public sector reflected the growing political power of the Democratic machine, which remained Irish dominated. But the machine's hold on local government was met by opposition from WASP reformers. Seeking to break the machine's power by severing the link between political activity and government employment, the reformers installed a civil service system—to little avail. The Irish encountered few effective competitors for city jobs. There was never any serious threat that WASPs would dislodge the Irish. Moreover, the increasingly numerous Poles, Jews, Italians, and others who were just off the boat had little chance of doing well in essay-type exams against the Irish, who were, after all, native English speakers.

The liabilities of the new immigrants lasted hardly a generation; with the Jews' rapid educational and occupational advancement, another competitor entered the scene. But as long as the Irish, through Tammany Hall's grip over city government, could control municipal hiring, interethnic competition posed little threat. Competition was structured in such a way as to minimize the value of Jews' educational advantages. The patronage system functioned unencumbered throughout Tammany's dominance between 1917 and 1933.

The depression severely challenged Irish control over public jobs; LaGuardia's election in 1933 delivered the coup de grace. Keeping control of City Hall required LaGuardia to undermine the material base of Tammany's power and consolidate his support among groups not firmly under Tammany's tow—the most important of which were the Jews, who had split between LaGuardia and his Tammany opponent in 1933. Both goals could be accomplished in the same way, namely pursuing the administrative changes long championed by the reformers.[2]

The depression and LaGuardia's reforms made city jobs more attractive to highly educated workers, which, under the circumstances, mainly meant Jews. One door at which Jewish competitors knocked was teaching, previously an Irish reserve (as the 1900 statistics show). If Jewish entrance into teaching produced antagonism, far more explosive was the situation in the police force. Twenty-nine thousand men sat for the exam held in April 1939, from whom three hundred were selected to enter the department in 1940. Of these, over one-third were Jews. Not surprisingly, this class of 1940 constituted the first significant proportion of Jews to enter the police.[3]

Jewish-Irish competition produced some other episodes, but conflict between them abated, thanks to the prosperity of the postwar era and the new opportunities it provided. Outmigration to the suburbs and the Sun Belt and mobility into the middle class depleted the ranks of the city's Irish population. By the late 1950s, as Nathan Glazer and Daniel Moynihan noted, so profound was the sense of displacement that the remaining Irish New Yorkers reminded themselves, "There are still some of us left."[4]

Those who are left have kept up the long-established Irish occupational ways. Although the commissioners of the police and fire departments are black and Puerto Rican, respectively, the top brass retains a strongly Irish cast, as does the rank and file. Indeed, the fire department presents a glimpse of New York gone by, with a workforce that is 93 percent white and 80 percent Catholic. Some unions still have a distinctly Irish makeup.[5]

In the 1980s, some of the old niches at last gained new blood, as an influx of new, illegal Irish immigrants fled unemployment in the Republic of Ireland for better times in New York. Whereas black Americans still found the doors of construction unions closed, the new arrivals, dubbed "JFK carpenters," were warmly welcomed by their aging compatriots. Women also retraced the steps of the past, as could be seen from the classified pages of the *Irish Echo,* with its columns of ads for nannies, babysitters, and housekeepers.

The Jews

Although the Jewish presence in New York extends far back, almost to the city's founding, Jews did not become an important, visible element in the city's economic life until the 1880s. Rising anti-Semitism, combined with the pressures of modernization, led to a huge outflow of Jews from Eastern Europe. By 1920, New York, with two million Jews, had become the world's largest Jewish city.

The new arrivals came just when the demand for factory-made clothing began to surge. Many had been tailors in the old country, and although most had worked with needle and thread, they quickly adapted themselves to machine production. As the various components of the clothing industry grew in synergistic fashion, the opportunities for mobility through the ethnic economy multiplied. Through rags, some immigrants found riches: the sweatshop workers who moved to contracting and then to manufacturing, or possibly careers in retailing, filled the newly formed ranks of New York's *alrightniks.*[6]

The Jewish concentration in commerce and clothing manufacture defined their initial place in the ethnic division of labor. Jewish specializations seldom overlapped with the Irish: domestic service and general labor were rarities among the Russians but were common Irish pursuits; by the same token, tailoring and retailing, whether by merchant or peddler, were far more likely to engage Russians than Irish.

As Jews sought to move beyond the ethnic economy, interethnic competition and antagonism grew more intense. The relatively rapid educational progress of younger immigrants and of the second generation prepared them to work outside the ethnic economy, but gentile employers were rarely eager to hire Jews. One study, completed just before the Great Depression, found that the doors of New York's large, corporate organizations — "railroads, banks, insurance companies, lawyers' offices, brokerage houses, the New York Stock Exchange, hotels ... and the home offices of large corporations of the first rank" — were infrequently opened to Jews.[7] The surge into the schools, and through the schools into the professions, met with resistance from the older, largely Protestant population that dominated these institutions.

In the 1930s, depression and discrimination outside the ethnic economy led many second-generation Jews to seek an alternative in public employment. Although the quest for government jobs, and in particular teaching positions, had started earlier, the straitened circumstances of the 1930s accelerated this search. The quality and quantity of Jews vying for government employment increased, heightening the competitive pressure on the Irish and yielding the antagonism we've already observed.

Jewish-Irish conflict reached its height in the late 1930s; it gradually subsided, replaced by a more explosive, deeply antagonistic relationship with blacks. Although black occupations were more similar to those of the Irish than they were to the Jews', the economic pursuits of Jews put them at odds with blacks on various counts. The Jews dominated small retail activity throughout the city and were particularly prominent in Harlem. The Jewish storeowners in Harlem sold to blacks but preferred not to employ them until protests in the mid-1930s finally forced them to relent. Antagonism toward Jewish shopkeepers in Harlem rose during the 1930s, fueled by the depression and by Jews' broader role as middlemen in the Harlem economy. Frustration boiled over in the riot of 1943, when black Harlemites burned down the stores of Jews in a fury that presaged events to come.[8] Hostility simmered thereafter, reaching the boiling point during the 1960s.

The transformation of the ethnic economy also engendered black-Jewish conflict. Rapid Jewish social mobility meant a dwindling Jewish working class; the diminishing supply of Jewish workers had a particularly notable effect on the garment industry, where Jewish factory owners were forced to hire outsiders in growing numbers — first Italians, then blacks. In World War II, desperate for workers, Jewish employers hired blacks in great numbers. By 1950, there were 25,000 African American garment workers, 20,000 more than were working in clothing factories ten years before.[9]

But relations between blacks and Jews proved uneasy. Blacks moved into less-skilled, poorer-paying positions, from which mobility into better-remunerated positions proved difficult. Although the garment unions made explicit efforts to organize black workers and integrate them into union structures, few blacks moved up to elected offices, and none high up in the union hierarchy. To protect jobs from southern competitors, the unions adopted a policy of wage restraint, which inevitably meant a softened stance on union employers at home—much to the dismay of black New York garment workers.[10]

The garment business was the Jewish enclave of the past; Jewish mobility into the middle class had made teaching the Jewish niche of the mid-1960s. As the schools came to serve a growing black population, their role was increasingly contested by black students, parents, and protest organizations. The complaints were various, and not all directly linked to the Jews' prominent role in the school system; but the situation in which so many Jews were teachers and so many schools in black neighborhoods were staffed by Jews inevitably led to conflict. In 1968, a black-dominated school board in Brooklyn dismissed a group of white, largely Jewish teachers and replaced them with a mainly black staff; these actions set off a three-month-long strike by the Jewish-led teachers' union. Although the union eventually won, its victory was pyrrhic, at least concerning black-Jewish relations. Memory of the strike and the resentments it fueled have not significantly changed, even a generation later.[11]

What has altered, however, is the economic position of the Jews. The ethnic economy of the immigrant days remains, but in vestigial form. Although Jews are still active in the garment industry, they mainly concentrate in the designing and merchandising ends. "Goldberg" no longer runs clothing factories; his place has been taken by "Kim" and "Wong," who only employ compatriots, not blacks. The same transformations have changed the face of petty retailing and small landlording—the older flash points of black-Jewish conflict. The Jewish presence in the public sector is also fading fast: working as a city engineer or accountant used to be a Jewish occupation; now these careers engage far many more Patels than Cohens.[12] Only in teaching and in higher education do the Jewish concentrations of the past remain in full force.[13]

A distinctive Jewish role in New York's economy still lives on. It is to be found in the professions, in the persistently high rate of Jewish self-employment, in the prominence of Jews in law, real estate, finance, and the media. But the current Jewish pursuits differ crucially from the older ethnic economy in that they are detached from the dynamics of interethnic competition that characterized earlier periods. In a sense, the material basis that underlay anti-Semitic currents in New York for most of the twentieth century is gone. But its legacy and the many other resources around which groups can compete—status, politics, and territory—ensure continued conflict between Jews and their ethnic neighbors.

The Blacks

In 1890, the black share of the New York population was 1.6 percent—just about what it had been on the eve of the Civil War. But in the 1890s the South started losing blacks due to outmigration, and that loss quickly translated into New York's gain. By 1920, New York housed 150,000 black residents—who, although only 3 percent of the city's population, made New York the country's largest black urban concentration. In the next twenty years, as European immigration faltered and then stopped, and bad conditions in the rural South provided additional reasons to leave, the number of black New Yorkers tripled. Postwar prosperity and a new wave of mechanization down South launched a final, massive flow northward: by 1960, the African American population of New York numbered 1,088,000, of whom approximately 320,000 had moved to the city from other areas (mainly the South) in the previous ten years.[14]

It was not until 1940 that black New Yorkers moved out of the peripheries of the New York economy. At the turn of the century, blacks mainly found work in domestic labor, with 90 percent of black women and 55 percent of black men working in some type of domestic service occupation. Blacks' confinement to domestic service reflected, in part, the unfavorable terms of competition with immigrants, who had evicted them from trades where they had previously been accepted. The continued expansion of New York's economy slowly opened doors in a few manufacturing industries; the shutoff of immigration during World War I and its permanent demise after 1924 further accelerated dispersion into other fields.[15]

But the depression largely put an end to these gains. By 1940, 40 percent of blacks still worked in personal service—a far greater proportion than among the workforce overall.[16] With the advent of World War II doors to other jobs were finally unlocked; manufacturing, in particular, saw very large black employment gains. Yet unlike the case in Chicago or Detroit, the black sojourn in New York's manufacturing sector proved shortlived. Lacking auto factories or steel mills, New York's goods-producing sector was a concentration of low-wage jobs; white workers remained ensconced in the better-paying, more skilled positions. Opportunities for blacks were more easily found in the burgeoning service sector—for example, health care—and in government; hence, blacks quickly dispersed into other fields.

Government, where 35 percent of native-born black New Yorkers worked in 1990,[17] has become the black niche par excellence. The history of black employment in the public sector provides yet another example of the continuing, interethnic competitive conflicts over jobs and economic resources in which New York's ethnic groups have been engaged.

In the early years of the twentieth century, local government, like most other New York employers, closed its doors to blacks: in 1911, the city only employed 511 blacks, almost all of whom were laborers. In the early 1920s, Tammany installed the leader of its black client organization, the United Colored Democracy, as a member of the three-person Civil Service Commission, but black access to public jobs changed marginally. By the late 1920s, the city counted 2,275 black workers on its payroll, of whom 900 were in laboring jobs and an additional 700 were in other noncompetitive or per diem positions.[18] The reform regime did more for blacks, pushing black employment above parity by 1940.[19] But these effects occurred as a result of the government's burgeoning payrolls, and they were mainly felt in the black concentrations of hospitals, sanitation, and public works, where more than 80 percent of the city's black job holders worked in 1935.[20] Moreover, blacks remained vulnerable to discriminatory practices, as in the city-owned subway system, where blacks only worked as porters, with the exception of a few stations in Harlem. Most important, the employment system that emerged during the depression put blacks at a structural disadvantage in competition with whites. Lacking the educational skills and credentials needed to qualify for most city jobs, blacks and Puerto Ricans found themselves channeled into noncompetitive positions, of which the single largest concentration was found in the municipal hospital system. From here there were few routes of movement upward, as these bottom-level positions were disconnected from the competitive system, which promoted from within.

Race didn't reach the top of the government's agenda until 1965, when John Lindsay arrived in office, the first reformer elected mayor since La-Guardia.[21] Elected with the votes of liberals and minorities, Lindsay lacked his predecessors' commitments to the interests of the largely white, civil service workforce and pledged to increase black and Puerto Rican employment in city agencies. But the new mayor quickly discovered that the civil service structure was not easily amenable to change. Lindsay gradually made progress in reducing the inflated eligibility requirements inherited from the depression, but resistance proved severe when his reforms threatened established white ethnic workers in the better-paid ranks.

Lindsay's main focus, in contrast to earlier reform administrations, was to evade the civil service system and its unionized defenders. The Lindsay administration created new, less-skilled positions for which minority residents could be more easily hired. But this approach never involved large numbers and, more important, left existing eligibility requirements unchallenged, shunting minority recruits into dead-end jobs, where they were marooned.

Lindsay backed off from his confrontations with the civil service system and its defenders in the aftermath of the disastrous 1968 teachers' strike. Where the mayor could both accommodate the unions and pursue his earlier goals of increasing minority employment, he did — mainly by tripling the number of exempt workers and shifting them from agency to agency to avoid the requirement of taking an examination. But in other instances, pressure from civil service interests proved overwhelming. With Abraham Beame's accession to City Hall in 1973, followed in 1977 by Edward Koch, mayoral support for black employment gains vanished for the next sixteen years.

The 1970s and 1980s nevertheless saw dramatic gains in black government employment. Like earlier white ethnic groups that had developed a concentration in public jobs, blacks benefited from simultaneous shifts in the structure of employment and in the relative availability of competing groups.

Changes in the structure of employment came from a variety of sources. The Equal Employment Opportunity (EEO) Act of 1972 prohibited discrimination in local government. By requiring local governments to maintain records on all employees by race and gender and to submit them to the Equal Employment Opportunity Commission, with the clear expectation that governments would show improvement over time, the act also led to institutional changes. As EEO functions were established in each city agency, recruitment and personnel practices changed in ways that benefited previously excluded groups, as recruitment became focused on minority and immigrant communities.

Moreover, the 1972 act provided minority employees with levers to act on more recalcitrant agencies, which they used with greatest effectiveness in the uniformed services. For example, in 1973 the Vulcan Society (the organization of black firefighters) successfully challenged the results of a 1971 exam, leading to an imposition of a 1:3 quota for the duration of that list

(1973–79). In 1979, the Guardians and the Hispanic Society challenged the 1979 police officer's exam; court findings of disparate impact led to the imposition of a 33.3 percent minority quota for the duration of the list.

While the advent of affirmative action helped increase access for blacks and other minorities, other changes on the supply side hastened the growth of black employment. Although the city's attraction to its traditional white ethnic labor force had begun to diminish by the 1960s, the fiscal crisis of the mid-1970s decisively exacerbated and extended the city's recruitment difficulties among its traditional workforce. By the time large-scale hiring resumed in the early 1980s, public employment had become a less attractive option than before. Moreover, municipal salaries and benefits took a severe beating during the fiscal crisis; although compensation edged back upward during the 1980s, real gains never recaptured the losses endured during the 1970s. The strength enjoyed by New York's private sector during the 1980s pulled native white workers up the hiring queue and out of the effective labor supply for many city agencies.[22]

In a situation where "the City was hiring a great deal and not turning away anyone who was qualified," as one deputy commissioner told me in an interview, the disparity in the availability of minority and white workers led to rapid recruitment of minority workers. Minorities had constituted only 40 percent of the new workers hired in 1977, making up the majority in only two low-paid occupational categories. By 1987, minorities made up 56 percent of all hires, dominating the ranks of new recruits in five out of eight occupational categories.[23]

Thus, the Koch years of 1977 to 1989 saw the ethnic composition of the municipal workforce completely transformed, notwithstanding the mayor's opposition to affirmative action and the disfavor with which minority leaders greeted his hiring policies. By 1990, whites constituted 48 percent of the 375,000 people working for the city and just slightly more—50 percent—of the 150,000 people working in the agencies that the mayor directly controlled.[24] The declining white presence in municipal employment chiefly benefited blacks. Blacks constituted 25 percent of the city's population and a still smaller proportion of residents who were older than eighteen and thus potentially employable, but made up 36 percent of the city's total workforce and 38 percent of those who worked in the mayoral agencies. Although blacks were still underrepresented in some of the city's most desirable jobs, the earlier pattern of concentration at the bottom was overcome. The municipal hospital system, which employed two-thirds of the city's black employees in the early 1960s, in 1990 employed less than one-fifth, reflecting the dispersion of blacks throughout the municipal sector. And higher-level jobs showed clusters of considerable black overrepresentation as well, with blacks accounting for 40 percent of the administrators and 36 percent of the professionals employed in the direct mayoral agencies.

By 1990, when David Dinkins became New York's first black mayor, the phase of black-for-white succession in municipal employment was nearly complete. Blacks held just over 35 percent of all city jobs; although unevenly represented among the city's many agencies, they were often a dominant presence, accounting for more than 40 percent of employment in six of the ten largest agencies, and more than 50 percent of employment in three of the largest ten.

The comparison with Latinos underlines blacks' advantage in the new ethnic division that has emerged in city government. Whereas the city's Latinos and black populations are equal in number, Latinos hold one-third as many municipal jobs as do blacks. The discrepancies are even greater as one moves up the occupational hierarchy into the ranks of managers and professionals. And blacks have been far more successful than Latinos in gaining new permanent civil service jobs, rather than the provisional appointments on which Latinos have mainly relied. The disparity has not gone unnoticed, as the Commission on Hispanic Concerns pointed out in a 1986 report.[25] Of course, other answers might be invoked to explain Latino's municipal jobs deficit relative to blacks. But whatever the precise explanation, Mayor Dinkins's continuing conflicts with the Hispanic community suggest that earlier patterns of interethnic competition over municipal jobs remain alive and well.

The Koreans

In the mid-1960s, just when New York could no longer retain its native population, it reverted back to its role as an immigrant mecca. Immigrants began flocking to New York immediately after the liberalization of U.S. immigration laws in 1965. Their arrival has been the principal driving force of demographic and ethnic change in New York ever since — and will continue to be for the foreseeable future.

In 1965, what no one expected was the burgeoning of Asian immigration. The reforms tilted the new system toward immigrants with kinship ties to permanent residents or citizens. Since there had been so little Asian immigration in the previous fifty years, how could Asian newcomers find settlers with whom to seek reunification? The answer is that kinship connections were helpful, but not essential. The 1965 reforms also created opportunities for immigrants whose skills—as engineers, doctors, nurses, pharmacists—were in short supply. Along with students already living in the United States and enjoying easy access to American employers, these professionals made up the first wave of new Asian immigrants, creating the basis for the kinship migration of less well educated relatives.

Thus, well-educated, highly skilled immigrants have dominated the Korean influx to the United States and to New York in particular. Although Koreans constitute a small portion of New York's new immigrants—rarely more than 3 percent of the eighty thousand to ninety thousand legal immigrants who come to New York each year—they play an important and very visible role. As middle-aged newcomers with poor English-language skills and often lacking professional licenses, relatively few Koreans have managed to steer a route back into the fields for which they trained. Instead they have turned to small business, setting up new businesses at a rate that few other groups can rival.

Koreans started in fruit and vegetable stores, taking over shops in all areas of the city, regardless of neighborhood composition or customer clientele. From there, Koreans moved on to other retail specialties—dry cleaning, fish stores, novelty shops, and nail salons. By 1980, a third of New York Korean males were already self-employed. The *1991 Korean Business Directory* provides a ready indicator of commercial growth over the 1980s, listing over 120 commercial specialties in which Korean firms are to be found.[26]

The roots of the Korean ethnic economy are found in several sources. The competitive field was open. By the middle to late 1960s, the sons and daughters of Jewish and Italian storekeepers had better things to do than mind a store, and their parents, old, tired, and scared of crime, were ready to sell out to the newcomers from Korea. By the 1980s, the supply of new, native-born white entrepreneurs had virtually dried up. One survey of neighborhood businesses in Queens and Brooklyn found that almost half of the white-owned shops were run by immigrants and that most white businesses were long-established entities, in contrast to the newly founded Korean shops with which they competed.[27]

Another spur to growth came from within the ethnic community. Koreans, like every other immigrant group, have special tastes and needs that are best served by an insider: the growth of the Korean population has created business for Korean accountants, doctors, brokers, hair stylists, and restaurant owners. Although the Korean community is too small to support a huge commercial infrastructure oriented to ethnic needs, the community has utilized its ethnic connections to Korea to develop commercial activities oriented toward non-Korean markets. Active trade relations between South Korea and the United States have provided a springboard for many Korean-owned import-export businesses, of which 119 are listed in the *1991 Korean Business Directory.*

Finally, the social structure of the Korean community itself generates advantages for business success that few other immigrant groups share. Many Koreans emigrate with capital, and those who are cash poor can raise money through rotating credit associations known as *gae.* Because Koreans migrate in complete family units, family members provide a supply of cheap and trusted labor. The prevalence of self-employment means that many Koreans have close ties to other business owners, who in turn are a source of information and support, and the high organizational density of the Korean community—which is characterized by an incredible proliferation of alumni clubs, churches, businessman's associations—provides additional conduits for the flow of business information and the making of needed contacts. These community resources distinguish the Koreans from their competitors, who are less likely to be embedded in ethnic or family ties that can be drawn upon for help with business information, capital assistance, or staffing problems.

The Koreans have discovered that conflict *need not* be interethnic; there are other sources of threat, and in the 1980s they mobilized Korean merchants on a considerable scale. Like other small business owners, Koreans were unhappy with local government, usually with something that government was doing or was threatening to do. Fruit and vegetable store owners felt that sanitation officials were too conscientious about sidewalk cleanliness, especially since the result of the officials' demands was often a fine that the Korean store owner had to pay. Pressuring the city to relax inspections became a high priority for Korean organizations. In the late 1980s, as the city's fiscal crisis led it to search for new sources of revenue, fiscal planners thought of placing a special tax on dry cleaners. So Korean dry cleaners entered an unusual coalition with the white owners of commercial laundries, and the union that represented the laundryworkers, to roll back the planned tax. Like other small business owners, Korean merchants could also become dissatisfied with government's *failure* to act. The prosperity of the

1980s gave commercial landlords license to raise rents to the maximum, much to the distress of small business owners throughout the city. Koreans joined with their non-Korean counterparts to push for commercial rent control — to no avail.

Although Italians and Jews have largely deserted petty retail trade, they have remained in wholesaling, where the businesses are larger and profits more sizable. Thus Jewish and Italian fruit and vegetable or fish wholesalers have acquired a substantial Korean trade. The encounter has not always been a happy one, as Illsoo Kim recounted in his pathbreaking book: "Especially in their first years of emergence into the fruit and vegetable business, Koreans reported many incidents at the Hunts Point [wholesale] Market. The incidents ranged from unfair pricing and sale of poor-quality produce by the Italian and Jewish wholesalers, to physical threats and beatings administered by competing white retailers."[28] Such conflicts sparked the first mass demonstration by Koreans ever in New York. Although Kim reports that Koreans were subsequently accepted by the wholesaling community, there have been continued incidents and protests, including a recent boycott by Koreans of one of the city's largest fish wholesalers.[29]

In New York, as in almost every other major American city, black neighborhoods have provided new immigrants from Asia and the Middle East with an important economic outlet. To some extent, Koreans and other immigrants have simply replaced older white groups that had long sold to blacks and were now eager to bail out of an increasingly difficult and tense situation. By opening stores in black neighborhoods Koreans were also filling the gap left by the departure of large, nonethnic chain stores, which were steadily eliminating the low-margin, high-cost operations involved in serving a ghetto clientele. Selling to black customers proved fraught with conflict. Small protests erupted in the late 1970s. In 1981 a boycott erupted along 125th Street, Harlem's main commercial thoroughfare, with black leaders calling Korean shop owners "vampires" who came to Harlem to "suck black consumers dry."[30]

Repeated security problems as well as more organized clashes led Korean store owners to establish neighborhood prosperity associations, in addition to those organizations that grouped merchants in a particular retail branch. Thus, alongside groups like the Korean Produce Association or the Korean Apparel Contractors Associations, one finds neighborhood groups like the Korean Merchant Association of the Bronx or the Uptown Korean

Merchants Association, which seek "to improve Korean merchants' relations with local residents or communities" while lobbying local police for more effective support.[31]

In 1990 antagonism between black shoppers and Korean merchants erupted in picket lines set up in front of two Korean stores in the Flatbush section of Brooklyn. The clash started with a dispute between a Korean store owner and a black Haitian customer who charged assault; that claim then provoked black activist groups — of fairly dubious repute[32] — to establish a boycott that targeted not only the offending owner, but a neighboring Korean merchant against whom no injury was ever charged.

The boycott lasted for months, choking off business at both stores. Although customers disappeared, the two stores were kept alive by contributions from the organized Korean community, which perceived a broader danger to its economic viability should the boycott succeed. As time went on, government officials were inevitably involved. The boycott became a crisis for Mayor Dinkins, who was widely criticized for not actively seeking an end to the dispute.

The boycott ground to a halt, and a court threw out the legal suit brought by the aggrieved Haitian shopper. Other, fortunately short-lived boycotts were started in New York even while the Flatbush dispute lingered on. A clash in a nearby Brooklyn area between blacks and a small group of Vietnamese refugees — possibly mistaken for Koreans — showed how quickly tensions generated in one arena could move to another.

Conclusion

The story of New York's Irish, Jews, blacks, and Koreans is richer and more complicated than the occupational histories I've recounted in the preceding pages. But if the chapter's deliberately one-sided focus provides only a partial account, it reminds us of ethnicity's continuing importance, and not simply because of feelings for one's own kind or animosities toward outsiders. Rather, ethnicity's centrality stems from its role as the mechanism whereby groups of categorically different workers have been sorted into an identifiably distinct set of jobs. In this sense, the ethnic division of labor has been the central division of labor in modern New York. Now, as in the past, distinctive roles in the ethnic division of labor impart a sense of "weness" and group interest — ensuring the persistence of ethnic fragmentation and conflict.

Notes

1. Stephen Erie, *Rainbow's End* (Berkeley: University of California Press, 1988), 88–89.

2. Thomas Kessner, *Fiorella H. LaGuardia* (New York: McGraw-Hill, 1989); Charles Garrett, *The LaGuardia Years* (New Brunswick, N.J.: Rutgers University Press, 1961).

3. A survey of the surviving members of the class indicates that 38 percent were Catholic and 36 percent Jewish, with Russia and Ireland the leading countries of origin of the respondents' grandparents (Richard Herrnstein et al., "New York City Police Department Class of 1940: A Preliminary Report" [unpublished manuscript, Department of Psychology, Harvard University, n.d.]).

4. Nathan Glazer and Daniel P. Moynihan, *Beyond the Melting Pot* (Cambridge, Mass.: MIT Press, 1969).

5. Data on the ethnic composition of the fire department are from *Equal Employment Opportunity Statistics: Agency Full Report* (New York: New York City Department of Personnel, 1990); data on the religious composition are from Center for Social Policy and Practice in the Workplace, *Gender Integration in the Fire Department of the City of New York* (New York: Columbia University School of Social Work, 1988), 41.

6. Roger Waldinger, *Through the Eye of the Needle* (New York: New York University Press, 1986).

7. Heywood Broun and George Britt, *Christians Only* (New York: Vantage Press, 1931), 244.

8. Dominic Capeci, *The Harlem Riot of 1943* (Philadelphia: Temple University Press, 1977), 172.

9. Waldinger, *Through the Eye of the Needle,* 109–10. Employment data calculated from the census apply to employed persons twenty-five to sixty-four years old only. "Blacks" refers to native-born African Americans only. Data calculated from the Public Use Microdata Samples (U.S. Bureau of the Census, *Census of Population, 1940,* Public Use Microdata Samples [Computer file] [Washington, D.C.: U.S. Dept. of Commerce, Bureau of the Census, producer, 1983; Ann Arbor, Mich.: Inter-university Consortium for Political and Social Research, distributor, 1984]; U.S. Bureau of the Census, Census of Population, 1950, Public Use Microdata Samples [Computer file] [Washington, D.C.: U.S. Dept. of Commerce, Bureau of the Census, and Madison: University of Wisconsin, Center for Demography and Ecology, producers, 1984; Ann Arbor, Mich.: Inter-university Consortium for Political and Social Research, distributor, 1984]).

10. Hasia Diner, *In the Almost Promised Land* (Westport, Conn.: Greenwood Press, 1977), presents a favorable account of the response among the Jewish trade union elite to the black influx into the garment industry; see chap. 6. Herbert Hill has offered a far more critical account in numerous writings, most important, "The Racial Practices of Organized Labor: The Contemporary Record," in *Organized Labor and the Negro,* ed. Julius Jacobson (New York: Doubleday, 1968), 286–337. For a judicious balancing of the issues, see Nancy Green, "Juifs et noirs aux etats-unis: La rupture d'une 'alliance naturelle,'" *Annales, E.S.C.,* no. 2 (March–April 1987): 445–64.

11. Diane Ravitch, *The Great School Wars* (New York: Basic Books, 1974).

12. Roger Waldinger, "The Making of an Immigrant Niche," *International Migration Review* 28, no. 1 (1994).

13. "The Debate Goes On," *Alumnus: The City College of New York* 87, no. 1 (Winter 1992): 8–11.

14. Emmanuel Tobier, "Population," in *Setting Municipal Priorities,* ed. Charles Brecher and Raymond Horton (New York: New York University Press, 1981), 24.

15. Data are from U.S. Bureau of the Census, *Occupations at the 1900 Census* (Washing-

ton, D.C.: GPO, 1904). See also Herman Bloch, *The Circle of Discrimination* (New York: New York University Press, 1969).

16. Data are from the U.S. Bureau of the Census, *Census of Population, 1940.*

17. Calculated from the U.S. Bureau of the Census, *Census of Population and Housing, 1990,* Public Use Microdata Sample (a Sample): 5-Percent Sample (computer file) (Washington, D.C.: U.S. Dept. of Commerce, producer, 1993; Ann Arbor, Mich.: Inter-university Consortium for Political and Social Research, distributor, 1993).

18. Colored Citizens' Non-Partisan Committee for the Re-election of Mayor Walker, *New York City and the Colored Citizen* (n.d. [1930?]), LaGuardia Papers, Box 3530, New York Municipal Archives.

19. Calculated from U.S. Bureau of the Census, *Census of Population, 1940,* Public Use Microdata Samples. Also see Edwin Levinson, *Black Politics in New York City* (New York: Twayne, 1974).

20. Ira Katznelson, *Black Men, White Cities* (New York: Oxford University Press, 1973), 82.

21. For a more detailed discussion of the Lindsay period, see Roger Waldinger, "The Ethnic Politics of Municipal Jobs," working paper no. 248, UCLA Institute of Industrial Relations, Los Angeles, 1993.

22. Raymond Horton, "Human Resources," in Charles Brecher and Raymond Horton, eds., *Setting Municipal Priorities* (New York: New York University Press, 1986). See also Roger Waldinger, "Changing Ladders and Musical Chairs," *Politics and Society* 15, no. 4 (1986–87):369–402, and "Making of an Immigrant Niche."

23. City of New York, Citywide Equal Employment Opportunity Committee, *Equal Employment Opportunity in New York City Government, 1977–1987* (New York: Citywide Equal Employment Opportunity Committee, 1988), 6.

24. Data are from unpublished EEOC reports from the New York City Department of Personnel, New York City Board of Education, New York City Transit Authority, and New York City Health and Hospitals Corporation.

25. City of New York, Mayor's Commission on Hispanic Concerns, *Report* (New York: Mayor's Commission on Hispanic Concerns, 1986), 109.

26. *1991 Korean Business Directory* (Long Island City, N.Y.: Korean News, 1991).

27. Roger Waldinger, "Structural Opportunity or Ethnic Advantage: Immigrant Business Development in New York," *International Migration Review* 23, no. 1 (1989): 61.

28. Illsoo Kim, *The New Urban Immigrants* (Princeton, N.J.: Princeton University Press, 1981), 51.

29. Pyong Gap Min, "Cultural and Economic Boundaries of Korean Ethnicity: A Comparative Analysis," *Ethnic and Racial Studies* 14, no. 2 (1991), 235.

30. Lucie Cheng and Yen Espiritu, "Korean Businesses in Black and Hispanic Neighborhoods," *Sociological Perspectives* 32, no. 4 (1989): 521.

31. Illsoo Kim, "The Koreans: Small Business in an Urban Frontier," in *New Immigrants in New York,* ed. Nancy Foner (New York: Columbia University Press, 1987), 238.

32. Tamar Jacoby, "Sonny Carson and the Politics of Protest," *NY: The City Journal* 1, no. 4 (1991): 29–40.

14 / Beyond "Politics by Other Means"?

Empowerment Strategies for Los Angeles'
Asian Pacific Community

Harold Brackman and Steven P. Erie

Introduction

Asian Pacific politics has been characterized as "politics by other means," for example, indirect influence through interest group lobbying, targeted campaign contributions, litigation, and protest rather than through the traditional direct electoral routes of voting and officeholding. This model of indirect group influence puts the best face possible on the fact that, historically, Asian Pacifics have been highly underrepresented among voters and elected officeholders.[1]

In the 1990s, are Asian Pacifics successfully making the transition to electorally based empowerment, as the nation's other ethnic groups have done? In this chapter we examine the electoral empowerment prospects of Asian Pacifics in seemingly the best case for a breakthrough outside of Hawaii: the Los Angeles metropolitan area. Measured by officeholding, minority political influence is more advanced in the Los Angeles metropolitan area than elsewhere in California. In 1991 over 40 percent of the state's forty-eight Asian Pacific elected officials came from the Los Angeles area. In Los Angeles County, California's demographic future already has arrived. By 1990 the metropolitan area contained over one-third of the state's Asian Pacific residents.

Analyzing both obstacles to minority electoral empowerment and strategies to overcome them in an important metropolitan test case, we will also argue that, normatively, "politics by other means" cannot substitute for full democratic participation by Asian Pacific Americans.

Unlike the Bay Area, where Chinese Americans make up over one-half of the Asian Pacific community, in southern California no nationality group constitutes over 30 percent of the overall Asian Pacific population. The Chinese, Filipino, Korean, and Japanese communities each have 125,000 to 250,000 members, followed by smaller numbers of Vietnamese, Asian Indians, Cambodians, Thais, Laotians, and Pacific Islanders. This diversity offers unique challenges for pan-Asian coalition building.

Asian Pacific Electoral Behavior

The Pyramid of Voter Participation

Electoral power can be conceived of as the peak of a pyramid that is very difficult for Asian Pacific Americans to climb because of distinctive patterns of age, citizenship, voter registration, and turnout. Asian Pacifics — deriving either by birth or ancestry from East and Southeast Asia, the Indian subcontinent, and the Pacific Basin archipelagos — made up 10 percent of California's 1990 population. Yet they represented only 7 percent of the state's vote-eligible adult citizens and 3 percent of its actual voters. Partly as a consequence of limited group electoral power, there were no Asian Pacific state legislators between 1980 and 1992.

The dynamics of Asian Pacific voter underrepresentation in California are both similar to *and* different from those of Latinos, the state's other highly underrepresented ethnic group. Both Asian Pacifics and Latinos are proportionately — and substantially — handicapped by young populations. In 1990 adults made up only 61 percent of the Asian Pacific and Latino communities compared with 74 percent of the black and 85 percent of the Anglo populations. Among adults, Asian Pacifics had higher citizenship rates than Latinos — 73 percent versus 62 percent. Among *adult citizens,* however, Asian Pacifics had lower voter registration rates than Latinos — 35 percent versus 42 percent. Registered Asian Pacifics and Latino voters, though, had similar depressed turnout rates — 33 percent. The cumulative effects of the barriers of age, citizenship, voter registration, and turnout on minority empowerment are staggering. The number of Asian Pacific voters would increase by nearly fivefold if the community's age, citizenship, registration, and voter profiles matched those for the Anglo population.[2]

Asian Pacifics have greater need for voter registration campaigns, while Latinos are more in need of citizenship drives. This differential mobilization logic is underscored when we analyze the changes over time in Asian and Latino citizenship and registration rates. Citizenship rates for adult Asians have increased significantly—both absolutely and relative to Latinos—since 1986. In that year the adult Asian citizenship rate closely mirrored that for Latinos—60 percent versus 57 percent. By 1990, however, the Asian citizenship rate jumped to 73 percent while the Latino rate had barely increased to 62 percent. Conversely, the Asian voter registration rate for adult citizens plummeted from 45 percent to 35 percent between 1986 and 1990 while the Latino registration rate remained relatively constant at slightly over 40 percent.

The UCLA Asian Pacific American Voter Registration Study estimated that in 1984 Japanese Americans, with the highest citizenship rate, had the highest voter registration rate—43 percent—among adult Asian Pacifics in Los Angeles County. In contrast, only an estimated 35 percent of the region's adult Chinese, 29 percent of Samoans, 27 percent of Filipinos, 17 percent of Asian Indians, 13 percent of Koreans, and 4 percent of Vietnamese were registered voters. There are also significant group differences among Asian Pacifics in party allegiance as well as turnout rates. Compared with Anglos, however, Asian Pacifics are both less partisan and less likely to vote.[3]

A Political Balance Sheet

The still prevalent image of Asians as a model minority is actually a double exposure. It pictures them as both economic overachievers and political underachievers. Observers offer a wide variety of explanations—and even differ over whether political quiescence really is a cause for concern—but virtually none challenges the view that Asian Pacifics remain politically a population of silent Americans.

As the 1990s opened, there was some evidence to support a more positive assessment. Despite limited Asian Pacific voting strength, Asians were beginning to be elected to local office. In 1980 Filipino Tony Trias, appointed to fill a vacancy on the Los Angeles Unified school board, was the sole Asian Pacific to hold a major city or county elected office. Ten years later, Warren Furutani had won a seat on the school board and Julia Wu on the Community College Board. Elected in 1985 in a 10 percent Asian Pacific district, Michael Woo became Los Angeles' first Asian Pacific councilman. In 1993, however, Woo failed in his bid to become the city's first Asian American mayor.

Building on earlier officeholding gains in the incorporated suburbs of the San Gabriel Valley, Monterey Park in 1990 became the first mainland U. S. city to have two Chinese Americans serving on its city council. Unfortunately, local Asian Pacific officeholding gains did not extend to state and federal offices. Between 1962 and 1992, no Asian Pacific from southern California served in the House of Representatives. Given these still limited realities of minority voting and officeholding, Asian Pacific politics, even in the supposedly breakthrough Los Angeles region, has primarily remained "politics by other means," namely, indirect group influence rather than electoral representation. For example, Asian Pacifics nationwide contributed $10 million to the 1988 presidential candidates and in California gave $1.5 million to the 1990 gubernatorial candidates.

Explaining the Asian Pacific Participation Deficit

We will consider the most often identified barriers to the electoral empowerment of Asian Pacifics under two explanatory headings: "Old World" imports or attitudes and experiences brought here by the immigrant generation and "New World" impediments, including internal disunity as well as the impact of discrimination. Three "Old World" factors limiting Asian Pacific political participation stand out in the literature: antidemocratic civic traditions, excessive preoccupation with home-country politics, and non-English monolingualism.

Antidemocratic Norms

Low participation rates ostensibly reflect the enduring imprint of the Buddhist-Confucianist culture emphasizing hierarchy, subordination to authority, passivity, and resignation. Stanley Sue and Devald Sue observe a "traditionalist" Chinese-American personality type—deferential, reserved, inhibited, and passive—that shapes political behavior as well as social interaction. Among Japanese Americans, Harry Kitano finds an apolitical orientation rooted in such Japanese values as *enryo* (nonagressiveness) and *gaman* (uncomplaining acceptance). Regarding Korean immigrants in Los Angeles, Yung-Hwan Jo traces their "unassertive, indifferent and even fatalistic posture" back to the neo-Confucian ethic. Similar cultural-religious interpretations have been applied to Filipinos, Laotians, and Samoans.[4]

In a pioneering study of the political participation of California's minorities, Carole Uhlaner, Bruce Cain, and Roderick Kiewiet have attempted to isolate the influence of imported cultural norms on group political behavior. Controlling for citizenship, age, and socioeconomic status, they found that the participation gap between Latinos and Anglos virtually disappeared. Among Asian Pacifics, however, there remained a small but significant residue that might possibly be due to cultural factors. It remains a daunting task, however, to operationalize and test the influence of such amorphous cultural factors.[5]

Home-Country Politics

Homeland ties have an effect that is easier to document although complicated to interpret. From earlier studies describing Chiang Kai-shek's Kuomintang—the Chinese nationalist party—as "the real power" in Los Angeles' Chinatown to more recent studies assessing homeland politics as "the most vital force shaping Koreatown," this explanation figures prominently in accounts of the political dynamics of various Asian Pacific communities. In the early twentieth century, Asian Pacific communities in West Coast cities became incubators of overseas nationalist movements. Their purpose was to reform or revolutionize China and Japan, as well as to liberate Korea from Japan and India from the British. Gradually, the initiative passed from activist exiles to repressive home-country governments intent upon politically containing their overseas populations.

During the Vietnam War these containment tactics were copied by military regimes in Seoul and the Marcos martial law government in the Philippines. In conjunction with intelligence agents, consular bureaucrats penetrated the politics of Asian Pacific American communities. They typically were abetted by the ethnic media (subsidized by or even headquartered in the home country) and by local ethnic business elites dependent upon foreign bank loans and government subsidies. The resulting pattern of blocked political autonomy—what has been termed "sponsored immigrant politics"—forced ethnic concerns about the welfare of the ancestral homeland into narrow and rigid progovernment channels. Authoritarian governments in Taiwan, Korea, and the Philippines promoted reflex loyalty to anticommunist orthodoxy.

In the 1970s Asian Pacifics belatedly began an internal debate about whether inordinate preoccupation with home-country affairs served as a distraction from the challenges of participating in U.S. politics. Recoiling from foreign governmental domination of their communities, Asian Pacifics embraced an assimilationalist strategy of group empowerment through greater electoral participation and officeholding. The 1980s challenged two major assumptions of the assimilationist model: first, that home-country political preoccupations would entirely wither away in the second and subsequent generations, and, second, that there was a zero-sum relationship between Asian Pacific involvement in foreign versus domestic issues. Beginning with the 1979 Koreagate scandal and the 1980 Kwangju Uprising, the Korean communities of Los Angeles and New York each threw off consular domination in favor of community activism. They became simultaneously involved in both local political issues and overseas human rights concerns. The Koreans set the precedent for parallel home/abroad hybrid activism in the 1980s among other Asian Pacific groups. This suggests an additive rather than a zero-sum model of domestic/foreign political concerns.

Language Difficulties

Virtually all Asian Pacific observers consider lack of English proficiency a significant empowerment problem. According to the 1980 census, one-half of Los Angeles County's Asian Pacifics listed as primary a language other than English. There are enormous differences in the English language capabilities of different Asian Pacific groups. Of predominantly native-born Japanese Americans, 32 percent classified themselves as "not speaking English very well," compared with 69 percent of the predominantly foreign-born Koreans and 82 percent of the Vietnamese. Filipinos and Asian Indians were as proficient in English as the Japanese because they came from countries with strong bilingual traditions.

The Immigration Reform and Control Act (IRCA) of 1986 imposed English literacy as a requirement for amnestied aliens seeking permanent residence and, ultimately, citizenship. These literacy barriers contradict the spirit of the 1975 Amendments to the Voting Rights Act mandating bilingual ballots for each language spoken by 5 percent or more of the local voting population.

Government policy, however, is not solely responsible for the divisive political consequences of language patterns among Asian Pacifics. Language diversity is both cause and correlate of political factionalism within and between Asian Pacific communities. The question of who speaks for Chinatown or Monterey Park is a matter not just of political opinion but of language. Mandarin speakers from Taiwan, Cantonese speakers from Hong Kong, and "ABC" (American-born Chinese) English speakers have problems communicating, politically and otherwise. In addition to this factionalizing Tower of Babel effect, non-English monolingualism constricts the flow of political information to Asian Pacifics. Almost one-half of Los Angeles Koreans have never read an English-language newspaper. Even more politically disadvantaged are the one-third of Laotians and Cambodians illiterate in their own language.

Language barriers to Asian Pacific empowerment are real, but their impact should not be exaggerated. Among Asian Americans, a consensus seems to be emerging around support for "English Plus." This calls for concerted efforts to acquire English while retaining and transmitting the home-country language. Grassroots implementation of the English Plus philosophy is dramatically increasing the English proficiency of Asian Pacifics both absolutely and relative to Latinos.

The following explanations of the Asian Pacific electoral participation deficit emphasize New World impediments rather than foreign causes.

Discriminatory Burdens

Virtually every chapter in national and state history until after World War II was a lesson in political exclusion for Asian Pacifics — from the Gold Rush Foreign Miners Tax and the 1879 state constitution's anti-Chinese provisions, to the anti-Japanese Alien Land Law of the Progressive Era, to the Immigration Restriction Acts and the U.S. Supreme Court's *Ozawa* and *Thind* decisions of the 1920s denying Asian Pacifics the rights of immigration and naturalization, to the Tydings-McDuffie Act of the New Deal effectively extending the immigration ban to Filipino nationals, to the culminating tragedy of the World War II internment.

Racial prohibitions on the acquisition of citizenship were not removed until 1943 in the case of foreign-born Chinese, 1946 in the case of Asian Indians and Filipinos born abroad, and 1952 in the case of Japanese immigrants and other Asian Pacifics. It is important to remember that today's native-born, middle-aged Asian Pacifics were born into a society that granted them citizenship but that had denied their immigrant parents the rights to naturalize, to vote, to hold public office, to qualify for civil service jobs, and even to receive federal welfare relief during the depression.

The conventional wisdom is that the "enforced passivity" characteristic of the immigrant generation begins to give way in the second generation to a politics of "reactive ethnicity" or collective self-assertion. However, this occurred only to a limited degree among Asian Pacifics. The formation of the Chinese American Citizens Alliance in 1904 and the Japanese American Citizens League in 1930 reflected organized attempts to implement this second-generation logic. However, the power structure outside and inside the Asian Pacific community stunted these early political efforts. Beginning in the 1950s, there were individual Asian Pacific—particularly Japanese American—political success stories. But not until the third and fourth generations emerged during the 1960s and 1970s did the politics of Asian Pacific self-assertion enjoy a real upswing.

Despite political gains culminating in the passage of the Redress and Reparation Act of 1988, discrimination continues to have a chilling effect both on native-born Asian Pacifics and on newer immigrants who manifest the political insecurities typical of the first generation. The perceived anti-Asian backlash of the 1980s—for example, the dramatic rise in anti-Asian hate crimes and the unfriendly English Only movement—and more subtle forms of discrimination—for example, the glass ceiling effect—keep alive even among third- and fourth-generation Asian Pacifics a sense of political alienation.

Demographic and Socioeconomic Depressants

Underlying demographic and class patterns create significant political differences between and within Asian Pacific groups, further depressing participation rates. The 1980 foreign-born proportion among Los Angeles County's Asian Pacifics ranged from a high of 93 percent among the Vietnamese to a low of 29 percent among the Japanese. The median age of the region's Asian Pacific population was twenty-eight compared with thirty-six among Anglos. Noncitizenship and non-voting-age status dramatically reduce the proportion of eligible voters in various Asian Pacific communities, particularly those from Southeast Asia.

Leaving aside the Pacific Islanders, the native-born proportion among Asian Pacifics correlates fairly closely with median family income—with Japanese at the top and immigrants from Southeast Asia on the bottom. Within Asian communities, the proportion of foreign-born can also mark a significant economic-political demarcation. Native-born Chinese and Koreans are still better off overall than newcomers, despite the high profile of the so-called Cadillac immigrants from Korea, Taiwan, and Hong Kong. In contrast, the most disadvantaged groups among Filipinos are drawn disproportionately from native-born cohorts with roots in the migratory farm labor experience. These complex internal group differences sometimes obscure the existence of what has been called "an invisible poor" Asian Pacific population, which includes unemployed Hmong, downtown Chinese, the elderly Japanese, and aging Filipino farm laborers.

The popular image of Asian Pacifics as a superachieving minority is contradicted by the economic experiences of Pacific Islanders and Southeast Asians. In 1980 Samoans, for example, had a 30 percent poverty rate and a 33 percent dependency rate on welfare, social security, or disability pensions. Overall, Pacific Islanders and Southeast Asians were more dependent upon public assistance than were African Americans and Latinos. Throughout the 1980s the Asian American poverty rate remained one and one-half to two times the rate for non-Hispanic whites, hinting at the existence of an underclass. High levels of poverty and welfare dependency among some Asian Pacific groups serve as barriers to political mobilization.

Electoral Empowerment Strategies

Asian Pacific activists are increasingly preoccupied with reapportionment and leadership development as strategies to achieve political incorporation. This reflects the recognition that mass empowerment is stillborn without elite facilitation.

Reapportionment and Redistricting

Asian Pacifics lagged in connection with boundary redrawing following the 1980 census. They concentrated instead on lobbying for the adoption of the new "Asian and Pacific Islander" umbrella classification that gave their nine major nationality groups stronger government affirmative action claims. Relative inattention to city, county, state, and federal electoral boundaries carried a price tag reflected, for example, in the gerrymandering of Los Angeles' Koreatown into three city council, two state senate, and three U.S. House districts.

In the early 1990s, the Coalition of Asian Pacific Americans for Fair Representation (CAPAFR) joined the NAACP Legal Defense Fund and the Mexican American Legal Defense and Education Fund (MALDEF) as a player in the state and federal reapportionment-redistricting games. At the local level, one key question involves at-large versus district elections. The conventional wisdom holds that the lack of geographic concentration makes ethnic politics more expensive and less valuable for Asian Pacifics. This is certainly true for some Asian Pacific groups like Asian Indians, who are not numerous enough to overcome their substantial residential dispersion. But it does not necessarily hold true when a diffusely settled Asian Pacific population grows large enough to become a plurality within community boundaries.

In fact, there is a consensus in suburban Monterey Park and Gardena that at-large elections enabling Asian Pacifics to marshal their broad-based strength have served them well. For example, Monterey Park City Councilwoman Judy Chu opposed district elections both on the philosophical ground that it racially polarizes and on the pragmatic ground that at-large Monterey Park had two Asian Pacific councilpersons while district-based Alhambra had none. In the city of Los Angeles, however, a concentration strategy exploiting the logic of district representation might make more political sense. In the case of Greater Chinatown, for example, relatively small boundary modifications—together with a major voter registration effort— might give a future Chinese American candidate the inside track in a first councilman district race.

But the concentration strategy is not without problems. First, should it aim at single or at multiple Asian Pacific groups, for example, Chinese Americans or a pan-Asian coalition? Second, is this strategy really superior to a more inclusive rainbow strategy that creates districts where cross-ethnic, cross-class coalitions can win? Bruce Cain and Roderick Kiewiet's 1984 study shows that two-thirds of winning Asian Pacific candidates in California came from districts less than 10 percent Asian Pacific, yet these same winning candidates represented districts with at least a 40 percent minority population. An Asian Pacific candidate like Michael Woo wanting to be elected mayor of Los Angeles has to be a crossover politician.[6]

Leadership Development

The paucity of political leaders is a key barrier to Asian Pacific empowerment. Career politicians represent the most obvious source of community political leadership. The Asian Pacific community has produced a sizable business and professional class but—perhaps as a consequence—few political leaders. Moreover, the few Asian Pacific career politicians have exercised what Kurt Lewin has called "leadership from the periphery." That is, the most successful politicians of Asian Pacific background are crossover leaders who identify least with the Asian Pacific community. Examples from the recent

California past include former U.S. senator S. I. Hayakawa and former Democratic state senator Alfred Song—both of whom had quite chilly relations with the organized Japanese and Korean communities, respectively.

A potential source of future political leadership is the growing pool of Asian Pacific political aides, especially the sixty-four serving in the state legislature. The southern California Asian Pacific Legislative Staff Caucus— comprising federal, state, county, and municipal aides—alone has some fifty members. As Fernando Guerra has shown, over one-third of minority officeholders statewide—and all six of Los Angeles' urban and suburban Asian Pacific councilpersons in 1990—began their careers as political aides. Because of the scarcity of Asian Pacific officeholders, however, their mentors generally have not been Asian Pacific. All too frequently Asian Pacific aides have not been groomed as protégés or successors.[7]

Despite Republican-sponsored "how-to" campaign seminars designed to overcome middle-class Asian Pacific resistance to more active participation in politics, the Asian Pacific business class still is not generally receptive to career opportunities in politics. There is more receptivity on the part of Asian Pacific professionals; indeed, even Asian Pacific office seekers who come from the "for-profit" sector are more likely to be self-employed engineers or accountants than entrepreneurs. Well-worn professional routes into a political career include human services and teaching. High poverty rates among Pacific Islanders and Southeast Asians provide an opening for Asian Pacific social service providers to act as gatekeepers between the community and government.

Whatever the source, empowerment will remain an uncompleted process until Asian Pacifics produce a generation of leaders capable of putting to rest the community's reputation as a politically passive population. The theory that such leaders are not born but can be made inspires the strong commitment to leadership development by such organizations as Leadership Education for Asian Pacifics (LEAP). Paralleling Latino leadership development programs are the Chinese American Policy Internship Program and the structured internship program of the Korean American Coalition.

Community Organizing

A new wave of electorally oriented Asian Pacific community organizations has been created since 1970 in response to demands for group self-assertion. Founded in 1983, the Korean American Coalition combines an explicit function as a recruiting channel for political aides and potential candidates. Other examples of new-wave community organizations include the Chinese American Association of Southern California, the Taiwanese American Citizens League, the Indo-American Political Association of Southern California, and the Union of Democratic Filipinos. Also included are ethnic political action committees (PACs) like CAPAC among the Chinese, FAPAC among the Filipinos, KAPAC among the Koreans, and the pan-Asian APAC. In addition to targeted campaign contributing, the Asian Pacific PACs may help produce new political leaders. Particularly influential among local Asian Pacific community organizations is the Asian Pacific American Legal Center (APALC), which lobbies and litigates on immigration, civil rights, and empowerment issues.

Asian Pacifics would especially benefit from registration-and-turnout campaigns to help them enter the house of full democratic participation. For example, modeled on the Latino Southwest Voter Registration Education Project, the UCLA Asian Pacific Voter Project has mounted nonpartisan voter registration drives in Monterey Park but with only limited success. A real breakthrough will probably require partisan campaigns mounted by the Democrats and the Republicans; both parties could gain by greater targeting of Asian Pacifics, but neither has yet shown much interest.

Intergroup Coalition Building

In their influential study *Protest Is Not Enough,* Rufus Browning, Dale Rogers Marshall, and David Tabb have portrayed coalition building across ethnic, racial, and class lines as the best vehicle for a minority group to move from political exclusion to inclusion and empowerment.[8] The challenge of intergroup outreach is both unique and compelling for Asian Pacifics.

Pan-Asian Coalitions

A pan-Asian coalition faces the formidable task of melding together a dozen larger and three dozen smaller nationalities from East Asia, Southeast Asia, the Indian subcontinent, and the Pacific Islands. This formulation, however, begs the anterior question of how disparate Asian Pacific groups can overcome internal divisions before they can unite with one another. The severity of the problem of internal unification around a national self-identity is partly a function of the homogeneity—or lack thereof—prevailing in the country of origin. At one end of the spectrum are Japanese and Koreans, who come from strong like-minded national cultures. At the other end are Filipinos, Asian Indians, and Southeast Asian groups who have to overcome the pluralist mosaic of regional, religious, and linguistic differences they bring from the old country. Even the Chinese community—which often looks monolithic to outside observers, including other Asian Pacifics—is viewed quite differently by insiders.

There are, however, strong countervailing pan-Asian tendencies. These coalitional tendencies date back to the 1960s, when the "Asian Power" battle cry was raised in emulation of the Black Panthers. Pan-Asianism was institutionalized in the 1970s by Asian Pacific groups lobbying for government affirmative action and group entitlement programs. Both nationality group loyalties and transnational commitments are likely to continue to coexist in uneasy tension among Asian Pacifics. The office of Los Angeles Mayor Tom Bradley, for example, recognized the pervasive influence of nationality by maintaining four group liaisons—Chinese, Japanese, Korean, and Filipino—with the Filipino given the additional responsibility for representing the smaller Vietnamese and Thai communities.

Ivan Light and Edna Bonacich's pathbreaking study of the Los Angeles Korean community highlights the multiple—and instrumental—layers of group identification that shape political behavior. To protect their major group interest in the garment industry, Korean manufacturers have organized on an ethnic-specific basis by forming the Korean Sewing Contractors Association. Because a more inclusive pan-Asian strategy was needed to compete for federal set-asides for minority contractors, Korean entrepreneurs joined wider Asian Pacific groups lobbying before Congress and the Small Business Administration. Finally, in the retail liquor industry, the Korean presence was not large enough for an ethnic-specific organization and group preference was not a policy objective. Hence Korean-American liquor store owners chose as their preferred lobbying vehicle the Southern California Retail Liquor Dealers Association—a rainbow trade association.[9]

Asian Pacifics and Other Minorities

The downtown Anglo business community remains an important part of the city's governing or policymaking coalition, but electoral power within the Anglo community has shifted away from WASP suburbanites toward Jewish voters on the West Side and in Fairfax and the San Fernando Valley. The black-Jewish coalition that dominated Los Angeles politics during the five terms of Mayor Tom Bradley has developed severe strains. This unraveling process has fueled hopes for the emergence of a new rainbow alignment in which Asian Pacifics would subordinate both nationality and pan-Asian concerns to the imperatives of a black-brown-yellow coalition.

The rainbow model, however, is an ideological gloss that obscures as much as it illuminates the realities of ethnic power in Los Angeles. In terms of their relations with African Americans, Asian Pacifics have long-standing roles as junior partners in the Bradley coalition. Mayor Bradley's cultivation of Asian Pacific businessmen began when he served on the city council in the 1960s. Asian Pacifics contributed 10 percent of the campaign funding for the Bradley gubernatorial attempts of 1982 and 1986. Also, by the 1980s Asian Pacifics had become major contributors to Bradley's mayoral reelection campaigns.

The tragic intergroup tensions that caused a near meltdown of black–Asian Pacific relations during the 1992 Los Angeles riots can best be understood in terms of an ethnic succession model involving conflicts over neighborhood turf, business opportunities, and political preferment. During the 1970s and 1980s, Koreans, Pacific Islanders, and Indochinese joined Latinos in moving into once solidly black South Central Los Angeles. Merchant-customer frictions became the flash point for violence that overwhelmed the conciliatory efforts of organizations like the Black Korean Alliance (BKA).

Even before the 1992 riots, affluent Asian Pacifics in the multiethnic South Bay showed minimal interest in politically coalescing with African Americans. City Councilman Michael Woo did better among black voters in his 1993 run for mayor because of his high-profile role in the ouster of Police Chief Daryl Gates following the Rodney King beating. However, a broad-based Asian Pacific rainbow alliance with African Americans seems less plausible than ad hoc, piecemeal coalitions limited to certain areas such as the inner city, where economically depressed Filipinos, Pacific Islanders, and Indochinese may make common cause with blacks around a social services agenda.

Parallel hopes for a durable political marriage between Asian Pacific money and Latino votes also may be difficult to fulfill. The more likely outcome is a multiplication of covert liaisons, such as that between pro-growth councilman Richard Alatorre and Chinese American developers, and single-issue alliances, such as the countervailing slow-growth Latino and Asian Coalition to Improve Our Neighborhoods (LACTION).

Public Policy and Asian Pacific Empowerment

Given the limited success to date of Asian Pacific electoral empowerment, "politics by other means" continues to be the primary strategy of group influence. Asian Pacific political organizations—whether utilizing lobbying, litigation, or protest tactics—have been active in shaping civil rights, economic, and foreign policy issues of particular concern to their communities.[10]

Civil Rights

Civil rights issues are a major preoccupation of the Asian Pacific community. Memories of past mistreatment are given new resonance for Asian Pacifics by discrimination currently suffered by both immigrant newcomers and the upwardly mobile native-born. For the Japanese American community, past injustices were the central contemporary civil rights issue until amends were made for World War II internment with the passage of the reparations bill. Under sansei, or third-generation, leadership, the National Coalition for Redress/Reparations (NCRR) became the model for new-style civil rights advocacy organizations among Asian Pacifics, such as the National Network for Immigration and Refugee Rights (NNIRR), the Alliance of Asian Pacific Americans, and the National Civil Rights Legal Consortium. These groups are involved in efforts to forge a common Asian Pacific agenda around an umbrella package of civil rights issues, including immigration reform, bilingualism, educational and employment discrimination, and the battle against antiminority hate crimes.

Asian Pacific lobbying groups moved from a secondary and uncertain role in connection with the Immigration Reform and Control Act (IRCA) of 1986 to a primary and dynamic role in connection with the Immigration Act of 1990. Asian Pacific organizations—notably the Pacific Leadership Council of Los Angeles—helped shape key compromises embodied in the 1990 act.

For the predominantly newcomer Asian Pacific communities like the Koreans and Vietnamese, civil rights tends to be synonymous with the twin issues of immigration reform and language rights, defined as opposition to English Only but support for English Plus. But for native-born, more established Asian Pacific communities such as third- and fourth-generation Japanese and Chinese, affirmative action is the pivot of the Asian Pacific civil rights agenda. There is widespread agreement that minority preferences remain a necessary tool for advancing Asian Pacific economic interests.

In the educational area, Asian Pacific support for affirmative action is qualified by fears of de facto admissions quotas or ceilings. The crux of the matter in California has involved the University of California admissions process—especially at Berkeley and UCLA—where the Asian Pacific proportion of the student body rose to more than 20 percent in the early 1980s while the Anglo proportion dropped below 50 percent. In response, the two campuses reclassified Asian Pacifics as overrepresented rather than underrepresented minorities and altered their admissions policies and practices accordingly. Asian Pacific enrollment at both campuses declined in the mid-1980s as token preferences given Filipinos, Southeast Asians, and Pacific Islanders masked the sharp cutbacks in slots allocated to Chinese and Japanese Americans. In 1987 Asian Pacifics began a political long march that has reversed what has been called "the unwritten law by the admissions offices" against Asian Pacific applicants to the University of California.

Economic Development

Growth and ethnic succession long have been intertwined in California. As California enters the Pacific Rim era, an ethnic dialectic between established Anglos and emerging Asian Pacifics has become a central issue of metropolitan growth in the Los Angeles area.

Downtown Redevelopment / While Asian Pacifics heretofore have taken a back seat to African Americans and even to Latinos in the electoral arena, their visibility as interest groups is much higher in the politics of downtown redevelopment. The reason is the centrality of Little Tokyo and Chinatown to Los Angeles' audacious effort since the 1960s to "invent a modern downtown" for itself. Created in 1948, Los Angeles' powerful Community Redevelopment Agency (CRA) has concentrated its renovation efforts on the North Central–Civic Center area, which is the historic core of Japanese and Chinese Los Angeles. The 1965 Los Angeles Master Plan and the 1972 Central City Plan both envisaged coordinated development of an "International Zone" in which Little Tokyo, Chinatown, and Olvera Street would serve a tourist-and-amenities function in relation to the central business district.

Little Tokyo was promised affordable housing, small business assistance, affirmative action preferences in construction hiring, and the establishment of a new community center. Federal urban redevelopment funding cutbacks, however, defeated or delayed these priorities, despite the lobbying efforts of the Little Tokyo People's Rights Organization, the Little Tokyo Development Corporation, the Affirmative Action Task Force, and the Japanese American Cultural and Community Center (JACCC).

To expand the community's economic base, the CRA in the early 1970s proposed a high-rise hotel. The New Otani Hotel was built by Kajima International and financed by the East-West Development Corporation—a consortium of thirty of Japan's largest financial institutions. Opened in 1978, the Japanese Village Plaza rehoused some of the displaced businesses. The Plaza, however, was quickly overshadowed by the new Weller Court shops "Little Tokyo's Rodeo Drive"—which were largely owned by Japanese nationals. A more positive development from the standpoint of community activists in the 1970s was the building of three hundred units of senior citizen housing in the Little Tokyo Towers and the completion of the JACCC building. By 1981 the parameters of Little Tokyo redevelopment were set, with three-quarters of the forty-seven-acre "action area" either redeveloped or planned for redevelopment.

Little Tokyo redevelopment provides a window into the complex political dynamics and conflicts within the Japanese American community, as well as within broader Asian Pacific communities. First, there was considerable tension between commercial and community-oriented definitions of "redevelopment." The sansei—many of them gentrifying "yappies" (young Asian Pacific professionals)—sought expanded neighborhood social services and cultural institutions rather than new business opportunities. Local neighborhood revitalization campaigns during the 1970s served as a training ground for young Japanese American activists who, during the 1980s, spearheaded the national campaign for redress and reparations.

Second, Little Tokyo experienced the increasing influence of Japanese multinationals and their overseas representatives. Anchored by Little Tokyo, Japanese investment in downtown Los Angeles has been massive. According to one 1989 estimate, the Japanese owned 30 percent of prime downtown office space. Little Tokyo community activists and small business owners have enjoyed only modest successes fighting "Big Tokyo" business interests and city hall.

Unlike Little Tokyo, Chinatown has a long-standing indigenous tradition of redevelopment dating back to the establishment of "New Chinatown" in 1938. In parallel with Little Tokyo, Chinatown revived these traditions during the 1970s with the Mandarin Plaza, the first of many shopping-and-office complexes. During the 1980s Chinese investors from East and Southeast Asia purchased banks, trading companies, and media outlets in the community. Whereas in San Francisco the major overseas Chinese investment influx has been from Hong Kong, in Los Angeles it has come from Taiwan.

As with Little Tokyo, Chinatown developers and community activists have had different definitions of desirable redevelopment. CRA generosity to Chinatown developers has made the community the major arena for redevelopment for inner-city Asian Pacifics. Chinatown community activists have fought the CRA, city hall, and state government over a range of projects, including plans to double the size of the county men's jail—already "the largest standing prison in the free world"—on the southern fringes of Chinatown.

Suburban Development / In recent decades the San Gabriel Valley has emerged as the new Asian Pacific suburban frontier. The Valley's Asian Pacific population mushroomed from 114,000 in 1980 to an estimated 273,000 in 1990. Monterey Park has become the model in miniature and in extremis for the overlapping ethnic succession and economic development battles being fought throughout southern California's suburbs. In 1982 an Asian Pacific–Latino alliance that promised moderate growth and increased crime control defeated an antidevelopment slate of Anglo city council candidates put forward by the Residents' Association of Monterey Park (RAMP). Later that year RAMP forced a special election on two antigrowth propositions requiring voter approval for major zoning changes. The propositions passed over the opposition of the city council majority. However, under the leadership of Mayor Lily Chen—America's first Chinese woman mayor—the city council in 1983 began granting wholesale zoning variances for the construction of mini-malls and condominiums.

RAMP made the 1986 council election a referendum on "throwing the big buck developers out of City Hall." Mayor Chen and two Latinos were swept from office. In power, however, RAMP proved to be an unstable coalition of Anglo populists primarily concerned with controlling land use and nativists intent on imposing language uniformity.

The resultant ethnic polarization sparked the counterorganization of a multiracial alliance called the Coalition for Harmony in Monterey Park (CHAMP). CHAMP lobbying pressure blocked a two-thirds English sign ordinance and forced the city council to rescind an English Only resolution. The Chinese community—backed by developer money—then launched a voter registration campaign spearheaded by the Asian Pacific Voter Registration Project (APVRP), modeled after the Southwest Voter Registration

Education Project (SVREP). In 1988 the Asian Pacific community produced a strong candidate for the city council, clinical psychologist Judy Chu. Campaigning as a moderate on the growth issue, Chu finished first in a field of eight candidates. The 1990 municipal elections, with two more minority councilpersons victorious, represented another resounding victory for racial pluralism.

Asian Pacific voters in both the inner city and the suburbs prefer to steer clear of the extremes in the growth politics debate. In the inner city, they gravitate toward multiracial moderate-growth coalitions that support limited commercial development provided it generates minority jobs and underwrites affordable housing. Asian Pacifics who have moved to the suburbs also seem to be more tolerant of new development than are established Anglo residents. They are attracted to a moderate growth platform that promises quality development to help pay for city services and to keep the tax rate down. However, they are unwilling to sacrifice residential livability for development. Obviously, the reconciliation of these diverse priorities becomes a difficult task when a politician turns from making campaign promises to trying to deliver on them in office.

Foreign Policy Issues

We look here at the efforts by current generations of Asian Pacifics to build transpacific political and economic connections and thereby to help create a new Pacific Rim–based future for California.

Political Linkages / Rather than a politically random movement between countries equilibrated only by supply-and-demand pressures, Asian Pacific immigration is very much directed along political, military, and economic salients connecting the United States to specific countries. For example, it is impossible to imagine that the Philippines, Korea, and Taiwan would be such major immigration sources except for the defense and trading partnerships forged between these countries and the United States after World War II. These partnerships put into a different perspective the home-country political preoccupations of Asian Pacifics.

The policy issues involved range from basing rights in the Philippines, to arms aid for Pakistan, to troop deployments in Korea, to defense commitments in Taiwan, to U.S. control of Guam and Samoa, to the reestablishment of diplomatic relations with Vietnam. These home-country issues — which also are U.S. foreign policy issues—are of lively concern to L.A.'s Asian Pacific communities.

Democratically involved, highly educated Asian Pacifics have also moved the human rights agenda to the center of Pacific Rim concerns. They have pressured not only the U.S. government but repressive regimes in the Philippines under Marcos, South Korea under Chung Hee Park and his successors, India under Indira Gandhi, Pakistan under General Zia-ul-Haq, Taiwan under the KMT, and mainland China after Tiananmen Square. Although the effectiveness of Asian Pacific human rights pressures has been highly uneven, Asian Pacifics are likely to continue to be an important two-way communication channel promoting democratic dialogue throughout the Pacific Rim.

Foreign Investment / As the 1980s ended, Japanese banks controlled 25 percent of California's banking assets and 30 percent of outstanding loans. Japanese corporations employed seventy thousand Californians, and Japanese investors were investing six billion dollars a year in the state's burgeoning real estate market. The acquisition of a significant share of California's assets by Japanese as well as Chinese and Korean interests has revived a controversy over foreign ownership that had been dormant in California since the era of the alien land law.

The "middleman minority" theory that has been widely applied to Asian Pacific entrepreneurs has both a domestic and a foreign component. On the one hand, such entrepreneurs are portrayed as merchant intermediaries between the Anglo majority and nonwhite minorities, particularly African American ghetto dwellers. On the other hand, they occupy an intermediate position between Asian capital and the American market.

U.S. immigration law, in fact, codifies the international version of the middleman theory by converting the economic capital and overseas connections of Asian Pacific immigrants into a national asset. Economically based "priority worker" quota preferences are available to certain multinational business executives and to aliens with special business expertise. The economic logic of the immigration law is most direct in the case of the "immigrant investor preference." This preference has recently been liberalized to create seven thousand openings a year for immigrants prepared to invest at least one million dollars in businesses employing ten or more workers.

Joel Kotkin argues that while the 1980s represented the decade of Japanese investment in California, the 1990s promises to be the decade of the overseas Chinese. He adds, however, that "even defining the nationality of these Chinese—Americans, Taiwanese, Hong Kong—is virtually impossible.... These transpacific nomads, known in Taiwan as *tai kun fai jen* or 'spacemen,' represent a new breed—Chinese entrepreneurs shuttling between Taipei or Hong Kong and such California cities as Torrance, Monterey Park, and Mountain View."[11]

Political movements embracing economic populism or nationalism can fuel nativist hostility to the indigenous Asian Pacific community. In 1989, before the speculative California real estate bubble burst, Congressman Mel Levine argued, "I can easily imagine Asian investors being pointed out as scapegoats for rising prices in the residential real estate market." Ironically, in the early 1990s these same Asian Pacific investors may be blamed for withdrawing capital from the declining California market.

International Trade / Nearly one half of California's sixty-three billion dollars in exports in 1989 went to Asia, making the Golden State second only to the United States itself as a trading partner of Japan. Estimates are that by 1995 one in six jobs in Greater Los Angeles will depend upon foreign trade, up from one in ten in 1990. Willingly or not, Asian Pacifics have been injected even more centrally into the debate over foreign trade than over foreign investment. One the negative side, they have been pictured as a weapon in the arsenal of overseas producers who, for example, give wholesale preferences to Korean import-export businesses in Los Angeles in order to flood the American market.

On the positive side, Asian Pacifics are being given a starring role in combating the trade deficit by the California Commission for Economic Development's Advisory Council on Asia. According to Lieutenant Governor Leo McCarthy, "The Asian American population in this state is our greatest asset in competing on the Pacific Rim. People who have been born and raised in an Asian environment and know the language, culture and all the nuances of doing business are very anxious to help California compete."

As the 1990s unfold, California's world position may owe much more to Asian Pacifics than merely the capital brought by immigrant investors. Relocating Hong Kong Chinese, for example, may utilize their wide-ranging connections to open up vast reaches of Southeast Asia to California economic penetration. Looking even further ahead, young Vietnamese may help the United States to peacefully return to Indochina through trade in the early twenty-first century.

But prosperity without empowerment is a precarious basis for social peace, as Asians on the other side of the Pacific Rim—particularly Chinese throughout Southeast Asia—have sadly learned. Despite the policy successes of a strategy of "politics by other means," California's Asian Pacific community remains politically vulnerable to backlash. The social compact appropriate for California's multiethnic future can only be built on the secure foundation of full democratic participation.

Notes

1. We wish to acknowledge the financial support of the California Policy Seminar for our research. For fuller documentation of our research, see Steven P. Erie, Harold Brackman, and James Warren Ingram III, *Paths to Political Incorporation for Latinos and Asian Pacifics in California* (Berkeley: California Policy Seminar, 1993).

2. Field Institute, "A Digest of California's Political Demography," *California Opinion Index,* August 1990, 5.

3. Don T. Nakanishi, *The UCLA Asian Pacific American Voter Registration Project* (Los Angeles: Asian Pacific American Legal Center, 1986).

4. Stanley Sue and Devald W. Sue, "Chinese American Personality and Mental Health," *Amerasia Journal* 1, no. 2 (July 1971): 36–49; Harry H. L. Kitano, *Japanese Americans: The Evolution of a Subculture* (Englewood Cliffs, N.J.: Prentice-Hall, 1976): 191–92; Yung-Hwan Jo, "Problems and Strategies of Participation in American Politics," in *Koreans in Los Angeles: Prospects and Promises,* ed. Eui-Young Yu, Earl H. Phillips, and Eun Sik Yang (Los Angeles: Koryo Research Institute, Center for Korean American and Korean Studies, California State University, 1982): 203, 208.

5. Carole T. Uhlaner, Bruce E. Cain, and D. Roderick Kiewiet, "Political Participation of Ethnic Minorities in the 1980's," *Political Behavior* 11, no. 3 (September 1989): 212, 217–18; Alejandro Portes and Ruben G. Rumbaut, *Immigrant America: A Portrait* (Berkeley: University of California Press, 1990), 11, 114, 125, 134–35.

6. Bruce E. Cain and D. Roderick Kiewiet, "Minorities in California" (paper presented at the California Institute of Technology Symposium, Seaver Institute, (March 5, 1996), 1-28.

7. Fernando J. Guerra, "The Emergence of Ethnic Officeholders in California," in *Racial and Ethnic Politics in California,* ed. Byran O. Jackson and Michael B. Preston (Berkeley: Institute of Governmental Studies Press, University of California, 1991), 126.

8. Rufus Browning, Dale Rogers Marshall, and David Tabb, *Protest Is Not Enough* (Berkely: University of California Press, 1984).

9. Ivan Light and Edna Bonacich, *Immigrant Entrepreneurs: Koreans in Los Angeles* (Berkeley: University of California Press, 1988), 322–27.

10. See, for example, *The State of Asian Pacific America: Policy Issues to the Year 2020* (Los Angeles: LEAP Asian Pacific American Public Policy Institute and UCLA Asian American Studies Center, 1993).

11. Joel Kotkin, *Tribes: How Race, Religion, and Identity Determine Success in the New Global Economy* (New York: Random House, 1993), 168.

15 / Political Capital and the Social Reproduction of Inequality in a Mexican Origin Community in Arizona

Edward Murguia

Introduction

In this study, we will examine theories concerned with the social reproduction of inequality in education and occupation, and will determine their applicability to the situation of a Mexican origin community in Arizona. Using Bourdieu's ([1973] 1977) theory of cultural capital and theories of labor market segmentation by Piore ([1970] 1977), Bluestone ([1965] 1977), and Reich, Gordon, and Edwards ([1973] 1977), we will see more clearly why the township of Guadalupe has been and remains toward the bottom of the socioeconomic order. Subsequently, by extending Bourdieu's theory and introducing a new concept, that of "political capital," we will demonstrate how the community has been able to survive and even to improve in some areas in the face of serious obstacles.

The Township of Guadalupe

Guadalupe, Arizona, is a township of about 5,000 people of Yaqui and Mexican origin in the southeastern section of the Phoenix metropolitan area, which has a population of about 2 million. The western border of the community is Interstate 10 and the city of Phoenix; on all other sides, it is surrounded by the city of Tempe. More specifically concerning population,

Guadalupe's population in 1990 was 5,458, while the population of the city of Phoenix was 983,408 and Tempe's was 141,865. The population of the Phoenix Metropolitan Statistical Area (MSA), which includes all of Maricopa County, was 2,122,101, or about 60 percent of the total population of Arizona (3,665,228) (U.S. Bureau of the Census 1992a, 1–3).

The Yaqui are Catholic Native Americans who came from the Mexican state of Sonora, directly south of Arizona. Originally farmers, they were forced from their lands in Sonora during the consolidation of Mexico under Mexican president Porfirio Diaz, and they settled in Guadalupe in 1910. Shortly after, with the growth of the Yaqui community, ethnic institutions emerged. Their church, Our Lady of Guadalupe, was established in 1916. Ethnic businesses providing services to the community developed during this period, but they were established largely by non-Yaqui Mexican origin families who settled around the original forty-acre Yaqui community. After sixty-five years as an unincorporated village, the community was incorporated in 1975. Based on a probability survey conducted in 1990–91, the community is about 60 percent Mexican and Mexican American and about 40 percent Yaqui in ethnic composition (Murguia and Bernasconi 1992, 87).

The Social Reproduction of Inequality

Education

One focus of this study is on a clearer understanding of the social reproduction of inequality as it applies to this and to other poor communities. Although Bourdieu's ([1973] 1977) study is concerned largely with higher education and with the reproduction of inequality in higher levels of society in France, this does not preclude our using and extending his framework to the study of Guadalupe and to similar low-income Mexican origin communities in the United States.

A central theme of Bourdieu's theory is that in a democratic society there has to be a seemingly meritocratic mechanism of selection for upward mobility. To do otherwise would be intolerable, given our belief that all should have a chance to rise. Bourdieu believes, though, that there exists a concealed transmission of power and privilege, the hiding of which is necessary in democracies. Education is that hidden mechanism. Rather than being the great equalizer of society, schools instead exacerbate original inequalities. While individuals with "cultural capital" acquired in the home do well in school, those with little of the required cultural capital are forced out. His theory does allow for some upward mobility by some nonelites, and, although a few carefully selected individuals may rise, this "creaming" does not take away from the relative permanence of the structure of social inequality.

Bourdieu has several concepts useful in this context. First is the afore-mentioned term, *cultural capital*. By cultural capital, Bourdieu means approaches, values, knowledge, and work habits that make individuals a part of the elite. Since Bourdieu is dealing with elites, his measures of cultural capital include theater, concert, and museum attendance. His concept can be modified, though, to include resources and activities in the home that result in success in school. This could encompass parents who speak standard English, who are knowledgeable as to what is being taught in school, and who are able to help their children with their homework. It could also entail such things as books and magazines in the home and, for example, closer to Bourdieu's original concept, such items as home computers and home encyclopedias. In Bourdieu's model, the family is the possessor of cultural capital. The more cultural capital a family has, the better the child does in school. Families of elites continually transmit background and actual knowledge useful for school to their young.

Bourdieu discusses "codes," that is, preknowledge necessary to understand and decipher materials to be learned in school. Families with a great deal of cultural capital are able to provide their offspring with codes necessary to do well in school. An appreciation of Shakespeare, for example, is facilitated by parents who have had some familiarity with his writings and can explain his plays and sonnets to their young. According to Bourdieu, cultural capital received at home provides advantages in school that the school then reinforces.

According to Bourdieu, those without cultural capital and without codes to understand material being taught at school are pushed out of school. They realize that they have no chance of doing well in school and rationally decide that they can't make it. We should not make the mistake of blaming children who lack the kind of cultural capital required by those in power for their negative view of school. Their experience in school tends to be one of recurring failure. A major share of the blame should be placed on the schools themselves, which produce failure under the guise of meritocracy.

Although Bourdieu's theory is insightful, we must be careful in applying it to the Mexican-origin population in the United States. We are not saying that working-class families in low-income Mexican origin communities are "deficient" in terms of academic potential. Certainly, children from low-income communities have as much intellectual potential as those born in more affluent areas. What we are saying is that the educational system in the United States is organized in such a way that experiences of families in middle and upper classes who speak "standard" English are valued, while experiences of those in working and lower classes whose language at home is not English are not valued in school. Rather than saying, as does Bourdieu, that children in the lower and working classes lack cultural capital, a more accurate statement of the problem is that children in the working and lower classes have cultural capital, but the knowledge they and their families possess is not valued by the society in which they live. As it is, those without a middle-class, English-language background are largely doomed to fail educationally. Failure by children of the lower classes is not an inevitable reality, but a political decision made by those in power. After all, those in power determine the language and content of standardized tests. One need only look at the experience of Canada and the decision to make French the language of commerce in Quebec to see that this is so. Knowing French became important instead of knowing English in Quebec. In the United States, knowing Spanish could be made valuable in schools, as could the experiences of children of the working and lower classes.

Ideally, instead of penalizing children who do not come from families with middle-class, standard-English backgrounds, schools could adapt to the communities in which they exist and use backgrounds gained in such communities in the learning experience. For those living in areas where those of Mexican origin predominate, the goal should be bilingual, bicultural individuals who can appreciate the language, culture, and customs of their families, as well as the English-based "standard" language and culture of the United States as a whole.

Occupation

After education, a second and related area we choose to address, which also informs us as to the social reproduction of inequality, concerns occupation. Specifically, we look at labor market segmentation. Piore ([1970] 1977) has conceptualized this segmentation as a "dual labor market," made up of "primary" and "secondary" markets. The primary sector is characterized by high wages, good working conditions, employment stability and job security, equity and due process in administration of work rules, and chances for advancement. The secondary sector is characterized by low wages, poor working conditions, considerable variability in employment, harsh and often arbitrary discipline, and little opportunity to advance. The poor are locked into the secondary labor market with little chance of advancement into the primary sector.

There are structural reasons inherent in the economy for low wages paid in the secondary sector. According to Bluestone ([1965] 1977), low-wage industries tend to have both lower amounts of capital and lower productivity rates and thus tend to be less profitable than industries in the high-wage sector. Additionally, low-wage industries face more competition than do industries in the oligopolistic primary sector. Competition keeps profit margins low for secondary-sector industries, and a small profit margin results in a reluctance to raise wages. Workers in the secondary sector tend to have less human capital than workers in the primary sector and, therefore, can be replaced more easily than those in the primary sector, which fact also tends to keep wages low in the secondary labor market.

Bluestone concludes that the working poor should not be blamed for their inadequate incomes. If anything, he comments, they should be "blamed" for not having the good luck to complete their education and move into the primary sector, an interesting observation given the analysis by Bourdieu. Bourdieu, of course, believes that, overall, the working poor have little chance to achieve elite status by way of education. Overall, Bluestone faults an economic system unable to provide adequate people with adequate jobs.

Reich, Gordon, and Edwards ([1973] 1977), in their study of labor market segmentation, indicate that minorities, women, and youth predominate in the secondary labor market. They add that unstable working habits are fostered in the secondary labor market given the nature of the market, and, as a consequence, individuals are handicapped in trying to move from the secondary into the primary sector. They believe that along with segmentation by sex, educational credentials, and industry grouping, there is labor market segmentation by race. Historically, because of segmentation by race, class conflict often has been diverted into race conflict.

Bluestone's view of adequate people working for inadequate wages and Reich, Gordon, and Edwards's belief that there are racial barriers to movement from the secondary to the primary labor market sector are particularly appropriate in the case of Guadalupe.

Relationships between Occupation and Education

Let us examine relationships between education and occupation to understand more clearly the structure of the social reproduction of inequality. In the status attainment model (Blau and Duncan 1967; Featherman and Hauser 1978), occupation and education are intimately related. Parents' education and parents' occupation strongly predict the educational attainment of their children, and the educational attainment of the children strongly predicts children's occupations. To put this in Bourdieu's terms, parents' education and occupation are equivalent to the amount of cultural capital possessed by the family, and the greater the cultural capital, the greater the chances for offspring of that family to be successful in school. These findings fit well with findings of the Coleman Report (Coleman et al. 1966), in which class background was the strongest predictor of performance on standardized tests. Success in school, which at this time we can define as a college degree, is increasingly becoming a prerequisite for entry into the primary occupational sector. The difficulty of large-scale upward mobility for the people of Guadalupe into the primary occupational sector becomes apparent.

Political Capital

An exclusive emphasis on the social reproduction of inequality would make advancement seem hopeless for those at the bottom of the socioeconomic order. They would seem to have little chance for advancement either in the educational or in the occupational sphere. However, two observations can be made. First, despite the overall structure of the system, empirical studies of status attainment tell us that some are able to rise educationally and occupationally, although the rise may not be great (Blau and Duncan 1967; Featherman and Hauser 1978). Secondly, because of an ideology of egalitarianism (Lipset 1967), economic forces are not allowed to grind to their inexorable conclusion, but rather, occasionally, there is intervention in the political arena to support the ideology of equality of opportunity.

With this in mind, let us now introduce a new concept, that of "political capital," which can inform us as to the situation in Guadalupe and in similar communities. The concept is an extension of Bourdieu's concept of cultural capital, itself an extension of the concept of capital as economic wealth that can create more wealth. Political capital is defined as power, or the potential for power, in the political and judicial domain. This power is used to maintain privilege among the elites or to gain an improved quality of life among nonelites. The source of political capital for communities at the bottom of the socioeconomic order is a sense of a need for justice and for equality of opportunity in a democracy. The source of political capital for elites is an ardent desire to maintain privilege, and it is implemented through their ability to select and to control those who make and interpret laws. Our subsequent discussion of political capital concerns nonelite communities. We speak of community, first, in terms of oppressed minorities across the nation and then of the community of Guadalupe in particular.

One difference between political capital and cultural capital as defined by Bourdieu is that whereas cultural capital resides in the family, political capital resides in communities or groups as a whole. An interesting aspect of political capital is that it can precede and foster additional economic and cultural capital. Political capital can foster changes in the social structure and provide either direct assistance, such as direct monetary payments, or indirect assistance, such as giving a group some advantage in employment, as is done with veterans in civil service employment or both. Political capital can change the rules under which the socioeconomic game is played.

We are able to subcategorize political capital into two types, extrinsic political capital and intrinsic political capital. Extrinsic political capital is that given to a group by politically powerful and sympathetic outsiders while the group itself is still largely economically and culturally powerless. For example, abolitionists, who supported freedom for slaves before the Civil War, and Presidents Kennedy and Johnson, who supported the civil rights movement of the 1960s, could be considered examples of sympathetic outsiders. This extrinsic support, however, often is generated by insider leadership. Insiders tend to see social ills not as resulting from individual weakness but as systemic and structural. Rather than being overwhelmed by societal problems, they are moved to try to do something about them. This is so because they often are better educated and have had more contact with the outside world than most within the community. Successful education and contact with outsiders leads to a realization that community betterment is possible. Insiders often serve as brokers between the community and sympathetic outsiders who have expertise the community can use.

In the context of minority communities, there are two types of insiders, ethnic insiders and nonethnic insiders. Ethnic insiders are those of the same ethnicity as those in the minority community. Nonethnic insiders are those who are nonminority but who have largely acculturated into the minority community and have self-identified with the community.

During the civil rights movement, Martin Luther King provided ethnic insider leadership. Similarly, Cesar Chavez contributed ethnic insider leadership in the struggle to improve the quality of life of farmworkers in the United States, a struggle that received support from numerous sympathetic outsiders in such activities as grape and lettuce boycotts. The oppressed can possess extrinsic political capital because their situation can arouse sympathy and support from which, subsequently, can come real gains in life chances.

Intrinsic political capital can develop within the group itself once it extrinsically has been given some ability to participate in the political system, although, for minority groups at least, some extrinsic political capital must remain. For example, substantial changes in the political structure of the American South came after the Civil Rights Act of 1964, which enabled African Americans to vote in larger numbers. Past oppression can create solidarity within a group, and solidarity can yield political returns. Because some politicians want the support of the group's potential intrinsic political capital, they work toward changes that ultimately result in some educational and economic improvement of the group.

Disadvantaged groups can come to possess intrinsic political capital with the help of extrinsic political capital either because of their numbers, where they constitute a numerical majority or, if not a majority, because of their solidarity and militance, which can give them a considerable amount of political capital. Intrinsic political capital supported by extrinsic political capital can affect the occupational and educational outcomes of the group.

Education and Occupation in Guadalupe

The people of Guadalupe have experienced the most severe kinds of social inequality in both education and occupation. Because they did not speak English, because many of them worked in low-level agricultural jobs, and because they were racially different from the Caucasian majority, the kinds of obstacles faced by people in Guadalupe have tended to be extreme. The kinds of problems faced by people in the township are much more extreme than the kind envisaged by Bourdieu in his theory of cultural capital, and, of all the types of labor in the secondary labor market, conditions in agriculture for laborers have been among the most oppressive.

Examples given by Bourdieu in his study of cultural capital have to do with frequency of opera attendance, of listening to classical music, and of going to museums. In Guadalupe, for many, the lack of cultural capital involves a much more basic problem of serious poverty and having a language different from the language of the nation. Concerning labor market segmentation, no sector is more deeply into the secondary labor market with all of its problems than agricultural, particularly seasonal, farm labor. What has been experienced, then, in Guadalupe has been "off-the-chart" social inequality, and, consequently, problems of stopping the social reproduction of inequality and moving toward upward mobility have been extraordinarily difficult.

Political Capital and the Community of Guadalupe

As previously noted, political capital can precede and assist in developing economic and cultural capital. Before economic and cultural capital of individuals in a community can be generated, the community itself must acquire and provide basic services. In the early 1960s, relative to what was standard and expected in the United States at the time, Guadalupe was severely lacking in services. In 1962, with the exception of one road, and this only because it was the major county road connecting Phoenix and Tucson, none of the streets in the community were paved, nor were they marked with stop signs or street signs. The water system in the community was inadequate, there was no mail delivery to houses, and police protection, under the jurisdiction of Maricopa County, was almost nonexistent. Health care was seriously substandard, and even ownership of land on which houses had been built was in question (Cortright 1967; Garcia 1973; Murguia and Bernasconi 1992).

With reference to our political capital model, the key ethnic insider was Lauro Garcia. Garcia was a Korean War veteran who subsequently attended Arizona State University in Tempe. In 1960, because trailer-space rentals around campus were relatively expensive, he bought a lot in nearby Guadalupe and, with his family, established residence there (Cortright 1967, 13; Garcia 1973, 11). He became an active member of the Guadalupe Health Council, organized in August 1961. Members of the organization recognized the need for improving the community and decided that although there was need in many areas, health would be a priority (Garcia 1973, 14).

Medical services in the community were severely lacking. In 1963, county medical services in the community consisted of one clinic a month. The building in which the clinic was held was cockroach and rat infested, with poor ventilation. Heating and cooling systems in the building were in need of repair, and the building was almost unbearable, particularly in the summer. The County Health Department wanted to close it down, an action that would have created a burden for people in Guadalupe because the closest county hospital was over twenty miles away in Phoenix. Garcia and the Guadalupe Health Council cleaned and repaired the building. Instead of it being closed down, in March 1964, services were increased from once to twice a month. Additionally, the Health Council bought supplies, a refrigerator, and an examination table for the clinic (Garcia 1973, 18).

The key outsider was Fred Ross, who arrived in Guadalupe in April 1964. Previously, Ross had been schooled by Saul Alinsky and was working for Alinsky's Industrial Areas Foundation (Cortright 1967, 12). One of Ross's most noteworthy achievements had been discovering and instructing Cesar Chavez while Ross had been organizing farmworkers in California (Levy 1975).

Since the 1920s, the Presbyterian Church had held one hundred acres of land in Guadalupe in trust, the acreage subsequently settled by families in the community. The church wanted to transfer ownership of land to families living on lots in the acreage and invited Ross to Guadalupe to help with the process. Ross, however, felt limited working on only this one problem, given all the other community problems, and requested free rein to assist the community as a whole (Cortright 1967, 13).

Ross's organizational technique was to hold numerous house meetings, the advantage of this type of meeting being the social comfort engendered. In this relaxed setting, individuals in the community felt free to express their opinions honestly as to what the needs of the community were. He held forty meetings to this end, although many needs had already been identified by the Guadalupe Health Council. In May 1964, a preorganizational meeting for a new community-based organization, in many ways a successor to the Guadalupe Health Council, was held. This new organization, with Lauro Garcia as its director, was called "The Guadalupe Organization," or GO (Garcia 1973, 18–19). Under Ross's guidance, the Guadalupe Organization's first priority was to develop political power. Ten voting registrars from GO were dispatched to register voters in the community. In 1962, before the voting registration drive, Guadalupe had 182 registered voters, with 140 actually voting. In 1964, after the drive, that number had increased to 715, of whom over 80 percent actually voted in general elections in November 1964, all largely in the same direction (Democrat) with the effect of a block vote (Garcia 1973, 19). At that time, given the relatively sparse population of this part of the county, which was still heavily agricultural, this was a significant increase.

One of the ways sympathetic outsiders can help insiders is with professional expertise. Lauro Garcia stated, "We had feelings of how you help your community. But we didn't have the professional touch and he gave us that" (Garcia 1973, 18).

An important episode in the sociohistory of the community illustrates clearly the role intrinsic political capital can play in improving the community. It also demonstrates the effectiveness of Ross's methods. In 1964, Ross and Garcia met with a member of the Maricopa County Board of Supervisors. Since Guadalupe was unincorporated at the time, the local governing entity of the community was the County Board of Supervisors. The board member, although not entirely unsympathetic to the needs of the community, indirectly indicated disinterest in the meeting by continuing to shuffle papers after Ross and Garcia's entrance. They proceeded to inform the board member that as a result of their voter registration efforts, Guadalupe now had over seven hundred registered voters. When the board member heard that the community had over seven hundred registered voters, he froze, stopped shuffling papers, and instructed his secretary not to take calls. Attentively, he listened to Ross and Garcia's requests concerning lack of paved streets and lack of police protection. He agreed to commence paving two and one-half miles of road a year in the community, promised improved police protection, and promised to get an officer from the community in the police force. Garcia tells us that the board member delivered on his promises (Garcia 1973, 19–20).

A second example of political capital in Guadalupe involved an educated ethnic insider with outside contact who used the courts to improve life chances in the community (Guadalupe Organization 1973; Murguia and Bernasconi 1992). This example, more clearly than the first, demonstrates the kinds of obstacles those working for social change have had to face.

Socorro Hernandez, a young woman from one of the leading families in Guadalupe, already possessed some cultural capital. As a member of the Community of the Sisters of the Precious Blood, she received her bachelor's degree in 1966 at Dayton University, the first person from Guadalupe to receive a college degree. She left the Precious Blood Sisters and entered a master's program at Texas Tech University, receiving training in educational counseling. In 1970, she returned to the community and began work as a counselor at Veda B. Frank Elementary School in Guadalupe, a part of Tempe Elementary School District No. 3, which included Guadalupe. All of the children at Frank School were from Guadalupe at the time.

In her work, she became aware of practices that seemed to her to be unfair. The district was administering IQ tests in English to children in second grade. According to Hernandez, the children did well on the exams to the extent that they understood instructions or if the teachers demonstrated what they wanted done. Failure on the tests largely was the result of a language barrier, not the children's lack of ability (Johnson 1979, SS-1). Tests administered in English could not analyze fairly the abilities of the children, since many came from homes in which little English was spoken. As a result, a disproportionate number of children from the community scored low on the tests and were labeled "mentally retarded" and placed in special education classes. In Bourdieu's terms, the children did not have the cultural capital of mastery of English and, as a result, were stigmatized and sentenced to educational failure. Of children in special education classes in the district, 67 percent were of Mexican origin, although students of Mexican origin made up only 17 percent of children in the district. Also, Hernandez discovered that the district was receiving approximately twice the funds per child for a student placed in special education. There was a vested interest, then, on the part of the school district to have children in special education classes because of the additional funds they generated. It also was apparent that the additional funds were not going to the school in Guadalupe.

When Socorro Hernandez, by then Socorro Hernandez Bernasconi, informed district administrators as to the situation, they refused to look into the matter and instructed her not to say anything more about it. Hernandez Bernasconi informed the Guadalupe Organization as to what was occurring in the district. The Guadalupe Organization strongly supported Hernandez Bernasconi, and she and nine members of GO who were parents of children in the school became coplaintiffs in a class action lawsuit against the district on August 10, 1971.

The Guadalupe Organization was successful in its suit, which resulted in the "Guadalupe Regulations" of the State of Arizona. The Arizona State Board of Education mandated a fairer way of testing abilities of bilingual children. The result of this suit affected children in communities throughout Arizona, Native American as well as those of Mexican origin, assuring that children would be tested in their functional language.

After the filing of the lawsuit by members of GO, administrators in the school district retaliated against the organization and against Hernandez Bernasconi. GO had been using buildings of Frank School to offer adult education classes free of charge to members of the community to obtain high-school equivalency degrees (GEDs). District administrators revised their policy to require that GO pay $250 a week in rent for use of Frank classrooms. GO then moved its classes to rooms in the Catholic church complex in the community. Hernandez Bernasconi was removed from her position as counselor at Frank School, even though she was the only bilingual counselor in the district, and was placed as a teacher at an all-Anglo school outside of Guadalupe. The move from counselor to teacher was, in effect, a demotion because the position of counselor generally is regarded more highly in the schools than that of teacher. A counselor, for example, could move more easily into administration than a teacher. Hernandez Bernasconi again filed suit, claiming, first, discrimination on the part of the district because of the demotion and, second, that her right to freedom of speech had been violated (Guadalupe Organization 1973). The district's position was that Hernandez Bernasconi had not suffered discrimination because there had been no loss in pay, and that she had "no right to discuss the practices of the district, either during school hours or on her own time" (Howard 1978, 7). Hernandez Bernasconi felt that she had been demoted in the move from counselor to teacher and that she was attacking a practice detrimental to children and so had the right to do so (Howard 1978, 7).

In 1979, after seven years of litigation and ten thousand dollars in court costs, a heavy burden for a family of modest means to bear, the Supreme Court of the United States upheld the decision by the Ninth Circuit Court of Appeals, which had found that the district had denied Hernandez Bernasconi her First Amendment right to freedom of speech (Johnson 1979, SS-1). The next step was to be another trial to determine the issue of discrimination. If discrimination were found, the district would be required to pay damages, including court costs. At that point, the district decided to settle out of court. It paid Hernandez Bernasconi for court costs and sent her a contract to teach kindergarten at Frank School part time. By then, however, because of an integration plan for schools in the district, two-thirds of the children from Guadalupe in Frank School were going to other schools outside of the community and non-Hispanic white children were being bused to Frank School. Hernandez Bernasconi decided to work at an alternative school for the children of Guadalupe, which had been established by the Guadalupe Organization (Johnson 1979, SS-4).

A third example of political capital in Guadalupe involves Colette Mc-Nally-Cruz, a nonethnic insider and program coordinator of Centro de Amistad, the successor organization to the Guadalupe Organization (McNally-Cruz 1993; Ulik 1993). Born in Ireland, McNally traveled to Spain as a young woman to study Spanish as a second language. In Spain, she joined the Spanish order of the Sisters of Loretto and taught English in Spanish schools for almost twenty years (from 1958 to 1977). In 1977, the Sisters of Loretto in Arizona requested assistance from the Spanish sisters for their work with Mexican origin and Native American populations in Arizona.

McNally was sent, and she spent ten years in Arizona before coming to Guadalupe and the Centro de Amistad in 1988. During those ten years, she received her B.S. from Northern Arizona University in 1981 and, by means of summer work, a master's degree in school administration from the University of San Francisco in 1987. She was principal of a school in Flagstaff and, in 1988, arrived in Guadalupe. In the township, she became program director of Centro de Amistad. She subsequently left the order, became an American citizen, and married a Hispanic from Honduras.

From Bourdieu's perspective, McNally accumulated an immense amount of cultural capital, having a total of thirty years in teaching and administration in the schools. When faced with the dismal record of achievement of the children of Guadalupe in the schools, particularly in the high school, McNally-Cruz decided on a radically different approach. The attrition rate of students from Guadalupe in the high school had been very high. In 1988, 125 children from Guadalupe entered the high school, and four years later, in 1992, only 24 of this group graduated (Ulik 1993, 1).

Instead of a remedial approach, in which children who already had experienced failure would be put into classes to "catch up," her approach became one of prevention. She called her program "Academia," and it consists of two parts. In the mornings, eighth-grade graduates from Guadalupe attend physical education class at Marcos de Niza High School in neighboring Tempe. (Guadalupe itself does not have a high school, so children attend high school in an affluent area in Tempe.) The program is voluntary and free of charge to the participants and gives participants the opportunity to earn a full physical education credit in the summer before entering school as freshmen. In subsequent years of high school, instead of taking the required P.E. course, they are able to choose an elective in its place. They are also able to become familiar with the high school before fall classes begin. Again, the key insight is that instead of Guadalupe children being placed in *remedial* classes to try to catch up, they are given the opportunity of gaining a head start in *advanced* classes. In other words, the process is one of "acceleration" instead of "remediation" (Ulik 1993, 1). Psychologically, there is a world of difference between the two approaches. In acceleration, the self-concept is enhanced. In remediation, the self-concept is battered, first, by the original failure that caused the remediation; second, by being placed in a remediation class with other "failures"; and, third, by being placed with teachers who know that their students have a history of failure and who, therefore, will expect little of them.

One might inquire as to why physical education was chosen as the vehicle for the program rather than other, more academic, classes. The request for physical education classes came from the parents and students themselves. Physical education has been problematic for students from Guadalupe for financial reasons because of the expense of uniforms and locker and towel fees and for social reasons because in physical education classes students have to interact (for example, in choosing teams), and the social distance between students from Guadalupe and Anglo students from Tempe sometimes makes such interaction uncomfortable. Also, physical education has been problematic for cultural reasons of modesty because of common showers (Ulik 1993, 1–2).

After spending the morning at the high school, students ride a bus back to Guadalupe, eat lunch, and attend the second part of the program at Centro de Amistad in the afternoon. The goal of the second part of the program is to help the children see what is possible for them in the future. The students attend presentations by successful Latinos in all walks of life. The students can identify with the speakers, some from Guadalupe itself, who can tell them what it will take to attain a measure of success in American society. One speaker, for example, was a marine from Guadalupe who emphasized staying in school and away from drugs. Another was an assistant director of financial aid and scholarships at Arizona State University who had had to live in his car for a time while attending Arizona State. A third speaker was one of eighteen children in a migrant family, was twenty-two years old when he graduated from high school, and currently is an associate professor of multicultural education at Arizona State University (Ulik 1993, 2).

In the summer of 1992, the first year of the program, 37 youths participated in the advanced P.E. classes and 34 received high-school credentials in P.E. Thirty-three of the students completed their freshman year in high school. In the summer of 1993, 73 youth began the program, 64 received high-school credentials in P.E., and all 73 remain in school as of late September 1993. What is significant about the program is that in monitoring the progress of children from Guadalupe in the high school, heavy attrition among the group continues except for the class group that went through the program. Of course, this is a social program, not a scientific experiment. It could be argued that because of self-selection, those participating in the program most likely would have been successful anyway. However, should the program continue to expand and include more and more of the children of Guadalupe and should the attrition rate with those going through the program remain low, this would give strong evidence of the success of the program.

The Limits of Political Capital in Guadalupe

While the Guadalupe Health Organization and the Guadalupe Organization in the past and the Centro de Amistad in the present have fought to improve conditions in the community, it must be realized that the agents of political capital, the insiders and sympathetic outsiders, have had to face and continue to face considerable obstacles. The forces involved in the social reproduction of inequality remain formidable. Using data from the 1990 census (U.S. Bureau of the Census 1992b, 6–46), we can make some comparisons among Guadalupe and adjoining Phoenix and Tempe along several socioeconomic dimensions.

Concerning language, 24 percent of persons 5 to 17 years of age in Guadalupe speak a language other than English at home, compared with only 4 percent in Phoenix and 2 percent in Tempe. For those 18 years and older, 55 percent of those in Guadalupe speak a language other than English, compared with 13 percent in Phoenix and 11 percent in Tempe. Although from a cultural maintenance perspective, it is positive that people in Guadalupe maintain their use of the Spanish language, from the cultural capital perspective, use of Spanish in the home, unless it is accompanied by knowledge of standard English required in the schools, will lead to academic failure and, subsequently, to low occupational prestige (Tienda and Neidert 1985). Concerning education, and confirming Bourdieu's thesis, of persons 25 years and over, 33 percent in Guadalupe are high-school graduates or higher, as compared with 79 percent in Phoenix and 90 percent in Tempe. (However, this probably does not mean that 33 percent of people living in Guadalupe actually completed twelve years of schooling, because one of the Guadalupe Organization's projects was in adult education and numerous people in Guadalupe received their high-school equivalency degrees.) Only 2.2 percent of those in Guadalupe have a bachelor's degree or higher, as compared with 20 percent in Phoenix and 37 percent in Tempe. This is significant because, as previously mentioned, primary sector jobs currently tend toward requiring a college degree. (Tienda and Neidert [1985] present evidence as to how strongly college attendance and, especially, college graduation add to the occupational prestige of Mexican origin males.) With reference to employment, in 1990, 47 percent of those in Guadalupe were in the labor force, while 61 percent of those in Phoenix and 67 percent of those in Tempe were in the labor force. Of persons 16 years and over in the civilian labor force, 16.6 percent in Guadalupe were unemployed, compared with 7 percent in Phoenix and 5 percent in Tempe.

In terms of income, the per capita income of Guadalupe was $4,939, for Phoenix it was $14,096, and for Tempe, $15,530. In other words, per capita income in Guadalupe was only about one-third that of Phoenix and Tempe. A parallel statistic to per capita income is the rate of poverty. In the three areas, with reference to persons with income in 1989 below the poverty level, Guadalupe had a 40 percent poverty rate, Phoenix had a 14.2 percent poverty rate, and Tempe had a 13.6 percent poverty rate. Thus, the poverty rate in Guadalupe was three times greater than that of Phoenix and Tempe.

It becomes clear that socioeconomically, Guadalupe has not caught up with its neighbors. What remains to be seen is the extent to which political capital is able to narrow the present gap between the people in Guadalupe and those in surrounding communities in spite of structural forces that militate against the closing of disparities. Sufficient political capital may be able to assist individuals within a community to reach a level where they can begin to compete for resources that have been going almost automatically to the more elite.

Conclusion

In the United States, while it is believed that all should have "equal opportunity" to rise socioeconomically, respected theorists and numerous studies have indicated that this is not the case. They indicate instead a social reproduction of inequality that resembles the mechanisms of the popular game of Monopoly, where the tendencies are for the wealthy to get wealthier and for those with little to have less and less. These structural tendencies fly in the face of a fundamental value in the United States, that of egalitarianism (Lipset 1967). Therefore, a counteracting tendency is allowed occasionally to operate whereby systemic rules are modified to keep some lines of upward mobility open and to fight the tendency of the poor to become a permanent underclass. What we have demonstrated in the case of Guadalupe is that the countertendency of egalitarianism does not operate on its own in low-income communities, but requires political capital activated through insider and outsider agents of political change. It is the insider agents of political capital who are of particular interest, because our analysis indicates that pressure for change comes from them, assisted by external agents. Insider agents are individuals who identify with their community and who, if they are ethnic and from the community, have escaped poverty and risen to middle-class status. If they are nonethnic insiders, they have, for some reason (often religious), chosen to cast their lot with the poor. They act as mediators between their community and sympathetic outsiders and bring processes in motion that improve life chances of people in their communities. They are intimately in contact with the needs and wants of members of their community. They also understand that a better life than that of poverty is possible, and they work for the betterment of their community.

This analysis indicates that the future of Guadalupe and similar communities depends in part on the presence of educated middle-class insiders as agents of political capital, who can mobilize intrinsic and extrinsic political capital for community improvement. Wilson (1987) demonstrated that part of the reason for the desolation of black inner-city communities was the exodus of the black middle class to more affluent areas. Similarly, Friedman ([1966] 1977) argued that public housing in the United States was effective to the extent to which its clients were members of a "submerged middle class" during the depression. Public housing deteriorated after the depression when the vocal and politically active middle class moved out. The future of Guadalupe and like communities depends on having sufficient numbers of educated insiders such as Lauro Garcia, Soccoro Hernandez Bernasconi, and Colette McNally-Cruz to continue the struggle for social justice and to enlist the support of sympathetic outsiders for the improvement of the community.

References

Blau, Peter M., and Otis Dudley Duncan. 1967. *The American Occupational Structure*. New York: Wiley.

Bluestone, Barry. [1965] 1977. "The Characteristics of Marginal Industries." Pp. 97–102 in *Problems in Political Economy: An Urban Perspective*, 2nd ed., edited by David M. Gordon. Lexington, Mass.: Heath.

Bourdieu, Pierre. [1973] 1977. "Cultural Reproduction and Social Reproduction." Pp. 487–511 in *Power and Ideology in Education*, edited by Jerome Karabel and A. H. Halsey. New York: Oxford University Press.

Coleman, James S., Ernest Q. Campbell, Carol J. Hobson, James McPartland, Alexander M. Mood, Frederic D. Weinfeld, and Robert L. York. 1966. *Equality of Educational Opportunity*. Washington, D.C.: U.S. Government Printing Office.

Cortright, Barbara. 1967. "Guadalupe, Arizona: Scar City." *Reveille* 2:12–15.

Featherman, David L., and Robert M. Hauser. 1978. *Opportunity and Change*. New York: Academic.

Friedman, Lawrence M. [1966] 1977. "Public Housing and the Poor." Pp. 507–12 in *Problems in Political Economy: An Urban Perspective,* 2nd ed., edited by David M. Gordon. Lexington, Mass.: Heath.

Garcia, Lauro. 1973. "An Interview with Lauro Garcia, November 19, 1973." Interview by Ella Varbel. Unpublished manuscript.

Guadalupe Organization. 1973. "Guadalupe." Guadalupe, Ariz.: Guadalupe Organization.

Howard, Jane. 1978. "Seven Year War Rages On, Still Unsettled." *Arizona Forum,* March, 7–8.

Johnson, Ann. 1979. "Battle Brings Partial Victory." *Phoenix Gazette,* July 4, SS 1,4.

Levy, Jacques E. 1975. *Cesar Chavez: Autobiography of La Causa.* N. Y.: Norton.

Lipset, Seymour Martin. 1967. *The First New Nation.* Garden City, N. Y.: Anchor Books.

McNally-Cruz, Colette. 1993. Telephone interview by Edward Murguia. Centro de Amistad, Guadalupe, Arizona, September 28.

Murguia, Edward, and Santino Bernasconi. 1992. "Guadalupe in Time: The Past, the Present and the Future Development of an Indo-Hispanic Community in Arizona." Pp. 83–99 in *Harmonizing Arizona's Ethnic and Cultural Diversity,* edited by Leonard Gordon, John Stuart Hall, and Rob Melnick. Tempe: Arizona Town Hall, Arizona State University.

Piore, Michael J. [1970] 1977. "The Dual Labor Market: Theory and Implications." Pp. 93–102 in *Problems in Political Economy: An Urban Perspective,* 2nd ed., edited by David M. Gordon. Lexington, Mass.: Heath.

Reich, Michael, David M. Gordon, and Richard C. Edwards. [1973] 1977. "A Theory of Labor Market Segmentation." Pp. 108–13 in *Problems in Political Economy: An Urban Perspective,* 2nd ed., edited by David M. Gordon. Lexington, Mass.: Heath.

Tienda, Marta, and Lisa J. Neidert. 1985. "Language, Education, and the Socioeconomic Achievement of Hispanic Origin Men." Pp. 359–76 in *The Mexican American Experience: An Interdisciplinary Anthology,* edited by Rodolfo O. de la Garza, Frank D. Bean, Charles M. Bonjean, Ricardo Romo, and Rodolfo Alvarez. Austin: University of Texas Press.

Ulik, Clare. 1993. "Different Drill: Town, School Try PE to Ease Transition for Minority Teens Who Don't Last in High School." *Arizona Republic/Phoenix Gazette* (Tempe Community section), June 28, 1,6.

U.S. Bureau of the Census. 1992a. General Population Characteristics: Arizona. *1990 Census of the Population.* 1990 CP-1–4, table 1. Washington, D.C.: GPO.

———. 1992b. Summary Social, Economic, and Housing Characteristics: Arizona. *1990 Census of the Population.* 1990 CPH-5–4, tables 2, 4, 6, 10, 12. Washington, D.C.: GPO.

Wilson, William Julius. 1987. *The Truly Disadvantaged: The Inner City, the Underclass, and Public Policy.* Chicago: University of Chicago Press.

16 / The Continuing Legacy of Discrimination in Southern Communities

James W. Button

There has been a white backlash on race recently. Whites have a strong feeling that blacks are getting too many privileges, and that whites are suffering from reverse discrimination.

White city administrator, Daytona Beach, Florida[1]

Racial attitudes are better today. Blacks and whites work and play together more. The races are closer and more doors are open now for blacks. Even some of our churches are integrated.

Black public official, Crestview, Florida[2]

The civil rights movement of the 1960s was considered one of the most important social movements in this country's history. With a particular focus on the South, whose history of antiblack violence and segregation was unparalleled, the movement's primary goals included political power and social and economic equality for blacks. Some thirty years later, however, it is still not clear what the total impact of the movement has been in the South and how close (or far) blacks are from achieving these fundamental goals.

A number of scholars have lauded the movement as a significant catalyst to reshaping the South and removing forever the barriers that have separated the races. Historian Robert Weisbrot, for example, has claimed that "if America's civil rights movement is judged by the distance it traveled ... a record of substantial achievement unfolds."[3] The walls of segregation in public facilities have tumbled, schools and most places of work are integrated, black public officials are commonplace, and perhaps most important, racial fear and hate have been reduced. Black economist Thomas Sowell echoes this claim and states even more forthrightly that "the battle for civil rights [for blacks] was won, decisively, two decades ago."[4]

Yet not all accounts of the black movement have been so sanguine. William Chafe, after studying Greensboro, North Carolina, both before and after the civil rights movement, concluded that "inequality and discrimination still suffuse our social and economic system, buttressed by informal modes of social control even more powerful than the law."[5] And a recent close analysis of Atlanta, the epitome of black progress in the South, shows "not only that full equality of opportunity has eluded Atlanta, but that some of the gains made during the civil rights era are eroding rapidly," particularly in education and the economic sector.[6] Thus while substantial racial progress has been made in the South, race continues to preoccupy the public mind, and in many respects the separation between blacks and whites is still pervasive and deep-rooted.

To explore more fully the issue of black progress in the South, this chapter reports the results of a long-term study of the status of blacks in six Florida communities. Florida contains the necessary range of political and socioeconomic environments typical of the South,[7] and the cities were carefully selected to represent both variations in political culture (especially Old South–New South differences) and in the relative size of the black population (table 16.1).[8] In terms of culture, the northern part of the state is representative of the mainly rural, relatively poor, agricultural-based Old South, while the southern (mainly coastal) region is typical of the more urbanized, faster-growing, and relatively middle-class New South. In each city, I examined the most significant municipal services (police and fire protection, streets, and recreation), as well as private sector employment and other indicators of conditions for blacks.[9] In most instances, I have been able to chart changes in these services and opportunities for blacks over the past three decades, and I have attempted to link these changes with various political, economic, and contextual factors. This unique approach has enabled me to see not only *what* changes have occurred in the lives of blacks in these communities, but also *why* and *how* these transformations have taken place. The focus of this chapter will be on the degree of change since the civil rights era of the 1960s and the status of blacks in the 1990s.

Table 16.1. Typology of communities

Region	City characteristics	
	Population (1990)	Percent black (1990)
Old South		
Crestview	9,886	20
Lake City	10,005	38
Quincy	7,444	61
New South		
Titusville	39,394	11
Daytona Beach	61,921	31
Riviera Beach	27,639	70

Municipal Services and Employment for Blacks

One of the most immediate goals of the black political movement in the South was the improvement of local public services.[10] Police protection and the reduction of police brutality were a high priority in almost all black neighborhoods. Streets and public works were also major issues in many communities; it was common to have street paving and maintenance end at the black section. Even parks and recreation, often considered more "quality of life" than basic services, were historically sources of deep dissatisfaction for many southern blacks. Parks, playgrounds, beaches, and other public recreational facilities were usually closed to blacks, and many blacks could not afford commercial entertainment or transportation to lakes, beaches, or other sources of leisure.

The value of these municipal services went well beyond their functional importance, however. Improvements in these services for blacks had a psychological and symbolic significance that should not be underestimated. In the minds of many blacks the inadequate provision of streets, parks and recreation, police protection, and other services had clearly denoted the inferior status assigned to blacks in the South.[11] As a black public official in Crestview put it: "Street paving has been particularly poor for blacks, and street maintenance as well. Many whites just feel they don't need to give blacks as much."[12]

The employment of blacks in municipal jobs was also a goal of the civil rights movement. Historically such employment was a familiar avenue of economic advancement for disadvantaged groups. Public employment, moreover, conferred a degree of status or prestige not found in low-paying private sector jobs usually held by blacks. Yet southern cities traditionally had either not employed blacks at all or hired them only for the most menial positions.[13]

Among city services, police and fire, or human safety services, are often most important. Historically, poverty-stricken black neighborhoods have suffered from high rates of crime and fire, and black citizens typically have endured a great amount of police brutality. The black political movement of the 1960s, however, brought some significant changes to most of these protective services. Improved street paving and water services, housing rehabilitation programs, and the construction of substations in or near black areas all tended to enhance fire service. By the early 1970s, moreover, most fire departments had hired their first blacks (table 16.2). This was a major breakthrough, since these departments were often the most resistant to black employment.

As for police departments, the proportion of black officers increased moderately during the 1960s and 1970s (table 16.2). By the early 1970s police patrols were usually integrated and black officers were allowed to arrest white citizens (neither practice was common prior to this period). New South communities tended to develop police-community relations programs and to increase patrolling in high-crime black neighborhoods. Improvements in black employment and often protective services were greatest in majority-black cities, reflecting the influence of demands by black citizens and the political power of black city officials.[14]

Perhaps most important, reported incidents of police brutality toward blacks declined in almost every community by the late 1970s and early 1980s. Most significant in helping to bring about this reduction in brutality was the presence of more black police and black elected officials.[15] Besides being generally more empathetic toward blacks, minority police often influenced departmental policy and general police relations with the black community. And with blacks in political power, the police could no longer assume an atmosphere of white supremacy in their treatment of black citizens.

Yet by the 1990s, the proportion of black police and firefighters was still surprisingly low (table 16.2). In no department had blacks gained proportional equality, and in several cities (Crestview, Titusville, and Daytona Beach) the percentages of black personnel were similar to those for the 1960s. This notable lack of progress in employment was due to a variety of factors, including relatively low pay (starting salary in most departments was less than twenty thousand dollars annually), better job opportunities in the private sector, strict codes of behavior and discipline requirements, and negative feelings expressed by many black citizens toward black officers (they are

Table 16.2. Percentages of black police and firefighters (1960–91)

Communities	1960		1970		1980		1991	
Crestview	0[a]	(0)[b]	11	(0)	13	(0)	6	(7)
Lake City	13	(0)	19	(19)	13	(19)	13	(22)
Quincy	0	(0)	9	(0)	17	(9)	26	(17)
Titusville	7	(0)	3	(3)	4	(7)	8	(0)
Daytona Beach	8	(0)	2	(0)	15	(9)	11	(8)
Riviera Beach	17	(0)	19	(7)	30	(4)	44	(25)

[a]Percentage of blacks in police department.
[b]Percentage of blacks in fire department.

still often called "Uncle Toms" and viewed as traitors). In addition, city affirmative action programs were less rigorously enforced in the 1980s and were usually broadened to include other minorities, particularly white women. The economic recession and resulting local budget cutbacks also affected black employment, since the last hired were typically the first to be fired.

Allegations of police brutality and harassment of blacks have continued to be a significant issue in most communities.[16] Clearly the dramatic increase in the later 1980s in drug trafficking and drug-related crimes in black neighborhoods has exacerbated conflict between blacks and the police. As a black leader in Lake City stated it: "Blacks still dislike the police, and the police are fearful to patrol black areas where the majority of violent crimes and drug trafficking occurs."[17] Police-black conflict in several cities has resulted in major protests by blacks. The most serious of these was in 1987 in Titusville where a youth riot and several rock-and-bottle-throwing disturbances erupted following charges of police mistreatment of blacks.[18]

Streets and Recreation

Other municipal services, particularly streets and recreation, have also been valued by blacks, and their improvement was a goal of the civil rights movement as well. Prior to the 1960s movement, the condition of streets in most black neighborhoods was very poor, especially in the Old South. Relatively few streets were paved—an average in 1960 of approximately 20 percent in black neighborhoods in these cities. At the same time the estimated average of paved streets in predominately white neighborhoods was 64 percent.[19] Poor roads usually denoted a variety of other conditions that also affected living conditions. Areas that lacked paving were typically deficient in drainage, sidewalks, streetlights, and street signs, conditions that threatened the safety of citizens and hampered responses of emergency vehicles, including police and fire services. During the rainy season, standing water on unpaved streets with no drainage was a potential health hazard. Finally, the lack of such basic services tended to retard community growth and discourage new and beneficial commercial development.

In the decades following the civil rights movement, street and related services for blacks improved markedly. In every community more street paving occurred in black than in white neighborhoods. The more affluent New South cities showed the greatest improvement in street services, with almost all streets paved in the black areas by 1980. Progress was evident in the Old South as well, but these impoverished cities still lacked paving for approximately 10 percent of roads in black neighborhoods as of the early 1990s. Relative size of the black population had little bearing on these capital improvements. In terms of employment in public works departments, blacks traditionally worked in large numbers in the streets division, typically performing the most menial jobs. This tradition was apparent in each of these cities except Crestview, and was a practice that has continued without major change throughout the last several decades.

As for recreation and park services, blacks also lacked basic facilities in the early 1960s. In the relatively poor Old South communities there were no developed parks for blacks or whites. Although blacks in the New South cities enjoyed municipal parks at this time, such parks were relatively small and not as well maintained as those in white neighborhoods. In accordance with southern tradition, moreover, all parks and recreation programs were totally segregated.

Blacks experienced modest improvements in recreation programs and facilities over the next several decades. Once again, New South cities increased park acreage and programs the most. In the Old South, lingering racism and poverty combined to limit public improvements, but self-help efforts by blacks sometimes produced increased recreational opportunities. Perhaps the most significant recreation issue, however, was the desegregation of facilities. Integration often provoked intense racial anxieties for whites, and thus proceeded slowly and with difficulty, especially at traditionally all-white municipal beaches and swimming pools. As expected, integration was initiated sooner and achieved more easily in the New South. Although most recreational programs were desegregated to some degree by the late 1970s, many beaches, pools, and even neighborhood parks were still used in the 1990s almost exclusively by only one racial group.

As in the case of police and fire protection, blacks in elected local office were the most important political factor in bringing about these changes in streets and recreation. Black officials played a crucial role in upgrading services and increasing employment for blacks. Of significance, too, were federal grants for street paving and infrastructure, and these programs included Community Development Block Grants and federal revenue sharing.[20] As these federal dollars became increasingly scarce because of cutbacks in the later 1980s, some basic services for blacks lagged behind those for whites, especially in the poorer Old South communities that were dependent on federal aid.

By the 1990s it is clear that the blatant inequities of the past in municipal services are no longer a significant issue. In fact, only 35 percent of the community informants interviewed recently perceived that there were any differences in the quantity or quality of city services provided to blacks and whites.[21] The differences today have more to do with disparities in living standards and styles between the races than with racial discrimination in the distribution of services. In recreation, for example, most whites have a choice between municipal and private facilities — a choice most poorer blacks do not have. And in street services, paving and drainage are increasingly provided by private developers, who pass on these costs to relatively affluent whites. As a result, the issue increasingly is not whether public services are allocated equally, but whether the level of services provided blacks compensates sufficiently for their lack of alternatives.

Lingering Discrimination in the Schools

Public schools, since they are the greatest contact points for blacks and whites, are very much a barometer of race relations in southern communities. A look at the schools vividly reflects the uneven progress afforded blacks. While public schooling was totally segregated prior to 1954, this racial separation continued in practice for a number of years after the Supreme Court decision in most of these cities. Black demonstrations and especially federal court orders were necessary to bring about substantial desegregation, which did not occur in the Old South until the early 1970s. The more racially moderate New South communities were able to desegregate their public schools earlier, but not without significant challenges from blacks and severe racial conflict in most instances.

After two decades or more of school desegregation, however, white and black students (and most parents as well) are generally more accepting of each other, and black high-school graduation rates have continued to climb. Yet both white and black informants claimed that racial problems in the schools were the most common racial issues in their communities in the last several years. In most of the schools, issues of second-generation discrimination have plagued black youths.[22] Thus blacks often suffer disproportionately from high rates of corporal punishment and suspension. Furthermore, the number of black teachers has declined significantly in many schools as fewer minorities decide to pursue careers in education. As a result, the schools are increasingly made up of white middle-class teachers and black (and other minority) students. The essential problem with this situation, according to a black school official in Titusville, is that "most white teachers don't know how to relate to or deal with black students, and black students get very discouraged."[23] Moreover, significant "resegregation" of many public schools has occurred, especially in the predominantly black cities of Riviera Beach and Quincy, as whites have continued to flee to private schools or left the community altogether.

In some communities there have been serious black-white confrontations recently over issues in or related to schools. In Crestview, for instance, where the black population is relatively small and quiescent, significant interracial fighting (some called it a "riot") occurred at the high school in the spring of 1992. This conflict, the first in more than a decade in the school, involved the issues of interracial dating and racial symbols (like "X" and the Confederate flag) worn on student clothing.[24] Even more serious, however, was the 1991 firing of the only black principal in Lake City schools and his replacement with a white administrator. Blacks saw the dismissal and replacement as not only unjustified in itself, but as reflecting an egregious insensitivity to the school's tradition of always having had a black principal (the school is located within a black neighborhood).[25] In reaction, blacks staged numerous protests, including a major march through the heart of the city, and boycotts of selected white businesses. The protests were to no avail, but the scene was reminiscent of the 1960s civil rights era of intense racial conflicts.

Uneven Progress in the Private Sector

While the civil rights movement in the South has been important in improving public services and employment for blacks, the economic advancement of blacks has generally been more difficult to achieve. Thus fundamental political rights have not always been translated into economic improvements for blacks.[26] Yet, perhaps the most important long-term goal of the movement was the betterment of the black community's social and economic conditions.

Prior to the 1960s, public accommodations in these communities were almost always segregated racially. In many cases blacks were denied a service altogether, such as admission to motels, apartments, and country clubs. In other instances they were served separately from whites, as in the case of restaurants that offered blacks carry-out service but no seating. With the advent of the civil rights movement and subsequent federal legislation, the walls of segregation in these accommodations began to crumble and eventually disappear. By the mid to late 1970s, most private establishments, including movie theaters, restaurants and motels, were desegregated. This was apparent even in the Old South cities where more traditional racial norms made the transformation more difficult to achieve.[27]

Public accommodations today are formally open to blacks, and generally black customers are treated fairly. Business owners are especially motivated by the desire to increase profits and increasingly perceive blacks as avid consumers. Thus it appears that economic incentives have supplanted certain racial fears, even in the Old South. As a black informant in Riviera Beach put it, "Businessmen look at the color of money more than the color of skin today."[28]

Yet some businesses still tend to treat blacks as second-class citizens, according to informants.[29] Some black interviewees reported instances of black customers being treated "rudely," experiencing "slow service," and being "watched" more closely than whites. Store owners in particular often disclosed that they fear black males in their establishments as potential thieves. And a few private establishments, such as country clubs and some recreational places, continue to be mostly segregated, although seemingly more for economic than for purely racial reasons.

Equality in private services for blacks, however, was always believed easier to achieve than equality in employment. Nevertheless improved jobs were seen not only as the primary path for blacks to escape economic impoverishment, but also as a means of enhancing black pride. Traditionally, blacks were relegated to the most menial and the lowest-paying jobs in these southern communities. But with the black political movement and federal legislation barring racial discrimination in employment, the record of blacks in the workforce improved. In a survey of businesses in these six cities, it was reported that few (12 percent) employed any blacks prior to 1960. But by the mid-1970s, 81 percent had hired one or more blacks, with the average proportion of blacks in the workforce being 19 percent (table 16.3).[30] Yet blacks were seriously underrepresented in high-level positions — they made up only 2 percent of those holding professional or managerial positions and 12 percent of those in skilled or semiskilled jobs. Most businesses still tended to hire blacks as menial workers such as dishwashers and cooks in restaurants, maids in motels, and janitors.

While economic empowerment and decent jobs have been the primary emphases of blacks over the last decade or more, the employment situation of most blacks has changed little in these communities. Another survey of the same or comparable businesses in the early 1990s shows only a modest increase in the proportion of professional or managerial positions held by blacks (now 8.5 percent) and of blacks in skilled or semiskilled jobs (now 16 percent) (table 16.3).[31] Overall employment for blacks in these businesses has actually *declined* 2 percent in the last fifteen years because of a significant decrease at the unskilled level (black employment at this level dropped 11 percent from the 1970s). Low-level jobs in general showed a decline among these businesses, and since blacks make up a relatively high proportion of these workers, they suffered greatly from these changes. The serious recession of the early 1990s also disproportionately affected blacks (once again, the last hired were often the first to be laid off). Despite assumptions to the contrary, increased competition for jobs from other minorities and new immigrants did not have a major impact on black employment.

The factors that are most important in explaining rates of black employment in the 1990s are black resource variables such as relative size of the black population, black customers, and black job applicants.[32] The black population is the basis for a potential black workforce and customer base, and as a result, the majority black communities had by far the best black employment record. Black customers seem to motivate black applicants by creating conditions known to favor the hiring of blacks. Employers frequently claimed, for example, that it was "good for business" to hire more blacks when there was a noticeable black clientele. These factors, moreover, are significant regardless of level of employment and community characteristics.

This finding contrasts sharply with the results of the comparable survey in the 1970s. Political variables, especially affirmative action programs and local black representation, were significant determinants of black employment in the 1970s, yet are not significant today. Moreover, the current data reveal an important barrier to black hiring. The claim by a number of employers that there is a lack of qualified blacks to fill jobs has proved to be a major

Table 16.3. Mean percentage of black employees in surveyed businesses

Time period	All businesses	Old South businesses	New South businesses
1976–77[a]	19[b] (2,[c] 12,[d] 31[e])	24 (3, 16, 42)	14 (1, 7, 21)
1991–92[f]	17 (9, 16, 20)	19 (12, 20, 20)	15 (5, 11, 21)

aTotal number of businesses surveyed in this period was 163.
bMean percentage that are black of all employees.
cMean percentage that are black of professional or managerial employees.
dMean percentage that are black of skilled or semiskilled employees.
eMean percentage that are black of unskilled or menial employees.
fTotal number of businesses surveyed in this period was 157.

impediment for blacks, but this claim is often linked to racial attitudes among employers. Thus business owners or managers with the strongest antiblack feelings were most likely to state that blacks were not fit for employment and were therefore less likely to hire them. This suggests that a number of employers are racially discriminating against black applicants but camouflaging this action under the guise of blacks not being qualified.

The good ol' boy system continues to favor friends and relatives for many jobs, and there is little emphasis today on affirmative action except in the larger businesses and firms with government contracts. In fact, only 12 percent of employers stated that they had implemented an affirmative action program and were actively seeking to hire blacks. There is clearly a more negative attitude about affirmative action today than in the 1970s. "Many businessmen see it as unfair," claimed a business manager in Crestview. "They feel that discrimination has been remedied and now everyone should compete on an even keel. Plus they don't like to be told by government that they still have to hire blacks."[33]

Surprisingly, black employment is decidedly better in Old South than in New South communities (table 16.3). This finding, which was apparent in the 1970s survey as well, suggests that the New South might not be as progressive in offering economic opportunity to blacks as is commonly believed. This finding is consistent through all levels of employment and all types of businesses with the exception of motels and apartments, where the tourist-oriented New South cities have the better record. Once again the importance of black resource variables is highlighted, as the Old South businesses have more black applicants and customers than businesses in the New South.

In addition to employment, another major issue in the private sector has been residential housing and neighborhood living patterns. As in most communities in the South, blacks and whites in these cities historically lived in highly segregated neighborhoods. While most neighborhoods are still racially distinct, there has been some shifting in the last decade or so of mainly middle-class blacks to predominantly white areas. Such blacks can afford to move to more affluent neighborhoods, and often they face little resistance from whites. On the other hand, the wealthiest sections, especially beachfront areas, remain essentially white. The cost of housing in these areas is prohibitive for all but a few blacks, and there are also informal sanctions against minority encroachment. In addition, almost one-third of the interviewed informants claimed that realtors or whites selling their homes still do things to keep blacks from buying or renting in white neighborhoods. The favorite tactic of such realtors, they suggested, was "steering" blacks to nonwhite areas. Moreover, blacks were much more likely than whites to be turned down for home loans, although these rejection rates seemed to be due more to economic circumstances than to race per se.[34] Nonetheless this has been another important barrier to the attainment of better-quality housing for a number of blacks.

Conclusion

While the nature and influence of the civil rights movement varied somewhat from one community to another, the effect of the movement was notable everywhere. Most evident were the improvements in basic municipal services and employment for blacks. Increased street paving, desegregated parks and pools, improved law enforcement, and more black police and firefighters — all such changes were due in large part to the black political movement, especially the election of blacks to local public office. More recently, many white officials, as well, have been supportive of improved services for blacks, but black representation (including black city administrators) has been crucial in protecting minority interests and insuring that black citizens receive decent services.

Yet even in the public sector progress has been inconsistent. Clearly it has been easier to improve capital-intensive services like street paving and parks than those services that are primarily human-intensive such as police and fire protection. The redistribution of funds and basic services is always politically less controversial than the reallocation of human resources. The latter change often requires difficult readjustments in behavior and attitudes.

Thus blacks have achieved near equality in street conditions in every community, but lag well behind whites in police and fire personnel and in top-level positions in most departments. Police brutality toward blacks, moreover, continues to be an important issue, while a number of parks and public swimming areas are still segregated. In addition, blacks in public schools often confront various forms of second-generation discrimination. Clearly blatant racial discrimination in the distribution of public services has ended, but significant class differences between blacks and whites and institutionalized forms of racism continue to thwart black progress.

While blacks have achieved some marked gains in the public arena since the 1960s, improvements in the economic and social sectors have been somewhat less common and often more difficult. The desegregation of public accommodations was the most obvious and clear-cut change. However, in private establishments where more personal contact between blacks and whites might occur — in country clubs, recreational places, motels, and residential housing — there has been relatively little desegregation, particularly in the Old South. Advances in black employment, perhaps the best indicator of economic progress, have been marginal at best. Most workforces of any size have been desegregated for some time, and blacks have slowly gained higher-level positions in some businesses. Nevertheless businesses that employ blacks still hire them mainly as unskilled or menial laborers, an employment level where jobs in general are shrinking.

Most important, it seems that the era of political conservatism of the 1980s, particularly the reduced emphasis on affirmative action, has clearly affected black employment opportunity. With less government intervention into private sector employment, blacks have been forced to rely on self-initiative and their own resources to a greater extent than previously. This suggests that potential black employees can no longer rely on the federal government or even black representation to aid in their employment as they once did in the 1960s and 1970s. Instead they must depend on the general black influence in the local economy to provide them with employment opportunities. For most southern blacks, typically residents in communities where blacks are clearly in the minority and are often dependent on the government to create more equal opportunities, this trend is an ominous one indeed.

Clearly a racial chasm continues to exist in each of these communities. As a thoughtful white official in Crestview expressed it: "There is still some deep-seated animosity between blacks and whites. Most whites want to treat blacks fairly and with respect, and blacks do have a greater chance than ever before for education and jobs. But whites resent blacks being given special opportunities, and blacks feel that whites still treat them poorly, don't like them, and don't give them the opportunities they should have."[35] And so the legacy of discrimination remains, and the long and difficult struggle for black equality in the South continues.

Notes

1. Interview, Daytona Beach, Florida, October 24, 1991.

2. Interview, Crestview, Florida, April 1, 1992.

3. Robert Weisbrot, *Freedom Bound: A History of America's Civil Rights Movement* (New York: Plume, 1991), 312.

4. Thomas Sowell, *Civil Rights: Rhetoric or Realism?* (New York: William Morrow, 1984), 139.

5. William H. Chafe, *Civilities and Civil Rights: Greensboro, North Carolina, and the Black Struggle for Freedom* (New York: Oxford University Press, 1980), vii–viii.

6. Gary Orfield and Carole Ashkinaze, *The Closing Door: Conservative Policy and Black Opportunity* (Chicago: University of Chicago Press, 1991), 2.

7. V. O. Key Jr., *Southern Politics* (New York: Vintage, 1949), 92.

8. William R. Keech, *The Impact of Negro Voting: The Role of the Vote in the Quest for Equality* (Chicago: Rand McNally, 1968), 99–101; Donald R. Matthews and James W. Prothro, *Negroes and the New Southern Politics* (New York: Harcourt, Brace and World, 1966), 117.

9. James W. Button, *Blacks and Social Change: Impact of the Civil Rights Movement in Southern Communities* (Princeton, N.J.: Princeton University Press, 1989), 23–25.

10. Keech, *Impact of Negro Voting*; Frederick Wirt, *Politics of Southern Equality: Law and Social Change in a Mississippi County* (Chicago: Aldine, 1970), 166–75.

11. Gunnar Myrdal, *An American Dilemma: The Negro Problem and Modern Democracy* (New York: Pantheon, 1944), vol. 1, 346–47.

12. Interview, black informant, Crestview, Florida, September 15, 1977.

13. Myrdal, *An American Dilemma*, vol. 1, 335; Harrell R. Rodgers Jr. and Charles S. Bullock III, *Law and Social Change: Civil Rights Laws and Their Consequences* (New York: Mc-Graw Hill, 1972), 122–23.

14. Button, *Blacks and Social Change*, chap. 4.

15. Ibid., 134–35.

16. Among the 116 informants (59 blacks, 57 whites) interviewed in these six cities in 1991–92, conflict between blacks and the police was the second most common racial issue cited. The only issue mentioned more frequently was racial conflict in the schools.

17. Interview, black informant, Lake City, Florida, January 11, 1992.

18. *Florida Today*, August 17, 1987, 1A, 1–2B; August 25, 1987, 2B.

19. Button, *Blacks and Social Change*, 149–51.

20. Ibid., 164–72.

21. There were significant racial differences in this perception, however. Of black informants, 53 percent thought there were still differences that favored whites in city services, but only 16 percent of white informants shared this perception.

22. Kenneth J. Meier, Joseph Stewart Jr., and Robert E. England, *Race, Class, and Education: The Politics of Second-Generation Discrimination* (Madison: University of Wisconsin Press, 1989).

23. Interview, black informant, Titusville, Florida, March 25, 1992.

24. *Okaloosa News Journal,* March 25, 1992, 2A.

25. *Lake City Reporter,* July 8, 1991, 1–2; July 10, 1991, 1–2; July 29, 1991, 1–2; and August 22, 1991, 1–2.

26. Chandler Davidson, *Biracial Politics: Conflict and Coalition in the Metropolitan South* (Baton Rouge: Louisiana State University Press, 1972), 123–40; Keech, *Impact of Negro Voting,* 96–99.

27. Button, *Blacks and Social Change,* 178–86.

28. Interview, black informant, Riviera Beach, Florida, April 21, 1992.

29. Of interviewed informants, 41 percent claimed that blacks are sometimes treated differently from whites in public accommodations.

30. Button, *Blacks and Social Change,* 187.

31. James Button and Matt Corrigan, "Blacks and Economic Opportunity in the South" (paper presented at the annual meeting of the Southern Political Science Association, Atlanta, Georgia, November 5–7, 1992.

32. Ibid.

33. Interview, white informant, Crestview, Florida, June 25, 1992.

34. *Daytona Beach News Journal,* January 22, 1989, 4A.

35. Interview, white informant, Crestview, Florida, June 25, 1992.

Contributors

Sophie Body-Gendrot is a professor of political science and American studies at the Sorbonne and the Institute of Political Science in Paris. She is the editor in chief of *Revue française d'études américaines* and the author of *Les Etats-Unis et leurs immigrants: Des modes d'insertion variés* (1992), *Ville et violence: L'irruption de nouveaux acteurs* (1993), and *Ensemble, cela fait une différence* (1994). She has been a visiting scholar at Columbia University; New York University; Wesleyan University; the University of California, Berkeley; and the University of California, San Diego.

Harold Brackman is a consultant on intergroup relations for the Simon Wiesenthal Center in Los Angeles. He is the coauthor (with Steven P. Erie) of *Paths to Political Incorporation for Latinos and Asian Pacifics in California* (California Policy Seminar, 1993) and of "The Once-and-Future Majority: Latino Politics in Los Angeles," in *The California-Mexico Connection* (1993), edited by Abraham F. Lowenthal and Katrina Burgess. He is also the author of *A Measure of Justice* (1977), a study of criminal justice policymaking in California.

James W. Button is a professor of political science at the University of Florida. His areas of specialization include black politics, urban politics, and political gerontology. He has published numerous articles and two major books, including *Blacks and Social Change* (1989), winner of the V. O. Key Award.

Sharon M. Collins received her Ph.D. in sociology from Northwestern University and is currently an assistant professor at the University of Illinois, Chicago. She studies racial segmentation in labor markets, with a focus on the aspects of black economic mobility that are politically mediated. Her research on black managers looks at the relationship between new job opportunities for middle-class blacks and post-1965 civil rights policies and pressures. Her latest article, "Blacks on the Bubble: Fragility in Black Jobs in White Corporations," appeared in August 1993 in *Sociological Quarterly*.

Steven P. Erie is an associate professor of political science at the University of California, San Diego. He is coauthor (with Harold Brackman) of *Paths to Political Incorporation for Latinos and Asian Pacifics in California* (California Policy Seminar, 1993) and of "The Once-and-Future Majority: Latino Politics in Los Angeles," in *The California-Mexico Connection* (1993), edited by Abraham F. Lowenthal and Katrina Burgess. He is also the author of an award-winning study of urban ethnic politics, *Rainbow's End: Irish-Americans and the Dilemmas of Urban Machine Politics, 1840–1985* (1988), plus numerous articles on urban, ethnic, minority, and gender politics. He currently is writing *Imperial Los Angeles: Public Enterprise and the Politics of Growth, 1880–1993* (forthcoming).

Norman Fainstein is dean of the faculty at Vassar College, where he is a professor of sociology. He has written extensively in the area of urban political economy, planning, and race. His recent publications include "Race, Class and Segregation: Discourses about African Americans," *International Journal of Urban and Regional Research* 17 (1993). Professor Fainstein is currently studying the relationship between class segregation and black social mobility in New York during the postwar period. He is also writing a book on the politics of the ghetto and the underclass.

Joe R. Feagin is the graduate research professor in sociology at the University of Florida. He does research on racial and gender discrimination issues. This research can be seen in *Racial and Ethnic Relations* (1993; with Clairece Feagin); *Living with Racism: The Black Middle Class Experience* (1994; with Melvin Sikes); and *White Racism: The Basics* (1995; with Hernan Vera). *White Racism* draws on in-depth interviews with whites and on case study analyses of black-white conflict in U.S. cities. Feagin is currently working on a book on black students at white colleges and another on black capitalism. Feagin has served as scholar-in-residence at the U.S. Commission on Civil Rights. His book, *Ghetto Revolts* (1973), was nominated for a Pulitzer Prize.

Cedric Herring is an associate professor in both the Department of Sociology at the University of Illinois at Chicago and in the Institute of Government and Public Affairs at the University of Illinois. He is also a faculty associate at the Irving B. Harris Graduate School of Public Policy Studies at the University of Chicago. He received his Ph.D. at the University of Michigan in 1985. His research interests include political sociology, labor force issues and policies, stratification, and the sociology of black Americans. Among his recent publications are *Splitting the Middle: Political Alienation, Acquiescence, and Activism among America's Middle Layers* (1990); "Skin Color and Stratification in the Black Community" (*American Journal of Sociology*, 1991); "Racially Based Changes in Political Alienation in America" (*Social Science Quarterly*, 1991); and "Preference or Necessity? Changing Work Roles of Black and White Women, 1973–1990" (*Journal of Marriage and the Family*, 1993). He recently became president-elect of the Association of Black Sociologists.

Michael Hodge is an assistant professor of sociology at Georgia State University in Atlanta. He received his Ph.D. from the University of Florida in Gainesville. His research focuses on the cultural ideology of American society that perpetuates and advances racial, ethnic, and class stratification. His recent work has dealt specifically with the resistance strategies of middle-class African Americans to this domination. He is a member of a research team of the Program for the Study of Social and Cultural Change in the sociology department and is currently examining issues of workforce diversity. He is currently writing a book on black entrepreneurship with Joe R. Feagin and Nikitah Imani of the University of Florida.

Leslie Baham Inniss is an assistant professor in the department of sociology at Florida State University, Tallahassee. She received her doctorate from the University of Texas at Austin in 1990. Her teaching and research interests are race and minority group relations and sociology of education. She is currently writing a book on the long-term effects of being a school desegregation pioneer.

Martín Sánchez Jankowski is an associate professor of sociology and a research associate of the Institute for the Study of Social Change at the University of California at Berkeley. He is the author of *City Bound: Urban Life and Political Attitudes among Chicano Youth* (1986) and *Islands in the Street: Gangs and American Urban Society* (1991), the latter the winner of the Robert E. Park Award.

Michael Kearney, professor of anthropology at the University of California, Riverside, has a long-term research and collaborative involvement with indigenous peoples of Oaxaca, Mexico, and their organizations in Mexico and in California. He is especially interested in transnationalism as expressed in migration, grassroots politics, identity, and human rights.

Edward Murguia is an associate professor of sociology and a research associate at the Laboratory for the Studies of Social Deviance at Texas A & M University, College Station. His books include *Assimilation, Colonialism, and the Mexican American People* (1989) and *Chicano Intermarriage: A Theoretical and Empirical Study* (1982). Among his articles are "Phenotypic Discrimination and Income Differences among Mexican Americans" (with Edward E. Telles), *Social Science Quarterly*, 1990; "Ethnicity and the Concept of Social Integration in Tinto's Model of Persistence" (with Raymond V. Padilla and Michael Pavel), *Journal of College Student Development*, 1991; and "On Latino/ Hispanic Ethnic Identity," *Latino Studies Journal*, 1991.

Adolph Reed Jr. is a professor of political science and history at Northwestern University. He is the editor of *Race, Politics and Culture: Critical Essays on the Radicalism of the 1960s* (1986) and the forthcoming collection *With Friends Like These: The "New Liberalism" and the New Assault on Equality*, and is the author of *The Jesse Jackson Phenomenon: The Crisis of Purpose in Afro-American Politics* (1986), as well as two forthcoming volumes, *Fabianism and the Color Line: The Political Thought of W. E. B. Du Bois* and *Stirrings in the Jug: Black Politics in the Post-Segregation Era*. He also is a regular columnist for the *Progressive* and serves on the boards of the Public Citizen Foundation and the Chicago-based Coalition for New Priorities.

Néstor P. Rodríguez is an associate professor in the Department of Sociology at the University of Houston. Working with other researchers, he has focused on Central American immigration and settlement, evolving intergroup relations between established residents and new immigrants, psychological trauma among Central American immigrant children, higher-education barriers among undocumented youth, and Latino political mobilization. Working with the Tomas Rivera Center, his most recent research involves an assessment of priorities and needs of different racial and ethnic communities in the Houston area.

Michael Peter Smith is a professor of community studies and development at the University of California, Davis. Formerly he taught political science at Tulane University and at Boston University and Dartmouth College. He has held visiting appointments in the social and political sciences at the universities of Cambridge and Essex and in planning and public policy at the University of California, Berkeley. He has published extensively in the areas of urban political economy, ethnicity and migration, and social theory. His books include *The City and Social Theory* (1980), *The Capitalist City* (1987), *City, State, and Market* (1988, 1991), and *After Modernism* (1992). His most recent research on the formation of transnational identities has appeared in such journals as *Theory and Society, Social Text,* and the *International Journal of Urban and Regional Research.*

Bernadette Tarallo is a lecturer and research associate in the Department of Applied Behavioral Sciences at the University of California, Davis. Her research on transnational migration has appeared in the *International Journal of Urban and Regional Research; The Annals of the International Institute of Sociology; Racism, the City, and the State* (1993), edited by Malcolm Cross and Michael Keith; and the popular press. She is currently coauthoring a book on the social practices of California's new immigrants and refugees.

Roger Waldinger, professor of sociology at UCLA, is the author of *Through the Eye of the Needle: Immigrants and Enterprise in New York's Garment Trades* (1986) and, with Howard Aldrich, Robin Ward, and associates, *Ethnic Entrepreneurs: Immigrant Business in Industrial Societies* (1990).

Howard Winant teaches in the Department of Sociology at Temple University in Philadelphia, where he has also served as director of the Latin American Studies Center. He is coauthor (with Michael Omi) of *Racial Formation in the United States* (1986) and author of *Stalemate: Political Economic Origins of Supply-Side Policy* and *Racial Conditions: Politics, Theory, Comparisons* (1994), as well as numerous papers on race and ethnicity, Latin American issues, social movements, and public policy. He received his Ph.D. from the University of California, Santa Cruz.

Index

Compiled by Douglas J. Easton